U.S. Steel and Gary, West Virginia

U.S. Steel and Gary, West Virginia

Corporate Paternalism in Appalachia

Ronald Garay

THE UNIVERSITY OF TENNESSEE PRESS • KNOXVILLE

Copyright © 2011 by The University of Tennessee Press / Knoxville.
All Rights Reserved. Manufactured in the United States of America.
First Edition.

The paper in this book meets the requirements of American National Standards
Institute / National Information Standards Organization specification Z39.48-
1992 (Permanence of Paper). It contains 30 percent post-consumer waste and is
certified by the Forest Stewardship Council.

Library of Congress Cataloging-in-Publication Data

Garay, Ronald.
U.S. Steel and Gary, West Virginia: corporate paternalism in Appalachia /
Ronald Garay.
       p. cm.
Includes bibliographical references and index.

ISBN-13: 978-1-57233-730-5 (hardcover)
ISBN-10: 1-57233-730-3 (hardcover)

 1. Steel industry and trade—West Virginia—Gary—History—20th century.
 2. Coal mines and mining—West Virginia—Gary—History—20th century.
 3. Gary (W. Va.)—Social conditions.
 I. Title.
II. Title: US Steel and Gary, West Virginia.

HD9518.G37G37 2011
338.7'669109754'49—dc22
2010030037

*To the Goads, Garays, Brewsters, and Flatts of Gary Hollow,
and to Mike Hornick, Friend and Historian*

Contents

Acknowledgments

My interest in writing this book dates to the 1980s when I began research-ing the relationship between the coal mines of Gary, West Virginia, and the mines' owner, U.S. Steel. I am a third-generation Gary native—born in Elbert, to be precise, but Elbert has now been incorporated into Gary proper—and so the project became both personal and professional.

The closure of one of the Gary Hollow mines in 1960 and a resulting job loss convinced my family to make a long move from the mountains of southern West Virginia to the high plains of West Texas. I was pre-paring to enter high school at the time and had little interest in knowing anything more specific about why the Gary mine had closed than what seemed obvious: The coal mining business was suffering, and Gary's fu-ture appeared bleak at best.

That explanation was sufficient for the moment, but as time passed I began searching for something more definitive. After joining the faculty at Louisiana State University in 1971, my search became more of a quest. Over the next several years that quest took me back to West Virginia, Virginia, and Pennsylvania, where details of the story in this book came together. Assistance in making sense of these details came from persons who guided me to sources and, most important, from persons who shared their first-hand accounts of living and working in Gary.

First among those helping with this project were members of my family, my mother Iris Miller, and my grandparents Roy and Opal Goad, especially. Their personal knowledge of Gary Hollow and its coal mining was invaluable. So much of what I learned from them came indirectly, hearing and observing things about the area's mining business that would be stored in my memory for years to come.

I also turned to long-time family friend Mike Hornick. Mike worked for many years as an engineer for U.S. Steel and was an authority on local history. He maintained a remarkable collection of documents, artifacts, photographs, and scrapbooks of newspaper clippings that chronicled the development of Gary Hollow mining. My sincere thanks to Mike for shar-ing his knowledge of the area and for stoking my enthusiasm for this project.

Thanks also to family friend Henry Paul, a long-time resident of Gary, former U.S. Steel employee, and one-time mayor of incorporated Gary.

Henry provided helpful input on life in Gary Hollow and conditions there in the post–U.S. Steel years.

Besides my thanks to individuals directly associated with Gary, appreciation goes to librarians and archivists who helped build the story I was hoping to tell. Heading the list is Stuart McGehee, archivist of the Eastern Regional Coal Archives (ERCA), and Eva McGuire, director of the Craft Memorial Library where the ERCA is housed in Bluefield, West Virginia. Stuart's and Eva's keen interest in and knowledge of the coal mining history of southern West Virginia led me to a bounty of helpful resources. I thank both of them for their help, time, and patience.

Among the many other librarians and archivists to whom I extend thanks for their personal assistance and direction are Gail McMillan and Joyce Nester at Virginia Tech's Newman Library Special Collections; Pam Seighman and Elaine DeFrank at the Coal and Coke Heritage Center, Penn State University, Fayette; June Piasecke at the Carnegie Free Library, Connellsville, Pennsylvania; Bob Turnbull at the J. Frank Marsh Library, Concord College, Athens, West Virginia; and Eleanor Beckner at the McDowell County Public Library, Welch, West Virginia.

Thanks also to the library and archival staffs at the following: West Virginia Archives and History Library, The Cultural Center, Charleston; West Virginia Collection and Wise and Evansdale Libraries, West Virginia University, Morgantown; Arthur Lakes Library, Colorado School of Mines, Golden; John Heinz Pittsburgh Regional History Center, Pittsburgh; Hunt Library, Carnegie-Mellon University, Pittsburgh; Hillman Library, University of Pittsburgh; Carnegie Public Library, Pittsburgh; DeGolyer Special Collections, Perkins Library, Southern Methodist University, Dallas; and Middleton Library, Louisiana State University, Baton Rouge. A special thanks to personnel of the McDowell County Clerk of Court, Welch, West Virginia.

I remain indebted to Scot Danforth, director of the University of Tennessee Press, for his interest and encouragement and to members of his staff and to reviewers whose comments and recommendations helped shape the book's final form.

Finally, what can I say to thank my wonderful wife, Mary Sue? She never protested when I insisted on spending vacation time researching this book. Mary Sue likely would have preferred traveling to some other destination and engaging in something more relaxing and entertaining than meeting persons to talk about Gary, coal mining, and steel making, or peering through dusty stacks of books and other assorted things found at libraries and archives. She tolerated all this and endured the inconveniences and disappointments of my research taking precedence over her own interests. I am eternally grateful to Mary Sue for putting up with my admittedly selfish determination to see this project through to its completion.

Acknowledgments

Introduction

Gary, West Virginia, did not exist as the nineteenth century gave way to the twentieth. In its place was nearly untouched wilderness, yet elsewhere much of America was booming. The misery and displacement occasioned by the Civil War was nearly two generations in the past, and as much of rural America became urbanized, small settlements bloomed into big cities. Rapid growth meant new construction, and buildings were going up—higher and higher—as quickly as space could be cleared for them.

People were on the move, too. America was expanding in all directions, and faster and more efficient means of transportation, primarily the railroad, were taking the country where it wanted to go. The railroads moved not only people but also the goods and supplies necessary to sustain America's growth and vitality. There were, in fact, few places the railroads seemed incapable of reaching. Rails ran everywhere. Rivers and mountains seemed little or no barrier to railroad construction. After all, one could be bridged and the other tunneled.

Much of the building that occurred in late-nineteenth-century America, whether skyscraper or railroad, required steel. Steel girders formed buildings and supported bridges. Steel rails carried locomotives and their trains of passengers or freight. But steel could not be produced without one of its most important ingredients: coke, a by-product of coal. Because coal and coke were most easily transported from mine to steel plant by railroad, steelmaking, railroading, and coal mining formed an industrial triad.

United States Steel, whose power and prestige was apparent from its very beginning, was incorporated on February 25, 1901, in New Jersey. "The corporation almost immediately acquired the capital stocks of nine large independent steel companies, a steamship company and an ore mining company."[1] Originally Carnegie Steel Company, U.S. Steel rose to a new form of corporate entity because of its acquisitions. Carnegie Steel was known as an "integrated" (or, more precisely, a "vertically integrated") corporation, meaning that Andrew Carnegie through the years had acquired either outright ownership of or exclusive access to everything needed "to make the firm immune to outside business pressures."[2] Carnegie controlled the sources of raw material (coal and iron ore, for example) necessary for steelmaking; the transportation systems (by land and water) needed to move the raw materials; the steel plants themselves; the systems for delivering his company's full line of manufactured products; and the distribution, marketing, and sale of those products. Thus, U.S. Steel inherited from Andrew Carnegie a sprawling integrated corporate enterprise that was virtually self-sufficient from top to bottom.[3]

Self-sufficiency, though, meant that U.S. Steel would always be looking to expand its ready supply of steelmaking raw material. Coal being one of the most important, U.S. Steel focused on the rich bituminous deposits of southern West Virginia as a prime acquisition target. In particular, U.S. Steel intended to operate what would be called captive mines to extract the kind of high carbon, low-sulfur coal found in the Pocahontas coal field—a massive coal formation that spreads through southern West Virginia and southwestern Virginia.

A farsighted move had brought title to much of this coal-rich land to the Norfolk & Western (N&W) Railway Company. But shrewd business dealings not only allowed U.S. Steel to secure lease rights to some fifty thousand acres of the N&W land, but also established N&W as the steel company's primary coal carrier. N&W built railroads into the Pocahontas field and transported coal to U.S. Steel's blast furnaces in Indiana and Pennsylvania. And while N&W constructed the railroads, U.S. Steel built the mining plants and town sites and then imported the men and their families needed to work the mines and grow the towns.

By 1902 N&W had made steady progress on its railroad, and U.S. Steel was constructing the first of several mines in McDowell County, West Virginia. The company actually had created a subsidiary called the U.S. Coal and Coke Company (USCC) to oversee its McDowell County operations. USCC's task required, on the one hand, construction and operation of coal mines, and, on the other hand, construction and operation of several towns situated near the mines and inhabited almost exclusively by company mine workers and their families. Several satellite towns eventually developed around the hub town that came to be called Gary, after U.S. Steel's first chairman of the board, Judge Elbert H. Gary. In fact, one of the satellite towns just two miles south of Gary acquired Judge Gary's first name of Elbert.

Gary and its sister towns rose quickly among all the industrial structures and mining facilities that also were filling the landscape. Gary was regarded as a model establishment within the coal mining region. The town was carefully planned and overseen by USCC to provide miners and their families with comfort and convenient access to schools, businesses, recreational facilities, and places of worship. The arduous and dangerous business that employed most of Gary's male population was hardly reflected in the spirit and ambience of the town at large. Incredibly, within these mountain hollows (or "valleys" to outsiders), where few people had ever lived, Gary was by 1910 booming just like the rest of America.

Finding Gary on the Map

Gary's population was bound inextricably to the fortunes of its colossus, benevolent patriarch, U.S. Steel. The "company," as U.S. Steel was known in these parts, integrated the needs and requirements of a commercial enterprise with those of a diverse population. Few of the town's original

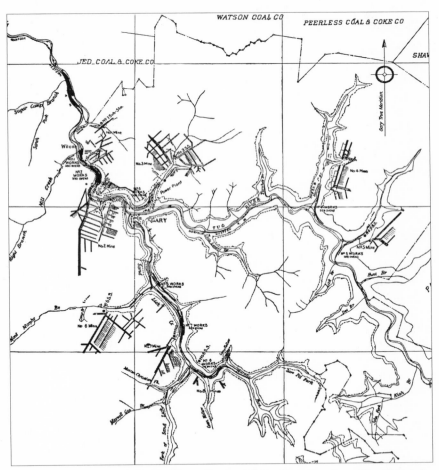

General Plan of Plants of United States Coal and Coke Company, Gary, West Virginia. From George R. Wood, "Electrical Equipment," *Mines and Minerals*, December 1906, 194.

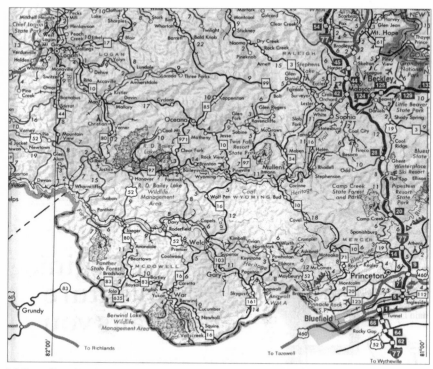

McDowell and Mercer County, West Virginia, 2010.

inhabitants came from West Virginia, and some came from eastern and southern Europe. This infusion of nationalities, racial and ethnic groupings, languages, cultures, and customs created a melting pot that was unusual for such a small place.

Travelers to Gary usually make their way from Bluefield, West Virginia's southernmost city located some forty miles to the southeast in neighboring Mercer County. Bluefield rose to prominence as a strategic rail and trade center in the late 1880s and became known as the "gateway to the Pocahontas coal field."[4] The title is a fitting one. All N&W rail traffic moving into the Pocahontas field from the east has always passed through Bluefield. Moreover, automobile travel on the main highway leading into the coal field from the east (or southeast) generally passes through Bluefield via U.S. 52.

N&W rails and U.S. 52 both wind around and through mountains once they exit Bluefield, but they converge less than ten miles to the northwest, at Bramwell. Bramwell is a quiet town of few residents, some of whom occupy opulent houses that speak of a storied past when the town was reportedly home to fourteen millionaires. Its wealth made Bramwell's "per capita income the highest in America for a time" during the early twentieth century. Coal barons and those who struck it rich doing business in the coalfields were Bramwell's upper crust. They settled there after the Flat Top Coal Land Association, owner of most of the Pocahontas coalfield land, made the town its headquarters. The association made leases to independent coal operators who built mining operations along the N&W. The Bank of Bramwell's demise in the 1930s, however, ended the town's glory days.[5] Still, the mansions that remain standing on the banks of the Bluestone River symbolize the wealth that at one time was drawn from the coal mines of the area.

Southwest of Bramwell and U.S. 52 is Pocahontas, Virginia, whose significance, like Bramwell's, lies in its past. If Bluefield can be considered the "gateway to the Pocahontas coalfield," then Pocahontas can lay rightful claim as its actual portal, since it was here in 1882 that the first portal was constructed to extract the millions of tons of coal mined in nearly every part of the Pocahontas field.[6]

Outside of Bramwell, U.S. 52 begins ascending Flat Top Mountain. Travelers in automobiles pay little attention to the climb, but the Flat Top proved a formidable barrier to the N&W during rail construction. A tunnel bored through the mountain in 1887 finally allowed rail service to and from the interior of the Pocahontas coalfield.[7] The towns of Elkhorn, Northfork, Keystone, and Kimball sit along the Elkhorn Creek valley. The creek, the highway, and the N&W railroad weave through town after town, each settlement owing its existence to coal and each one seeming to have reached whatever prominence it might have occupied at some point in the distant past.

Roughly thirty-two miles northwest of Bluefield is Welch, county seat of McDowell County. Although Welch is decidedly smaller than Bluefield, the two became notable as commercial and trade centers for the coal industry. Bluefield is situated at the periphery of the coalfields, whereas Welch is smack in the middle. One of Welch's most famous residents, writer Kermit Hunter, spoke of his hometown as "the industrial center of the coal empire" and a "coal metropolis" where "countless deals for timber and coal lands" were made in the city's early days.[8] Both Welch and Bluefield grew with the coal industry, and when the industry faltered, so did Welch and Bluefield.

State highway 103, south of Welch, leads to Gary. The highway—and the N&W—follow roadbeds constructed along the banks of the Tug River (more accurately, the Tug Fork of the Big Sandy River). The Tug joins Elkhorn Creek at Welch and flows northwesterly to eventually converge with the Big Sandy. The N&W extension to Gary and its satellite towns joins the railroad's main line where the Tug and Elkhorn Creek converge. Both Gary and Welch are in the eastern portion of McDowell County, which borders Virginia and dips into the crook of the state's southwestern panhandle. To the northwest, McDowell County comes within only a few miles of Kentucky. Gary may appear close to Welch on a map, but the appearance is deceptive. The map's flat surface belies the rugged mountainous terrain of the area. Gary actually is not close to anything. And the drive there is similar to a roller coaster ride full of twists and turns, climbs and dips, with little break. Stephen and Stacy Soltis described it this way: "Almost immediately you'll notice how the mountains begin to close in on one another; the valleys narrow to small canyons and the sky disappears under heavily canopied forests. It's a claustrophobic feeling that's common to this part of the world. You start wondering how folks got into this remote country, let alone exploited it with coal operators."[9]

Throughout these mountains are miles of parallel and perpendicular tunnels that crisscross one another at various intervals. How many miles of tunnels there are within the mountains of West Virginia probably have never been calculated. The number probably would reach into the thousands. All were meant to (and some still do) serve as corridors for shuttling miners to and fro. And each tunnel gradually lengthened as miners chipped away at the face of the coal seam.

Above this subterranean maize, the McDowell County region where Gary is located is a tangle of ambiguities for any newcomer or even native. Winding through the hollows on the twisting, bumpy highways, a driver encounters the ultimate in environmental devastation, where strip mines have torn away huge chunks of the mountainside in order to access the elusive coal seam. Below the strip mine, near the railroad track, there may be a rusting mine tipple ready to crumble. Somewhere in the vicinity, too, the viewer may see a mountain of slate and debris that are the by-products of mining. Then there are the shacks that dot the mountainside, precariously clinging to the angled plot of land on which they sit, with little paint to cover their rotting boards. Discarded appliances sit on their porches, and rusting bodies of ancient automobiles pepper the overgrown yard.

To many first-time visitors, this scenery may seem like classic West Virginia. It is the image portrayed in magazines, newspapers, and books across the nation. Denise Giardina's *Storming Heaven* and *Unquiet Earth* give fictional story lines to the real-life persons, places, and events of her youth in this part of coal country. And Harry Caudill's *Night Comes to the Cumberlands* tells the stark reality of the business of coal mining and the lives of coal miners and their families in the southeastern Kentucky Cumberland Plateau.[10] Regardless of the change of locale, the coal mining stories of one place are interchangeable with the other. Caudill leads readers on a journey through "his" coal country that is similar to the journey from Bluefield to Gary. He describes "mile after dreary mile of patched and cratered 'highways,' their ditches choked with mud and their banks and shoulders thick with weeds" and mountains "strewn with rotted, collapsing coal tipples, chutes and bins and pimpled with ugly slate dumps of every size and shape." He tells of the "scores and hundreds of abandoned houses. The windows fall out, the chimneys topple, the roofs leak and in the grip of decay they sag ever closer to the earth."[11]

But travelers who witness all the blight are just as apt to see unexpected things as they move along a winding hollow road. At one turn there may be rows of attractive, well-maintained homes surrounded by neatly manicured lawns. Another turn may reveal a world of indescribable natural beauty, especially in the spring, when the mountains are radiant with blooming rhododendron and dogwood. The forests are full of deep green leaves and aromas of new growth. Rabbits, woodchucks, foxes, and deer abound. And bright red cardinals, chattering robins, and majestic hawks crowd the thin strips of sky that open above the numerous ridges.

This beauty—and not the ugliness of industrial blight and manmade squalor—is what makes the area so special, so inviting, and so intriguing. It is a land apart from what persons who have never set foot in southern West Virginia might read about or know of the place. The deep friendships and unique experiences of growing up in a coal mining town, coupled with unsurpassed natural beauty, are what pull mind, if not body, back to Gary—back to the mountains.

Gary as Town

Something that needs to be clear to the reader at the outset is that the name "Gary" identifies two things. Gary is indeed the name of a town, but it is also the collective name for several "satellite" towns. Each of these towns—eventually numbering twelve—had its own name: Elbert, Filbert, Thorpe, Wilcoe, and Munson, for example. And each had grown up near one of the USCC coal mines. Like suburbs surrounding a city, these satellite towns often were clumped with the slightly more prominent Gary and treated as one and the same. Gary and its satellite towns also shared something in common with reference to their names that probably made them unique among other American towns. Because each USCC town was associated with a coal mine, and because each mine was numbered consecutively from when it first became operational, these numbers were interchangeable with town names. The first mine to open was, fittingly, Number One. The town that grew near the mine was Wilcoe. Alpheus grew around the Number Two mine, and Gary actually grew around the Number Three mine. Thus, Gary residents understood perfectly well that a reference to "Number Two" was a reference to the town of Alpheus.

Something else that needs to be clear is the designation of Gary as a town. This study defers to the judgment of Crandall Shifflett, whose authoritative book, *Coal Towns*,[12] would seem to settle the issue of what to call Gary. However, a sizable body of literature has developed over the years on the subject of employer housing for employees and the generic "company towns" where such housing most commonly exists. Research writers have referred to these settlements as coal camps, mining towns, mining settlements, mining communities, and mining villages, to name a few.[13] According to Gladys Tolleen Ahrenhols, "the terms camp, town, and community [were] used interchangeably and no differences in either degree or kind [were] attached to them."[14] Even Crandall Shifflett alternates from one designation to another when speaking of coal towns. Mack Henry Gillenwater also used a variety of referents in his extensive study of mining settlements. His rationale for using "town," though, was based both on population (a town was required to have between 1,000 and 2,500 residents) and the community's level of commercial activity.[15] Gary and its satellite communities certainly would qualify as "towns," although population fluctuations through the years have moved one or more of them outside of Gillenwater's specific definitional boundaries.

Considering all the above, reference to Gary as a coal town would seem perfectly acceptable. Arguments to the contrary are only academic, save for two exceptions. C. A. Cabell, a coal operator himself in the early 1920s and a builder of coal towns, stated emphatically that "'mining camp' is not the proper name for a community where mining operations are carried on. A mining town is the name that should be applied. A camp carries with it the suggestion of a temporary place; built to be abandoned in a short time. Such is not the case with mining towns. They are well constructed, and much better suited for the convenience and happiness of citizens than are most of the small towns I have seen."[16] The second exception comes from Shifflett and, like Cabell, also considers the concepts of permanence, emotional attachment, and sociocultural connections that in the past tended to elevate coal towns to the level of community. "Indeed," says Shifflett, "mining towns were communities: births, baptisms, marriages, anniversaries, and deaths formed the life cycle of thousands of families in coal towns. Children were reared in this environment, and all moments of life, big and small, which give to every family, great and ordinary, a cherishable history, likewise grew into a collective experience. The perspectives of former miners on life in the company town sometimes contrast sharply with conventional images of company towns."[17]

Gary may have been a coal camp in its early history, but it quickly moved to a much more permanent existence. As a town, Gary had many of the attributes of other towns of comparable size, but there were important differences. While certain businesses and services existed in Gary, they served only the very basic needs. There were schools, churches, grocery stores, gas stations, medical facilities, and even for a short while a bank, but the real commercial trade centers existed in Welch or Bluefield. Regardless of dependence on the outside, Gary residents possessed the mind-set of community. Mind, body, and soul could be nurtured here. Neighbor knew and cared for neighbor. Children were not always anxious to leave Gary once they were of the age to do so. And many stayed to raise families of their own. Gary the town, by all means, was also Gary the community.

Gary Hollow as Place

In a strictly geologic sense, a hollow is a declivity in the earth's surface formed by thousands of years of the eroding force of water as it eats its way deeper and deeper into that surface. Eventually, mountain walls form at very steep angles on each side of the stream bed. These V-shaped declivities are familiar to inhabitants of the southern Appalachians. They are somewhat similar to valleys, but valleys often have a wide, relatively flat spot here and there and generally run in a more uniform direction than hollows that have few, if any, wide or flat spots and seem to meander about the landscape in no particular direction. Geographer Raymond Murphy described the origin of the land and its hollows this way: "In southern West Virginia, Tug Fork and its many tributaries have dissected the original surface of the Appalachian Plateau into an area of sharp divides which rise 800 to 1,000 feet above a well-developed stream system, markedly dendritic [i.e., a nonsymmetrical branching similar to tree limbs connecting to a trunk] in pattern."[18]

Most persons who live in or near Gary live in a hollow. Unless one chooses to live on the top or side of a mountain, there is nowhere else to live. And whereas "hollow" as a reference point may imply a substandard, backwoods, off-the-beaten-path sort of place to outsiders, the term's use to locals in identifying where someone lives or where something is located is quite common and perfectly acceptable. Saying, for instance, that this study will be examining conditions that existed in Gary Hollow is a shorthand way of collectively pulling together all the persons and towns comprising Gary into a simplified referent that would be easily understood by most folks living in McDowell County. As such, the reader will see "Gary Hollow" frequently used to designate place.

Gary and Industrial Feudalism

Gary was the creation of U.S. Steel. The company was the sole reason for Gary's existence. The valuable coal flowing from the area's captive mines was the only link that connected U.S. Steel via its USCC subsidiary to the community. The kind of proprietary or paternalistic relationship that existed in Gary between company and employee was essentially that of a benevolent landlord where both parties were mutually agreeable to both working and living arrangements. U.S. Steel did not require that its coal mine employees live in company houses, trade at company stores, or engage in any particular company activity (besides employment responsibilities). And while most persons who lived in company housing indeed did work for U.S. Steel, there were those, such as schoolteachers, who were not company employees but who nonetheless lived in Gary. Additionally, nothing bound an employee or his family to the company. Gary residents who worked for U.S. Steel mines were free to leave if they chose.

There was no city government in Gary during most of its history. Duties of a mayor, city council, and all city officials actually were fulfilled by the single most influential person in Gary, the USCC general superintendent. A volunteer firefighting unit and emergency ambulance personnel were available during most of Gary's early history, and police protection was divided between the county and a company employee known as a "conservator of the peace," whose position was similar to that of a county deputy sheriff. Also, for much of Gary's early history, the company employed doctors who manned several clinics and frequently made house calls. The company deducted from pay about fifty cents per month per unmarried employee or one dollar per month per married employee to help subsidize the cost of medical care. A nominal payroll deduction of between one and two dollars per month also covered an employee's household water and electricity. Finally, a town site superintendent was in charge of house and roof repairs and painting. Houses were usually repainted every five years.

Although living conditions in Gary were lacking in some basic conveniences (not until the 1960s, for example, were sewer lines constructed that could connect households with a new sewage treatment plant to make indoor toilets possible),[19] there never was any mass protest to suggest that conditions had become intolerable or even unacceptable. Any unease or discomfort over such matters simply was tolerated and taken as part of life not uncommon to coal towns in general. Life in Gary was not ideal, but living was as comfortable, as predictable (to a degree), and as activity filled as most other industrial communities in this country.

The marriage between U.S. Steel and Gary might best be described as a "marriage of convenience." There was no compact or covenant that legally bound the company to Gary, other than U.S. Steel's original lease arrangement with the Flat Top Coal Land Association. Neither was there an emotional attachment that bound U.S. Steel to Gary. The only thing linking the two was business. And from 1902 through the 1950s business nurtured and sustained that bond. But, in the late 1950s downturns in the steel industry began to chip away at U.S. Steel's interest or even need to maintain a relationship with Gary to the same level as in the past. Within the coming decades, a series of events and circumstances continued to erode the relationship of company and town. Finally, in the 1980s the bond that held U.S. Steel to Gary for over eighty years dissolved altogether.

The Story

"Coal is the most valuable mineral in the world," concluded Malcolm Keir in 1926.[20] Some years later Winthrop D. Lane remarked, "West Virginia is the Eldorado of the soft coal industry."[21] Speaking of coal, and of West Virginia's soft coal in particular, in such superlatives was not unusual. Early twentieth-century histories of the state were full of similar language that celebrated coal and the coal industry.[22] The effusive image of coal early on may have been appropriate if somewhat overdone for the time, but it soon faded. The truth was that coal's real importance, its real economic value, was determined at some distance beyond West Virginia's borders. Much, if not most, of that value resided in the steel industry. And much, if not most, of the control over the coal industry of West Virginia resided in the corporate boardrooms of America's major steel companies. These two industries—coal and steel—were linked to one another. The economic viability of one was entirely dependent on the economic viability of the other. The dependent partner, though, was always the coal industry.

In a narrow sense, this book tells the story of U.S. Steel's relationship to its captive coal mining operation at Gary. It is the story of how industry-altering decision making by U.S. Steel executives reverberated within the mountain hollows and quiet neighborhoods of Gary. It is the story of change and reaction to change. In a broad sense, this book tells a story of how the early twentieth-century model of industrial organization and manufacturing dominance simply could not resist forces unleashed by a late twentieth-century global economy and technological revolution. More stringent government regulation of the workplace and of the environment, greater international competition in practically every economic sector, but most particularly in steel and energy production, diminishing relevance of organized labor at a time when production efficiency was more often measured not by tonnage but by less tangible metrics, and greater need for worker ability based not in physical but rather in intellectual skills gave rise to changes that left persons in America's coalfields reeling.

These two perspectives, then, frame the story that follows. It is not a story whose parts have not been told before. As source citations throughout this book will attest, much has been written about the hundreds of coal mining operations that have endured a fate somewhat similar to Gary's. George O. Torok, in fact, leads readers in his *Guide to Historical*

Coal Towns of the Big Sandy River Valley through a fascinating tour of many such coal towns, including Gary.[23] Crandall Shifflett's *Coal Towns* adopts a more scholarly perspective on the subject. Thomas E. Wagner's and Phillip J. Obermiller's *African American Miners and Migrants* tells the story of Gary's sister town, Lynch, Kentucky, which was also a product of U.S. Steel.[24] Alex P. Schust's *Gary Hollow* is a prodigiously illustrated, near encyclopedic source of information about Gary that leads readers through the early rise of the entire USCC operation.[25] This book draws from these sources, but it diverges from previous studies to examine more closely the nature and dimensions of the long-term industrial relationship that existed between U.S. Steel and its Gary, West Virginia, coal mining subsidiary and, ultimately, how and why that relationship came to an end.

Chapter 1

Origins and Settlement

Darkness shielded their presence as the Shawnees quietly advanced across the open field. They moved initially on tiptoe and then, as though choreographed, began a slow, rhythmic run. A small Indian band like this usually was led by a fellow warrior skilled in the hunt. But this band was different. At its head was none other than the Shawnee chief Black Wolf. This was, as a matter of fact, the sixth consecutive night that Black Wolf had appeared in the same place, at the same time, right on cue. He was neither a real chief nor even a real Indian but an actor who graced Welch High School's Maroon Wave Stadium-turned-arena theater as part of a May 12–17, 1958 extravaganza commemorating the centennial of McDowell County, West Virginia. "Black Wolf's" performances were accompanied by singing, dancing, elaborate staging, and a grand fireworks finale.[1]

The McDowell County Centennial was a big event in this southern West Virginia county not accustomed to big events. Many residents working long hours had carefully planned the centennial celebration to reflect not only the county's past but also what they assumed to be its future. The celebration had its serious side, but more than anything it was meant to be fun. There was a "Brothers of the Brush" beard-growing contest for the men, a centennial queen contest for women dressed as nineteenth-century belles, and scores of other activities spread throughout the official centennial celebration week. Most of the major centennial activities occurred in Welch, the county seat of McDowell County.[2]

The *Welch Daily News*, the county's only major newspaper, played a big role in the centennial by publishing a special commemorative edition on June 3. The hefty volume carried numerous photographs and articles that collectively provided an excellent overview of county history. Local readers probably found the articles interesting, amusing, informative, and perhaps even inspiring, but they also were keenly aware of the underlying message that flowed throughout the newspaper. The unmistakable story of McDowell County, to those even remotely acquainted with the place, was coal. More to the point, McDowell County was COAL COUNTRY— HARDCORE, IN-YOUR-GUT COAL COUNTRY!

The *Welch Daily News* provided all the statistics to drive home the point. "More than one billion tons of bituminous coal has been mined in McDowell County during the past 73 years, and more than two-thirds of the original reserve still remains underground," noted one of the paper's centennial edition articles. That one billion tons accounted for roughly one-fourth of the total coal tonnage mined in all of West Virginia during the same seventy-three-year period. For twenty-five years McDowell County had held the record as the "largest coal producing county in the nation." Statistics from the West Virginia Department of Mines continued to put the county in first place, even in 1958, although for the past few years the Federal Bureau of Mines' records had given that distinction to nearby Logan County. Even so, the coal mining output of the two counties remained close.[3]

The *Welch Daily News* illustrated in dramatic fashion the role that Gary coal mines had played in maintaining McDowell County's status as the nation's "Black Diamond Empire": "Imagine, if you will," said the newspaper, "a train of coal cars twenty-four thousand miles long circling the earth from Welch . . . and you will have the shipments of coal from U.S. Steel's Gary District since its beginning in 1902." These coal cars, according to the *Welch Daily News* story, had carried more than 200 million tons of coal to U.S. Steel plants during Gary's fifty years of coal mining.[4]

That half century for Gary had been remarkable in other ways. The mines, the town sites, and the persons working and inhabiting both had appeared, in Brigadoon fashion, almost overnight. In short order this out-of-the-way place nestled in the hollows of southern West Virginia was transformed into an industrial powerhouse. How that transformation occurred is where this story might ordinarily begin. But the real story of Gary's beginning stretches back not in half centuries but rather in increments measured only by geologic calendars—to a time when the coal that would be extracted from the Gary mines and the entire Pocahontas field was just forming.

Geologically speaking, nothing about the formation of this part of Appalachia happened quickly. Quite to the contrary, the events that made the mountains and the coal within them were products of massive changes that occurred over millions of years. Geologists have narrowed these millions of years into clumps of time called periods. One of these periods, the one most important to our story, was the Carboniferous, estimated to have begun about 360 million years ago and lasting for roughly 80 million years.[5] During the latter half of the Carboniferous period, most of what is now West Virginia was not mountainous at all, although a chain of mountains did exist farther east. The area also had a tropical climate as a result of continental drift. Such drifting carried North America far to the south. Eventually it reversed course and drifted back north. In time, rain swept down enough sediments from the eastern highlands to collect in the basin to their west and form a rich soil where a variety of tropical plants took root. Whole forests of these trees, ferns, and other prehistoric plants appeared. Then a shifting of the earth's surface allowed enormous amounts of water to flow into the basin and to form inland seas and lakes that transformed the forests into swamps. Eventually the plant matter died and decayed.[6]

Water drained from the swamps, and the resulting dry basins once more were covered with sediments carried down from the eastern highlands. Then, in cyclical fashion, water returned to the basins; swamps once more resulted; plant life flourished, died, and decayed; water receded; and sediments covered what remained. As the various layers of plant material separated by various layers of sediment began to build, a metamorphosis occurred. The chemical nature of the plant matter (a compound of oxygen, hydrogen, and carbon) began to change due to the heat and pressure to which the decayed plants were subjected. Oxygen and hydrogen gradually dissipated, leaving only the carbon. Over time the carbon deposits hardened into coal. Since some layers of coal were formed much earlier than others, the metamorphosis that purged the mineral of its hydrogen and oxygen was more complete in some places than in others. So, depending on where it is found today, coal will vary as to its carbon content. For example, one form of coal called lignite has a carbon composition of about 70 percent. Anthracite coal, on the other hand, contains as much as 95 percent carbon. Bituminous coal—most common to southern West Virginia—falls between lignite and anthracite, with a carbon content of about 80 percent.

The various layers in which coal deposits are found today are called seams. While coal seams vary in thickness (the average measuring about three feet in height), rarely do they reach more than nine feet.[7] The area size of a coal deposit or "field" conforms to the size of the swamp that millions of years ago formed that field. Some coalfields encompass the area of an entire state. More than one coal seam may be found at varying depths in a single field. The seams are separated from one another by various layers or strata of sandstone, shale, clay, and limestone. All of these rock types were formed from the sediments that originally covered the decaying plant matter that became coal. And in the same way that plant matter was compressed into coal, so were the mineral sediments compressed to form the sandstone, shale, clay, and limestone.[8] This layering, or stratification, occurred when the land surface of southern West Virginia was relatively flat.

Geologists surmise that several millions of years after the Carboniferous period the continental drift began moving the land mass that would become North America in a direction that placed it closer to its present location. Nearby land masses also slowly began shifting positions and in doing so bumped into one another. One such bump presumably was forceful enough to push the North American land mass inward, causing the heretofore flat land of the Appalachian basin to fold and lift, creating the Appalachian Plateau.[9] This folding and lifting continued for roughly 45 million years. The end product was a vast flat-topped mountain that probably resembled the mesas of today's American West. Once the uplifting subsided, nature began the process of carving the featureless Appalachian Plateau into more recognizable shapes. Water was the primary chisel that eroded away the soft rock, working its way downward to form the hollows of southern West Virginia. For over 200 million years erosion continued to create the valley and ridge topography that marks the present-day landscape.[10] As North America moved to its present position on the planet, plant life common to a more temperate zone began covering the emerging Appalachian Mountains.

The uplifting motion that created the Appalachian Plateau also lifted the coal and rock embedded in the earth to higher and higher elevations. Some of the uplifting also caused portions of once horizontal strata to tilt slightly in one direction or another. The erosion that cut through the earth and formed the hollows or valleys also cut through seams of coal, exposing the ends of the seams on opposite sides of the hollows. These exposed seams appeared as outcroppings and eventually brought geologists and surveyors to the area for a closer look.

The environs of present-day southern West Virginia and southwestern Virginia became "a nearly impenetrable forest of hemlock, white oak and poplar and a tangled wilderness of rhododendron and laurel."[11] Wild game was plentiful, with bears and panthers and even buffalo and elk roaming the countryside. Eventually Indians came to the area, mostly to hunt. Evidence of major Indian trails in present-day McDowell County suggest that Shawnees from villages in Ohio traveled along the Tug River as they moved to hunting grounds in present-day Tazewell County, Virginia.[12] Conflicts erupted between the Shawnees and white settlers who began to populate the area in the late 1700s. These conflicts ended, as did the Shawnees' presence altogether following their defeat by General "Mad" Anthony Wayne at the Battle of Fallen Timbers in 1794.[13]

Exactly when the first Anglos entered southwestern Virginia is unknown. Traders and hunters probably entered the area in the early 1700s, but the first recorded visit occurred in 1748 when James Patton led a group there to explore and survey some 120,000 acres of land that he had secured as a royal grant. Patton, Dr. Thomas Walker, and several of their friends secured another grant in 1749. Dr. Walker, a medical doctor by profession, led a group of surveyors into the area in 1750, and by accounts recorded in his journal was the first to discover and make mention of the coal deposits in the vicinity of present-day Pocahontas, Virginia.[14]

Dr. Walker, friend to Peter Jefferson and later his executor and guardian to his son, Thomas Jefferson, was a man of great accomplishment. The precise purpose of his 1750 exploration was to survey land as far west as Kentucky. On the return leg of his trip, Dr. Walker noted the following in his journal, dated June 19, 1750: "We got to Laurel Creek early this morning, and met so impudent a Bull Buffaloe that we were obliged to shoot him, or he would have been amongst us. we [sic] then went up the Creek six miles, thence up a North Branch of it to the Head, and attempted to cross a mountain, but it proved so high and difficult, that we were obliged to Camp on the side of it. This Ridge is nigh the eastern edge of the Coal Land."[15] A footnote in a reprint of Dr. Walker's journal explained that the "Coal Land" that Walker alluded to "was the outcrop of the Pocahontas coal field."[16] And while this indeed may have been the first mention of the coal here, Dr. Walker's language suggests that he had prior knowledge not only of the "Coal Land's" existence but also its boundaries.

Nearly twenty years passed from the time of Dr. Walker's exploration and survey until Thomas Witten became one of the first Anglo settlers to move his family into permanent residence in present-day Tazewell County. The date of the Witten family's arrival is said to have been 1767, although records seem unclear on the matter. Witten built a cabin for his family at Crab Orchard, some twenty-five miles due south of present-day Gary.[17] Other settlers soon followed. John Greenup, Absalom Looney, Matthias Harman and his brothers Jacob and Henry, John Craven, Joseph Martin, John Henry, James King, and John Bradshaw all built cabins in close proximity to the Witten cabin.

Settlers also began moving to present-day McDowell County. Soon persons with names like Fletcher, Cartwright, Milam, Lambert, Totten, Belcher, Bailey, and Murphy lived there. In some cases several brothers within a single family brought their families to the area, all to live within a short distance of one another.[18] Whether any of these persons settled on land owned by one of the royal land grantees is unknown, but chances are that most settlers arriving in southwestern Virginia by this time ignored any such land grant claims. Such attitude and the family names themselves are indicative of the Scots-Irish ethnicity of those who migrated to this part of the country in the early eighteenth century. Upon arriving in America from their native Scotland or Ireland, the Scots-Irish quickly moved past the more populated coastal towns and chose instead to build their lives in the Appalachian wilderness. They were well suited to their new home, coming from what James Webb called "a culture of isolation, hard luck, and infinite stubbornness that has always shunned formal education and mistrusted—even hated—any form of aristocracy."[19] These highly independent first-generation citizens of southwestern Virginia probably cared little for claims on land where they lived or for decisions made in distant places that frequently redrew the political boundaries of their home counties. Nonetheless, major alterations beginning in 1799 and continuing to the end of the Civil War significantly shifted these invisible lines. Tazewell County, for example, was created from two other counties by the Virginia general assembly in 1799. Seven years later, in 1806, the assembly redrew the Tazewell County map once more into a nearly 3,000 square mile mega-county that included all of present-day McDowell County and parts of Mercer and Wyoming Counties in West Virginia, and parts of Buchanan, Giles, and Bland Counties in Virginia.[20] Another boundary change occurred in 1858 when the general assembly detached territory from Tazewell County to form McDowell County. The new county's contour was very much as it is today.[21]

Virginia's secession from the Union in 1861 met with resistance in Virginia's western counties. Resistance was such that citizens from several of these counties elected delegates to a convention meeting in Wheeling in May and June 1861 for the purpose of nullifying Virginia's secession ordinance and to consider breaking away from Virginia and the Confederacy altogether. A "dismemberment ordinance" and a plan to create a new state that would remain part of the United States resulted from the Wheeling conventions. Both plans won overwhelming approval of citizens from the proposed new state on October 24, 1861. Several counties, including McDowell, were not represented by delegates at the Wheeling convention. The counties nonetheless were annexed to the new state of West Virginia, admitted officially to the Union on June 20, 1863, by proclamation of President Abraham Lincoln.[22]

Little more than a year after the Civil War ended, Jordan Nelson moved his family to Powell's Bottom, a state-straddling piece of property that one day would be renamed Pocahontas. Nelson, of Scots-Irish descent and grandson of a Revolutionary War veteran, intended to farm and set up shop as a blacksmith. To his good fortune, Nelson found a sizable outcropping of coal, or coal bank, on a nearby hill and began to dig chunks of it suitable for fueling both his home fireplace and blacksmith forge. What Nelson did not realize was the immensity of the coal seam that lay beyond its outcropping. It has been described as "perhaps the richest seam in the history of the industry, the Pocahontas Number Three, which stood a remarkable thirteen feet tall at its outcrop near Pocahontas." The seam in years to come would be the "portal to the Pocahontas coal field." The mine built to extract the coal from the Nelson Seam operated for seventy-two years and yielded approximately 44 million tons.[23] The coal's value in dollars was enormous, but its value to the steel industry was incalculable. Whether Nelson was aware of Dr. Walker's earlier observations about coal in the area is unknown. Other persons, though, were keenly aware of the coal there, and when the time was right they paid Nelson a visit.

Chapter 2

Iron and Steelmaking Science and Manufacturing

Jordan Nelson probably would have preferred his privacy and quiet life to what lay ahead. But because of where he happened to be, Nelson was destined to be both participant and observer of an industrial revolution that had been transforming much of western Europe and the northeastern United States but that only lately had arrived in southwestern Virginia.

Historians have divided the industrial revolution into two parts, the first lasting from roughly the mid-eighteenth to the mid-nineteenth century and the second lasting from the mid-nineteenth to the early twentieth century.[1] Industry was changing the economy, the workplace, and the lifestyle of Europeans and Americans. And the driving forces of the new industrialism were coal and iron.[2] The origins of ironmaking as predecessor to steelmaking is unknown, but the industry's development centered among wealthy landowners in Great Britain. Thomas Southcliffe Ashton noted why that was so: The "apparatus of an ironworks represented a volume of capital that few save landowners could command. Moreover the industry was intimately dependent on the land for its raw material in the form of [iron] ore, limestone, and charcoal; and it was the demand of the landed classes for the implements of agriculture and war that constituted the main reason for its existence."[3] Casting guns, canon, and shot seemed to be the major products of these early ironworks or foundries.[4]

Iron makers, wealthy or not, were at the mercy of mother nature to supply the ingredients of smelting—iron ore, limestone, and wood. Most critical of the three, regarding availability, was wood, which was partially burned to produce charcoal of nearly pure carbon.[5] "Since ancient times, iron had been smelted with charcoal, which would be mixed in direct contact with the iron ore and then fired. Charcoal provided not only the necessary heat but also the carbon needed to promote the chemical reduction of the iron (the oxides in the ore would combine with the carbon and be released as carbon dioxide)."[6] Problem was, the trees from which charcoal eventually derived grew in forests that were quickly being depleted and not very quickly renewed. In addition, iron makers vied with shipbuilders for the same wood. And given Great Britain's status as a naval power, a reduction in wood necessary for shipbuilding was regarded as a threat to national security. As a result, the British Parliament began enacting laws in the mid-sixteenth century placing restrictions on iron makers' use of trees as "fuel timber."[7] Restrictions and potential scarcity of such an important ingredient forced iron makers to consider replacing charcoal with a more abundant raw material: coal.[8]

The idea of using coal to replace charcoal was not new. Coal had been used sparingly for such purpose early on, but it was discovered that coal contained impurities—sulfur chief among them—that would "contaminate the iron when the coal and iron ore were mixed together." Iron makers discovered, however, that the "key to making usable iron with coal was to first bake the coal to drive off the volatiles and turn it into 'coke,' much the way wood is turned into charcoal."[9] The coke-making, or coking, process was not a simple one to master, although a patent for manufacturing coke was awarded as early as 1589. Not until 1709, though, was Abraham Darby credited with actually "distilling" coke from coal and making it a "commercially viable product" for smelting iron at his ironworks in Coalbrookdale.[10] Darby's contribution came at a propitious moment in British history. Coal, plentiful and relatively inexpensive, already had supplanted wood (due to its growing scarcity) as the major heating fuel for both home and workplace. Even more important, it was easily transported from mine to town or city via Britain's numerous waterways, particularly its canals. In fact, the British parliament passed several navigation acts between 1758 and 1802 to create canal or river-improvement companies "whose primary aim was to carry coal."[11] Much of that coal—about a fifth of it by the early nineteenth century—was destined for ironworks. And, of course, the same vessels that delivered coal and other raw material to the foundry also carried what was produced at the foundry to the marketplace.[12]

Ironworks were also located near waterways to properly smelt the iron in blast furnaces, which were heated with blasts of air provided by "bellows worked by men, horses or a water-driven mill wheel."[13] The blast furnace was adequate for its time, but iron smelting awaited a mechanical means of supplying a stronger and more continuous blast to manufacture high-quality iron. The wait ended with the arrival of the revolutionary steam engine, patented in 1775 by James Watt and Matthew Boulton, who perfected the machine that many others had worked to invent. The steam engine was soon utilized as a railroad locomotive, but it proved itself first as the means necessary to produce the kind of blast iron makers needed. Phyllis Deane pointed to the installation of the steam engine as "the turning point in the history of the iron industry." Because of the steam engine, said Deane, "the iron industry lost its migratory character and began to concentrate in large-scale units of production grouped in regions where coal and iron were in ample supply and where water-borne transport was available."[14]

The iron industry was beginning to assume characteristics that would remain intact as it moved from Great Britain to America. The same was true of the iron maker (or ironmaster) himself. Building and operating a blast furnace was expensive, so the iron maker usually had to be quite wealthy. Some early iron makers, John Wilkinson as an example, also assembled other properties in such ways as to resemble the vertical integration of a modern corporation. Wilkinson's properties included "collieries, tin mines, iron foundries, forges, warehouses, and landing stages" spread over "Wales, Cornwall, the Midland, London and France."[15]

The iron maker required wealth both to build his business as well as to sustain its growth and operation. But if done well the products he manufactured could build wealth beyond imagination. Great wealth also awaited persons engaged in another business with origins in the first two decades of the nineteenth century: railroading. Railroading depended entirely on iron and, later, steel. And iron makers and steelmakers became nearly as dependent on the railroad industry. Locomotives made of iron pulled cars whose undercarriage and wheels were made of iron along two parallel rails made of iron. The rails could be laid practically anywhere and when a waterway or ravine was encountered, an iron bridge could be built to allow easy crossing. Additionally, locomotives could pull cars loaded with raw material such as coal from the mines to the ironworks and then haul finished iron products to the marketplace.

The idea for constructing a steam-powered locomotive took hold in Great Britain following the pioneering lead of such inventors as Richard Trevithick and George Stephenson. Horse-drawn wagons had been employed since the late 1700s to move coal along wooden rails from collieries (or coal mines) to canal or river barges. The steam engine provided a different kind of motive power for moving the wagons—one whose boilers could be fueled by the very coal that was being moved. The railway age had begun, and by 1825 some three hundred to four hundred miles of railroad had been built in Great Britain. That number increased to over two thousand miles by 1845. The railroad building boom was under way. Closely allied to that boom was investor interest in mining and the iron industry. "By the 1850's," said Phyllis Deane, "twenty-seven blast-furnaces a year were being built and new fields of coal and iron ore were being rapidly opened up."[16]

The push to industrialize America was similar to that in Great Britain. To a great extent industrial development in America was stimulated by the British and assisted greatly by British engineers and inventors who were more than willing to share what they could with Americans. As a result, Americans were able to bring a wealth of knowledge across the

Atlantic concerning building and manufacturing products that eventually competed with their British counterparts. The steam engine was one such product. Robert Fulton turned his knowledge of the British invention to full advantage when he was the first to build and demonstrate the utility of a steam-powered boat in 1807. The "success of the steamboat," said Gavin Weightman, "very rapidly began to transform America as it became the most important form of transport before the arrival of the railways."[17]

Eyeing the steamboat's success, Americans were even more intrigued by the potential for a steam-powered railroad locomotive. A flock of American engineers traveled to Great Britain to study the new technology. Horatio Allen was one of them. He traveled to Great Britain in 1828 and met with George Stephenson to learn all that he could about the steam-powered locomotive. Before his return to America in 1829, Allen had purchased a Stephenson-built locomotive. The machine's trial run on a wooden rail track was set for August 8, 1829. The run was a success, and in less than a year Peter Cooper of New York demonstrated the first American-built locomotive also running on a wooden track in Baltimore. This track shortly became the first leg of the Baltimore and Ohio Railroad. From this point on, interest in railroading grew exponentially, stimulated by America's westward expansion and the need for a transportation system that could carry travelers, goods, and raw material from one point to another quickly and economically.

Enthusiasm for railroading, stoked immensely by the continuing success of the steamboat, was dampened somewhat by what Gavin Weightman called a "striking anomaly: A rapidly industrializing world largely made of wood and fueled by it."[18] Both uses, though, had limitations that were readily apparent. Wooden rails, even when topped as some were by metal strips, simply were inadequate to carry the weight of a locomotive and train of cars over a prolonged period. Substituting iron rails for the wooden ones was the only solution to the problem. But since existing foundries at the time were incapable of producing rails of the sort needed, American railroad builders were forced to import the rails from Great Britain. What's more, though some locomotives indeed were built in America, most had to be purchased from British manufacturers.[19]

Purchasing iron products from abroad demonstrated the shortcomings of America's own iron industry while also showing its enormous need for a steep growth curve. Such growth quickly occurred, driven in great part by the inexorable proliferation of steamboats and railroads. One source, in fact, described America's "metallurgical industries" at the time as "first and foremost the handmaids of transportation," and characterized the relationship this way: "During the early decades of the [nineteenth] century, foundries and shops for the manufacture of steamboat machinery were to be found at every important river town of the interior, while larger engine works were established at our leading seaports. Indeed, the period when steam was applied exclusively to water transportation might be called the foundry era of the American iron industry. Then came railways. . . . Thereafter, for most of the remainder of the century the market for rails was the barometer which measured the prosperity or depression of iron and steel manufacturing."[20]

But all of this was far in advance of the origins of the first ironworks in America, believed to have been a blast furnace built in Saugus, Massachusetts, in 1645. Ironmasters shortly established foundries in other colonies. Not until 1716, though, was iron manufactured in Pennsylvania, in what was "destined to be the leading iron and steel manufacturing state in the nation."[21] Most colonies were blessed with a "relative abundance" of the raw materials necessary to produce iron. "There were iron ore deposits and extensive tracts of woodland for the manufacture of charcoal, the principle blast furnace fuel of the era."[22]

Charcoal remained the chief fuel for smelting iron ore into pig iron for well into the nineteenth century. Unlike in Great Britain, where wood scarcity was forcing ironmasters to convert to coal, wood was plentiful and inexpensive in America. Moreover, charcoal, for the moment at least, seemed to be of a sufficient quality of fuel to produce castings for household utensils, farm implements, and nails. One downside, however, was the seasonal nature of charcoal's production, which was between May and October when conditions normally were dry. The quality of the wood also affected the charcoal's quality. According to Paul Paskoff, "The harder woods, such as hickory, oak, beech, ash, and black walnut, because of their tight grain, low water content, and resulting high specific gravity, made the best charcoal per cord."[23] Fortunately for the iron industry, these tree species were fairly common in the Northeast.

Charcoal continued as the exclusive fuel for American ironmaking until about 1830, when experiments began for using coal as a fuel.[24] This was well past the time when British ironmasters had converted to coal and well after the spurt of canal building in Great Britain. America had its own rush to canal building, though at a later date than Great Britain and with considerably less urgency. American canals typically were meant for barges and boats carrying products of practically every kind, but only occasionally was there a need to transport coal.[25] Coal as fuel had a very slow start in America. Not only did the vast wilderness woodlands seem to provide an infinite source of fuel, but the country's many rivers and streams also provided water power to operate the machines of industry operated by steam power in Great Britain. Coal's potential as a fuel nonetheless was known to early explorers of America's interior. Sightings of coal seams became a prominent part of their reports. And when the village of Pittsburgh grew at the convergence of the Allegheny and Monongahela rivers in western Pennsylvania in the 1700s, merchants and home owners took advantage of coal in nearby hills to use for both heating and manufacturing. This was bituminous coal, drawn from the outcroppings of a vast coalfield that stretched south along the spine of the Appalachians from Pennsylvania into Alabama. But Pittsburgh was alone in its heavy use of coal, as there was no practical way of transporting coal across the Allegheny Mountains. Nor was there much interest in the coal anyway.

But it was not long before anthracite coal "transformed a virtual wilderness into an industrial superpower with astonishing speed."[26] Anthracite coal, discovered in eastern Pennsylvania in the late 1700s, had fewer impurities, higher carbon content, lower hydrogen content, and little smoke when burned compared to bituminous coal. However, unlike bituminous coal, which lies in vast quantity beneath the earth's surface, most of the world's anthracite coal is confined to roughly five northeastern Pennsylvania counties. Still, the transformation began in earnest when American ironmasters came to realize, as their British counterparts had realized many years earlier, that the laws of supply and demand in the evolving iron industry were beginning to push manufacturing needs beyond the ability of charcoal makers to produce this vital fuel. Simple calculations showed why. A blast furnace producing a thousand tons of pig iron annually required charcoal made from 150 acres of timber. Since a stand of timber takes approximately twenty years to regenerate, the blast furnace would require some two thousand to five thousand acres of timber to maintain a steady supply of fuel.[27] This was an enormous burden on woodlands that were quickly disappearing as the population moved West. Moreover, the demands of industrialization meant that production of more and more iron was required each year.

The result was an iron-making industry that by the late 1830s had begun replacing charcoal with anthracite coal. From about 1855 to 1875, anthracite coal became the principal fuel for iron making until surpassed by the coke that came from bituminous coal. Also, because of the proximity to the anthracite coalfield, the iron-making industry, until the last quarter of the nineteenth century, was centered in Pennsylvania's Lehigh and Susquehanna valleys as well as locations in New Jersey and New York, where the anthracite coal could be transported easily by barge or rail.[28]

The anthracite region became the center of early American railroading, and coal became one of the first commercial products hauled by the budding railroad companies. In addition, the railroad companies purchased the region's coal-rich property, and ironworks began specializing in rolling mills, where heavy rails—called T-rails because of their shape—were produced.[29] At least two mills, one in Danville, Pennsylvania, and the other in Allegany County, Maryland, were the first to produce T-rails in 1844. Most rails had been imported from Great Britain, but the

U.S. Congress gave American rail makers an advantage in the domestic marketplace by placing a tariff on rail imports in 1842.[30]

Eastern Pennsylvania's dominance as America's iron-making capital was short lived, however. When the Clinton Furnace became the first blast furnace built in Pittsburgh in 1859, the country's iron-making hub was soon to move to western Pennsylvania. The rapid growth of the iron industry in the Pittsburgh vicinity also meant the decline in use of anthracite coal and the rise in bituminous coal's distillate (or carbon residue) coke as a blast furnace fuel.[31] While a process for making coke had been perfected in the early eighteenth century in Great Britain, Americans had failed to copy the process well enough to create usable coke in sufficient quantity until after the Civil War. Peter Temin described the process this way:

> It was the chemical properties of coke that retarded its introduction before the Civil War, but its physical properties assured its dominance as a blast-furnace fuel after the war. The process of coking was valuable for its effects on the sulphur content of the coal, but its main importance lay in its creation of a porous, yet sturdy physical structure. . . .
>
> When Bituminous coal is coked, its volume does not fall. Rather than collapse upon itself, the remaining material in a good coking coal forms a fine honeycombed structure with air spaces in between. This means that coke has a higher surface area in relation to its volume than anthracite, and that it can burn faster. If a greater volume of air is blown into a blast furnace, coke will burn faster, while anthracite will speedily reach a limit set by the maximum rate of combustion on its restricted surface area.[32]

Bituminous coal suitable for coke making was found in hills surrounding Pittsburgh, but just a short distance to the city's southeast, in the vicinity of Connellsville, lay the richest veins of superior coke-making coal known at the time. It is to the abundance of this "relatively sulphur-free" coking coal within such easy reach of Pittsburgh that historians contend the city owed its prime stake in the iron-making and steel-making industry.[33]

The coke-making process itself was relatively simple:

> [Coke] was produced in beehive ovens, whose shape was indicated by their name, varying from 11 to 12 feet in diameter and from 5 to 6 feet high. The coal was dumped

through a hole in the crown of the furnace and spread
evenly on the floor to a depth of 2 or more feet. The front
opening, through which the coke was discharged, was
nearly closed with bricks. The heat retained in the thick-
walled oven from the previous coking fired the charge,
but complete combustion was prevented by excluding
more and more air until it was cut off completely. After
coking about 48 hours the charge was drawn. The product
of such an oven for each heat was 120 bushels, or nearly
a quarter of a ton.[34]

The one flaw that existed in the beehive oven process was the loss of gases
that contained valuable by-products. Specially designed retort ovens eventually remedied the problem.

Other coal mining regions produced their own coke through the end
of the nineteenth century, but "the Connellsville region, some 50 miles
long and 3 miles wide, continued to turn out more than half the total." And
the extent of that production was impressive. Connellsville coke ovens in
1876 "had an annual capacity of about a million tons; four years later the
number of ovens approached 8,000 with an output of over 2,000,000 tons,
and by 1890, when there were 15,000 ovens, the product was more than
5,500,000 tons."[35]

All of this had enormous income potential, something industrialist
Henry Clay Frick had taken advantage of in 1871. By 1880 his H. C. Frick
Coke Company controlled roughly 150 acres of coal mining land and
about fifty coke ovens near Connellsville. Within two years the number
of Frick-owned ovens had increased to more than a thousand, with about
ninety railroad carloads of coke shipped daily to fuel Pittsburgh blast
furnaces. In time, Frick would own 80 percent of the coke-producing
capacity of the Connellsville region. For ironmasters and steelmakers
alike, the price they paid for coke was the price set by Henry Frick. As
one writer said, "Frick stood in undisputed command of the sources of
their fuel."[36] A coal baron extraordinaire, Frick was one among several
others who made their fortune in the coal business, particularly the bituminous, or soft coal, side of the business. And since bituminous coalfields
could be found in many parts of America, there was abundant opportunity for persons to open mines of their own. This "far-flung soft-coal industry," as Barbara Freese pointed out, "did not lend itself to monopoly
or oligopoly control. Soft coal, in fact, became one of the nation's most
fiercely competitive industries."[37]

Henry Frick's prominent position did not escape the attention of a
particular group of Pittsburgh industrialists determined to partner with
the coal baron. Andrew Carnegie beat his competitors to the punch.
Intending to transform America's use of iron into America's use of steel,

Carnegie purchased roughly 11 percent of H. C. Frick Coke Company's stock in 1882. That ownership portion rose to 50 percent in 1884, and by 1888 Carnegie owned 74 percent of the Frick Company. Frick, for his part, did not fare badly, becoming a Carnegie partner and, in the words of Carnegie biographer David Nasaw, grew "immensely rich and powerful doing so."[38]

Andrew Carnegie had a keen eye for finding what was necessary to make the company that bore his family name the best and the biggest it could be. The company engaged in iron making at first and incorporated all the latest manufacturing techniques that the well-traveled Carnegie discovered. His travels often took him home to his native Scotland and south to England, where he never failed to make a "pilgrimage to iron and steel foundries" and talk with their owners about manufacturing innovations. In 1872 Andrew Carnegie called upon Henry Bessemer to discuss Bessemer's experiments with a new steelmaking technique. He stood, so the story goes, "before the blazing cauldron of the Bessemer converter, and then 'jumping on the first available steamer, he rushed home' to his Pittsburgh ironworks crying: *The day of Iron has passed— Steel is King!*"[39]

Steelmaking was an ancient art practiced in many places but particularly in the Far East. Only small amounts of steel could be made at one time because the process of producing malleable steel by heating iron to a level that removed all impurities was tedious and time consuming. Until Bessemer revolutionized the process, European steelmaking required removing carbon from pig iron to produce wrought iron and then reintroducing carbon into the wrought iron by heating it with charcoal. Bessemer simplified this two-step process by first smelting iron in a furnace called a converter and then blowing cold air over the molten iron. If the iron ore used to produce the iron was free of chemical impurities, phosphorous especially, then the converter blow miraculously would produce steel. The key to this industrial miracle was nonphosphoric iron ore. And where but Great Britain and the United States was such ore found in greatest abundance.[40] Already the ore coming from the Lake Superior region of Michigan was known to be low in phosphorous. Any steelmaker having ready access to this ore in addition to the Connellsville coal was at a particularly advantageous position over his competitors.[41]

Andrew Carnegie had access to the coal, but he did not immediately have access to all the Lake Superior ore his company needed, nor was it available at what Carnegie considered a reasonable price. Adding to both problems was a fear that the owner of much of the most productive iron ore mines in the Lake Superior region—none other than oil tycoon John D. Rockefeller—might take his near-monopoly control of the ore into a steelmaking enterprise of his own. The situation was resolved in 1896 when Carnegie and Rockefeller signed a lease agreement giving

Carnegie full output of all Rockefeller mines at a minimal royalty pay-
ment. Carnegie also agreed to use only Rockefeller railroads and Great
Lake steamers to ship the iron ore to the Carnegie steel plants. In return,
Rockefeller agreed not to enter the steel business.[42]

Andrew Carnegie began his steelmaking career in 1872, building his
first steel plant at Braddock, a few miles from Pittsburgh on the banks
of the Monongahela River. The plant, modeled after those of Henry
Bessemer's, was in operation by 1875. Within three years Carnegie's
share of the steelmaking business rose above all his competitors.[43] By
1891 Carnegie's combined steelworks were "the dominant force in the
nation's fastest growing, most significant industrial sector."[44] From their
beginning through much of the 1880s, the Carnegie steelworks primarily produced rails for the railroad industry. By 1890, though, Carnegie
had diversified into other steel products, including "beams, bars, angles,
sheets, rods, pipes, nails, plates, and structural shapes for bridges, buildings, skyscrapers, and ships."[45] Skyscrapers had begun to appear in New
York and Chicago, and as cities grew so did the boom in steel construction. In addition, the automobile, making its first appearance in the 1890s,
was destined to create yet another enormous use for steel. America, as
Thomas Misa remarked, was taking "institutional and physical form as
a nation of steel," and the major supplier of much of that steel was none
other than Andrew Carnegie.[46]

From the beginning, Carnegie determined to acquire his wealth in
steelmaking only. But he came to realize that he needed to invest in other
facets of the business—ownership of mines where important raw materials were found, ownership of transportation links to carry raw material
to his steel plants and to carry finished steel products to market, and the
marketing means to sell his steel. Carnegie eventually came to appreciate the value of vertical integration.[47]

As big as Carnegie Steel was, the company continued to share a competitive stage with smaller steel companies. The companies were nomi-
nally independent of Carnegie Steel, but in reality Carnegie could indirectly control competitors via an arrangement called a pool. Pools were
loosely connected companies that manufactured similar products like steel
who agreed to maintain a certain price level so as not to undercut competitors in order to gain an unfair market advantage. The steel industry was
notorious for creating pools only to have them disintegrate when one of
the pool members decided to unfairly drop prices. Andrew Carnegie, as it
happened, was well known for creating pools and then lowering prices so
far that smaller steel companies were driven out of business.

The ineffectiveness of pooling was such that a new and more effective kind of business arrangement appeared in the 1890s. Enterprising
individuals created holding companies, or giant corporations that "held a

controlling share of the securities" of several smaller companies. When the "New Jersey legislature passed a general incorporation act favoring holding companies" in 1899, "the holding company soon became an extremely popular form of organization, and a large number of the nation's firms incorporated in New Jersey. This technique was also popular because it gave control of a large number of companies to a single unit by a transfer of stock and great concentration could be achieved by a relatively small capital outlay."[48] The single unit thus resulting from these mergers or integrations of smaller entities often became a giant corporation representing both "a concentration of productive power as well as a concentration of selling control."[49]

The first and most prominent construction of a corporate holding company in the steel industry happened not in Pittsburgh but in Chicago. The iron and steel industry had developed there in nearly parallel fashion to its development in the East. And similarly, railroads lay at the heart of that development. It was said that Chicago and its surrounding environs in Cook County "had outdistanced Allegheny County [Pennsylvania] as a Bessemer rail producer" by 1879. Joliet, Illinois, in fact, was home to one of the earliest Bessemer steel plants erected in America. And the "first rail rolled in the United States was made at Chicago from an ingot cast at Wyandotte."[50] By 1889 the several major steel companies in Chicago and vicinity were consolidated into a vertically integrated corporation similar to Carnegie Steel in Pittsburgh. The corporation, or holding company, the Illinois Steel Company, comprised five steel plants; iron ore mines in Minnesota, Wisconsin, and Michigan; and "a large tract of coking coal in the Connellsville district."[51] A considerable amount of the Connellsville coke came from the H. C. Frick Coke Company via contracts that Frick held with several of the Chicago steel companies prior to their 1889 merger.[52]

Illinois Steel was one of the earliest corporate creations of someone destined for much, much bigger things. Elbert H. Gary, or "Judge" Gary, as he was better known, was an attorney who practiced law in his hometown of Wheaton, Illinois, some twenty miles west of Chicago. Gary's brief service as a county judge from 1882 to 1890 earned him the "judge" sobriquet by which he was known the rest of his life. Returning from the bench to his law practice, Judge Gary soon developed a reputation for his expertise in corporate law and was retained as general counsel by several Chicago companies, including Illinois Steel. At the time of Judge Gary's arrival, the company was struggling financially, and Gary suggested that the corporation resolve its plight by boldly growing bigger, merging with competitors, acquiring more iron ore properties, and improving its manufacturing infrastructure. Such a move, according to Gary biographer Ida Tarbell, "would bring about what [Gary] called 'a rounded proposition,'" or something akin to a "super-sized" vertically integrated steel corporation that could "meet the formidable and threatening competition of the greatest iron master in the country, Andrew Carnegie."[53]

The Illinois Steel Board of Directors was agreeable to what Judge Gary proposed but only if one of America's most preeminent financiers, J. Pierpont (J.P.) Morgan, would be willing to underwrite its cost. Gary, working nearly single-handed, took approximately three months to make all merger and other business arrangements. The end product was a new company, Federal Steel, which Illinois Steel now would join as a subsidiary. Federal Steel was capitalized at $200 million. So successful was Judge Gary in creating this new corporation that J.P. Morgan asked him to become its president. And so, in September 1898 Elbert H. Gary stepped from his career as a corporate attorney to his new job as president of the Federal Steel Company.[54]

Federal Steel's charter, according to Victor S. Clark, "was broad enough to cover the most varied operations: 'Mining of all kinds, manufacturing of all kinds, transportation of goods, merchandise, or passengers upon land or water; building houses, structures, vessels, ships, boats, railroads, engines, cars, or other equipment, wharves or docks, or constructing, maintaining, and operating railroads, steamship lines, vessel lines, or other lines for transportation; the purchase, improvement or sale of lands.'"[55] David Nasaw noted that Federal Steel's creation in 1898 was only the first great development in this new kind of business organization and that "with accelerating ferocity in 1899 and 1900, the merger movement transformed the steel industry."[56]

J.P. Morgan occupied a pivotal role in this merger movement. He had a virtual lock on America's financial institutions through his ownership or majority control of the nation's leading banking and insurance institutions. Morgan's initial ties to the steel business were indirect but formidable. He invested heavily in the ever-expanding railroad business in the late nineteenth century, and, as it happened, many of the railroads controlled by Morgan had coal connections. Since it was commonplace for railroads serving coal mines to actually own the mines and much of the adjoining properties, Morgan's control of the New York Central, the Pennsylvania, the Lehigh Valley, the Lackawanna, Erie, and New Jersey Central gave him a virtual mine-owning, coal-carrying monopoly in the anthracite region. Influence in the bituminous coal region was not as complete, though it was extensive, via control of the Baltimore & Ohio, the Chesapeake & Ohio, and the Hocking Valley Railroad.[57]

Railroads had proved to be outstanding investments while America was growing westward, but growth was slowing and the economic uncertainties of the late nineteenth century had caused J.P. Morgan to expand his investments into steel. The steel industry suffered the same economic ups and downs as railroads, particularly since the fortunes of both industries were so closely linked. But Morgan saw a very bright future for steel. The one obstacle to that future, though, was the ability of small independent steel companies to underprice the bigger companies and cause havoc in the marketplace. Andrew Carnegie solved that problem somewhat with his integrated company. To a great extent, the Federal Steel Company brought even more pricing stability to the industry. Either of these two giant companies, though, now could undermine the other. There was only one way to short-circuit that from happening: Morgan would have to buy out Carnegie and, in so doing, Judge Gary would have to mold Federal Steel and Carnegie Steel into a corporation unlike anything that ever had existed.

J.P. Morgan, Andrew Carnegie, and Elbert Gary all knew intuitively that an overture of some kind to merge Federal and Carnegie Steel would be forthcoming. The overture, as it happened, commenced on December 12, 1900, during a dinner attended by Morgan in honor of Carnegie Steel president Charles Schwab. Morgan and Schwab talked briefly at the dinner and agreed to talk more during the next two months about the merger possibility. Finally, in February 1901, J.P. Morgan informed Schwab that he was ready to buy Carnegie Steel. Morgan reportedly told Schwab, "If Andy wants to sell, I'll buy. Go and find his price."[58] Jean Strouse described what happened next: "Carnegie deliberated overnight. The next day—apparently disregarding moral qualms—he handed Schwab a single sheet of paper with his terms spelled out in pencil: the price he wanted for the Carnegie Company and all its holdings was $480 million. Since the company made approximately $40 million a year, the purchase price amounted to about twelve times earnings. Schwab drove downtown and presented the paper to Morgan, who took one look and said, 'I accept this price.'"[59]

Carnegie's asking price is in dispute. One writer placed it as low as $400 million, but several placed it as high as $492 million.[60] Dispute or not, the price was impressive and was said to be "the largest price that up to that time had ever been paid in the history of the world for a business enterprise."[61] On February 25, 1901, a charter was granted for the corporation that now emerged from the Carnegie transaction—the United States Steel Corporation. Official business for the new U.S. Steel began on April 1, 1901. With capital valued at just over $1.4 billion, the company became the world's first billion dollar enterprise. Judge Gary had "conceived the possibility of building a large steel empire, or as someone put it, a steel republic that would have worldwide influence."[62] Now, Gary's ambitious vision had happened. As his reward, J.P. Morgan named him to chair U.S. Steel's Executive Committee, a position roughly analogous to today's corporate CEO. Charles Schwab was named the corporation's president. And Morgan himself along with twenty-four others comprised U.S. Steel's board of directors.[63]

The "first and most notable effect of the [U.S. Steel] consolidation was to stabilize the price of iron and steel."[64] And how could it not? Certainly there were several big steel companies not included under the U.S. Steel umbrella, but the biggest, Carnegie Steel and Federal Steel in particular, were there. Just a brief glimpse of U.S. Steel's inventory and its manufacturing potential give some indication of how its massive size and tendrils that reached into every facet of the steel business must have overwhelmed smaller competitors. At its earliest days, U.S. Steel owned "73 blast furnaces, steel works, [and] rolling mills" capable of producing nearly 70 percent of all of America's steel rails. By virtue of its production capacity of roughly "7,400,000 tons of pig iron, 9,400,000 tons of steel ingots, and 7,900,000 tons of finished steel per annum," U.S. Steel "controlled 60 per cent of the structural steel product, a large fraction of the output of steel plates, sheets, bars, hoops and cotton ties; nearly the entire output of tin-plates and tubes; 60 per cent of the output of wire and wire rods; 95 per cent of the output of wire nails, and practically all of the barbed wire and woven-wire fence business, of which it had a virtual monopoly through the ownership of patents."[65]

U.S. Steel's transportation subsidiaries consisted of 1,500 miles of railroad, 428 locomotives, and 2,300 railway cars. The company also owned 112 ships and five docks at two harbors. In fact, its Great Lakes ore carrying "steamers and barges constituted the largest fleet engaged in any one traffic under the American flag, and [comprised] all the largest vessels in the trade." U.S. Steel mined more than half of the iron ore (approximately 13 million tons annually) mined in the Lake Superior region. And of the 21,000 coke ovens in the Connellsville region, U.S. Steel owned all but 1,200 of them.[66]

This steelmaking colossus appeared to have everything it needed to begin business on a grand scale. Yet, within two months of U.S. Steel's beginning Elbert Gary was negotiating to lease a sizable area of land in southern West Virginia where his company might have access to the rich Pocahontas coalfield.

Chapter 3

Pocahontas Coalfield and the N&W

Jordan Nelson was the first to actually exploit the splendid resource of Pocahontas coal that lay all around him, but he was not the first to know of its presence. Dr. Thomas Walker had written about the coalfield over a hundred years before. Thomas Jefferson, possibly drawing from Walker's journal, even referred to the coal rich area of western Virginia in his *Notes on the State of Virginia* in 1782.[1] Apparently, the first actual geological survey of the area comprising the Pocahontas field was made by Dr. William Barton Rogers, director of the Virginia Geological Survey from 1835 to 1841 and the first president of the Massachusetts Institute of Technology. In his "Report of the Geological Reconnoissance of the State of Virginia," published in 1835, Rogers said the following regarding his observations in western Virginia: "No section of the whole state offers perhaps so much that is characteristic, either in its physical geography or geological structure, and none holds out richer promise of valuable practical results as soon as it shall be systematically explored. By far, the greatest portion, if not all, of its strata belong to a group of formations, distinguished not only in America but throughout the world, as being the chief depositories of *bituminous* coal."[2]

Rogers made additional geological reports about western Virginia coal through 1841, but his and subsequent reports from other geologists emphasized the importance of coal in regions of the state that were more accessible to industrialists and mine operators. Navigable rivers such as the Kanawha, and railroads such as those built by the Baltimore & Ohio either before or during the Civil War, were providing necessary links from mine site to industrial user. Indeed, the possibilities for exploiting the raw materials of West Virginia led one writer to conclude, "A new era is now dawning. The capitalist has discovered, with keen vision, the abundant coal, iron, petroleum, and other wealth thus hidden, and the central location of the lands containing them; he has planted his money in these hills, and is determined to gather a golden harvest."[3]

But even after three-quarters of a century, *Resources of West Virginia,* a volume that claimed to give a comprehensive assessment of the state's mineral wealth, did little more than repeat what Rogers had reported earlier. The authors, M. F. Maury and William M. Fontaine, wrote, "This country [McDowell County] is accredited with seams as thick as 12 feet, but there are no reliable observations to justify more than a mere mention of this fact." Maury and Fontaine concluded that McDowell County "is very inaccessible, as may be gathered from the fact that not a single answer has been obtained to fifty circulars sent into it, asking for information. In consequence of this, we cannot give any detailed account of it."[4]

Actually, had Maury and Fontaine been acquainted with Jedediah Hotchkiss they would have gotten a wealth of information. After Dr. Thomas Walker, Jedediah ("Jed") Hotchkiss was the second person of prominence to be associated with the Pocahontas coalfield. Others were soon to follow. Some visited briefly, some stayed, and some never saw the area at all but attached themselves to the coalfield via second-party investors or as absentee land, mine, or railroad owners.

An "author, lecturer, geological authority, editor of an industrial journal, entrepreneur, and friend of Northern and English capitalists" who "tirelessly promoted Virginia's natural resources and industrial potential," Hotchkiss was described by an acquaintance as "a delightful conversationalist, a charming lecturer, and a man of commanding presence."[5] Hotchkiss was a New Yorker by birth (in 1828), but a trip to the Shenandoah Valley in 1847 turned him into a Virginian. He developed considerable skills as a geographer and mapmaker, and when the Civil War came Hotchkiss furnished maps for several Confederate generals, including Stonewall Jackson and Robert E. Lee. He set up shop in an "engineering and topographical office" in Staunton, Virginia, following the war. More important was his near evangelistic effort to convince anyone who would listen of what the abundant raw materials in this part of the country offered investors. Hotchkiss was especially interested in drawing attention to an area he had mapped in what now was southern West Virginia, an area identified by the high and elongated Flat Top Mountain that ran through it in a near north-south direction. It was at the southern end of the mountain where Jordan Nelson had begun chipping away at the coal outcrop described earlier. Jed Hotchkiss was well aware of the outcrop, and, contrary to geologists like Rogers who held that the coal here was sparse and of little value, Hotchkiss was certain of just the opposite.

Determined to confirm his theory, Jed Hotchkiss hired former Confederate soldier turned coal prospector Isaiah Welch to survey the Flat Top region in 1873 and to assess the amount and quality of coal there. What Welch found left little doubt that not only would mountain after mountain yield an abundance of the mineral, but the coal was of the highest quality.[6] With Welch's survey report tucked in his pocket, Hotchkiss set out to promote investment in the coal-rich property. His effort was assisted by the prevailing attitude shared by many industrialists of the period, like that of their counterparts in Great Britain a century before, that a coal mine "was as magnificent an asset as a gold mine."[7] Mark Twain and Charles Dudley Warner, coauthors of *The Gilded Age: A Tale of To-Day*—a title that forever after would attach itself to late nineteenth-century America—were themselves promoters of coal mining, though with a more sarcastic tone. One of Twain and Warner's characters was introduced early in the novel as seeking his fortune searching for an elusive vein of Pennsylvania coal. When he discovers the coal as the novel draws to a close, the writers describe him as having "become suddenly a person of consideration, whose speech was freighted with meaning, whose looks were all significant. The words of a proprietor of a rich coal mine have a golden sound, and his common sayings are repeated as if they were solid wisdom."[8] Despite the author's less than complimentary intentions, their not-so-subtle message was obvious: coal was important.

Few familiar with coal in the Flat Top region needed convincing that it was a prize worth pursuing. But two problems lay before anyone hoping to exploit the coal deposits. One was the "chaotic state of land titles" leading to uncertainty about just who owned the property. Much of the land belonged originally to speculators who had purchased small tracts from Revolutionary War veterans and assembled them into huge landholdings. A considerable portion of the land, though, had been forfeited to the state of West Virginia following the Civil War due to nonpayment of taxes.[9] Ownership of small parcels of the land then passed to farmers interested only in living on and working their property. But by the 1870s companies and syndicates were dispatching agents to acquire the property. The traditional assumption has been that many of the farmers who owned the land often had no idea of its value; thus they were either poorly compensated for what they gave up or swindled out of their land by unscrupulous public officials who had little reluctance in agreeing to fraudulent property claims of wealthy speculators in exchange for hefty bribes.[10] And it is sad to say that the story of coal development in southern West Virginia requires acknowledgment that the great industry probably was founded largely on deceit and questionable real estate practices.

However, Randall Lawrence's investigation of land dealing in McDowell County found that a number of the "mountain landowners" were quite able to hold their own in the bargaining process when dealing with speculators. Lawrence also found that a considerable portion of McDowell County acreage had been purchased by as many as sixteen individuals and two companies prior to and during the Civil War. All were absentee owners with addresses as far away as New York, Philadelphia, Baltimore, Richmond, and even Paris, France. Why they purchased the McDowell County land is uncertain, but their ownership appeared legal. Company and syndicate agents arriving in McDowell County to buy land in the 1870s had to deal with these big land owners just as persuasively as they dealt with the small landowners.[11]

Regardless of how it was done, land somehow had to be purchased before the second of the two problems standing in the way of exploiting coal deposits could be resolved. That problem, of course, was creating a means to transport coal from the mines. The problem's solution was obvious: railroads. The first effort to build a railroad in the vicinity was initiated by a group of Virginia businessmen and investors in 1872. The group was led by Gabriel C. Wharton, then a member of the Virginia general assembly. Wharton, while serving as a Confederate general during the Civil War, had led troops into the Flat Top Mountain region and had seen firsthand numerous coal outcroppings there. He immediately grasped the commercial significance of what he saw. Shortly after voters elected Wharton to the Virginia legislature, he pushed for approval of a charter to incorporate the New River Railroad, Mining and Manufacturing Company. The charter, granted on March 7, 1872, empowered the new company, which comprised Wharton and his twenty-five business and investor friends, to build branch railroads in several southwestern Virginia and southern West Virginia counties for the purpose of transporting coal, iron, and other minerals to the main line of the Atlantic, Mississippi, and Ohio Railroad at Pulaski, Virginia.[12] The new railroad company actually predated by over a year the Hotchkiss release of the Welch survey report, which possibly explains why the railroad owners included nothing in their charter about specific places or mines that their railroad would serve.

Soon another group of investors appeared, these from Philadelphia, with interests in the coal mining potential of the area. Some confusion exists over just what precipitated their visit. One source says that the group's leader, Thomas Graham, and several of his associates decided to personally investigate the area in 1873 after reading about Isaiah Welch's survey. After visiting with Jordan Nelson and exploring some of the places Welch had claimed contained coal deposits, the Philadelphia group was convinced of the area's potential for coal mining and agreed that a railroad was necessary to connect various coal properties and to carry the coal away.[13]

Two groups now were vying for the same objective, and at least one writer charged that the Philadelphia group "cunningly devised" a scheme to gain control of the Virginia group's charter.[14] Whether or not that was the case is both uncertain and somewhat irrelevant, since economic conditions at the time precluded building the planned railroad.[15] By 1880, relations between the Virginia and Philadelphia groups appeared cordial enough for the two to merge and form the New River Railroad Company.[16] One of the new company's few actions following its formation was to acquire "valuable options" to nearly 100,000 acres of "cream of the coal and other mineral lands."[17] The intent of the New River Railroad Company's board of directors at this point seemed less focused on building a railroad than on holding their valuable charter and property options while awaiting a suitable buyer. The wait would be a short one, and the board would have Jed Hotchkiss to thank.

Hotchkiss, ever the promoter, launched in January 1880 a monthly magazine called *The Virginias: A Mining, Industrial, and Scientific Journal Devoted to the Development of Virginia and West Virginia*, which carried a wealth of geological and geographical information about the region. The subscription list included financiers, industrialists, and American as well as European investors. Once more, Philadelphians— most notably investment bankers at E. W. Clark and Company—paid particular attention to what Hotchkiss was publishing. Their interest intensified in February 1881, when the Clark group in partnership with investors from several British banks purchased the financially troubled Atlantic, Mississippi, and Ohio Railroad, whose route carried it from Norfolk in eastern Virginia across the state to Bristol in southwestern Virginia. The railroad was given the new name of Norfolk and Western Railway Company, or the N&W.

One of the Clark group's youngest associates, Frederick J. Kimball, who would rise to the N&W presidency in 1883 and remain there for the next twenty-one years, was soon requesting more information from Hotchkiss about Virginia and West Virginia coal deposits. By May 1881, Kimball, two associates, and, reportedly, Kimball's wife were traveling to the area to assess firsthand the quantity and quality of its coal. After inspecting the coal outcrop near Jordan Nelson's farm, Kimball remarked to one of his associates, "This may prove to be an important day in our lives."[18]

Frederick Kimball lost little time in convincing his E. W. Clark partners of the importance of the coal deposits he had seen. Not only could the coal be used to fuel N&W locomotives, but the railroad also could become a major coal carrier. But first the Clark group had to negotiate to purchase railroad rights of way and property options from the New River Railroad Company. With little apparent quibbling, buyer and seller signed an agreement on June 23, 1881. One important stipulation of the agreement was that a "proper corporation" independent of the N&W Railroad Company, but still largely controlled by persons connected with E. W. Clark and Company, be created to hold title to all coal properties that had been under New River's control. The corporation formed for such purpose in September 1881 was called the Southwest Virginia Improvement Company. Titles to all coal property now under the Southwest Virginia Improvement Company's control were cleared, and by January 1882 the company opened its first mine where Nelson once gathered coal by the bucket load. A company town named Pocahontas was built near the mine for the miners and their families who soon would be moving to the area.

Meanwhile, construction had begun in August 1881 on a nearly seventy-five-mile N&W rail extension to Pocahontas. The extension, to be called the N&W's New River Division, left the main line at New River Bridge near Radford, Virginia, and traveled northwest along the river-banks of the New, the East, and the Bluestone rivers until finally reaching Pocahontas. The coal that already had been mined in Pocahontas prior to the railroad's arrival was loaded into coal cars, and on March 12, 1883, an N&W locomotive pulled away with the first of many trainloads of coal that would come from the surrounding mountains.[19]

The Southwest Company provided N&W all land necessary for building spur tracks, but the railroad company was responsible for laying and maintaining its own rails. Southwest also agreed to develop its mining properties and to transport all coal subsequently mined via N&W rails exclusively. Legal exigencies forced the Southwest Company to reorganize itself as the Flat Top Land Trust by 1887. The company name shortly changed once more to Flat Top Coal Land Association. The company's reorganization also brought a change in direction. The Flat Top Coal Land Association continued its land acquisition, but rather than operate coal mines itself, the company leased land to other mine operators.

Flat Top's move was a good one. The company purchased land, some of it for as little as $1.50 an acre, whose value quickly appreciated. By 1888 the Flat Top Coal Land Association owned much of the land in the Pocahontas coalfield, an area of approximately 247,000 acres, about 150,000 of which was "underlaid with coal." Some 65,000 acres of the Flat Top land was in McDowell County. Quite possibly, though, the company did not yet own the land where Gary eventually would grow. Evidence of that comes from this vague reference to unsurveyed land on the Tug River in McDowell County, found in Flat Top's first annual report: "It is the policy of this Association to buy lands contiguous to those we now own when we find them valuable for coal, and they can be had at reasonable prices. A large body of coal lands acquired from the South West Virginia Improvement Company lies across Flat-top mountain from Pocahontas in McDowell County, on the waters of Tug River, and there is a considerable body of adjoining land underlaid with No. 3 coal from seven to nine feet thick and above water level. We have contracted for the purchase of several thousand acres of this land, and are examining titles and will complete surveys after the opening of spring."[20] Lessee coal companies usually signed thirty-year leases with the Flat Top Coal Land Association with an opportunity to renew leases for an additional thirty years. The coal companies also agreed to pay royalties to Flat Top based on tons of coal mined. Leases averaged one thousand acres each, and in order to assure a supply of coke for iron and steelmaking, each "lessee was required to build one bee-hive coke oven for each ten acres of lease."[21]

Completion of N&W's New River Division was not the company's ultimate goal. Its first annual report, issued at the end of 1881, stated that the N&W planned to extend its railroad all the way to the Ohio River, "thus forming a through line to the West and Northwest."[22] Hotchkiss had provided N&W President Kimball an analysis and map in 1881, with his recommendation for the best route to the Ohio,[23] but moving beyond the present terminus at Pocahontas would require a recommendation on how to deal with the Great Flat Top Divide that rose above the land like the spine of a giant razorback. N&W chief engineer W. W. Coe presented Kimball three options in April 1885: go north and cross, go south and cross, or bore through the mountain only a short distance from Pocahontas and follow the Elkhorn Fork of the Tug River on the west side of Flat Top.[24]

The tunnel option was chosen, and by the late 1890s the 3,100 feet Flat Top, or Coaldale, tunnel was ready for use, although its steep grade from both sides challenged locomotive engineers from that time forward.[25] The tunnel's completion was an engineering feat, but it also was a symbolic opening to what the N&W called its Ohio Extension. Considerable attention had been given to the best route for building the remainder of the railroad onward to the Ohio River. Added to Hotchkiss's 1881 recommendation were several coming from Coe.[26] And one favoring a particular route came from Clark, president of the Flat Top Coal Land Association. Clark, who had sent an agent to assess the Big Sandy and Tug Fork route, enclosed a copy of the agent's report with his letter to Kimball. He noted how the route would shorten the railroad distance for hauling coke—the N&W's "surest source of revenue"—to Chicago. He then drew comparisons between the more widely known Connellsville coal and coke region and the potential for coal and coke from the Flat Top region, noting several advantages potential buyers of Pocahontas coke would have over buyers of Connellsville coke:

> The demand for Connellsville coke has been so large during the past two years, mainly for the manufacture and melting of iron, that the [coal] operators have been able to obtain large prices for their product. Labour has for a long time been very unsettled in that field, and great loss and inconvenience resulted to consumers from partial or general strikes. The coke gives general satisfaction, but large consumers desire to find other sources of supply so that they may not be dependent entirely on the one field. They have not found elsewhere any coke as good as Connellsville excepting that from the Flat-Top field, which after repeated competitive tests, is now recognized as the best coke sent to market.[27]

The suggestion by Clark and others to follow that Pocahontas coal was a superior coking coal, better even than Connellsville coal, was not well received by folks who lived in the Connellsville region. The long history and proud tradition of coal mining in this southwestern corner of Pennsylvania has been well documented.[28] Suggesting that a superior coking coal existed in the Pocahontas coalfield would be a competitive bone of contention between the two regions for years to come. And, by an ironic twist of fate, Connellsville and Gary would come to share much in common once U.S. Steel expanded into southern West Virginia. In the 1880s, though, ranking the quality of Connellsville coal and coke *below* that of Pocahontas coal and coke was a blow to pride that likely carried significant economic as well as commercial implications.

Southern West Virginia happened to be blessed with geological conditions that produced coal perfect for not only coking but also heating and transportation fuel. As described by Charles Kenneth Sullivan, "The high quality bituminous is low in gases which the trade refers to as 'volatiles,' including methane, hydrogen, and ammonia, and in sulphur and ash. Fixed carbon content is high, as consequently in the mineral's BTU rating." Because of the coal's clean burning quality (earning the name "smokeless coalfields" for the several West Virginia counties where it was found), Pocahontas coal not destined for the coking ovens and then to the steel mills "became the standard fuel for the steam-powered American navy."[29] "The Pocahontas No. 3 seam was the one first worked" here, read a 1920s N&W brochure, "and upon the purity and general excellence of the coal from it was founded the enviable reputation of the field."[30]

The term "smokeless coal," according to William McKinley Merrill, "is a trade name in common use. . . . Technically, it is more correct to refer to the smokeless coals as low volatile or semibituminous." The chemical composition of low volatile coal makes it ideal for coke making, and according to Merrill, "the low volatile coals of Southern West Virginia are not surpassed by any other low volatile coals in the United States in those properties necessary for making the best coke."[31] The smokeless coalfields comprise three smaller fields—the Pocahontas, New River, and Winding Gulf—and they stretch northeastward from Tazewell County, Virginia, into McDowell, Mercer, Wyoming, Raleigh, and Fayette counties in West Virginia.[32] The Pocahontas is the westernmost of the three smokeless fields and quite possibly is the only one whose area has been delimited by judicial decree and defined by railroad lines. In *American Coal Company et al. vs. John R. Morris et al.*, the judge writing the decision described the Pocahontas field as "a certain definite territory which includes portions of McDowell, Mercer, and Wyoming counties, West Virginia and Tazewell County, Virginia, and is that territory served by the Norfolk and Western Railway by its main line and branch lines between Flat Top Yard and Iaeger, W.Va., and by its Dry Fork line from Iaeger, W. Va to Cedar Bluff, Va.; and that territory served by the Virginian Railway, main line, from Clark's Gap at Maben, and on its branch line from Mullens to Stone Coal Creek."[33]

Jedediah Hotchkiss was really the first to apply what Charles Kenneth Sullivan called his "industrial propagandist" encomiums to the riches of Pocahontas coal in the pages of his *Virginias* magazine. The June 1882 issue, for example, described the "coals of unsurpassed excellence for domestic, steam, metallurgical and other purposes, and especially for the making of pure, high-grade cokes."[34] In that same issue Hotchkiss reported the results of an analysis of Pocahontas No. 3 coal furnished to Kimball by Andrew S. McCreath. McCreath was identified as "the chemist of the Second Geological Survey of Pennsylvania." The coal composition he described was as follows:

Water	0.932
Volatile matter	20.738
Fixed carbon	73.728
Sulphur	0.618
Ash	3.984
Total	100.000

McCreath also determined that the coal once baked would yield 78.330 percent coke.[35]

Two years later, Kimball commissioned McCreath to expand on his analysis and then published McCreath's results in *The Mineral Wealth of Virginia*. The above figures remained unchanged in the expanded analysis. "Many of the leading Iron Masters of Pennsylvania" considered McCreath to be "eminently capable, trustworthy, and conservative" in his work.[36] For a Pennsylvanian of such impeccable credentials and standards to be giving such high marks to Pocahontas coal carried particular relevance.

Regardless of expertise, claims of superior coking coal coming from southern West Virginia were taken as a challenge in Connellsville, and at least one local newspaper—the *Keystone Courier* (later shortened to the *Courier*)—decided to hire an expert of its own to conduct an analysis of Connellsville coal. To no one's surprise the "expert" decreed Connellsville coal to be superior. The *Courier*'s results were hardly conclusive and indeed were criticized by an authority in metallurgy for the manner by which the analysis was conducted.[37] Moreover, the results published in the *Courier* pertained to the physical properties of Connellsville *coke*, not the chemical properties of Connellsville *coal*. *Courier* editor Henry P. Snyder was convinced that he had proved his point as to which part of the country produced the highest quality of both coal and coke. A 1914 retrospective of the controversy published in the Connellsville *Weekly Courier* said the article reporting the analysis results "was circulated all over the industrial world. The West Virginia interests made no answer to it; there was none. It did more than any other single circumstance to establish the superiority of Connellsville coke and to fix the growing value of Connellsville coal."[38]

The "no answer" claim was incorrect, although there is uncertainty as to whether the claim was made before the April 1883 issue of *The Virginias*. Nonetheless, subsequent reports of the chemical composition of Connellsville coal showed it to be slightly inferior to Pocahontas coal. In fact, an analysis of Connellsville coal for distribution at the 1893 Chicago World's Fair showed the following:

Water	1.130
Volatile matter	29.812
Fixed carbon	60.420
Sulphur	.689
Ash	7.949[39]

An analysis of coal from several Connellsville coal mines completed in 1900 gave similar results. Of the coal analyzed from ten mines, the following composition was the best of the group:

Water	0.000
Volatile matter	28.400
Fixed carbon	65.360
Sulphur	1.340
Ash	4.900[40]

Comparisons of the above composition analyses of Connellsville coal with the earlier one for Pocahontas coal seem conclusive with evidence that confirms claims made for the superiority of the Pocahontas coal. At any rate, competition between the two areas remained intense but friendly.

If the quality of Pocahontas coal was not reason enough for mine operators to flock to southern West Virginia, there was in addition the coal's accessibility and the control that operators could exercise over their employees. Sullivan described the "obliging geology" that had positioned the Pocahontas seams above the creek and riverbeds, and at a relatively level, horizontal plane, allowing "ease of entry to the miner, largely preventing the need for extensive shaft or slope-mouth excavation." A "well-behaved seam," said Sullivan, meant coal that "was easy to mine as well." And "easy coal is cheap coal, in terms of the money costs of production."

No less important was cheap labor. The mine operator could draw on not only indigenous workers but also "eastern European peasants and displaced blacks from the American South." Union organizers eventually came calling, but "in the early years these people remained unorganized and received the lowest wages in the industry."[41] Coal operators certainly had to look favorably at the labor situation, since there was ample evidence from the Connellsville region of just how disruptive labor unrest could be. This highly concentrated area comprised roughly fifty mines or "works," and with its 7,000 coke ovens it "produced over two-thirds of the nation's coke."[42] Yet, as one writer explained, "Labor troubles began almost with the time the coke trade assumed industrial proportions. From 1881 until 1894 the history of the region was one of almost constant strife. When the miners were not quarreling with their employers they were fighting among themselves."[43]

More peaceful conditions prevailed in the Pocahontas coalfield once mining was fully under way. The N&W was on the move by March 1890 to complete its Ohio Extension, and a bridge across the Ohio River at Kenova, West Virginia, was begun at the same time that grading and track laying on the rest of the line commenced. The Ohio Extension was complete and opened to rail traffic by November 1892.[44] Coal operators could hardly wait. Nearly thirty mines strung along the N&W railroad in McDowell County either were operational or nearing completion by the time rail service began.[45]

The fictional character in Twain and Warner's *The Gilded Age* who finally became wealthy when he discovered coal now was supplanted by real persons in West Virginia whose search for coal along the N&W was much easier and probably more lucrative. So much so, in fact, that they needed a suitable place both to transact business as well as to live the life worthy of a coal baron. Bramwell, West Virginia, became that place. Named for Flat Top Coal Land Association surveyor Joseph Bramwell, town site was founded in the early 1880s as the company's home base. Only a short distance from Pocahontas, Virginia, it was built on a rare flat horseshoe bend of land bordered by the Bluestone River. Besides opulent homes that housed coal operators and their families, Bramwell's most important commercial structure was its bank—the Bank of Bramwell, chartered in 1889, and destined shortly to become "the financial capital of the Pocahontas Coalfield in its glory days."[46]

The Bank of Bramwell would become one of the most successful banks in West Virginia, due in large part to the management skills of its president Isaac T. Mann. Mann arrived in Bramwell in 1889, became a teller at the Bank of Bramwell, and climbed quickly to become the bank's president. He eventually rose to the directorship of several local banks, the Continental Trust in Washington, D.C., and the N&W Railway. He became what some historians have called the "'leading financier' of the southern coalfields" and was in a perfect position to meet and confer with other top financiers and industrialists from West Virginia and elsewhere. Among those in whose circles he moved was Judge Elbert Gary.[47] Precisely how Mann and Gary met is uncertain, but the reason for their acquaintance is beyond doubt. Gary was interested in acquiring coal property in the Pocahontas field on behalf of U.S. Steel, and Mann was the preeminent person to help make that happen.

There are several reasons why Elbert Gary was interested in coal from this region. According to his biographer, Ida Tarbell, his interest in raw material sources began when he became counsel to the Illinois Steel Company. His concern over where the company acquired its coal and at what price most certainly brought him into contact with people well acquainted with the coking qualities of Pocahontas coal.[48] There is evidence, too, that Chicago was the test site in the late 1880s for comparing Pocahontas coal with Connellsville coal.[49] The test possibly had been sanctioned by Gary or perhaps another Illinois Steel official. Test results likely had been a factor in the company's decision to begin transporting coal from one of the newly opened Pocahontas coalfield mines.[50] Adding to Illinois Steel's decision was the fact that McDowell County was closer to Chicago than was the Connellsville area because of the N&W's Ohio Extension. A shorter route also meant potential cost savings to Illinois Steel.

Gary was also concerned that the Connellsville coal region was U.S. Steel's only source of coke. Such heavy reliance put U.S. Steel at the mercy of the region's unsettled labor problems, disputes that could result in strikes.[51] In addition, the area had been so heavily mined over the years that coal reserves were in danger of depletion. The situation was not immediately critical, but securing additional sources of coal would be a wise move.[52] Coal from U.S. Steel's mines in the Pocahontas field would give the company more source diversity and control over labor organizers.

Gary may also have been anxious to head off competing coal operators in securing prime coal mining property in McDowell County. While most mining in the county at the turn of the century was confined to operations close to the N&W's main line, that would not be the case for much longer. Even in 1893, in a publication prepared for distribution at the World's Columbian Exposition, McDowell County was touted as a coal mining mecca. Describing how the N&W had opened the area to world commerce, the piece read, "Practically a wilderness a few years ago with only a scattering population among the mountains and scarcely any degree of civilization, the county is now rapidly becoming one of the foremost in the State in a business way and the development of its coal is rapidly bringing the county into prominence."[53]

Gary and fellow U.S. Steel executive committee member William Edenborn joined with Mann to form the Pocahontas Coal Syndicate, or simply the Gary Syndicate. In *From Mine to Market*, Joseph T. Lambie describes in detail what happened next. The condensed version is that when the Gary Syndicate approached the Flat Top Coal Land Association, presumably to lease only a suitable acreage of land for coal mining, the association officers offered to sell Gary, and thereby U.S. Steel, all of the nearly 239,000 acres currently in its possession. On June 19, 1901, the Gary Syndicate was offered, for a $50,000 deposit, an option to buy all of Flat Top's property for $10 million. Prior to exercising its option the Gary Syndicate had acquired options to additional property that brought the total to about 300,000 acres, or approximately "82 per cent of the entire Pocahontas coal field," and brought the total price to $13.5 million. Gary and his partners lost little time in exercising their option. The landholding and mining company that now replaced the Flat Top Coal Land Association would be known as the Pocahontas Coal and Coke Company.[54]

But did U.S. Steel really intend to be such a prominent property owner in southern West Virginia, or was the transaction orchestrated by the Gary Syndicate simply a business maneuver? And where was the N&W whose board of directors had been roughly the same as that of the Flat Top Coal Land Association? Was the railroad company offered the same option as the one offered the Gary Syndicate? If so, then why did N&W executives and board of directors reject the deal? Lambie maintains that Kimball had always opposed the N&W assuming ownership of property the railroad served. But when that property came under control of a company like U.S. Steel, which had no ties whatsoever with the N&W, Kimball became alarmed. The careful control that the N&W management in cooperation with the Flat- Top group could maintain over the extent of leasing and the level of coal mining and coke production in the Pocahontas field now would be in jeopardy. Perhaps even more important was the possibility that U.S. Steel could entice another railroad company to compete with the N&W or, worse yet, U.S. Steel could build its own railroad into the region.

The possibilities were such that Kimball assembled the N&W executive committee, explained the consequences of the Gary Syndicate deal, and recommended that committee members immediately contact Gary with a proposal to buy the less-than-one-year-old Pocahontas Coal and Coke Company. Without hesitating, the Gary Syndicate agreed to negotiate a sell, but the price would be a hefty $20 million. Again, without hesitating, the N&W accepted. The railroad company assumed ownership of 300,000 acres of land and a land management company whose name would be changed to Pocahontas Land Corporation in 1939. The N&W executives had no intentions of entering the mining business and instead leased its land through the Pocahontas Coal and Coke Company to coal operators, just as the old Flat Top Coal Land Association had done. The N&W became what "essentially was a landholding company divided into land, coal, timber, and railroad divisions that controlled hundreds of thousands of acres."[55]

"Control" was the key word. Now the N&W could pick and choose its coal operator lessees, adjust freight and royalty rates whenever necessary, and, best of all, maintain a monopoly coal carrier railroad service in most of southern West Virginia. U.S. Steel, on the other hand, gained considerable profit on the N&W purchase. More important, though, was the thirty-year lease agreement, effective December 31, 1901, of 50,000 acres of land in McDowell County for coal mining and coke production. Both coal and coke had to be shipped via the N&W "and its designated connections" with "guaranteed freight rates as favorable as those of other routes and coal fields." The lease "also provided that not fewer than 1,000 [coke] ovens should be erected in 1902 and an additional 1,000 ovens in each of the next two years." U.S. Steel finally "agreed, reluctantly, that all coal mined and coke produced should be for its own use and not for sale." N&W executives were especially relieved to have this stipulation a part of the lease agreement, since it prevented U.S. Steel from dominating the marketplace and single-handedly affecting the production level and pricing of coal coming from other N&W-served coal operators.[56]

There is some question, though, of just how compliant U.S. Steel was with regard to the N&W. Had the big steel company refused to agree with any of the railroad company's demands, exactly what could the N&W have done about it? After all, the same J. P. Morgan banking empire that controlled U.S. Steel also controlled the Pennsylvania Railroad, which by 1900 had acquired approximately 30 percent interest in the N&W. That was not enough for Morgan to claim any controlling interest. But when the N&W was negotiating with the Gary Syndicate (representing, incidentally, J. P. Morgan's U.S. Steel) for purchase of the Pocahontas Coal and Coke Company in 1901, it was J. P. Morgan and Company to whom N&W turned to help finance the deal.[57] It would appear that Morgan held final say over any decision and any move made in the Pocahontas coalfield once the N&W/Gary Syndicate transaction was completed.

Money and ownership matters aside, the next step for U.S. Steel in 1902 was rapid development of its 50,000-acre McDowell County leasehold. Mine works and beehive coking ovens had to be constructed; town sites had to be surveyed; houses, stores, and other structures had to be built; the N&W had to extend a railroad connection south from its mainline at Welch; and workers and their families had to be persuaded to move into these wild environs to commence coal mining.

Chapter 4

Gary at the Beginning

Among the crazy quilt of companies gathered beneath the U.S. Steel umbrella, Illinois Steel took initial lease of the newly acquired McDowell County property. The connection with Illinois Steel was logical, since most coke produced in the county would be destined to Chicago area steel plants (and later to steel plants in Ohio), and Illinois Steel officials already were familiar with the coal mined in the area.[1] Corporate maneuvering, though, had moved management of McDowell County property to a new U.S. Steel subsidiary, the United States Coal and Coke Company (USCC), by June 1902. USCC would be responsible for constructing the coal works and town sites that soon would appear along the banks of the Tug River.[2] And as already stipulated in U.S. Steel's agreement with the N&W, USCC would supply coal and coke only to its parent company and would rely exclusively on the N&W to ship both.

The USCC's corporate headquarters was moved from its original location at Welch to Gary in 1913, and after a series of additional leases USCC expanded its total leased property in McDowell and surrounding West Virginia counties to nearly 118,000 acres. The company also leased some 40,000 acres in eastern Kentucky.[3] USCC's principal operation, though, remained in the area it began developing in 1902. A June 15, 1902, *Bluefield Daily Telegraph* story, appearing only one day after USCC's formation, introduced readers in this West Virginia coal region to the presence of their new neighbor. The story told of contracts for the construction of 950 coke ovens, all to be built by a Greensburg, Pennsylvania, company. In addition, "Three mines will be opened, work on which has already been started. The motive power for the operation of the mines, cars and tipples will be electricity. Plans for the erection of an electric power plant are now being drawn. Near the mines in the vicinity of Welch, the company will erect a 20 room club house, two stories high, for the use of the employees. The contract to put up this building has been awarded to A. T. Stevenson of Pittsburg [sic]. During the coming year the company will also put up 300 dwelling houses, to be occupied by its miners. In short, *what is now an almost broken forest is to be turned into a great mining center, and a great mining town is to be built there.*"[4] Actually, there were a few families scattered among several log cabins where Gary would soon grow. There was even a post office about a mile north of Gary at Tug River, which was renamed Wilcoe by USCC officials.[5]

While residents of the southern West Virginia coal region were reading about the new coal mining operation at Gary, so were coal mining and steel plant executives nationwide doing the same in the pages of various trade publications. The *Coal Trade Journal*, in February 1902, reported on U.S. Steel's lease of Pocahontas field property, noting that the company had secured "sufficient coal of the best character and quality to provide, on the present basis of consumption, for about 30 years. This, with the Connellsville coal now owned, will, on the same basis, furnish the necessary supply of coke for upwards of 60 years."[6]

The *Engineering and Mining Journal* reported in its February 1902 issue that William Glyde Wilkins, "the Frick Company coke and mining engineering expert" had examined U.S. Steel's Gary area and had arranged for opening several mines there in advance of USCC's formal creation.[7] The same publication reported in May 1902 that locations had been determined for eight mines and for roughly 1,000 to 1,200 coke ovens in the soon-to-be USCC operation. In addition, a contract had been awarded "for putting in a saw mill and for felling the forest near the mines." The article also mentioned that the N&W was building a branch line from Welch into the USCC operation, but the line would not be complete until September 1902. The line's completion was key to hauling heavy items to the USCC construction site.[8]

Another progress report, appearing in the *Engineering and Mining Journal's* June 28, 1902, issue, said that USCC was preparing to "spend in the next year not less than $3,000,000 in building new coke ovens, dwelling houses for the coal miners and installing machinery in the Pocahontas coal fields." The report also announced that "Thomas Lynch, president of the H. C. Frick Coke Company, and general manager of all the coal and coking operations of [U.S. Steel], and president of most of the subsidiary concerns engaged in the coal and coke production for the Steel Corporation, will be president of [USCC]."[9]

All of the construction planned by USCC awaited the railroad. A suitable highway from Welch into the Gary area would not be built until the 1920s, and the existing dirt trails meant only for foot, horse, and wagon traffic simply could not accommodate the kind of transportation now needed.[10] N&W was doing its best to serve those needs as quickly as possible. Starting at some point in 1902, the N&W created the Tug Fork Branch from Welch to Gary and beyond to the other USCC satellite towns. Spur and siding railroads were built along the banks of the Tug River southeast to Wilcoe and then to Gary and then on east to Venus and Thorpe. From Gary the N&W built a second spur called the Sand Lick Branch that ran nearly due south of Gary, following Sand Lick Creek to

Ream, Elbert, and Filbert. Railroads on both the Tug Fork Branch and the Sand Lick Branch were serviceable by mid-1903 and nearing completion by mid-1904.[11]

By summer 1903 construction of the USCC industrial facilities at Gary was well under way. USCC consulting electrical engineer George R. Wood of Pittsburgh reported in *Mines and Minerals* how the company's "new central electrical power plant . . . was successfully started on August 3, [1903]," and that three "coking plants" were "in partial operation" as of September 15, 1903. Expectations were that all ten of the proposed plants would be complete by the following October. The coking plants were the ovens, ranging from 250 to 450 per mine works built near the mine portals. A total of 3,600 such ovens was planned for the ten USCC mine works in and around Gary. "When it is recalled that the entire Pocahontas field has not over 8,000 ovens in blast," said Wood, "the magnitude of this new work is apparent." And if that failed to adequately impress readers, Wood added the following about the modern mining equipment and features to be employed in the USCC mines: "Electric locomotives will gather the coal from the rooms [or coal facings], larger locomotives will handle to the outside; at the bins will be electrically driven elevators and crushes; electric larries will deliver coal to the ovens; electrically driven centrifugal and deep-well pumps will supply water to ovens; electric motors of large capacity will drive ventilating fans for mines, . . and offices, stores, shops, and miners' houses will be lighted by electricity. The plant, as a whole, will, in short be *the most complete and largest electric coal-mining plant in the world.*"[12]

All of the building that was going on required manpower and money. George Wood estimated that as of September 1903 more than 3,000 men were "at work on construction of ovens and plants, and probably 2,000 additional could be employed if obtainable."[13] Data compiled from U.S. Steel annual reports show an estimated $4 million alone spent on the Gary operation by 1905, with roughly $2 million more spent by 1910.[14] The cost was high, but the reason seemed obvious. U.S. Steel was committed to building a first-class operation and model towns. The objective was unique for an industry where living conditions for workers and their families too often were less than ideal. Robert F. Munn, writing about the situation the West Virginia coal industry faced during the early 1900s, said the industry's "involvement in the housing and social welfare of its labor force was the result of historical accident rather than conscious choice." Munn pointed out that coal mines usually were located some distance from established communities and the amenities—houses, stores, schools, and churches—that communities typically provide. Poor road conditions, if roads even existed, and few automobiles meant that mine workers and their families had to live near the mines themselves. "Thus," said Munn, "if a company wished to attract and retain miners, it had no option but to provide at least basic housing and a store." Munn described how coal company owners reacted to their "unsought role as landlord":

> The majority clearly regarded the company town as a necessary evil, to which a prudent manager devoted as little time, energy and money as possible. Most company officials appear to have known little and cared less about the living conditions of their employees. There were, however, exceptions. Even in the early days of the industry, a small but growing number of bituminous coal operators were concerned with improving the quality of life of miners living in their towns. Motives were, of course, mixed. Some were moved by social conscience, other[s] by a conviction that benevolence was good business, still others by an unwillingness to have their names associated with an unkept [sic] cluster of shacks.
> . . .
> Thus [mine owners] argued that modest investments in better housing and recreational facilities would pay off by attracting the "better class of miners." This class, being responsible, sober and stable, would work hard and scorn the blandishments of "labor agitators."[15]

The need and desire to construct coal mining towns in the best possible way struck a responsive chord among officials who were responsible for such construction. Whether their intentions were fired by pure benevolence or by some less-than-admirable ulterior motive is difficult to judge. Whatever the motivation, it seems that U.S. Steel's determination to build a model coal mining operation in McDowell County came from the very top—from Judge Elbert Gary himself.

The story of Gary's role in the development of the town that eventually was named in his honor was told by Donald R. Beeson, a pioneer resident of Gary and native of Connellsville, Pennsylvania. Beeson was working at U.S. Steel's American Bridge Company (Ambridge) near Pittsburgh when he learned that engineers were needed at the company's new West Virginia coal mining operation. Beeson left his job at Ambridge in 1902 and traveled to Welch aboard a freight train and then on to Gary by mule. He lived there from 1902 to 1905, working as a draftsman in the USCC engineering department and then as company photographer. His first impression of what he called "that godforsaken corner of the world" was "a model of a tough and wicked community."[16] Clearly, changes needed to be made.

According to Beeson, Judge Gary visited the area on several occasions. He was interested, of course, in the progress workers were making on building the mining works. But he was just as interested in the progress toward construction of houses that were beginning to dot every available piece of level ground. Gary had traveled to Germany in 1902 to investigate living conditions of German steelworkers and coal miners. What he saw and learned there impressed him.[17] During the late nineteenth century, German industrialists saw the need to improve the living conditions of their workers. As one German mine inspector stated in 1902, "the provision of good housing for the workers is the best and only means in the Ruhr coal-mining district to settle the workers and limit the extremely strong labour turnover. . . . The building of good housing is thus as much to the economic advantage of the employer as to that of the workers."[18]

When Gary returned from Germany, he asked Donald Beeson and a colleague to provide him with draft plans "based on sketches of German 'miners' houses' with bath rooms and kitchen sinks"—accommodations that were unique for company houses at the time. Gary liked the plans Beeson submitted and ordered that several houses be built according to their specifications. Shortly after they were built and occupied, Gary paid a surprise visit to their occupants. To what might have been great dismay, he found in many cases that "the bath tubs were being used to store coal and the lavatories and sinks and closets were all stopped and out of use." According to Beeson, "We looked for the experiment to end there but the Judge paid close attention to all details, talked with the men and women at the houses and reserved his judgement till next day. Much to the surprise of everybody familiar with the matter, he came to the chief engineer next day and ordered that all workers houses then projected, something over a hundred, have bath rooms and kitchen sinks."[19]

Unfortunately, subsequent decisions limited most houses to outdoor toilets, with bathrooms reserved for superintendents and mine foremen housing. All houses, though, were connected to a "community water supply, with a pipe to every kitchen," and were wired for electric lights. Where possible, houses were "built on stone piers, requiring little excavation. Afterwards, steam shovels were used to excavate a terrace along the hillside, on which the houses were placed, with the roads back of them. The first houses cost about $250 a room, including all fixtures and facilities."[20] A writer who visited Gary in 1914, after many of the houses had been completed, described them as "well constructed and all frame lumber is of the best quality of hemlock. All the roofs are sheathed with 1-inch hemlock or poplar boards nailed to the rafters. The rooms, halls, and closets on the first and second floors are plastered with wood fiber plaster. The woodwork is stopped and painted with three coats of mixed paint."[21]

A number of important buildings, company offices for example, were built of stone brought to the site from a nearby quarry.[22] Practically everything else built in Gary Hollow, though, was made from wood. The

Gary at the Beginning

abundance of timber in the Tug River area was something that W. W. Coe had mentioned to Frederick J. Kimball when he surveyed the area for the N&W. "The timber in this section consists of poplar, hemlock and white oak in about equal amounts, with some chestnut and other varieties of oak and some black walnut, maple and beech."[23] With U.S. Steel's arrival, several lumber companies set up sawmills near the places where most of the construction in and around Gary was under way.[24] A photograph of one of the sawmills in the vicinity of Ream taken in September 1903 shows a mountainside nearly stripped of all timber.[25] Clear-cutting seemed an insignificant matter when compared with the cost savings of having most of the raw material for construction within easy reach.

Houses built in company towns tend to follow a uniform design that varies little if at all. In fact, Mack Henry Gillenwater, in his extensive study of housing in the Pocahontas coalfields, reduced the "total number of house types" in the region to what he called "eight morphologically similar groups."[26] U.S. Steel moved away from that pattern somewhat, choosing instead to create a variety of house plans for Gary, even though a single row of houses in a given town site still might follow the same plan. Some of the earliest house plans, all of which originated in the USCC chief engineer's office, included two-room cottages; six-room, two-story single-family dwellings; and eight-room, two-story double (or duplex) houses designed for two families occupying four rooms, each on either side. Alex Schust determined that the company "used at least 53 different housing plans and multiple variations of a plan to construct miners' houses, boarding houses and clubhouses. In many cases, the size of the building area and the need for particular types of housing determined the house plan to be used."[27]

There were a few houses planned for Gary Hollow, though, whose plans were distinct and whose size and prominent locations distinguished them from all others. These were the houses intended for the USCC officials—foremen, engineers, and superintendent. These houses not only provided more comfortable living arrangements for their occupants, but also physically and symbolically served to separate labor and management. Take, for example, the superintendent's house that was set upon a hillside within easy view of anyone living in or just passing through Gary. The two-story structure had a living room, dining room, kitchen, study, parlor, and bathroom on the first floor, with an outside porch and sun parlor. The second floor had six bedrooms and three bathrooms. The attic contained two bedrooms, trunk room, billiard room, and store room. All rooms, incidentally, had very generous dimensions and contained interior woodwork of the highest quality.[28]

Structures other than houses came from the USCC draftsmen. Among these were company stores, emergency hospitals, post offices, schools for both whites and blacks, churches, recreation buildings (with dance halls, pool halls, bowling alleys, and theaters), banks, ballparks, and even cemeteries. The stores were operated by the United Supply Company, a USCC subsidiary and sister to the Union Supply Company that operated stores in the H. C. Frick Coke Company region. USCC also provided its own firefighting, emergency, and security forces.[29]

By and by, coal works and towns were constructed alongside the Tug River from west to east and then south alongside Sand Lick Creek: Nos. 1, 2, and 3 in 1902, No. 6 in 1903, Nos. 4, 5, and 7 in 1904, No. 8 in 1905, Nos. 10 and 11 in 1907, No. 9 in 1908; and No. 12 in 1909.[30] Nos. 13 and 14 would not appear until much later. As nearby towns sprang up, most were named in honor of U.S. Steel officials. And as residential structures were ready for occupancy, miners and their families began to arrive. Population rose quickly, and by 1910 the number of persons living in Gary and its satellite towns was estimated at between ten and twelve thousand.[31]

By January 1903 the N&W provided a passenger service that connected all Gary Hollow towns, as well as Welch, Bluefield, and other destinations. In fact, N&W's time table, effective January 18, 1903, was the first to identify "Gary" by name, although it was misspelled "Geary."[32] By the end of the twentieth century's first decade the mining and residential infrastructure in Gary Hollow had blossomed into a nearly self-sufficient, self-contained industrial enclave. But the spirit of the place was captured after only its first year by an unknown writer in the *Bluefield Daily Telegraph*: "It almost staggers belief that one year ago the foundations of these towns were not laid. . . . Verily, verily has a miracle been wrought. The comfortable cottages, the contented air which prevails among the employes [*sic*]—all tell that the United States Coal and Coke Company have founded towns, not merely erected temporary settlements which will only last for a time and then pass away to be heard no more."[33]

Developing model towns and model coal mining works was serious business for U.S. Steel and USCC officials. Their effort happened to coincide with a time in the nation's industrial history when greater and greater attention was being paid to living conditions in company towns, particularly in the coal mining regions. Articles in trade publications, journals, and government reports documented conditions that ranged from squalid to exemplary. More often than not, whenever specific examples were cited, Gary appeared among the best of the best.[34] *Coal Age* magazine featured the unique activities of Gary Hollow, including annual contests for "the best lawns, flowers and truck gardens."[35] A two-part series described improved education conditions and the construction of a new consolidated school at Gary. A picture of one of the wagons used to carry students from surrounding towns to the Gary school accompanied one of the series' articles and carried the caption "Hauling Raw Material to Culture Factory."[36] Two other *Coal Age* articles described the

USCC special effort to educate foreign-born miners and their spouses. The company established night schools in 1913 to teach its male workers "to speak, read and write the English language." The next year, company nurses began instructing women homemakers "in sanitation and house-work."[37] It is no surprise, then, that a 1922 coal commission organized by Congress rated USCC towns among the highest of some "713 company-controlled bituminous coal mine communities." In fact, Filbert (No. 9 Works) and Main Gary (No. 3 Works) ranked 8 and 12, respectively, on the commission's rating scale.[38] USCC's Gary Hollow coal mining operation by itself was soon recognized for leading the way in innovation, productivity, and especially mine safety. New machinery, new uses of electricity, and new methods of mining in general were described in detail in several publications.[39] But the company's efforts toward mine safety seemed to receive the most attention and for good reason. One writer commented in a 1909 article, "The U.S. Coal and Coke Company enjoys the distinction of being considered by the State mine authorities one of the best equipped and safest properties in West Virginia."[40]

Crafting safe working conditions in one of the most hazardous industries was no small task. Judge Gary, though, once more taking his lead from German industrialists, decided that U.S. Steel employees would have the safest working environment possible. Shortly after 1906 he issued the following directive: "The United States Steel Corporation expects its subsidiary companies to make every effort practicable to prevent injury to employees."[41] Signs bearing the company slogan "Safety the First Consideration" began appearing at conspicuous places around Gary Hollow as greater attention was given both to making the workplace as safe as possible and to educating workers on the subject.[42] USCC also devised sets of safety rules covering practically every facet of the company's mining operation. These rules were distributed to all workers, but in order to enforce them USCC set up a system for rewarding mine foremen and assistant foremen for accident prevention.[43]

Similar rules and overall concern with safety applied to employees at the H. C. Frick Coke Company. In fact, now that Frick and USCC were both U.S. Steel subsidiaries, the two had long since overcome their competitive differences in order to work cooperatively. One of the most successful efforts at sharing ideas was production of mine safety movies. Using the nearly universal language of the cinema, the movies illustrated to workers, particularly miners less fluent in English, the right way and the wrong way to do something. The first such movies were produced in Pennsylvania in 1913 and screened in H. C. Frick mines before being shipped to USCC workers in West Virginia. Such a movie was produced in Gary and made available to fellow miners in Pennsylvania.[44]

The USCC and H. C. Frick Coke Company had more in common then just sharing ideas. The two companies had been drawn together in a corporate sense, but to a great extent USCC, as the younger of the two, was the recipient of considerable personal influence coming from the older company. When Thomas Lynch became president of U.S. Steel's coal mining subsidiaries, it was quite natural that his many years as an H. C. Frick Coke Company executive would affect his oversight of the additional companies that came under his leadership.[45] And USCC as the newest of these companies quite possibly received special attention from Lynch in the quality of personnel he dispatched from the Frick Company to travel south to Gary Hollow. They were of the highest caliber, personifying the importance U.S. Steel placed on making its southern West Virginia coal mining operation a model in the industry. Particularly noteworthy were William Glyde Wilkins, Howard Eavenson, and Edward O'Toole.

William Glyde Wilkins was a civil engineer whose Pittsburgh firm, W. G. Wilkins Company, specialized in building industrial plants "connected with bituminous collieries and coke works." He in fact was said to have "constructed the largest number of coke plants credited to any single engineer."[46] Wilkins had done extensive work for the H. C. Frick Coke Company, designing a number of plants for the company in the Connellsville region. One publication even referred to him as "the Frick Company coke and mining engineering expert."[47] Among the USCC plans attributable to Wilkins are Plan No. 1 (Two Room Miners House), Plan No. 2 (Three Room Miners House), Plan No. 4 (Six Room Miners House), Plan No. 5 (Eight Room Double House), Plan No. 8 (Ten Room Double House), Club House, Freight Ware House, and both general and specific plans for coke ovens. All plans were completed between February and October 1902.

What William Glyde Wilkins started, Howard N. Eavenson continued with his arrival in Gary in 1902. As USCC's chief engineer, Eavenson built the bulk of USCC's operation in Gary and Lynch, Kentucky. His training for the job came from seven years with Frick, where he served as a draftsman, division engineer, and assistant chief engineer. Eavenson oversaw construction of all coal works in Gary, from No. 1 through No. 12. Donald Beeson, who worked directly under Eavenson, described his boss as "probably the most brilliant member of the engineering profession in my long experience."[48] Eavenson returned to Pittsburgh after leaving Gary in 1920 and became an engineering consultant and prominent member of the community. He served as a trustee of Carnegie Institute and Carnegie Institute of Technology and received an honorary doctorate in 1928 from the University of Pittsburgh. He also served as president of the American Institute of Mining and Metallurgical Engineers in 1934.[49] Throughout his long career, Eavenson wrote three prominent books: *Coal through the Ages* (1935), *The Pittsburgh Coal Bed—Its Early History and Development* (1938), and *The First Century and a Quarter of American Coal Industry* (1942). He also published numerous articles.[50]

The last of the three connecting links between USCC and the H. C. Frick Coke Company was Edward O'Toole. O'Toole became the longest serving general superintendent in USCC history, moving into that position in 1904, following the departure of Jared M. B. Reis, the company's first general superintendent (or general manager, as the position was first titled). Colonel O'Toole, as he would become known, was an assistant to Reis for one year after his 1903 arrival in Gary. Beeson described O'Toole as a "rough, illiterate Irishman . . . from the Connellsville Coke Region . . . whose management proved itself in something like a year."[51]

Given the success of his nearly thirty years at the helm of USCC's Gary operation, it is inconceivable that Beeson's characterization of O'Toole as illiterate was accurate. Perhaps he gave that impression initially, but O'Toole spoke to many groups, prepared numerous company documents, and otherwise maintained communication with his U.S. Steel superiors, in addition to writing several trade publication articles and even serving as president of the local school board for nearly twenty-six years. He also was an inventor, perfecting a coal mining machine in the 1920s that was "used to cut and load simultaneously along the coal face" as the machine advanced through the mine.[52]

Apart from the greater paternalistic nature of his company town job, O'Toole's responsibilities as general superintendent were not unlike those of a small-town mayor. He was accountable to U.S. Steel for Gary's "mining operation and the physical infrastructure that supported the mining operation including the miners' houses, roads, sidewalks, sanitation, and garbage collections."[53] He also had the power to evict residents from their homes, usually because of the head-of-household's poor job performance, which gave him a unique, indirect influence over job performance among all USCC employees in Gary. Since O'Toole represented the company, it was important that he enforce company policy. In effect, the position of general superintendent was equivalent not only to mayor, but also to high school principal or, better yet, boarding school headmaster.

Much about the character of the USCC workforce can be determined from the USCC payroll books available at the Eastern Regional Coal Archive. One of the earliest payroll books, from June 1903, pertains to the No. 1 Works. Most of the names appear to be nonforeign, and the same surnames for quite a few of the workers suggests that perhaps many brothers and/or fathers and sons were employed at No. 1. A review of several payroll books also indicates that names quickly disappeared, which possibly accounts for USCC recruiting so heavily for replacement employees. According to Stuart McGehee, "[USCC] recruited its labor from two primary sources: Eastern Europe, where the late nineteenth century witnessed a mass emigration from political instability and religious persecution; and the Deep South, where thousands of black

Southerners escaped the 'Jim Crow' segregation, disfranchisement, and resulting poverty."[54]

Coal miners, primarily of English, Irish, Scotch, Welsh, and German ancestry, were recruited from other coal regions such as Pennsylvania, but most of the newly arrived mine workers came from eastern and southern Europe. Many of the Europeans arrived during one of the successive tidal waves of immigration between 1880 and 1920. From 1901 through 1911 alone, nearly 8.8 million immigrants arrived on America's shores.[55] Many of the new arrivals headed straight to industrial centers such as Pittsburgh and Chicago and became steelmakers; others headed to the coalfields to work in the mines. Some immigrants came from steelmaking or coal mining backgrounds, but many came to America with little previous experience in their new occupations.[56] Nevertheless, their labor was in demand. As one writer put it, "America could never have finished its transcontinental railroads, developed its coal and ore deposits, operated its furnaces and factories, had it not drawn upon Europe for its labor force."[57]

When miners arrived in the Pocahontas Coal District in late 1896, there were forty mines to choose from, a number that more than doubled by the 1920s.[58] But many chose to move beyond the mines spread along the N&W main line and settle in Gary Hollow. And so it was that by 1910 the No. 2 Works payroll carried such surnames as Pensula, Paola, Ngrovice, Kesistie, Covoch, Zobo, Manola, Tomosso, Santov, Zonel, Skovane, Alphonzo, Sarono, Quagalia, Dromstock, Vatch, Yocop, and Droglish.[59] In that same year O'Toole reported that twelve nationalities were represented in the Gary mines, calculating the following percentages for each nationality: American (white),17.8; American (black), 26.8; Hungarian, 22.2; Italian, 13.8; Slavs, 5.8; Roumanian, 5.5; Poles, 4.5; Russians, 3.0; German, 0.5; Greek, .06; Swede, .02; Spanish, .01; and French, .01.[60]

Once employed by USCC and settled into a company house or clubhouse apartment, the new worker, whatever his native land, was assigned a specific job from among several mine-related occupations. Occupations listed in the USCC payroll book for the No. 1 Works in January 1904, with their accompanying daily pay rate for inside and outside day laborers included: blacksmith ($1.60–$2.50); dumper ($1.50–$1.90); slate ($1.50–$1.90); slate picker ($1.35); cager ($1.50); fireman ($1.60); pumper ($1.60); hoisting engineer ($2.00); car carpenter ($2.25); shaft mining ($2.00–$3.00); track ($1.50–$2.25); timberman ($1.50–$1.90); driver ($1.65–$2.25); car dropper ($1.35); greaser ($0.75); trapper ($0.75); mason ($1.35); and carpenter ($1.75–$3.00).[61] Employee earnings during each biweekly pay period usually were determined after certain deductions were calculated. House rent that ranged from two to four dollars in 1904 was a major deduction, whereas a physician fee ranging from twenty-five to fifty cents was relatively minor. Generally, the biggest deduction came from payment on credit extended at the company store. Such payment sometimes was enough to leave the balance due a worker at less than a dollar.[62] Some USCC employees, such as the general superintendent and chief engineer, were salaried and paid an unrecorded (but likely, substantial) sum each month. What's more, there were several positions assigned to the chief engineer whose pay was based on a monthly rather than daily rate. Chief engineer Eavenson's staff, with their accompanying pay scale for January 1904, included chief draftsman ($150); division engineer ($109); draftsman ($87.50); prospector ($67.50); chainman ($40.50); and axman ($36).[63]

Some occupations—such as cager, hoisting engineer, and shaft mining—were unique to the No. 1 Works. This was the only mine in the entire USCC Gary Hollow operation that required a shaft entrance. Shaft mine workers had to ride an elevator-like cage from the surface to reach the seam. The No. 2 Works also was unique in being the only slope entrance mine in the operation. A slope entrance was slightly angled so that miners could reach a coal seam running just a short distance beneath the surface. All other USCC Gary Hollow mines had drift entrances that entered a seam laterally from some point on a hillside. The mine stayed on a nearly horizontal plane as it progressed through the hill. According to Edward O'Toole, about 97 percent of all mines in the Pocahontas region had drift entrances. Drift mines also had minimal need for "expensive ventilation and transportation equipment," according to Ronald D. Eller. "The drift mine not only drained well and was less gaseous, but because it required little machinery, operations could be undertaken with very little initial investment."[64]

Within the entire Pocahontas coalfield, only four seams, the Nos. 3, 4, 5, and 6, were workable. Two of the most abundant seams, Nos. 3 and 4, were mined by USCC. The thickness of the No. 3 seam reached by the Gary mines ranged from 3.0 to 7.5 feet. The No. 4 seam runs from 65 to 80 feet above the No. 3 seam. The earliest mines worked the No. 3 seam, although the shaft at the No. 1 Works, with its 180 feet depth actually penetrated both the No. 4 and then the No. 3 seams. The USCC Gary Hollow operation, according to Howard Eavenson, was the first in the entire Pocahontas field to "mine the No. 4 seam extensively."[65]

One of U.S. Steel's original objectives of building nearly three thousand beehive coke ovens at the Gary Hollow mines was soon abandoned after some two thousand ovens had been built. The reason for changing plans was the "speedy development of the by-product oven."[66] In fact, it was reported that by 1913 all production of coke at the USCC Gary Hollow mines "has now been discontinued, and the entire output of the mines is shipped to Gary (Indiana), Joliet, South Chicago and other points, where, mixed with other coals, it is coked in the more economic by-product oven."[67] However, West Virginia Department of Mines records show that coke production did not cease until as late as the 1919–20 fiscal year, and nearly 221,000 tons of coke were produced in Gary Hollow. Not until the early 1920s did USCC discontinue coking operations in Gary altogether.[68]

By-product coking allowed for the recovery of important chemicals and gases lost in the beehive oven coking process. Hardly revolutionary, by-product coking had been used extensively in Europe since the late 1800s, but it was slow to take hold in America because USCC president Thomas Lynch felt the H. C. Frick Coke Company was too heavily invested in beehive coke ovens to convert to another process. Lynch's attitude affected USCC's Gary Hollow operation. However, reluctance to invest in by-product coke ovens dissipated when U.S. Steel decided to build a battery of such ovens at its new Gary, Indiana, steel plant in 1905. From that point on, U.S. Steel suspended any further beehive coke oven construction and launched extensive construction and use of by-product ovens. Beehive oven coke production slowed nationwide in the coming years, but it did not cease altogether.[69]

Coal and coke production in Gary Hollow followed generally upward trajectories as one mine after another came on line. Annual production and employment figures exceeded the previous year, although with some exceptions. Statistics for July 1 through June 30 of the first fiscal year (1903–4) show Gary mines employed 1,015 workers who produced roughly 593,000 tons of coal. From the coal produced, nearly 227,000 tons of coke were produced. Coal production steadily increased to nearly 963,000 tons and about 633,000 tons of coke by 1905–6. Employment also was up to 1,381 by then. Employment increased the following year to 1,766, but coal and coke production dropped slightly to approximately 942,000 tons of coal and about 578,000 tons of coke. Employment rose to 2,076 in 1907–8, and coal tonnage for the first time topped 1.0 million, with coke tonnage slightly under 692,000. By 1909–10, there were 2,653 workers, nearly 2.6 million tons of coal, and nearly 847,000 tons of coke. The following year, though, employment was down to 1,770, with over 1.7 million tons of coal and roughly 281,000 tons of coke.[70]

The up-and-down nature of coal production and employment in Gary Hollow during USCC's first decade continued well into the future. Generally, USCC's coal production and workforce size was determined by U.S. Steel's production at its steel plants. When steel production was high, the need for coal and the workers to mine it were high. When steel production was low, so was the need for coal and coal miners. A variation of the equation also applied to steelworkers. High production at the steel plants usually meant high employment. When production was low, steelworkers were laid off.

U.S. Steel production was affected by many factors, including overall economic conditions. When a panic in 1907 threatened to close businesses, banks, and trust companies, steel purchases plummeted. U.S. Steel cut thousands from its workforce as J. P. Morgan's financial maneuvering pulled the nation from the brink of catastrophe. As a result, U.S. Steel's 1908 production, income, and employment numbers all were far below those of 1907. The income decline also included a drop in U.S. Steel's export sales from roughly $200 million in 1907 to approximately $151 million in 1908. U.S. Steel aggressively pursued a niche in the overseas market, particularly in Great Britain and Germany, and ran its plants at near capacity to produce enough surplus steel to sell overseas, at prices lower than American customers paid for the same products.[71] This early example of "dumping" haunted U.S. Steel when overseas steelmakers did the same thing later in the century. However, stiff U.S. government tariff protection prevented overseas steelmakers from making a similar entry into the American marketplace in the early twentieth century.

Domestic competition also affected U.S. Steel. Although the company was a giant, comparatively speaking, it nonetheless had formidable competition from other steelmakers such as Bethlehem, Jones and Laughlin, Midvale, and Republic. A competitor's pricing practices could affect U.S. Steel's ability to sell its products. Failure to implement new technology, or to build new plants, or to adapt to fabrication needs of customers could leave U.S. Steel at a competitive disadvantage and thus slow the company's steel production. Then there were the unexpected circumstances that pushed production to near peak levels. World War I, for example, came when U.S. Steel was working its way out of a major slump. Production in 1914 had dropped from 18.7 million tons to 13.2. By 1915, tonnage was back to 18.3 million tons, and in 1916 it zoomed to 23.4 million tons. U.S. Steel's income advanced accordingly, from $23.4 million in 1914 to $75.9 million in 1915 and $271.5 million in 1916.[72]

In years to come labor disputes and strikes affected both steel and coal production. But it was the economic depression of the 1930s that found the steel and coal industries at their lowest ebb. Rock bottom came in 1932, when U.S. Steel reported steel output at 5.5 million tons, income at a loss of $71.2 million, and number of employees down to approximately 164,000. Production was the lowest in U.S. Steel history, and only once before, in 1904, had company employment been any lower. Never had income appeared in the loss column. In similar fashion, USCC's Gary Hollow coal production dropped to 560,000 tons, with slightly more than 500 employees on the job in 1932. The two industries rebounded, though. By the time the United States entered World War II, steelmaking and coal mining were once again robust in every measure of prosperity—production, income, and employment.[73]

Chapter 5

Labor Issues and Labor Organization

Labor and management during much of the early days of corporate growth in both the steel and coal industries seldom were at ease with one another. This was especially true among the builders of massive enterprises such as Andrew Carnegie and Henry Clay Frick, both of whom historian Matthew Josephson called "robber barons." "In introducing technical economies, in adjusting wages, in the hiring or firing of their workers," said Josephson, "the barons exercised their sacred rights over colossal properties in a manner which closely paralleled the 'Divine Right' of feudal princes."[1]

Industrial workers of the late 1800s were beginning a slow but steady drift toward labor organizations or unions that could serve as agents of collective bargaining with employers. Most employers—Carnegie and Frick in particular—resisted attempts to negotiate with any union representatives, choosing instead either to fire employees connected with the unions or, in more dramatic fashion, to lock out employees by closing entire plants for the duration of a labor dispute. Employees were left with two alternatives: give in and return to work or strike. But the success of any strike required a strong union, representing as many workers as possible, that could bring strength in numbers to the bargaining table. There was a middle ground toward representation in the form of company unions. These gave workers the opportunity to discuss workplace concerns with management but never to make demands. Company unions obviously could never engage in collective bargaining.[2]

Henry Clay Frick was perhaps the most ardent opponent of unions. Numerous strikes among coal and coke workers at the H. C. Frick works during the 1880s and 1890s had erupted into violence. Long periods of shutdowns at the works showed how loss of production at the coal mines could affect steel production in the same way that a slowdown or lockout at steel plants affected coal production.[3] One of the most serious strikes against Frick occurred in February 1891, when 10,000 coal and coke workers walked off the job at Connellsville over low wages. When several of the strikers attacked guards stationed at the coke works, seven of the strikers were killed and many more were wounded. Henry Frick, though, at the urging of Andrew Carnegie, refused to give in to workers' demands. Frick hired a hundred Pinkerton agents to secure his property and then waited. By late May the strike ended when workers agreed to return to their jobs without winning any wage concessions.

Little more than a year later, in late June 1892, Frick and Carnegie utilized the same tactic when workers, led by officials of the fledgling Amalgamated Association of Iron and Steel Workers, went on strike for higher wages and a reduction in the twelve-hour-day, seven-days-per-week work schedule at Carnegie's Homestead plant. Pinkerton agents once again were employed to guard the Carnegie property. The ensuing violence was more vicious than at Connellsville, and the loss of life was greater on both sides. The strike dragged on until November 21, 1892. With little money left to live on, and the cold winter months fast approaching, Homestead strikers voted to return to work. Once more, Carnegie had made no concessions. One of the ironies of the situation was that steel orders for 1892 had declined to such an extent that closure of the Homestead plant caused minimal financial loss to Carnegie Steel.

The Homestead strike's aftermath was a major blow to steelworkers. The only union of consequence that represented them now was discredited. Wages remained the same as before the strike. The workday and workweek hours remained the same as before. And more and more European immigrants were hired for unskilled positions at Carnegie steel plants. Even before the strike a distinct ethnic division had begun appearing at the plants. "The skilled workers were native-born or first- or second-generation Germans, Irish, Welsh, or Scotsmen. The unskilled day laborers were almost all Eastern Europeans, mostly Slovak, though they were referred to as 'Hungarians,' 'Huns,' and 'Hunkies.'"[4]

These, then, were the labor conditions in the plants that U.S. Steel gained ownership of in 1901. They "presented the officers of the new corporation with both an immediate practical problem and a longer-ranged project in labor reform and public relations," said Gerald G. Eggert.[5] Critical to the new corporation's ability to steer its way through the thorny issues that lay ahead was its leader, Judge Elbert Gary.

As chairman of the board, Gary's power was further enhanced by chairing U.S. Steel's executive committee and finance committee, from which he built the organization as a reflection of his own character traits and values. His influence was not confined to U.S. Steel. Paul A. Tiffany remarked that Gary was the entire American steel industry's most "dominant personality over the first quarter of the new century."[6] U.S. Steel policies fostered by Gary were meant to appeal to the public, to U.S. Steel's competitors, and, perhaps most significant at the time, to the U.S. government. Gary promised and delivered on public disclosure of U.S. Steel's performance via quarterly earning reports and annual reports.

He also inaugurated cooperative competition whereby steel industry competitors discussed pricing and other such matters during industry get-togethers known as "Gary dinners." These gatherings had the appearance of collusion, but all attendees insisted such was not the case.

Gary's appeal to the government came largely in response to his concern that U.S. Steel not be viewed as a monopoly operating in violation of the Sherman Antitrust Act. Gary, in fact, had purposely maintained U.S. Steel's original size in order to keep the government at bay. Nonetheless, the U.S. Justice Department filed suit against the company in 1911, charging it with violation of the Sherman Act. The Federal District Court for New Jersey dismissed the suit, ruling that no evidence existed to validate charges of monopoly. On appeal, the U.S. Supreme Court, in a four-to-three decision rendered on March 20, 1920, agreed with the lower court.[7]

The long battle that U.S. Steel waged with the federal government was settled, but there remained a growing disharmony in labor-management relationships. The twelve-hour workday and seven-day workweek were the most contentious issues. Overlooked, insisted Gary, were the good wages, safer working conditions, company welfare programs and pensions that benefited U.S. Steel workers. As far as the working hours issue, Gary asserted that steel industry tradition had established the policy and that most workers favored it because of the additional pay they could earn. That pay would drop, said Gary, if the twelve-hour workday were reduced to eight hours. The reduction would create a three-shift workday and require hiring more workers. Whether or not steelworkers truly were interested in the working hours issue, labor organizers continued treating it as a wedge to gain standing among any disgruntled workers. However resourceful the organizers might prove to be, they still would have to contend with a U.S. Steel executive committee that already was on record as opposing unionization.[8]

In simple terms, collective bargaining and the twelve-hour day became the flashpoints of labor-management relationships at U.S. Steel well into the 1930s. Judge Gary actually capitulated somewhat to critics of the twelve-hour day in 1918 by announcing that the eight-hour shift thereafter would constitute the basic day at all U.S. Steel plants. But since wartime conditions prevented immediate implementation of the eight-hour day, the twelve-hour day would have to continue temporarily, with workers paid a time-and-a-half wage. Once the war ended, the overtime pay disappeared, but the twelve-hour day continued.[9]

Also at war's end came a renewed effort toward unionizing steelworkers. This time the effort was led by an arm of the American Federation of Labor called the National Committee for Organizing Iron and Steel Workers. National Committee leaders chose "eight hours and the union" as their rallying slogan. All efforts by AFL president Samuel Gompers to discuss the National Committee's position with Gary were rebuffed. Gompers felt that sentiment toward unionizing was sufficient enough among all steelworkers that if he were to call a strike, a substantial number of workers, even at U.S. Steel, would walk away from their jobs. Several National Committee members made one more effort to meet with Gary on August 26, 1919, in order to request that U.S. Steel accede to a list of committee demands. Heading the list were the "right to collective bargaining," the "eight-hour day," and "one day's rest in seven." Gary once more refused to meet, and when President Woodrow Wilson himself failed to convince Gary to at least speak with National Committee representatives, Gompers set a strike to commence on September 22, 1919.

When September 22 arrived nearly half of America's steelmaking workforce, an estimated 250,000 persons, walked off the job. Many of the workers were from U.S. Steel plants, although work continued with little noticeable interruption at most of the company's Pittsburgh vicinity plants. Regardless of the less than total success, the number of workers who did strike was impressive. Steel executives responding to the strike remained outwardly unswayed by strike demands. Gary in particular charged that several National Committee leaders—organization secretary William Z. Foster, for example—were radicals and intended to lead the country's laborers down the road of Bolshevism. By January 8, 1920, the National Committee ended what came to be called the Great Steel Strike of 1919.[10]

From all appearances striking steelworkers seemed to have gained little. None of their grievances had been resolved. But gradually the press, politicians, and even the clergy began to respond. Several post-strike investigations of steelworker conditions were undertaken. Reports of these investigations when made public rendered a most uncomplimentary critique of labor-management relationships. President Warren Harding and U.S. Secretary of Commerce Herbert Hoover were convinced enough by what they heard and read to make a forceful case to Gary to end the twelve-hour workday. Gary finally conceded defeat on the matter and announced in August 1923 that the twelve-hour day would end for good at U.S. Steel.[11]

Gary would not concede an inch in collective bargaining, though. One historian suggested that his opposition to unions was based on the threat they would pose to his authority as head of U.S. Steel. It was also Gary's contention that unions "would have introduced an element of uncertainty and instability to the industry."[12] Gary's unswerving defense of the "open shop" lasted some ten years after his death, but in the end U.S. Steel's fight against organized labor could not be sustained. The Wagner Act of 1935 "required an employer to engage in collective bargaining with any union demonstrating the support of a majority of his men."[13] The act's legality was challenged in court and eventually upheld by the U.S. Supreme Court in 1937. Shortly before the Supreme Court's decision, on January 9, 1937, Myron C. Taylor, Gary's successor at U.S. Steel, had a chance meeting with Congress of Industrial Organizations (CIO) head John L. Lewis in Washington, D.C. That meeting was followed by several days of private conversations, the result of which was an agreement to allow U.S. Steel employees' the right to collective bargaining by their choice of agent (or union) as long as a right to work for the company was not dependent on union membership. A contract outlining this agreement was announced on March 2, 1937. The Steel Workers Organizing Committee, whose name was changed to the United Steelworkers of America (USWA) in May 1942, became U.S. Steel employees' official bargaining agent.[14]

A postscript to the story of the 1919 steelworkers strike is Robert Asher's interviews of steelworkers who refused to strike. Many of the workers said they remained on the job because they feared the violence during the Homestead strike might happen in their situation. According to Asher, many of the "steelworkers concluded that the power of the steel companies was so great that the eight-hour day and union recognition could be obtained only with the assistance of federal legislation."[15] In the end, they were proved right.

The history of labor organization in America's coalfields, like that in the nation's steel plants, is full of violence and bloodshed. Union efforts to organize mine workers in southern West Virginia was perhaps the most violent of all. Books bearing provocative titles such as *Thunder in the Mountains, Bloodletting in Appalachia, Law and Order vs. the Miners*, and *Life, Work, and Rebellion in the Coal Fields* chronicle the struggle that played out between labor and management during the mine war years.[16] The first coal miners' union, called the American Miners' Association, formed in the Midwest in 1861. The union's main objectives remained unchanged from that time forward: better pay and safer working conditions. Both were accomplished briefly but soon disappeared as other upstart labor organizations engaged in a power struggle with the American Miners' Association. The resulting internecine struggles severely injured the union cause. Finally, delegates from two of the strongest miners' unions of their day met in Columbus, Ohio, in January 1890 to form the more permanent United Mine Workers of America (UMWA). Their purpose in forming the UMWA and what they hoped to achieve was underscored in the following words drawn from the preamble to the union's 1890 constitution: "There is no fact more generally known, nor more widely believed, than that without coal there would not have been any such grand achievements, privileges and blessings as those which characterize the nineteenth century civilization, and believing as we do, that those whose lot it is to daily toil in the recesses of the earth, mining and putting out this coal which makes these blessings possible, are entitled to a fair and equitable share of the same."[17]

The UMWA's first major victory came in 1897, when union leaders signed an agreement with coal operators in Pennsylvania, Ohio, Indiana, and Illinois (called the Central Competitive Field) that guaranteed an eight-hour workday and higher wages to bituminous coal miners. Just as important, though, was the agreement's stipulation that the UMWA organize West Virginia miners. The reason was purely economics. The nonunion West Virginia mines were beginning to market their coal in the Midwest and now could afford to sell coal for less than the unionized mines of the Central Competitive Field could charge.[18] As such, the Central Competitive Field group "insisted . . . that it was the duty of the union to protect them by organizing the non-union fields . . . so that all States should be upon as equal a basis as possible."[19]

What these coal operators were demanding in this unusual alliance with the UMWA did not come easily. West Virginia operators understood clearly that by organizing miners in their state the Central Competitive Field operators working in tandem with the UMWA could demand "interstate wage agreements" that would then force price stabilization within the entire bituminous coal industry. Jerry B. Thomas described the conflict that arose from this situation: "The United Mine Workers' resolute efforts to bring West Virginia into the interstate system and the equally determined resistance of the Mountain State operators resulted in protracted disputes which embittered labor-management relations for decades."[20]

Nowhere in West Virginia was antiunionism so strong as in the Pocahontas coalfield. Coal operators there, in fact, were described by the Coal Commission staff in its 1923 report as "aggressively non-union."[21] Howard Lee, one-time West Virginia attorney general (1925–33) more specifically said the most "aggressively non-union" coal operators of all were those in McDowell County. They formed, said Lee, a "super-oligarchy" that dominated "every branch of the county government and every phase of the lives of the people" in what Lee called "a complete industrial autocracy."[22] Collectively, the McDowell County coal operators formed a highly effective phalanx in the early 1920s that was nearly impossible for union organizers to penetrate.

West Virginia coal operators also possessed important tools to help them fend off the advances of labor organizers. One of these was the operators' virtual control of local, county, and state government. And they were not reluctant to exercise all that such power allows. Most important, though, was their control of law enforcement. And if that were not enough, the operators could turn to the Baldwin-Felts Detective Agency based in Bluefield to furnish mine guards. Baldwin-Felts agents were deputized by the county sheriffs and placed in charge of preventing union organizers from meeting with miners. In the event that miners ever did strike, it was Baldwin-Felts's responsibility to root out the strike organizers and to break up the strike.[23]

Political power and enforcement power allowed southern West Virginia mine operators to exercise near total control over their employees' productivity. Control to them was everything; it was not to be relinquished, nor was it to be shared. A report by the Bituminous Operators' Special Committee to the 1923 Coal Commission put the control issue front and center as the reason for southern West Virginia mine operators not signing agreements with the UMWA. The operators "object to placing their labor relations with their men under the absentee control of the international officers of the United Mine Workers' organization," read a portion of the report. In addition, the report stated the mine operators' objection to any "closed shop" requirement whereby only UMWA members could be employed at the mines. Most important, though, the report said that the operators "are convinced that contracts with [the UMWA] are in the interest neither of the operator nor the miner, but tend to stifle efficiency and individual initiative, and to create a relationship based not on mutual confidence and sense of responsibility but on mutual hostility."[24]

UMWA officials did little in their organizing methods either to address or to dispel any of these concerns. According to Winthrop D. Lane, the union did not always employ "methods of persuasion and of an appeal to logic." Lane said that union organizers often were "provocative," threatening, "preached the gospel of discontent in some of its extreme forms," and "mingled doctrines of class warfare with their arguments for unionism." At the extreme, said Lane, organizers "represented the miner as the slave of a wage system that was robbing him of his share of the product of his labor."[25] However extreme the arguments might have been, coal miners in southern West Virginia were not necessarily in accord with the UMWA. Many of the miners were persuaded to join the union, but many more refused the call. Those who remained independent represented what David Alan Corbin called the "working class that possessed wants, needs, and goals that diverged dramatically from the UMWA and its policies."[26]

Such sentiment was especially present among Gary Hollow miners. Much of the UMWA's organizing efforts, even what little the union accomplished in McDowell County, occurred either before U.S. Steel began mining there or during the years when the USCC was just beginning to operate. Chances are that newly employed miners were not interested in labor organization anyway. Randall Lawrence concluded that one reason for this general apathy toward the UMWA was that so many miners in southern West Virginia—and this certainly applied to those in Gary—not only were first-generation miners but also first-generation Americans. "They were finding jobs, learning new skills, earning the money needed to support themselves and to provide transportation for family members left behind, and beginning new families," said Lawrence. "Once secure in a job and a town," he continued, "the miner had to learn to live and work with people speaking different languages, worshiping in different faiths, and living in different cultural traditions."[27]

There is uncertainty, too, as to just how apparent USCC's antiunion inclinations were and to what extent, if any, the company attempted to persuade its employees to avoid union organizers. U.S. Steel was described at one point as "a far-flung empire of semi-autonomous units."[28] That autonomy could imply that a U.S. Steel subsidiary might have been less rigid toward organized labor than Judge Gary would have liked or would have even found acceptable. But to whatever degree Gary's antiunion position had filtered down to the USCC general superintendent, there would have been little incentive on the superintendent's part to disagree with his boss. However Edward O'Toole communicated his position to USCC employees, he nonetheless was known to be staunchly antiunion. The political power he was able to amass during his many years as USCC general superintendent and the considerable influence he wielded over the local press certainly provided him the means to effectively disseminate his antiunion views. There is evidence, too, that USCC, because of the sheer size and power of the company it represented, was able to influence smaller independent companies to adopt U.S. Steel's antiunion position.[29]

Persuasion works in subtle, sometimes unpredictable ways, but U.S. Steel had the resources to practice an effective kind of employee persuasion via social welfare or welfare capitalism. The concept of welfare has come to mean something entirely different than what it meant to industrial America in the early twentieth century. The U.S. Department of Labor defined "welfare" in 1919 as "anything for the comfort and improvement, intellectual or social, of the employees, over and above wages paid, which is not a necessity of the industry nor required by law."[30] Providing adequate housing, good schools, recreational facilities, and health care were all part of what Stuart D. Brandes described as welfare capitalism that business leaders like Judge Elbert Gary practiced in order to keep mine workers and their families happy.

Social welfare, or labor capitalism, was nothing new. It simply was the most recent version of a practice begun in early nineteenth-century America when, shortly after the War of 1812, several New England businessmen formed a group called the Boston Associates to build and manage textile plants. Morrell Heald credits the group as being the first to apply "the corporate form of business organization to manufacturing" and the first also to display "an active interest in the lives and living conditions of their employees." In their effort "to attract reliable workers," the Boston Associates built such company towns as Lowell and Waltham, Massachusetts, which provided "housing conditions, as well as religious, social, and intellectual resources suited to the backgrounds and expectations of the prospective employees." Lowell, in particular, became a model town that eventually attracted visits from such luminaries as Andrew Jackson and Charles Dickens.[31]

Social welfare for workers took on added significance as industry of one kind or another grew more prominent. There were many practical reasons for companies to supply all basic worker needs. Forces of political progressivism as well as the social gospel religious movement also gave prominence to the manner by which workers and their families were treated.[32] For some time there even appeared a kind of competition among companies to outdo one another in just how well and to what extent social welfare was practiced. Pride in what had been accomplished was demonstrated at the St. Louis 1904 Louisiana Purchase Exposition via a photographic exhibit of American company towns prepared by the U.S. Labor Bureau. Company towns associated with a variety of industries were represented, and all photographic images were meant to convey the typical company town in near idyllic form.[33] The view presented by the exhibit failed to convey underlying strains between employer and employee in company towns. Even in one of the very first, at Lowell, Massachusetts, wage disputes, criticism of working and living conditions, and job competition from newly arrived immigrants combined to puncture the serene image that Lowell residents had so long presented to outsiders.[34]

Closer examination of how welfare capitalism was practiced in many company towns shows that good works often were accompanied by ulterior motives. According to Ronald Eller, "Moral considerations undoubtedly played a part in the new emphasis upon community welfare, but there were also sound business reasons for the improvement of social conditions. The desire to attract workers, to resist the encroachment of unions, and to stem the appeal of other 'radical' movements pointed in the same direction." Companies like U.S. Steel that entered into coal mining in the early 1900s "undertook a two-pronged policy to strengthen their relationships with their own employees and improve their image in the public eye, while continuing to mount an all-out campaign against the union movement." Eller cited Elbert Gary as "one of the first business leaders to recognize the value of public respect and confidence in deterring social criticism and government interference" and pointed to the construction of towns like Gary, with all the welfare efforts that applied to their maintenance, as manifesting the kind of favorable image policy that Judge Gary advocated and carefully nurtured.[35]

Indeed, with regard to the use of welfare to counter the influence of union organizers, Gary once said that U.S. Steel management "must make it certain that the men in our employ are treated as well as, if not a little better than, those who are working for people who deal and contract with unions."[36] Taking Gary's philosophy to the town of Gary itself, one unnamed USCC official was quoted as saying, with respect to the company's program to improve housing and encourage upkeep and gardening, "When employees of a company are made to take a great interest in their homes and to have pride in the appearance of them, there is but one result—they become happy and contented, and are not so susceptible to 'hard times' and anarchistic propaganda."[37]

Altruism or good business? Regardless of which of the two was the greatest motivator, there is little doubt that social welfare or welfare capitalism as practiced in Gary Hollow was successful. Were mine workers being manipulated by what appeared to be the good intentions of their employer? Perhaps they were, but the mobility of coal miners and the many mining companies that existed in the early twentieth century gave miners complete freedom to leave Gary whenever they wished. The fact that so many stayed, even through difficult times, suggests that life in Gary Hollow was good enough and work conditions were acceptable enough that there were few reasons to leave. Many men, in fact, arrived in Gary Hollow at a young age and never left. And families whose several generations called Gary Hollow home were testament to a lifestyle that— company induced or not—many found to their liking.

Even so, the UMWA finally arrived. The first concerted effort by the union to overcome its early failures to organize the southern West Virginia coal workers came during the uneasy years surrounding World War I. Wildcat strikes became almost commonplace at a number of southern West Virginia mines from 1919 through 1921. Key issues precipitating the strikes were higher wages and reduced working hours.[38] Neither of these issues seemed particularly significant to USCC mine workers. Nonetheless, they, along with other mine workers in the Pocahontas and Tug River coalfields, were awarded a pay increase and a reduction in official workday hours, effective August 1, 1919. Hours were reduced from nine to eight daily and pay rose to about thirty cents per hour more than unionized workers' pay.[39] The action allowed the Bituminous Coal Operators to report to the U.S. Coal Commission in 1923 that the "eight-hour day is universal among the non-union miners . . . earnings of miners in non-union fields are at least as high as those in union fields . . . [and] the miner is more nearly his own boss as to whether he will work when the mine is running, how long he will work and how he will work than almost any other class of laborer."[40]

There is scant evidence of any major push by the UMWA to organize mine workers in Gary Hollow. Such was not the case at the nearby USCC operation at Lynch in Harlan County, Kentucky. "Bloody Harlan" was the well-deserved name given the place where union organizers and miners often clashed with USCC guards over the right to unionize. Unlike their brother miners in Gary Hollow who apparently were less welcoming toward the UMWA, miners at Lynch were determined to force U.S. Steel to recognize their right to collective bargaining and their desire to be represented by the union.[41] They were assisted by the same 1935 Wagner Act that opened the door to collective bargaining in the steel industry. USCC mine workers in Gary Hollow also took advantage of the Wagner Act but instead of turning to the UMWA as their bargaining agent, they formed—at the apparent urging of captive mine owners—a competing union called the Independent Associated Miners Union. Coal workers at several other captive mines made a similar choice. How much control workers themselves had in the matter is uncertain, but UMWA president John L. Lewis was determined enough that his union be the lone collective bargaining agent throughout the coal industry that he threatened to call a strike in November 1941, to force captive mine owners to recognize the UMWA's primacy.[42] The timing was significant, coming not only when coal was needed for heating homes and businesses, but also when threats of war were pushing the steel industry to produce steel at maximum capacity. President Franklin D. Roosevelt persuaded the captive mine owners and the UMWA to arbitrate their apparent stalemate and to accept unequivocally the arbitration panel's decision. Whether by coincidence or by overwhelming need stemming from the cataclysmic events of the day, the arbitration panel voted on December 7, 1941, in favor of UMWA representation at all captive mines.[43]

The most effective benefit of the UMWA, according to Winthrop D. Lane, was the miners' "power to refuse to work" as a show of force and defiance. Elaborating on just how important this power was, Lane said the mine worker "can exercise this power to the great inconvenience of the operator. He can shut down plants. He can interfere with the production of coal. He can cause financial loss. He can also, through the union, make appeals to the class interest of his fellow workers; he can cause disaffection and stir up strife; he can make capital out of the hostility of the operator. His power is neither so many-sided nor so controllable as that of the operator, but it is effective."[44] Just how effective the UMWA might be in Gary Hollow soon would be tested.

The 1940s was a decade of promise for Gary mine workers and their families. Although there were struggles, Gary Hollow residents appeared to be satisfied about their community and their contribution to the country, even in the midst of a world war. An article about Gary Hollow in the July 1943 issue of the *West Virginia Review* captured a moment in time and painted a glowing image of the place. "Main" Gary was said to be "as pretty a town as you will find anywhere in the State." "On the hillsides," the article continued, "stretch rows of attractive homes, tree-shaded, wide-porched, with attractively planted yards." Company houses at the time rented for about $2.00 per room per month. Average monthly cost for electricity and water was $2.00 and $1.25, respectively. Garbage pickup was free and coal for heating was $3.60 a ton, including delivery. Company medical coverage for a single person, including "all medical fees, hospitalization, and doctors' fees," was $2.30 per month, and family coverage rose slightly to $3.20 per month. The total number employed in Gary Hollow at the time was about 4,800, of which about 700 were serving in the military. Most impressive about the community, according to the article, was its unity in a common cause. "Here, men of German, English, Italian, Mexican, Spanish, and south central European extraction go into the vast melting pot that is America. Groups form themselves because of speech, racial, or religious backgrounds but always there is a spirit of thankfulness which says proudly: 'I am an American!'"[45]

Chapter 6

Coal Power and Town Life

During the twentieth century Gary assumed the mantle of industrial powerhouse in the hollows of southern West Virginia. Gary mines were crucial to steelmaking in World War II, furnishing over 28 million tons of high grade metallurgical coal (called "met coal") to U.S. Steel. Gary's contribution accounted not only for roughly one-quarter of the entire coal tonnage mined in McDowell County from 1942 through 1945, but also for nearly one-quarter of the entire coal tonnage used by U.S. Steel during the same period.[1]

Trainload upon trainload of coal moved daily from Gary Hollow to the Northwest, but the average coal miner likely paid little attention to any connection between the raw product that he dug from the earth and the war-making machinery that now spread around the world. But there was an enormous contribution, and U.S. Steel made due mention of that fact at war's end: "Steel was used in the manufacture of most of the instruments of war by which victory over our enemies was achieved. U.S. Steel is proud of the very substantial contribution to the war effort of the thousands of men and women comprising its personnel, whose work and cooperation helped to produce U.S. Steel's share of the nation's steel requirements as and when needed. . . . Specialized materials made primarily of steel were required for tanks, trucks, planes, ships, shells, bombs, rockets, fencing, containers, wire rope, engines, guns, springs, and for hundreds of thousands of other items."[2] Judging which among these were the most crucial would be impossible, but emphasizing ships alone, U.S. Steel subsidiaries built over nine hundred vessels and floating structures that included destroyers, cruisers, landing craft, troop transports, tankers, and barges. Besides building the instruments of war, U.S. Steel's fabricating subsidiaries assisted other companies in constructing such wartime facilities as shipyards, power plants, plants for manufacturing aircraft and tanks, and material for building military camps in the United States and overseas. U.S. Steel also provided the steel used in producing building machines, railroad locomotives and cars, and trucks, all of which carried vital cargo of every description to wherever needed. Additionally, U.S. Steel either directly or indirectly assisted in both developing and manufacturing important coal chemicals and other coal by-products, such as "sulfa drugs, aspirin, nylon, aviation gasoline, synthetic rubber, plastics, perfumes, DDT, and fertilizers," that served military and civilian needs not only during the war but also for peacetime applications.[3]

The image of coal miners busily engaged in their daily work routine with sights squarely set on a "let's win the war" singular objective might have been good for propaganda posters and the national morale of World War II America, but it would be fair to suggest that Gary miners and, for that matter, miners from numerous other coal mining towns, were not absolutely at ease with that sentiment. There was no shortage of patriotism in Gary—plenty of fathers, brothers, sons, and other kin had left the coal mine to serve in the armed forces—but the tension between labor and management that had been part of coal mining in this country virtually from the industry's beginning did not take a holiday just because of war. After all, to the miner the urgency of the nation's wartime needs did not make his job any easier, nor did it lessen the risks of this most dangerous of occupations, nor did it nullify what the miner perceived as his obligation to family and self to expect fair compensation for a day's work.

And so Gary coal miners, along with bituminous coal miners from across America, followed UMWA's lead in four separate strikes in 1943. The union demanded a daily wage increase of two dollars per miner, premising its demand on what was said to be employers' failure to provide miners portal-to-portal pay—that is, pay for time spent in transportation to and from the mine's mouth and the miner's place of work. The seriousness of the matter to the existing national emergency eventually prompted President Roosevelt to intervene. The president ordered that the government seize control of all bituminous coal mines and requested that miners return to work. What followed was a series of work starts and stoppages orchestrated by the UMWA between late spring and late fall of 1943, and ending only when the union finally negotiated a contract that assured miners of receiving an additional $1.50 daily wage increase.[4]

Employees of a vital industry walking off the job during wartime hardly endeared those workers to the American public. But miners were not alone. The roughly 60,000 striking bituminous coal miners joined some 2 million other U.S. workers in approximately 3,700 strikes during 1943. And the number of strikes and strike-idled workers increased significantly during the next two years. Much of the impetus for such labor unrest grew from the National War Labor Board's strict wartime controls on wage increases—controls that for all intents and purposes froze bituminous coal miners' wages at 1941 levels. Frozen wages might have been acceptable had the cost of living held steady during the war, but inflation pushed prices beyond what coal miners and many other American workers could afford. Thus, work stoppage, if for no other reason than to draw attention to their plight, seemed justified. Striking coal miners were portrayed in the American press as jeopardizing the nation's security for monetary gain. The charge, however, was countered by at least one report stating that record coal production prior to the 1943 strikes had provided the United States with a coal reserve that easily would have met the nation's needs during the year.[5] At year's end, U.S. Steel ignored the matter of coal reserves but did estimate that the 1943 strikes had resulted in a loss of 2.6 million tons in coal production. With that in mind, the company's statement about labor relations in its 1943 annual report gave high praise to its achievements in general, but its comments directed toward the company's unruly miners were noticeably strained.[6]

Only a few months after World War II ended, the USCC announced plans to build a coal cleaning and preparation plant at Alpheus, between Gary and Wilcoe, that upon completion would be the largest plant of its kind in the world. It would take raw coal, clean it of rock and other impurities, crush it to a uniform size, blend it with coal from different mines, and finally spray the finished product with oil to minimize coal dust during shipment. Once the treatment process was complete, the cleaned and prepared coal was carried to holding bins positioned over railroad tracks, where it then was dropped into hopper cars as they moved along the tracks. When full, the hopper cars were transported to their steel plant destination. At maximum capacity the Alpheus central preparation plant could process 360 railroad cars of coal per day, or seven million tons annually.[7]

The coal preparation plant was becoming the symbol of the modern bituminous coal mining operation throughout America. Mining mechanization had made it so. Before mechanical loading machines made their appearance at the mine face, coal miners picked out as many impurities, such as shale and other rock, as possible. The coal then was loaded into cars and sent to the user without further processing. The speed of mechanical loaders made it impossible to clean the coal by hand, and the preparation plant became the only means by which impurities could be removed. The removal process was ingenious. Because the density of coal is less than that of the impurities surrounding and imbedded in it, floating the coal in a liquid pool allows unwanted residue to sink to the pool's bottom while the coal remains afloat. By 1947 preparation plants were using this or similar cleaning processes to prepare approximately 37 percent of all bituminous coal mined in the United States.[8] The refuse removed from the coal at the Alpheus preparation plant—roughly 350 tons of it per hour—was carried by conveyor belt to a nearby hollow and dumped.

Up and running by 1947, the Alpheus preparation plant was expected to operate for approximately twenty years, and as soon as the first load of coal came rolling in, the clock started ticking toward the plant's demise.[9] For now, however, the Alpheus preparation plant meant prosperity. A hellish war had just ended, the steel-making business was booming, and all seemed well with the world, not counting the work stoppages at the Gary coal mines, which had become an annual occurrence from 1946 to 1950. To the chagrin of wives and mothers, the strikes seemed always to occur during holiday periods, when the absence of a company paycheck pushed household budgets to their breaking point. The labor disputes were orchestrated by the UMWA and all had to do with wage increases. The stoppages lasted anywhere from two weeks to two months, and on a number of occasions the government had to step in to force both labor and management to settle their differences. Had the work stoppages not occurred, noted U.S. Steel in its 1949 annual report, the company's coal miners "could have earned the highest yearly wages in their history."[10]

Labor disputes aside, changes for Gary, both big and small and some with greater and some with lesser impact, were on the way. First came the announcement in November 1950 that the corporate name of United States Coal and Coke Company, a name that had been synonymous with Gary for nearly half a century, was being changed. On November 6, Irving S. Olds, U.S. Steel chairman of the board, announced that, effective January 1, 1951, the United States Steel Corporation would merge the United States Steel Corporation of Delaware, Carnegie-Illinois Steel Corporation, H. C. Frick Coke Company, and United States Coal and Coke Company into a single operating entity known as the United States Steel Company. The new combination would be a wholly owned subsidiary of its similarly named United States Steel Corporation of New Jersey parent company and would be headquartered in Pittsburgh.[11] And, some three hundred miles south of its new corporate home, U.S. Coal and Coke Company now would be known as United States Steel Gary District. The reason given for the consolidation was "simplification of the corporate structure" in order to centralize its operation and make it more cost effective.[12]

Existing mines in the now renamed Gary District had expanded for years as continuous coal removal pushed the mines deeper and deeper into the Gary Hollow mountains. A totally new mine, however, had not appeared here in decades. That changed in 1948 when U.S. Steel opened No. 14 mine and built the town of Munson nearby.[13] The new town took its name from John G. Munson, a U.S. Steel vice-president since 1939 who retired from that office in 1951.[14] The No. 14 mine actually had two entrances, or portals, one about 70 feet above the other, that allowed simultaneous access to both the Pocahontas No. 3 and No. 4 seams. The higher of the two portals was dubbed the "mine in the sky" due to its location at 2,160 feet above sea level. Within four years the No. 14 was producing four thousand tons of high-grade met coal per day. And the mine, said to be "completely mechanized" with combination drilling and cutting machines and loaders, was said to have a potential of producing at least 10,000 tons of coal per day. Every day loaded mine cars carried coal twenty miles underground to an outside tipple, where the coal was dumped onto a conveyor belt, carried nearly six hundred feet, and tipped into waiting N&W coal cars. The coal was then transported seven miles to the Alpheus preparation plant.

The seriousness with which U.S. Steel undertook development of its new mine was obvious. Over 1.5 million cubic yards of earth and rock were removed to transform a mountainside into not only the new No. 14 mine but also the town of Munson. An office building, lamp house, and bathhouse, as well as a unique ski hoist to move miners between the two No. 14 entrance levels were constructed for mining purposes. And to accommodate mine employees and their families, a company store, twenty-one six-room houses, two rooming homes, and an elementary school said to be "among the most modern in the county" also were constructed.[15] Munson's creation, like that of its Gary Hollow sister towns so many years before, was remarkably fast and by all appearances meant to last.

The No. 14 mine was only part of U.S. Steel's effort to expand its coal mining operations at a number of its properties. Wartime demands had caused depletion of metallurgical coal reserves at an "abnormal rate," according to U.S. Steel Chairman Irving S. Olds. In addition, the many UMWA strikes since the war had not allowed "Big Steel," as the trade press referred to U.S. Steel, to restore its depleted coal reserves quickly enough to bring them back to their normal level.[16] Besides the Gary District No. 14 mine, U.S. Steel's H. C. Frick Coke Company began plans to open a new mine near Fredericktown, Pennsylvania, and to reopen a mine near Uniontown, Pennsylvania, that had been abandoned for more than twenty years. All of this was to keep a sufficient flow of coal primarily to the U.S. Steel blast furnaces in the Pittsburgh area, which required 55,000 tons of coal per day.[17]

By 1958, when the McDowell County Centennial was under way, U.S. Steel Gary District was an industrial complex that included five mines (Nos. 2, 6, 9, 10, and 14) as well as the Alpheus preparation plant.[18] The preparation plant, though, was the one entity that most represented U.S. Steel's presence in McDowell County. The company's labyrinth of underground mining operations might have been impressive, but the mines were hidden, virtually invisible to the nonminer. The Alpheus preparation plant, though, was huge, impressive, and very, very visible. Even for persons who were completely unaware of what happened inside the plant or why it even existed, its mere presence symbolized power, prestige, and—quite likely to many—a degree of permanence. U.S. Steel's full-page advertisement in the *Welch Daily News* centennial edition carried a three-quarter-page mountainside view of the Alpheus plant.[19] The edition's first page carried another nearly quarter-page view of the plant. So important was the Alpheus preparation plant to the county's pride, and so symbolic had it become to this out-of-the-way section of southern West Virginia, that county officials shuttled Senator John F. Kennedy up the Tug River Valley to be photographed with Gary District general superintendent C. W. Connor while looking admiringly at the structure.[20]

Coal production put McDowell County on the industrial map during the 1950s. The county competed with neighboring Logan County throughout the decade to be the state's leading coal producer. And while the total tonnage mined in each county far outpaced other West Virginia counties, Logan took a slight edge over McDowell County in the late 1950s. Perhaps more important, though, was the lead that McDowell County safely held throughout the decade in total value of all coal coming from its mines.[21] Heading the list of mines contributing to this position were those of U.S. Steel Gary District. The U.S. Bureau of Mines, in fact, reported annually from 1952 through 1960 that Gary mines usually led all other McDowell County mines in total coal production and occasionally even cited the leadership role of individual mines, as in 1952 when No. 2 was cited and in 1954 when Nos. 2, 6, 9, 10, and 14 all were cited.[22] The National Coal Association reported that during most of the 1950s, the No. 2 mine (along with several other U.S. Steel mining operations at Lynch, Kentucky, and Robena, Pennsylvania) ranked among the top fifty bituminous coal mines nationwide according to annual tonnage produced. At the close of the decade, Gary's No. 14 mine entered the list as No. 2 dropped off.[23]

Significantly, U.S. Steel chose the Gary No. 2 and No. 14 mines to introduce new "continuous mining machines" in 1957.[24] Mechanical mining methods had become more and more prevalent throughout the bituminous mining industry nationwide. In fact, by 1952, 97 percent of all coal producers in West Virginia cut their coal by machines and 80 percent loaded their coal mechanically.[25] But most important was the amount of bituminous coal being mined nationwide by continuous mining machines. These machines accounted for less than 1 percent of all coal mined in the United States in 1950, but that figure increased to almost 20 percent near the end of the decade.[26] In a 1958 National Coal Association report, continuous mining machines were called "the most marvelous of all the industry's subterranean monsters. . . . These machines, of several types, eliminate the separate steps of cutting, drilling, blasting and loading. The continuous miner has multi-toothed cutting heads by which it eats its way into the coal seam, tearing loose the coal and passing it to the rear of the machine where it is transferred to conveyor belts or loaded into shuttle cars for movement to the surface by mine cars. These hungry machines can mine up to eight tons of coal per minute."[27]

Life outside the mines in Gary Hollow also began to change during the 1950s, although change was incremental and hardly noticed. Veterans returning from World War II brought Gary's 1950 population to approximately nine thousand. That seemed to be a good level, but it represented a drop of nearly six hundred from the 1940 population. Main Gary, as it was called, accounted for nearly a fourth of Gary Hollow's entire population.[28] As a result, Gary Hollow did not undergo the postwar building boom that many other American towns experienced. Returning veterans either moved into their families' homes or rented existing houses. Uniformity with respect to landscape and structure had been established for quite some time. Geography had seen to that. However, eight new houses were built in a subdivision north of Wilcoe called Talman Village in honor of U.S. Steel Gary District general superintendent Woods G. Talman. After the No. 14 mine was opened and the town of Munson and Talman Village were built, the company built nothing more. As of 1954, there were approximately 1,360 houses standing throughout Gary Hollow. Since a number of these were duplex houses, total dwelling units numbered nearly 2,100.[29]

Gary Hollow residents relied on nearby Welch to provide most commercial needs, but Gary Hollow towns were remarkably self-sufficient. Several company stores, all stocked with essential food and pharmaceutical items, were spread throughout the area. Within each household, though, residents unfortunately straddled the fence with regard to primitive versus modern conveniences. Not until the 1960s, for example, did many houses have indoor toilets. Even for those houses that did have indoor toilets prior to the company's construction of a common sewage system, raw waste was flushed into nearby creeks. Such pollution did little to enhance the area's aquatic life, which, for the most part, had long since disappeared.

Gary Hollow also was without a communitywide telephone service until the late 1950s. Before then only a few residents had phones, which they regarded as prized possessions. Neighbors, however, often made a nuisance of themselves by frequently using the phone, and incoming calls oftentimes forced the phone's owner into becoming a message service for the entire neighborhood. For long-distance calls, the company's main office building had a phone booth and users paid an office clerk for toll charges.[30]

There were other links to the world at large. The *Welch Daily News* and radio from Welch's WELC had been around for some time, and both provided a sufficient amount of local news. Television, however, was slow to grab hold in Gary Hollow since surrounding mountainous terrain prevented a strong signal from the nearest station, Bluefield's WHIS-TV, and few households had receivers anyway. But, in time, interest in television persuaded company engineer Mike Hornick to plant an antenna atop a mountain near Elbert and run a cable from that point to houses throughout the town. This precursor to today's cable television system was one of the first of its kind and succeeded in bringing a clear signal to Gary Hollow from as far away as Charleston and Huntington.

Television's arrival was in ironic juxtaposition to the departure of the N&W branch line which made its final run on April 1, 1951. The train, said to have been "a real money-maker for many years," pulled into the Gary terminal following its last trip south to Filbert with only a few passengers—all aboard more for nostalgia than for need—the locomotive's engineer and fireman, and the conductor, two brakemen, and the baggage master.[31] No bands played, no banners were hung, and few even noticed. Despite its discontinued passenger service, the N&W Railway continued to transport thousands of loaded cars to the Alpheus preparation plant. However, its fleet of steam locomotives were replaced by diesel locomotives by mid-1960. Several reasons accounted for the steam locomotive's demise, including N&W's inability to manufacture replacement parts for them. The most ironic reason, though, was the escalating cost of coal to fuel the steam locomotives.[32] While the move to the more efficient diesel locomotives made great economic sense, the steam locomotives were missed in Gary Hollow. True, the soot that poured from their smokestacks had ruined many a newly washed sheet hung on the clothesline to dry, but the locomotive's rumbling presence was somehow reassuring. And the regularity of the steam whistle on a weekday morning was just as good as any alarm clock to awaken children for another day at school.

And school in Gary Hollow was serious business. Teachers there were well trained and intensely dedicated. Even though many male students were determined to follow their father's occupational footsteps into the mines, the quality of education at Gary Hollow schools was such that graduating students could fit easily into the most demanding colleges in the country. Proof of this fact lies in the many doctors, lawyers, professors, engineers, ministers, and other professionals whose roots are in Gary Hollow, and whose intellect and ambitions were nurtured by a marvelous array of teachers.

Several elementary schools scattered throughout the area prepared students through the sixth grade, and then they were bussed to Gary for junior high and high school. Bussing did not carry the same connotation in postwar Gary Hollow as it did in many cities later on, although the problem of segregation certainly existed in Gary Hollow. White children went to white-only elementary schools and black children went to black-only elementary schools. The schools built for white children were constructed of brick; the ones built for black children were made of wood and usually were the schools originally built for the whites. Regardless of their exterior construction, elementary schools for both white and black children generally had comparable teaching and learning resources. White children eventually made their way to Gary High School, and black children enrolled in Gary District High School. Both were brick facilities, and both, according to all accounts, were equal in most respects.

When the U.S. Supreme Court's 1954 *Brown v. Board of Education* decision forced integration of public schools, McDowell County's compliance with the ruling was slow. But by 1956 the process of integrating elementary schools throughout the county, including Gary Hollow, began by moving black children into the previously all-white schools. Gary High School, however, did not enroll its first black student until 1958. The McDowell County Board of Education complied with *Brown v. Board of Education* by allowing voluntary as opposed to mandatory integration, leaving black parents with the option of moving their children to a new school or letting them stay in familiar surroundings. And, in fact, Gary District High School had served black students well for many years. Black students had their own traditions, their own organizations, their own sports teams, their own band, and a very devoted and supportive group of alumni. As such, by the end of the 1950s few students had elected to move from Gary District High to Gary High School.

The reluctance of black students to enroll at Gary High and the reluctance of their parents to force the issue frustrated the efforts of local leaders of the National Association for the Advancement of Colored People (NAACP) to fully integrate whites and blacks at a single high school. Not until passage of the 1964 Civil Rights Act, whose Title IV virtually mandated desegregation of all U.S. public schools, did the McDowell County Board of Education finally move all students from Gary District High to Gary High School. The move was accomplished in fall 1965, and the vacated building was converted into an elementary school.[33] Integration of Gary Hollow schools was orderly, calm, and generally without incident, although Alice Carter noted after a thorough study of the subject that one of only two countywide incidents related to school integration occurred on the first day of classes at Gary High School in 1958. A former biology teacher gave this account of the incident: "A lot of white kids were in front of the gymnasium yelling 'two, four, six, eight, we don't want to integrate' led by one of the stupidest kids in the world, absolutely. And the assistant principal was a very intelligent lady. She rang the bell about ten minutes early. Everyone went to class. That was the end of that."[34]

The relative ease with which Gary Hollow schools were integrated reflected a racial harmony unique about Gary and its satellite towns. This is not to say that Gary Hollow was a utopia where racial prejudice and intolerance did not occasionally rear their ugly heads. And certainly plenty of well-documented studies show that the history of coal mining in this part of the country included significant strains of racism, from the kinds of jobs that black miners had to perform to the kinds of living conditions their families had to endure.[35] Blacks moved to the southern West Virginia coalfields early in the twentieth century, and "the extensive use of black labor," noted Jerry Bruce Thomas, had become "a distinguishing characteristic of the southern smokeless coal fields" by the 1920s.[36] Many black mine workers who moved to McDowell County were drawn to USCC mines in Gary Hollow by the company's extensive and persuasive newspaper advertising campaign.[37] Blacks and immigrants alike filled jobs often vacated by white workers who departed the nonunion mines to work in union mines elsewhere. Many of the native whites who remained, said Thomas, moved "into supervisory or day-wage jobs such as motor and machine operation. Immigrants and Negroes did the rough work, particularly pick mining, loading, and coke drawing."[38] Conditions outside the mines for black mine workers and their families were briefly described by O'Toole in a 1923 article: "The Americans, both white and colored, and the foreign employees live together in harmony in [Gary Hollow]; the only segregation requirement is that white and colored shall not live in the same house."[39] In time, though, definite patterns of segregated housing began to emerge throughout Gary Hollow.[40]

Nonetheless, acceptance of school integration in the 1950s proved that Gary Hollow residents had come to terms with a problem that would continue to plague many parts of America far into the future. For years Gary coal miners, regardless of race or ethnicity, had worked alongside one another, performing equal tasks and earning equal pay (the UMWA had seen to that).[41] And while there were definitely enclaves of black households, as there were enclaves of white households, there also were many places in Gary Hollow where black families lived next door to white families. The company maintained all houses equally, so there was no "other side of the track" in Gary Hollow. Everyone lived both figuratively and literally on the same side.

Even though coexistence worked well in Gary Hollow, there nonetheless were pockets of segregation that seemed destined never to disappear. Churches, for instance, remained solidly black or white. The company maintained separate country clubs for blacks and whites. The one frequented by whites had a nine-hole golf course, a swimming pool, and a club house, whereas the one black club had no golf course but did have a swimming pool and a club house of lesser dimensions and architectural prominence than the white club. The company also maintained a Sportsman's Club for its employees atop what was called "No. 9 Mountain," accessible by a winding dirt road from Filbert. The club consisted of a rustic log cabin–like recreation hall used for dances, parties, and receptions, as well as an outdoor playground with swings, seesaws, and horseshoe pits. Though no "whites only" sign was posted at the Sportsman's

Club entrance, an understanding nonetheless existed as to who would and who would not be welcomed there.

The cultural milieu that came of Gary's mixture of racial and ethnic identities made it a kind of miniature melting pot. A stroll through Gary Hollow would bring one into contact with a variety of languages—including Italian, Hungarian, Polish, and Spanish. The children of immigrants were usually bilingual and could easily connect their parents' old world with the new. Other signs of a multiethnic presence were well-kept gardens full of exotic herbs and vegetables, as well as the aroma of freshly baked bread that filled the air. Not as common but still present were chicken coops that provided fresh eggs and sometimes fresh meat. And still to be found making their rounds in Gary Hollow were the modern descendants of the early peddlers who brought their wares straight to the doorstep. During the 1950s Nick Rucci drove his bakery truck throughout the hollow, selling a variety of fresh pastries. And salesmen from the Raleigh Company, the Jewel Tea Company, and the Fuller Brush Company made their rounds as well, selling home products on order or right from their truck. Another cultural icon that traced its origins to the early days of McDowell County coal mining was that of the hard-drinking, hell-raising miner whose lifestyle was only borderline civilized. Whiskey, and more often moonshine, indeed had been abundant at one time, and stills located in remote mountain hideaways continued to produce the stuff. And some foolhardy souls continued to buy it and drink it.

Gary Hollow, however, had mellowed considerably over the years, and it was a safe place in the 1950s. The front door to just about any home could be left unlocked at night with little chance of burglary. Children could play outdoors with little fear, and there were plenty of activities to keep them occupied. Gary Hollow youth, much like those in bigger towns and cities, joined the Boy Scouts and Girl Scouts, took piano and dance lessons, and joined numerous church and school activities. A traveling carnival visited Gary each year, and for one summer week the very young had access to the closest imitation of an amusement park they would encounter in this part of the country, while the older youth trekked to the sideshows and more daring rides. There to initiate the adventuresome adolescents into the forbidden sights of adulthood were burlesque dancers, who occasionally appeared outside their tents to give quick samples of the erotic moves that awaited patrons on the inside.

With fall in Gary Hollow came the ritual of Friday night football. The Gary High Coal Diggers took on nearby teams from Welch, Iaeger, Big Creek, Northfork-Elkhorn, Pineville, Bluefield, Princeton, Oceana, Beckley, and elsewhere. Basketball filled the gap for organized sports during the winter and spring, and little league baseball carried through the summer. These, of course, were boys sports. Girls sports at the time were confined to physical education classes. Community parks were non-existent in Gary Hollow, unless school playgrounds are counted, but they were not necessary. After all, the surrounding mountains provided the same kind of recreational activities that vacationers later would pay thousands of dollars to enjoy. For boys, at least, the freedom to roam the woods alone or with friends was a rite of passage. Trails that had been trod by Shawnee centuries before could be explored, and so what if they were really only animal paths, the imagination allowed them to be whatever a youngster wanted. There were unparalleled views from forest clearings atop the highest ridges. There were wild berries to pick, and deer to see, and great soaring birds of prey to behold. And best of all, this park was free and its gates were always open.

These things and more were part of Gary Hollow during the 1950s. As odd as it might seem, the coal mines that were the sine qua non of Gary's existence remained somehow removed from the lives of all but those who worked in them. The mines were omnipresent, but they were remote enough from the town centers to remain virtually invisible. Coal might have been the foundation upon which all livelihood in Gary Hollow depended, but there existed a collective identity apart from coal that made Gary and its satellite towns unique. Regardless of whether coal was on the periphery of discussion and activity, there still remained tucked away in the subconscious of many, if not most, Gary residents the uneasy certainty that coal mining in Gary Hollow was living on borrowed time.

Chapter 7

Steel Industry in Decline

Today Pittsburgh is a vibrant, modern metropolis shaped by mountains and the Allegheny and Monongahela rivers, which merge at "the Point" to form the Ohio. Home to world-class universities and museums, Pittsburgh features culture in its highest (and sometimes lowest) forms, as well as scores of ethnic neighborhoods that add flavor, color, and texture to one of America's great cities.

Set the clock back fifty years and a different Pittsburgh emerges. Steel mills dominated the landscape, strung along the riverbanks for miles with their blast furnaces continually aglow. U.S. Steel became synonymous with Pittsburgh, although New York City had been the company's corporate home from the very beginning. The reorganized U.S. Steel that emerged in January 1951 was headquartered in Pittsburgh, and in 1952 it moved into a gleaming forty-one-story skyscraper at 525 William Penn Place.[1] The "Big Steel" company had at last found its home in the "Steel City."

The relationship between U.S. Steel and U.S. Coal and Coke Company still existed, despite changes in corporate organization and names. Gary continued to thrive or wilt depending on the decisions that now came from Pittsburgh. As the health of the American steel industry in general determined the well-being of U.S. Steel, so did it also affect the well-being of every man, woman, and child in Gary. What made the U.S. Steel–Gary connection so crucial in the 1950s was that the American steel industry's health was not good. The industry showed great vigor at first. Business indicators in fact pointed to growth and prosperity. But the indicators proved deceptive. What soon became obvious as the 1950s wore on was that the industry had begun a slow but inexorable decline.

The Steel Industry Roller Coaster, 1960s–1980s

The integrated sector of the steel industry experienced one blow after another during the 1960s, 1970s, and 1980s. There were occasional glimmers of hope, if not signs of vigorous health, but they were illusory. The steel industry in reality had taken an economic turn for the worse. "The seeds of future problems for the American steel industry were sown in the choices made during the expansion of the 1950s; the harvest was reaped in operating losses, plant closures, and the lay-off of tens of thousands of workers through the 1970s and 1980s."[2] The industry's ailments were numerous. Some existed independently, but most affected or were affected by the others. When ailment A came into play, then ailment B was activated, and then ailment C, and so on, as if the entire steel industry were a living organism infected by some uncontrollable virus. Steel imports significantly eroded the strength of the integrated steel industry. Wage demands and wage concessions also played a part, as did economic recessions, upheavals in the energy industry, environmental activism, and "new information-based ways of generating income that did not consume steel."[3] And there was more. One analyst saw many of the industry's woes as self-inflicted through its failure to prepare for the long term, its failure to invest in technology, and its heavy investment in overpriced raw material.[4] Other analysts regarded the steel industry's troubles as part of a broader shift in the U.S. economy, "away from the basic manufacturing industries that have dominated and defined U.S. economic growth since the turn of the century. In the case of steel," the analysts added, "this shift began as far back as the 1950s, when growth in steel consumption slowed, and was clearly underway by the 1970s." These same analysts, reviewing conditions from their retrospective perch in the early 1980s, concluded, "Over the last thirty years, the American steel industry has been transformed from a symbol of industrial might into a symptom of industrial blight."[5]

There were signs that the American steel industry was destined to boom as the 1960s began. The Vietnam War required steel for armaments. Construction of the interstate highway system required tremendous amounts of steel, especially for bridge construction. And President Lyndon Johnson's Great Society pumped money into the economy that encouraged building and buying—buying that oftentimes meant automobiles and appliances made of steel.[6] But the positive signs failed to tell the whole story. Many of the manufacturers building steel products now demanded lighter steel, which meant essentially less steel, and some traditional steel users were beginning to use less expensive and more efficient building material. Demand from major steel users in the railroad, shipbuilding, and agricultural industries also began to decline.[7] By the 1970s, the Vietnam War had ended and the interstate highway system was complete. Infrastructure development in general slowed in America and left steel producers with fewer and fewer customers.[8]

Any suggestion that the steel industry's not-too-distant future might be heading into troubled waters would have been scoffed at during the heady years after World War II. "By the late 1940s, the American steel industry occupied an exceptional position in the world," wrote Kenneth Warren. "The material base of the military victory recently won by the

Allies had depended at least as much on the United States' preeminent position in iron and steel as on any sector of its economy."[9] Moreover, as the steelmaking capacity of much of Europe and Japan lay in ruins in 1945, American steel accounted for more than 60 percent of total world production.

But recovery was under way. Thanks in large part to American economic assistance, the industrial capacity of Western Europe and Japan, particularly with regard to steel production, was on the move by the mid-1950s. Most important was that the new European and Japanese steel plants were employing modern designs and modern technology. What was happening overseas was destined to catch a complacent American steel industry napping. During this period the industry suffered from what Warren characterized as an "overweening self-confidence combined with an incapacity to recognize that there were innovators, good practical steelmen, and expansion-minded companies elsewhere in the world." As a result, American steelmakers by 1960 "produced only 26 percent of the world's steel, a lower proportion than at any time since the early 1870s."[10]

How far the Europeans and Japanese had advanced since World War II was illustrated by the steadily decreasing amount of America's steel exports and America's steadily increasing amount of steel imports. Indeed, the balance of export to import always had favored America until 1959, when America imported more steel than it exported.[11] Perhaps it was inevitable that the balance would tip in favor of overseas producers. After all, imported steel now was cheaper than domestic steel, and the supply of overseas steel was less likely to be interrupted by labor disputes,[12] as was so emphatically illustrated by the nearly four-month-long 1959 UMWA strike. Whatever the dominant factor might have been, Paul Tiffany declared in *The Decline of American Steel* that the post-1959 import-to-export ratio "never again reversed itself, eventually plunging the [American] steel industry into a shattering collapse from its proud heritage."[13]

Why were foreign steelmakers so successful in putting their products into the hands of American customers? Generally, conditions within the major exporting countries such as West Germany and Japan created a comfortable incubator to grow the postwar steel industry. With help from their governments many countries developed steel industries that eventually accomplished three important things. First came the production of enough steel to satisfy their own country's needs, thus diminishing the need to import steel from America. Second was a surplus of steel, much of which was unloaded on the world market, thus competing head to head with American steelmakers and undercutting their prices. Third was the investment by foreign steelmakers in facilities and advanced technology, thus putting American steel producers at a strategic disadvantage.[14]

76

The new foreign steel plants, especially in Japan, were built at tide-water sites located near oceangoing vessels, which could bring raw materials to the plants and pick up finished steel products for delivery.[15] With few exceptions—U.S. Steel's Fairfield Works near Philadelphia being one of them—American steel plants were landlocked, bordering either the Great Lakes or the Ohio River.[16] Indeed, for purposes of world trade, being perched alongside a lake or a major river was hardly comparable to being located near an ocean. The European and Japanese steel industries also incorporated the newest and most efficient steelmaking technology into their new plants.[17] American steelmakers were either unwilling to adopt the new technology or were financially unable to make the transition from old to new technology in time to keep up with the foreign competition.

According to one industry observer, failure to incorporate the newest steelmaking techniques in a timely fashion proved costly. Said the observer, "In steel, truly important cost or quality differences can virtually always be traced to technology. The way steel is made—the choice of furnace and raw materials, the chemistry of the metal, the way it is cast, the way it is finished—lays a basis for defining a firm's competitive advantage."[18] The first major application of technology to steelmaking came from Henry Bessemer in 1856. The Bessemer furnace that he invented and that bore his name made possible for the first time the production of steel in uniform quality and in mass quantity. Bessemer furnaces were replaced early in the twentieth century by open hearth furnaces invented by Carl Wilhelm Siemans, a British citizen of German ancestry. The open hearth (OH) furnaces greatly increased the production capacity for steelmaking and became the standard steelmaking unit worldwide. In 1952 a new kind of steelmaking furnace, called the basic oxygen furnace (BOF), was introduced in Austria. The BOF allowed steelmakers to produce steel much faster and at less cost than the open hearth furnace. What's more, the BOF process allowed production of lighter steel products that were in much demand at the time. The new technology was characterized as a "major breakthrough in steelmaking" and was quick to catch on in Europe and Japan, though it was slower to grab hold in America. Not until 1963, for example, did U.S. Steel decide to install its own BOF.[19]

The failure of the American steel industry to more aggressively adopt the new BOF technology proved costly. It was a failure, however, that typified the industry's postwar technological conservatism born of America's steelmaking dominance. "In the absence of the pressure of competition," observed steel industry analyst William Scheuerman, "U.S. producers avoided the risks associated with new technology and took the safe and tried path of their previous success. During the 1950s, for example, while the rest of the Western industrial world was busy the [basic oxygen] process, U.S. producers invested in 40 million tons of open hearth capacity. According to *Business Week,* the decision to buy 40 million tons of the wrong kind of capacity' placed the industry at a technological disadvantage that it never overcame."[20]

Decisions on whether to stay with the open hearth or whether to move to the BOF process were slow to materialize throughout the American steel industry. The inevitability that BOF eventually would predominate was not evident until after 1958 when the last OH furnace was built in America. Even by 1965, however, the amount of American steel produced in BOFs still only slightly exceeded 17 percent.[21] Nonetheless, too many American steel companies were caught in a serious development conundrum. On the one hand, expanding facilities, albeit with nearly obsolete technology, was costly and would require sufficient time to amortize. On the other hand, if conversion to BOF was to occur, funding for such modernization meant raising the price of steel. Foreign steelmakers by 1959 already were undercutting American prices, so increasing the price of American steel would only intensify the stream of domestic customers buying steel from overseas. Fewer customers would mean less income, which in turn would mean too little money to support the considerable sums that American steelmakers would need to finance their BOF conversion.[22] Growth in overseas steel production from 1961 through 1985 was impressive. West Germany, Italy, and France were among the growth leaders, but the Soviet Union outdid them all, advancing from a 1961 steel output of nearly 78 million net tons to a 1985 output of over 170 million net tons. On the other side of the globe, however, Japan accomplished an equally dramatic increase, rising from a 1961 steel output of roughly 31 million net tons to an output of more than 116 million net tons in 1985. All the while, America's steel production was headed in the opposite direction. From a 1961 output of approximately 98 million net tons, America's steel production fell to little more than 88 million net tons by 1985. America's declining steel output was only part of the story, though. In 1961 American steelmakers were producing approximately 25 percent of all the world's steel. By 1985 that figure had fallen to approximately 11 percent.[23]

Steel production of such magnitude and on such an international scale did not happen just by chance. Rather, growth in steel as a major industrial commodity was more by design and as much political and symbolic as economic. Many countries over the years had come to regard "the state and the steel industry as one." To them "steelmaking [was] emblematic of industrial development."[24] As such, foreign steel producers were assisted by their governments in whatever manner necessary, for they became the flag bearers of their nations. And while steelmakers in countries like Great Britain, France, Italy, Japan, and Canada could rely on their governments for financial subsidies whenever and however needed,

American steelmakers' "dependence on private capital markets" during the recession-squeezed economy of the 1970s and 1980s left them vulnerable to foreign competitors bent on overproducing and underpricing.[25]

To counter the trade imbalance American steel producers did as their foreign competitors were doing and turned to government for help. And the help they most desired was implementation of trade restrictions that would limit foreign steelmakers' access to the American market or place a duty on imported steel that would force prices equal to what American steelmakers charged. As a result, President Lyndon Johnson announced in 1968 that he had forged what came to be called a Voluntary Restraint Agreement (VRA) with Japanese and some European steelmakers that would restrict their exporting certain kinds of steel products into the American market. "In short," declared Scheuerman, "to avoid restrictive trade legislation, foreign steel producers, acting in conjunction with the executive branch of the United States, agreed to divide the American market as part of an international steel cartel."[26] The VRA limited steel exports to America to roughly 14 million tons in 1970 and 15.5 million tons in 1971. Effective January 1, 1969, the agreement was supposed to extend for three years, and it seemed to have some initial impact.[27] Steel imports dropped in 1969 to nearly the agreed upon quota, and the 1970 level was actually lower than the agreed upon quota. The import decline was encouraging, but in reality the lower level of imports likely was due to heavy demands for steel in the exporters' own countries. Indeed, by 1971 America's steel imports were higher than ever, and exports had fallen substantially. Ironically, steel coming into America from the six leading exporting countries—Japan, West Germany, Belgium/Luxembourg (regarded as a single unit), France, Great Britain, and Canada—dropped in almost equal proportion in 1969 and 1970 but then rose in nearly equal proportion in 1971.[28]

The VRA experiment clearly did not achieve its objective, nor did it stimulate American steelmakers to invest in plant modernization. Investment dollars instead flowed overseas, where a number of the major American integrated steel producers either purchased or built steelmaking or steel fabricating facilities. Such ownership simply enhanced corporate portfolios that already contained extensive mineral holdings that many integrated producers held in every corner of the globe.[29] Even the apparent VRA success in 1969 and 1970 was deceptive, since import quotas were based entirely on tonnage. As the amount of steel had decreased, the value of the imported steel actually had increased. Specialty steel products that were more expensive for American customers now replaced the less expensive products that had arrived in greater bulk.[30]

President Richard Nixon renewed the VRA for another three years in 1972. Not only was the amount of foreign steel flowing into the United States restricted by this second VRA, but the type of steel was regulated as well. Once more the VRA appeared to be working as steel imports fell below their quota level and American steel exports rose. But once again the changing level of imports and exports was attributed primarily to the boom in steel demand in Europe and Japan.[31] Demand for steel worldwide dropped sharply in the mid-1970s, but even when it began to increase, steel imports once more plagued the American steel industry. As a result, President Jimmy Carter in 1977 pushed his advisors to develop and implement a trigger price mechanism (TPM). The TPM responded to a growing trend among domestic integrated steel producers of filing suits against foreign steel producers, charging them with illegally dumping their products in America. TPMs were supposed to set a pricing level for imported steel that would provide foreign steel producers a fair profit while resting steel prices at a level competitive with what American producers could charge. Whenever the price for imported steel dropped below the established level, the TPM was supposed to "trigger an accelerated and automatic dumping investigation."[32]

But the TPM, like the VRA, did not work. It was suspended in 1980 and reimposed in 1981, only to be suspended for good in 1982. Economic forces seemed arrayed against any government-imposed import restrictions helping the American steel industry.[33] Even when restrictions appeared helpful, the results could not be sustained. European steelmakers, for instance, seemed perfectly willing to reduce exports, but no sooner had some measurable evidence of their reductions appeared than the level of steel imports from such non-European countries as Canada, Brazil, Japan, and the Republic of Korea began to increase. In addition, the total level of steel imports coming into America increased in 1983 and rose to a record level in 1984. And all the while American exports kept dropping and dropping and dropping. In 1985 American steel producers exported less than a million tons of steel—a twenty-five-year low, while America received more than 24 million tons of steel from foreign producers. Little wonder that American steel exports were dwindling, though. The amount of steel produced in the United States in 1985 remained below 100 million net tons for the fourth consecutive year. Not since 1962 had American steel mills produced less than 100 million net tons of steel.[34]

Steel Pressures and Competition from Other Corners

Foreign competition was only one of the pressures that continued to complicate the steel industry. Steel was losing ground to other metals, as well as to plastic, as a basic component of construction.[35] Competition within the domestic steel industry itself had taken on added significance with the appearance of a new kind of steel production plant known as a "minimill." Environmentalism was pushing the steel industry to conform to new laws that placed constraints on pollution-producing mining and steel production methods. Economic and political conditions within the oil industry, whose connections with steel production heretofore had seemed slight at best, now were becoming exceedingly more relevant. Finally, steelworkers began flexing their union muscle when all the other pressures bearing down on the steel industry began endangering job security.

Minimills

Any impression that the *entire* American steel industry was suffering from the impact of foreign competition would be misleading. Indeed, the image of a steel industry that was somehow monolithic in nature and made up of companies that despite size were near mirror images of one another was also misleading. While it is true that most American steel companies were modeled after the integrated operation of U.S. Steel, smaller companies based upon a nonintegrated model had existed since the early 1950s.[36] The minimill was one such model. Beginning in the 1960s, minimills mounted a domestic challenge to the integrated steel-makers' control of the marketplace that, albeit on a smaller scale, resembled the more aggressive challenge mounted by foreign steelmakers.

The several differences between minimills and integrated operations fall into four categories: plant size, production technology, plant location, and product. As for size, minimills produce far fewer tons of steel per plant than integrated plants—300,000 ton capacity compared to 3.5 million ton capacity. And, of course, greater capacity equates to bigger plants that are more costly to operate. More important, though, is the need for integrated plants to have access to raw materials such as coal and iron ore for blast furnaces. Minimills have no such need, since they produce new steel by melting old steel or scrap in electric furnaces. For all intents and purposes, minimills are in the steel recycling business. Integrated plants also use scrap metal in producing steel but not nearly to the same extent as minimills. By relying on an abundant supply of scrap, minimills need not worry about sources or transportation of raw materials.

Without the need to access raw materials, minimills are able to locate throughout the United States, within easy reach of their intended market. Dependence on raw materials, transportation needs, and a widely dispersed marketplace have restricted integrated steel plants to parts of the country that often are quite distant from customers. And reaching these customers requires a complex system of distribution, warehousing, marketing, and delivery. Minimills can virtually deliver their products from the plant to the customer's doorstep. Finally, minimills concentrate their production to only a few specialized products for which a ready market exists—wire rods, flat-rolled sheets, bars, and pipes. Integrated plants, on the other hand, produce everything that the minimill produces but in greater quantity, size, and shape. In addition, integrated plants produce a variety of more complex products such as heavy steel sheets or slabs that may be pressed into whatever form the customer needs.[37]

Minimills produced approximately 5 percent of all raw steel in the American steel market by the end of the 1960s, and within another decade the minimill output increased to nearly 12 percent. That number jumped to almost 20 percent by 1985. This rapid expansion in output combined with continued product specialization allowed minimills to become competitive with integrated steel plants in a number of product lines.[38]

Environmental Issues

The environmental movement was well under way in the United States by the late 1960s. Persons and organizations within the movement were determined to reverse years of industrial pollution. Positioned high atop their hit list of most egregious offenders was the steel industry, which as of the early 1970s was contributing about 33 percent of all water pollutants and 10 percent of all air pollutants in the United States. The massive effort needed to clean up the air and water fell into the hands of the Environmental Protection Agency (EPA), created in 1970. The EPA put the steel industry on notice that it either could spend the necessary money in dealing with pollution control or pay hefty fines for violating EPA regulations. The steel industry reacted by closing steel plants whose "obsolete and inefficient" technology was environmentally unsound but whose replacement, given other problems that existed at the plants, would have been economically imprudent. Christopher Hall suggested that while critics blamed the high cost of complying with the EPA regulations for the plants' closures, the plants more likely had been scheduled for closing anyway.[39] The steel industry also responded with facility upgrades. A number of companies spent considerable sums of money to install BOFs, electric furnace (EF) units, and other pollution control technologies. In all, steel industry capital expenditures for both air and water pollution control from 1966 to 1970 totaled approximately $573 million. That amount more than doubled, to roughly $1.2 billion, from 1971 to 1975, and from 1976 to 1980 the industry spent an average of $529 million per year on air and water pollution control.[40]

Oil

"Oil is the American lifeblood," wrote Todd Brewster and Peter Jennings in 1998. "Like no other raw material, [oil] has contributed to the American ethos, most notably for its propulsion of the American dream machine, the automobile."[41] So important was the automobile to Americans that the one-automobile-to-every-four-persons ratio that existed in 1950 was reduced to a one-automobile-to-every-two-persons ratio by the 1970s.[42] The mobility of automobiles convinced many Americans to move from neighborhoods near their workplace into more distant suburbs. The end result was more and more automobiles carrying more and more passengers to and from work.[43]

The automobile needed gasoline, of course, and that made oil an increasingly valuable and necessary commodity. Oil also was needed for other consumer goods as well. Plastics, for instance, were oil-based, and there were few items in the mid-1970s American household that were not partially or entirely made of plastic.[44] Few Americans likely made the connection between plastics and oil, but the connection between oil and automobiles was another matter. And the big, heavy automobiles (lots of steel in their construction, keep in mind) that averaged about eleven miles per gallon in those days required plenty of gasoline.[45] But not to worry. At mere pennies to the gallon, gasoline was cheap and from all appearances plentiful.

Unknown to most Americans, though, the flow of oil was beginning to show signs of slowing down. Access to oil that for so long had seemed an American birthright was in fact about to become subject to economic and political upheavals of crisis proportion. The worldwide oil industry since the 1920s had effectively been under the control of seven giant corporations known as the Seven Sisters (from Greek mythology). The corporations—Exxon, Shell, British Petroleum, Gulf, Texaco, Mobil, and Socal (or Chevron)—were overwhelmingly American, but by the nature of their business in faraway places, particularly in the Middle East, it was easy to think of them as more international than domestic. These were the companies that early on grasped the importance oil would play in countries where the automobile and trucking industries were beginning to boom in the 1920s. It was also these companies that had the technological and financial wherewithal to search for oil wherever it might be.

Much of the oil during those early days came from America, but vast oil fields also lay beneath the desert sands of Saudi Arabia, Iran, Iraq, and Kuwait. The Seven Sisters successfully negotiated with leaders of these countries for rights to the oil in return for concessions, or royalty payments based upon a percentage of profits. Pumping, refining, shipping, and marketing was the Seven Sisters' responsibility. As such, governments and ruling families in these countries did little but collect hefty royalty checks. The Seven Sisters, on the other hand, also made enormous sums of money while also controlling the flow and thus the price of oil in the international marketplace.[46] This arrangement worked fine until 1973, when there was a pivotal shift in who would control oil flow and oil prices worldwide. Nearly fifteen years before, in April 1958, representatives from several of the Middle Eastern oil producing countries met to discuss ways by which they could wrest control of oil prices. A September follow-up to that meeting brought the representatives together in Baghdad, where they formed a cartel known as the Organization of

Petroleum Exporting Countries, or OPEC. OPEC membership eventually stretched beyond the Middle East and comprised thirteen nations: Algeria, Ecuador, Gabon, Indonesia, Iran, Iraq, Kuwait, Libya, Nigeria, Qatar, Saudi Arabia, United Arab Emirates, and Venezuela. Collectively, these nations controlled roughly four-fifths of the world's oil supply.[47]

OPEC members may have planned from the very beginning to use the cartel as a political tool; the organization's focus, however, appeared to most outside observers as economic only. OPEC's political side first appeared in June 1967, following the clash between Israel and her Arab neighbors—Egypt to the south and Syria to the north—in the Six-Day War. Israel's swift victory was impressive militarily, and the land seized from its neighbors (the Golan Heights to Israel's north and the Sinai peninsula to its south) stretched Israel's boundaries to more than three times the country's original size.[48] As a show of solidarity, other Arab nations banded together in opposing the support given Israel by the United States and Great Britain. A number of the Middle Eastern countries called for OPEC to place an oil embargo on Israel's Western allies. But too few of the OPEC members joined to make the embargo effective. The United States saw little effect whatsoever. Plenty of gasoline was available, and most Americans probably paid little attention to events that were happening halfway around the world.[49]

The Seven Sisters, on the other hand, were paying close attention. For the first time the tenuous nature of their relationship with oil-laden countries had been exposed. And it had come at a most inopportune time. American demand for oil was increasing at precisely the same time that American oil production was beginning to decline. By 1973—that pivotal year—the United States, whose oil fields had been abundant enough to allow the Seven Sisters to export American oil now became a "net oil importer."[50] As a country that imported most of its oil and "consumed one in every seven barrels of oil used in the world each day,"[51] the United States was now in a very vulnerable position.

Also of issue was the region's volatile politics. Wounds from the Six-Day War continued to fester, and in April 1973 Egypt and Syria met to once more plan war against Israel. The two nations struck on October 6, 1973—a day known as Yom Kippur, "the day of atonement, when even secular Jews fasted and prayed."[52] On October 14 the United States came to Israel's assistance by airlifting needed supplies into the country. Three days later, Arab members of OPEC met in Kuwait City and defied wishes of their Seven Sister partners by raising oil prices some 70 percent. The price increase was coupled with a threat to impose an oil embargo on any country that supported Israel. When President Richard Nixon pledged on October 19 to send Israel a $2.2 billion aid package, the Arabs followed through on their threat.[53] By October 21, all Middle Eastern members of OPEC had joined their Arab neighbors in supporting the embargo.[54]

The cost of oil skyrocketed as a result of the embargo. For countries not affected, OPEC raised the price of a forty-two-gallon barrel of oil from roughly two dollars to nearly twelve dollars.[55] American oil companies were forced to manage the crisis by increasing their gasoline prices and by decreasing the amount of gasoline they delivered to dealers. A cease-fire agreement signed by Israel and Egypt on November 11 seemed to have little impact on the embargo. By late November, service stations across America began to run short of gasoline. As a means of conserving the fuel, President Nixon ordered that service stations close on Sundays, heating oil companies limit their deliveries, and speed limits be reduced to fifty miles per hour on the nation's highways. Federal Energy Director William Simon developed a standby rationing plan that, if implemented, would have restricted automobile owners to roughly eight gallons of gasoline per week. Some states imposed their own conservation plans that either limited the amount of gasoline that could be purchased at one time or limited the time when such purchases could be made. The embargo lasted until March 13, 1974, when OPEC voted to end it. A request from OPEC customers to reduce oil prices, which had jumped by more than 300 percent during the embargo, was rejected. Little wonder why. After all, the price hikes were said to have earned OPEC members over a billion dollars by the end of 1974.[56]

Such wealth flowing to Middle Eastern countries steeped in tradition and heavily influenced by Islamic law and custom quickly began to create social fissures. Autocratic government leaders who controlled much of the oil wealth used it in some cases to begin rapid development of their countries, basing such development on the more advanced countries of the West. One such country was Iran. Iran's leader, the Shah, made great efforts to Westernize his country in the latter part of the 1970s, but in 1979 he was deposed by Islamic fundamentalists who rejected the Shah's efforts toward modernization and instead established an Islamic theocracy.[57]

Iran was said to be "a nation with more oil than almost any on earth," so when fighting in that country in 1978 began to close down oil production that by December had ceased altogether, oil prices that had risen so sharply only four years earlier now began rising sharply once more. Ironically, cessation of Iran's oil flow was not the reason for oil price increases, since other oil-producing countries such as Saudi Arabia increased production to offset any shortages. Oil prices instead were driven up by artificial forces. As Richard Holt described it, "Oil companies, governments, and wealthy individuals bought for speculative reasons, driving prices up further still. . . . So in 1979, it was the American and European oil companies—not OPEC, nor the Iranians—that tripled the price of crude oil. Oil companies and their big customers such as the chemical companies rushed to build up their inventories before the price went even higher—and thus drive it higher still. By March [1979], Iran was exporting again, at a healthy two thirds of its previous rate."[58]

Oil scarcity, whether actual or anticipated, had changed America in ways both dramatic and subtle. Inflation and recession, both of which already were problems, simply worsened during and after the 1973–74 embargo. Inflation that had begun to ease somewhat during the late 1970s began rising once more during the Iranian crisis in 1979.[59] Consumers, whose pocketbooks felt the brunt of inflation the most, reacted to higher gasoline prices in a number of ways. Driving habits changed nationwide. Many people walked more and turned to mass transit; others traded in their gas-guzzlers for more fuel-efficient models, usually foreign built. In fact, as one observer noted, "While sales of Volkswagens and Toyotas were booming, the American [automobile] companies were hectically retooling to make small cars."[60]

For the oil industry itself, matters could not have been rosier. OPEC's price hikes had set in motion a monetary gusher destined to bring unimaginable wealth to Saudi Arabia, Kuwait, and the United Arab Emirates.[61] American oil companies, far from losing money, actually earned huge profits from both the OPEC embargo and the Iranian crisis. Exxon, the world's largest oil company, reported a 59 percent profit increase during the last quarter of 1973, which led the company to significantly expand and accelerate oil exploration.[62] To help with such efforts, the U.S. Congress approved construction of the trans-Alaskan pipeline to carry oil nearly eight hundred miles from the North Slope fields near Prudhoe Bay to Valdez on the southern Alaskan coast, where it would be pumped aboard tankers and shipped to various American refineries. The pipeline was completed on June 20, 1977. The North Slope field was expected to produce some 1.2 million barrels of oil per day—enough to supply about 10 percent of the country's daily oil consumption. Such aggressive oil exploration and production led not only to a decrease in American dependence on foreign oil by the early 1980s, but also to a decrease in the price of oil.[63]

The events of the oil industry during the 1970s and early 1980s connected with the steel industry. The first link came from the downturn in the manufacture of automobiles and heavy machinery resulting from soaring oil prices. The steel industry suffered accordingly due to the declining steel orders from these two heavy users of steel.[64] Even when automobile manufacturing began to pick up, the cars and trucks that rolled off the assembly line were smaller and lighter and required less steel in their construction.[65] Offsetting the steel industry's uncertain situation, though, was the now urgent need for another product that the industry could supply in abundance: pipes. The surge in domestic oil exploration began almost immediately after the 1973–74 oil embargo. Steel pipes were needed for drilling and for constructing pipelines such as the trans-Alaskan pipeline. Structural steel also was needed to build drilling rigs and platforms and oceangoing tankers. Oil industry needs for steel were so great, in fact, that income from oil-related steel products during the 1970s often countered losses or stagnant growth in other segments of the steel industry.[66]

The second link between oil and steel pertained to the Iranian crisis of 1979. Speculation that the Iranian crisis was certain to cause oil shortages similar to those caused by the earlier OPEC embargo proved incorrect. There was no shortage; plenty of oil was available. Nonetheless, the speculation kept crude oil prices high and helped pump up confidence among oil company executives that they needed to continue drilling for oil. More and more steel was ordered as drilling rigs reached a record number in 1981. Ten years earlier, in 1971, American steel producers reported manufacturing 257,000 net tons of products destined to fulfill oil industry needs. That tonnage accounted for less than 1 percent of the total amount of steel shipped that year. By 1981 steel producers had shipped over 6.3 million tons of steel products to the oil industry. That substantial rise in tonnage now accounted for over 7 percent of all steel shipped by American steelmakers that year.[67] When forecasts for the coming year suggested that there would be even more drilling, American steel companies planned to meet what they assumed would be nonstop orders by boosting their capacity to turn out all the pipe and other oilfield products necessary to accommodate what appeared to be a frenzy to find oil.

But the frenzy ended in 1982. Drilling began to drop, slowly but certainly. From a record 91,600 wells drilled in 1981, the number fell by 8 percent to 84,729 in 1982. The number was down to 77,050 in 1983—9 percent less than the previous year and 16 percent less than 1981. Hope probably rose in 1984 when drilling jumped to 86,412 new wells, but the hope was short lived as the drilling count dropped to 71,650 new wells in 1985.[68] The flagging interest in drilling coupled with a decline in the price of a barrel of crude oil. From a high of $31.77 per barrel in 1981, the price dropped steadily—to $28.52 in 1982, $26.19 in 1983, $25.88 in 1984, and $24.09 in 1985. In 1986 the price for a barrel of crude oil plunged to $12.51.[69]

When the cost of drilling for oil exceeded its profit potential, drilling naturally began to slow. Steel pipes were no longer in great demand—there was a tremendous surplus of pipes already available that probably never would be used—so oil companies canceled contracts with steel producers across America.[70] Oil industry–related products produced by American steel companies dropped from roughly 6.3 million tons in 1981 to less than 2.8 million tons by 1982 and to less than 1.3 million tons by 1983.[71] Pipe producing units that had become such an important asset to steel plants now were being shut down, and steelworkers who had produced the pipe were being laid off.[72] This reversal of fortune had repercussions throughout the steel industry. While it would be an exaggeration to suggest that the manufacture of steel goods for the oil industry was the ingredient that kept some steel companies solvent, it certainly would be fair to say that it boosted earnings, output, and hope.

Labor

The word "labor" is peculiar in that it most often is regarded as a noun, referring to the economic component of capitalism that produces a company's product. Management and company stockholders often see labor as something that costs money and that translates as a business expense. Theoretically, when the cost of labor rises, so must the cost of what labor produces also rise in order for a company to make a profit. In a purely economic sense, one might conclude that, to management and stockholders, the value of labor is its ability to generate money. Workers, however, view labor as who they are and what they do. To workers, what they do—the work itself—has a value all its own. Its worth is measured not in generating profits but in generating fair pay and reasonable working conditions. Which measurement of value should predominate is the driving force behind the labor union movement in the United States, and reconciling the two views is at the heart of collective bargaining. When reconciliation fails, strikes often result.

The original USWA contract signed in 1937 by U.S. Steel Chairman Myron C. Taylor and labor leader John L. Lewis contained specific provisions spelling out wages and benefits agreed to by union and steel company leaders. The contract was effective for a three-year period, at the end of which a new contract was negotiated.[73] And while the USWA represented labor during these negotiations, U.S. Steel, "in its position as industry leader, generally acted as bargaining agent for the [steel] companies."[74] As soon as World War II ended, the whole matter of collective bargaining in the steel industry began taking on a familiar pattern. From 1946 through 1959, every new USWA contract period was preceded by a strike. Usually disputes over wages or benefits or both were at issue. Steelworkers were idle for progressively longer periods of time during the first three strikes. The 1946 strike lasted for twenty-seven days; the 1949 strike lasted for forty-two days; and the 1952 strike lasted for fifty-four days. The 1952 strike was particularly irksome to President Harry S. Truman, who actually nationalized all American steel companies for a short time to avoid disrupting steel production during the Korean War. The president's action was found illegal when challenged in court, and he was forced to relinquish control of the industry to the steel companies. The 1959 strike, whose 116-day duration was the longest in USWA history, was possibly the most costly, with some 519,000 steelworkers idled and numerous steel-dependent companies throughout the nation forced to suspend production as their stockpiles of steel dwindled to nothing. Approximately 250,000 more workers had to be laid off.[75] William T. Hogan referred to 1959 as "one of the most significant and most trying years in the history of labor-management relations in the United States."[76] The typical wages and benefits issues were on the bargaining table, but so were union concerns over the impact of workplace technology on employee job security. Management negotiators, on the other hand, were concerned with rising steel prices, overseas competition, and the role that escalating wages played in both.[77]

Every USWA strike since 1946 had been settled by a new contract in which steelworker wages and/or benefits had risen, and usually the raise had been accompanied by increased steel prices as a way to offset the rising wages.[78] The formula seemed to work in theory, but steel company executives claimed that employment costs over the years had risen at a level disproportionate to the prices the companies charged their customers.[79] Such an imbalance may have bothered corporate managers, but it was not the concern of USWA members, whose unanimous call for "'substantial' improvements in wages, hours, and working conditions" during their 1959 convention set the stage for the union's devastating strike.[80] The strike set in motion a ritual that had accompanied each of the preceding strikes. Actually, the ritual would begin somewhat in advance of the strike itself. Major steel customers such as automakers, anticipating the triennial steel strike, with its resulting shutdown of steel production, began stockpiling steel products in order to have enough on hand until steel production resumed. This hedge-buying meant that pre-strike steel production was far above normal output as steel companies paid workers overtime, hired extra workers, and even fired up long-dormant furnaces to fill the glut of hedge-buying customer orders. Ironically, strikes of short duration oftentimes found customers with such a surplus stockpile of steel that steelworkers who ordinarily might have been returning to work remained laid off until customer demand once more built to a normal level.

This ritual was anticipated for the 1959 strike, but after failed negotiations pushed the strike well beyond its expected length, steel customers found their stockpiles dropping to unacceptable levels. That is when customers were forced either to lay off their own employees or look to overseas steel suppliers. Long-term contracts demanded by the overseas suppliers cemented this relationship for some years to come. However, such a contract stipulation became moot in view of the customers' security in knowing not only that a dependable source of steel was available elsewhere, but also that prices paid for that steel were far less than those charged by domestic steel producers.[81]

Ritualization of the USWA contract negotiation process effectively pushed the management side of the steel industry to make certain that the industry's labor side was well compensated. American steelworkers, in fact, became "the highest paid industrial workers in the United States, if not the world."[82] But such wages and the certainty of their escalation were viewed by some analysts and by many steel company executives as a major impediment to the integrated steel industry's well-being during the recessionary 1980s. Several industry executives went so far as to say in 1982 that all eight of the major American integrated steel companies—U.S. Steel; Bethlehem; Jones and Laughlin; National; Republic; Armco; Inland; and Allegheny-Ludlum—"would vanish by the end of the decade unless the steep upward trend of labor costs were leveled off."[83] Whether exaggeration or a statement of fact, the point about the cost of labor was unambiguous. Steelworker wages had risen to their lofty level through a mixture of careful labor-management negotiation and forceful display of just how easily the workers could shut down the industry if their demands went unmet. Reference need only be made to the five USWA strikes between 1946 and 1959 that had consumed a total of 278 days—days when American integrated steel companies were not manufacturing steel and days when these companies lost money.[84] The strikes also had the indirect effect of stimulating trade in steel imports.

Strikes and the threat of strikes played a crucial role not only in the economic status of the steel industry itself but also in the economy of the entire nation. There were very few American manufacturers producing durable goods that did not use steel in some way. They depended on the steel companies to provide steel when needed. And manufacturers also depended on these companies to provide steel at an affordable price so that the goods they produced could be sold to consumers at a similarly affordable price. Any increase in steel prices to manufacturers generally meant increases in prices to consumers. Small increases could be absorbed easily, but substantial increases sometimes caused inflationary spirals that could and often did lead to economic recessions. Given steel's pivotal role in such an economic equation, the government paid particular attention to the industry's pricing structure, often applying direct or indirect pressure on steelmakers to keep their prices as low as possible. Steel companies pointed to the increased USWA wage and benefits demands during the triennial labor contract negotiations as their primary reason for needing to raise prices. Ironically, the government sided with labor in its contract demands for higher wages.[85] Government officials presumably regarded the potential shutdown of the entire integrated steel industry as such a real and continuing threat to the U.S. economy that they were willing to do what they could to keep the workers satisfied and on the job.

The USWA, backed by a supportive government and armed with the memory of how the lengthy 1959 steelworker's strike had impacted the steel industry, extracted better and better wage and benefits contract packages from the integrated steel producers throughout the 1960s. By

1972 steelworker compensation topped that of any other industrial group in America.[86] And in 1973 USWA president I. W. Abel and U.S. Steel officials introduced the Experimental Negotiating Agreement (ENA), which guaranteed steelworkers would not strike and that their wages would rise annually by 3 percent, with an additional cost of living adjustment to match the current inflation rate. Any contract matters in dispute were to be decided through binding arbitration. The ENA effectively pushed USWA member hourly wages from $4.81 in 1972 to $13.01 in 1982.[87]

Automatic wage increases at these levels hardly could be sustained in the integrated steel industry. The industry's eroding market position vis-à-vis foreign steel competitors made the situation particularly troublesome. Losing customers to foreign competitors was one thing, but American steelmakers were forced to keep steel product prices high in order to cover the ENA wage requirements. The dramatic industry downturn in 1982 finally brought the wage issue to a head. The ENA essentially was scuttled when USWA contract negotiations began in 1982. Steelworker wage concessions were inevitable, and the new contract approved on March 1, 1983, with a 9 percent reduction in wages, reflected a new reality where wage and benefit demands and cost of living adjustments were aligned to keep plants open and steelworkers working.[88] The wage concessions did not come easily, however. At the Basic Steel Industry Conference (BSIC), about four hundred local USWA chapter presidents rejected the contract package crafted by union president Lloyd McBride and steel company officials. According to John Hoerr, a festering mistrust between management and labor had surfaced at the local plant level. The workers blamed management for practices and behavior that were hardly conducive to company loyalty. And, if the companies were suffering financially—something that not all steelworkers accepted as fact—then it was only because of mismanagement. Company executives, on the other hand, regarded workers as overly protected by their unions, whose rules had forced companies to engage in unrealistic and unnecessarily expensive workplace practices.

The ENAs evidently kept at bay what Hoerr referred to as "polite belligerence" between management and labor. The workers did not strike, and they were able to get wage and benefit increases without a fight. But whatever doubt there had been about the financial plight of the American integrated steel industry was swept away when steelworkers experienced firsthand the devastating results of the economic recession that had begun in 1981. There were 153,000 laid-off steelworkers, thousands of whom were no longer eligible to receive unemployment benefits or stood to lose their homes to foreclosure. Such circumstances finally left the BSIC little choice but to vote in favor of wage and benefit concessions.[89]

Downsizing, Mergers, and Closures

There was clear evidence that the worldwide steel business was changing during the 1960s, 1970s, and 1980s, and in so many respects the American integrated steelmakers were losing in an industrial contest whose rules they had written. The industry had to change, and in dramatic fashion, if it intended to survive. Such change began to appear in the late 1960s and early 1970s in the form of mergers and plant closures.[90] The mergers were of two types: intraindustry, where one integrated steel company was purchased by another; and interindustry, where a corporate conglomerate whose chief business was not in steel nonetheless purchased a steel company to add to the corporation's portfolio. The interindustry merger often resulted in squeezing of the steel company's assets by the parent company without the parent making any real effort to improve the steel company. Plant closures that could result from either of the two merger types meant either that total plant operations were shut down or that maybe only portions of several jointly owned operations were shut down. The extent of closure was based on whatever might yield the optimum economic result. Ironically, the reduced steelmaking capacity that resulted from partial plant closure often resulted in profits for the steel company, since prices for its product remained stable while cost of running its diminished operation dropped. And whatever profits came from such downsizing quite often were not reinvested within the company but invested in foreign steel companies or in businesses either closely or loosely associated with steelmaking.[91]

Closures and downsizing eventually reached outside the steel mills themselves and into the integrated steel producers' subsidiary companies. Among the most vulnerable were the captive mineral operations—the iron ore mines of the Great Lakes region and the coal mines of Appalachia. The expense of operating captive coal mines in particular and then of transporting the coal to the steel plant continued to rise, while steel companies producing less steel were needing less iron ore and less coal, and spending less to acquire either one.[92] The amount (in tons) of metallurgical coal, such as the kind mined in southern West Virginia, consumed by American steelmakers to produce coke dropped by 36 percent from 1981 to 1982. That number dropped by another 7 percent in 1983. A difference of much greater proportion occurred over a ten-year span from 1973 to 1983. During that time, the amount of coal consumed to make coke dropped from approximately 86 million tons to approximately 31 million tons—a difference of more than 64 percent.[93] The more immediate impact of this declining need for coal to the coal operations, coal workers, and families of coal workers in Gary will be examined shortly.

Economic problems continued to plague the American steel industry during the late 1970s and early 1980s. The oil-induced miniboom of that period was short lived. By 1982 steel shipments from American producers fell to their lowest level in nearly half a century. As a result, according to Christopher Hall, the "integrated companies lost $3.3 billion, or 11 percent of their total equity."[94] And steel imports could be blamed for only so much of what was happening. Added to the mix of woe was a recessionary roller coaster whose twists and turns encountered double-digit inflation, high interest rates, lower spending, a pumped-up value of the American dollar, and lower priced foreign consumer goods such as automobiles.[95]

The result of all this was an American steel industry that in 1982 was producing at less than 50 percent capacity.[96] Ironically, the 50 percent level was nearly identical to another statistic that resulted from steel's plunging fortunes. Taking the total number of nonsalaried American steelworkers who had been laid off since plant closures had begun, the number stood at nearly 153,000 by the end of 1982. This number accounted for roughly 53 percent of all nonsalaried steelworkers.[97] However else the status of the American steel industry might be characterized, such a staggering unemployment rate now gave the situation a human dimension, which consisted of "unemployment, depression, and despair," representing "the most visible reminders of the domestic steel crisis."[98]

A Phoenix Too Late Rising

Perhaps it was inevitable that in only a few years the major American integrated steel companies that had weathered the economic storm would transform themselves into a once more prosperous, albeit downsized, industry. The companies were more efficient, boasted greater productivity with fewer workers, and competed both with domestic minimills and foreign suppliers. The American integrated steel industry, in short, had been "reorganized for success."[99] But this success came at a tremendous price. Measured in the broad strokes and unemotional language of economic theory, downsizing had translated into "shedding unprofitable operations."[100] Such actions had ramifications that stretched beyond the abstract indifference of economic theory and into the homes and livelihoods of real people.

Chapter 8

An Era Begins to Close

The fortunes of U.S. Steel during the 1960s and early 1970s paralleled those of the American integrated steel industry in general. To many, in fact, U.S. Steel *was* the steel industry. Since its beginning, the company had played a dominant leadership role in the affairs of the industry. That role began to decline during the 1960s. Other integrated steelmakers found that deferring to the dictates of U.S. Steel did not always work to their advantage and seemed on occasion to cause more harm than good. Ironically, though, the breach that occurred between U.S. Steel and its domestic competitors during the late 1970s was not so much their moving away from U.S. Steel as it was U.S. Steel moving away from them. And the reason was quite simple. U.S. Steel was diversifying; it was remaking itself, moving gradually away from steel as the company's primary product. U.S. Steel managers had taken a hard look at what was in store for the steel industry in the near term, and what they saw was bleak. The company's survival was at stake. So, U.S. Steel became a different company, and in the process it lopped off all nonessentials. Among them were the coal mines and employees in Gary.

Early Years of Growth and Expansion

U.S. Steel, from the company's very beginning to 1950, led all of its domestic competitors "in terms of rated annual steel ingot capacity."[1] Put in simpler terms, U.S. Steel had the tools to outproduce the competition by a mile. Only one other American steel company, Bethlehem Steel, came even close in ingot capacity, and the closest that Bethlehem could get was no greater than half the capacity of U.S. Steel.[2]

How a company comes to be so big, according to economist Gertrude Schroeder, happens "either by itself constructing or purchasing new production facilities, such as buildings, machinery, and equipment, or by merging with or acquiring the properties of other business firms." The first of these is called "internal" or "natural" growth, and the second is called "external" or "acquisitional" growth. Of the two, U.S. Steel chose the acquisitional route, having "acquired the assets of at least 31 previously independent business enterprises from 1901 through 1950."[3] Many of these, such as Union Steel Company; Clairton Steel Company; Tennessee Coal, Iron and Railroad Company; and Columbia Steel Company, were additions to U.S. Steel's already immense steelmaking enterprise.[4] But some were from outside the steelmaking tradition. The Atlas Portland Cement Company, purchased in 1930, was by no means engaged in steelmaking. Nonetheless, since cement is a "by-product from blast furnace slag," U.S. Steel actually had been in the business of manufacturing and selling cement from the company's earliest days. So, the addition of Atlas Portland to U.S. Steel's corporate family was a natural.[5]

Oil Well Supply Company was another U.S. Steel acquisition in 1930. It built and marketed products used in the burgeoning oil exploration and pumping business.[6] As in the case of the Atlas Portland Cement Company, there was complete logic in U.S. Steel's move into a business that manufactured oil field equipment. U.S. Steel, by anyone's measure, was gigantic at birth. So, there was little need for the company to grow any bigger. And indeed it was Elbert H. Gary, U.S. Steel's first president, who laid down the policy that if and when growth were to occur, it would be a slow, deliberate growth. To Gary, though, the size of the company was fine just as it was.[7]

By 1950 U.S. Steel was booming. Its annual report for that year was full of superlatives for company performance: ingot production totaled almost 32 million net tons, a new company record; sales reached nearly $3 billion, another company record; and income was roughly $216 million, as compared with the previous year's income of approximately $166 million.[8] Steel as an integral component in automobile manufacturing and other durable goods accounted for a portion of U.S. Steel's high demand and high profits. Another portion came from the building boom that had swept across postwar America. Office buildings, apartment complexes, department stores, warehouses, and bridges were crowding the landscape, and construction of all of these required tons and tons of steel.[9] The company was also beginning to expand its production to meet the military requirements of the Korean War. The production of special-grade steels to accommodate war needs accounted for approximately 40 percent of U.S. Steel's total production output by early 1951.[10]

U.S. Steel launched a multimillion-dollar program in late 1945 to expand and modernize its facilities to keep up with current as well as projected demands for steel that were expected to grow exponentially. Part of U.S. Steel's upgrade expenditure, amounting to over $35 million by 1950, was reserved for developing new coal mines and building coal preparation plants. New coal mines were needed to help replenish the company's coking coal reserves that had been nearly depleted during World War II. Much of the coal mine expansion occurred at mine facilities in Gary, including construction of the Alpheus coal preparation plant. Coal preparation plants also were built to service U.S. Steel mines in Pennsylvania. U.S. Steel found that the plants were necessary for removing the higher amounts of slate and other impurities that now accompanied coal as a result of newly introduced mechanized mining techniques.[11]

Expansion continued in other ways when U.S. Steel broke ground on March 1, 1951, for its new Fairless Works near Morrisville, Pennsylvania. The new steel production plant was said to be "one of the largest single expansions of steel producing capacity ever undertaken" and upon completion would annually produce 1.8 million net tons of steel ingots, along with "a wide range of finished steel products." The plant, named for U.S. Steel President Benjamin F. Fairless, began operation on December 11, 1952.[12]

Groundbreaking for the new Fairless Works was but one of the reasons that 1951 proved so special to U.S. Steel. Its annual report told why: "The year 1951, in which U.S. Steel completed fifty years of service to the nation, was marked by the achievement of new production records at a time when an adequate supply of steel was of maximum importance to this country. U.S. Steel's production, its sales, its shipments, its rates of operation, its movement of iron ore from mines to furnaces, all were greater than in any previous year of its history."[13] Ingot production for the year amounted to 34.3 million net tons, income was approximately $184 million, and sales reached in excess of $3.5 million. In addition, the company operated at full capacity for the entire year—something that it had done only twice before, in 1906 and 1916.

In 1952 U.S. Steel celebrated pouring its billionth ton of steel at the Homestead District Works near Pittsburgh. But two steelworker strikes that year lowered U.S. Steel's annual production, sales, and income figures, and customers were unable to replenish their steel inventories on schedule. U.S. Steel's push to fill back orders along with new orders made 1953 another record-breaking year for ingot production, sales, and income. And once more the company's steel plants were operating at more than 98 percent capacity.

From 1954 to 1957 patterns set during the decade's first four years continued. Ingot production, shipments, sales, and income all were down in 1954, but rose once more in 1955. A five-week steelworker strike in 1956 interrupted what probably would have been another record-breaking year for U.S. Steel. A record was set, however, in total sales. That record was eclipsed in 1957 with sales at more than $4.4 billion. A new U.S. Steel income record of roughly $419 million also was set. Ingot production of 33.7 million net tons was somewhat better than the previous year, but it was below the company's record level. The one figure that caught the attention of U.S. Steel officials in 1957 was the level of product shipments. "The trend of shipments within the year," noted the company's annual report, "was steadily downward."[14]

An Era Begins to Close

The trend quite likely was a precursor to the reversals that a nation-wide business recession brought to U.S. Steel in 1958. Ingot production and shipments for the year both were down considerably, as were sales and income. Company steel plants were working at less than 60 percent capacity.[15] The recession had been bad enough, but what occurred the next year was even worse. Steelworkers rejected the terms of their new labor agreement and voted to strike in July 1959. The strike lasted for 116 days, ending on November 7, 1959. The end came only after President Dwight Eisenhower obtained an injunction under provisions of the Taft-Hartley Act that forced steelworkers to resume work. The strike kept U.S. Steel operations at less than 60 percent capacity for the second year in a row. However, the company's ingot production and sales for 1959 actually increased somewhat over the previous year. A rush by customers during the first half of the year to stockpile steel inventory in anticipation of the looming strike accounted for most of the increases.[16]

All in all, U.S. Steel had seemed to weather the industrywide up-heavals caused by the 1959 strike. The company had weathered previous strikes, and at least by outward appearances it seemed capable of doing so again. Something was different this time, however. The nature of the American steel industry's bounce-back in general and of U.S. Steel's in particular was not nearly as elastic as in years past—mainly because of competition from abroad.

U.S. Steel in the 1960s

The symbolic power and presence of U.S. Steel was evident in every part of America during the 1960s. The 600-foot-high space needle center-piece of the 1962 Seattle World's Fair was a product of U.S. Steel. So was the 2.5-mile-long Varrazano-Narrows Bridge spanning New York Harbor that opened in 1964. In the same year, U.S. Steel began construction of the Vehicle Assembly Building at Cape Kennedy, where Saturn moon rockets would be assembled. The building would be the largest in the world when completed.[17] Chicago's John Hancock Building and Sears Tower, built during the late 1960s and early 1970s, and the tallest buildings in the world at the time, also were largely built of U.S. Steel manufactured girders and beams. The company also broke ground in downtown Pittsburgh in March 1967 for construction of its own image-enhancing corporate headquarters building.[18]

In 1962 U.S. Steel finally converted to the BOF steelmaking process at its Pittsburgh plants, with plans to convert its Chicago area plants the following year. The company announced plans in 1965 to spend an average $600 million a year for the next three years—"a rate about double that of the average of the past five years"—on facility upgrades. U.S. Steel CEO Roger Blough noted that the expenditure would help the company "excel in the competitive race and to increase participation in the growing steel market."[19] The enthusiasm of Blough's upgrade announcement was out of character for a company known for being overly cautious about both innovation and expansion.

U.S. Steel came by its technological conservatism naturally. Andrew Carnegie, whose massive steel company was the nucleus around which U.S. Steel was built, once remarked that "pioneering don't pay." And in that spirit it was widely believed that one of U.S. Steel's standing policies was "no inventions, no innovations."[20] The policy may have been not altogether true, but the sentiment nonetheless sometimes did reflect the company's decision making. "U.S. Steel, as the unquestioned leader of the industry," reflected Kenneth Warren, "was especially delinquent and lax in its approach toward technological innovation."[21]

U.S. Steel had made a serious mistake in its steel plant expansion program during the 1950s. While the company did build the new Fairless Works, the rest of its expansion was accomplished by rounding out or adding to the capacity of existing sites. Cost was a major factor in choosing to round out rather than build a new facility (the difference amounting to "$200 a ton of finished steel capacity" for rounding out, as compared to $300 a ton for a new plant). But rounding out meant that U.S. Steel, as well as most other American steel producers who followed the company's lead, simply "preserved old patterns of production and distribution."[22]

In a manner that underscored not only the predicament in which U.S. Steel found itself in the later 1950s, but also the conservative-laced defense that the company applied to its adoption of the BOF process, board chairman Roger Blough said in 1968 that "to have scrapped hundreds of millions of dollars worth of good and serviceable open hearth furnaces in order to replace them with a process that was then in its relatively primitive stages, would have been actually wasteful."[23] Such myopic rationalization was, in Kenneth Warren's words, "an example of entrepreneurial failure."[24] Still, U.S. Steel's economic health as the new decade dawned seemed to exceed expectations. In comparison with the final four years of the 1950s, the company's health might even have been described as borderline robust. Its 1960 income of $304 million indicated recovery from the financial hit sustained during the 1959 steelworkers' strike. Income for that year had dropped to roughly $255 million from the previous year's $302 million. Recovery was elusive, though, and by 1970 U.S. Steel's annual income had plunged to $148 million—the lowest since 1952, when a fifty-five-day USWA strike dropped company income to $144 million.[25]

Eroding income was problem enough, but U.S. Steel also was struggling with internal turmoil. John Hoerr described what was happening as "a creeping rot" that "eroded competitive ability and stymied innovation in the most vital of areas, human relations." One former U.S. Steel plant superintendent characterized the company's operations by the end of the 1960s this way: "The way they [U.S. Steel] made steel was crummy, the way they operated was crummy, and the way they handled labor relations was crummy."[26] What had happened to change the attitude of steelworkers who once had been so proud to work for U.S. Steel was traceable in part to the early 1960s experience of foreign steel competition.[27] The company's annual report, generally full of uplifting news for its stockholders, began to include items in the early 1960s that foreshadowed turbulence ahead. CEO Roger Blough referred to the "highly competitive atmosphere" in which U.S. Steel now was forced to operate, but he then noted with almost gushing optimism that the company was up to the challenge.[28] The following year Blough's optimism had disappeared. He blamed U.S. Steel's declining 1961 income level on, among other things, "strong competitive forces both at home and abroad."[29] By 1962 U.S. Steel was ready to announce a "competitive offensive" that included opening new plants, closing obsolete ones, producing a wider range of products, and improving its marketing apparatus. Such efforts, declared the company, "may well prove to be a turning of the tide which has adversely affected steelmaking over the last several years."[30] Remarking on the continuation of its "intensified cost reduction program" in 1964, U.S. Steel noted that actions it had taken as part of the program were making the company "a leaner, tougher competitor in today's intensely competitive markets."[31]

Foreign competition had become a chronic rather than an occasional nuisance, and its presence seemed particularly obvious during those hedge-buying months surrounding USWA labor agreement negotiations. U.S. Steel never was pleased with being compelled to raise wage and benefit levels in response to the veiled threats that potential strikes posed. But there were other problems associated with the ever-upward trend of steelworker wages that also bothered the company. A lengthy "Wages and Progress" statement included in U.S. Steel's 1967 annual report, in fact, warned in so many words that if wage increases continued on their present course without an accompanying rise in productivity, then the United States—and U.S. Steel in particular—would lose the competitive race and jobs would disappear.[32]

Gloom and doom might have been the order of the day for steelworkers, but Blough let it be known to stockholders during the company's 1968 annual meeting that silver linings surrounded the darkened financial clouds. Said Blough, "While the production and marketing of steel continues to be the principal function of [U.S. Steel], profit opportunities in related activities are being pursued vigorously in markets that are growing significantly."[33] These well-chosen words underscored how U.S. Steel was beginning to pay greater attention to the range of goods and services that the company had manufactured and/or marketed for years and that either directly or indirectly were related to its steel business. U.S. Steel for quite some time had invested significant sums of money overseas in joint ventures, including manufacturing special steel fabrication products (in Italy and Spain), producing cement (in the Bahamas), and mining important metal-producing ores (in Gabon, Quebec, South Africa, Venezuela, and Brazil).[34] Perhaps Blough intended to expand these overseas holdings and to invest in more. Or perhaps he was intimating U.S. Steel's move into new directions domestically. Whatever the immediate intent of his message, the U.S. Steel CEO's long-term projection was clear: a declining future for the one-time steel industry Juggernaut and all that had kept it afloat appeared likely. Prudence required that the lifeboats be readied.

Gary Hollow in the 1960s

Mine closings are fairly routine in coal mining country. And mines are closed for a variety of reasons. A mine might be worked out to the extent that its yield of coal simply is too low to justify the expense of keeping the mine in operation. Or an accident or explosion might make the mine unsafe or possibly destroy it entirely. Unless a mine closes because of unsafe working conditions or because of an accident or explosion, the closure rarely makes news outside its community. That is why the article appearing in the July 21, 1960, edition of the *Welch Daily News* was so unusual. There on page 1 was the headline "U.S. Steel to Close Gary No. 6 Operation." The story was brief, but it packed a wallop:

> U.S. Steel Corp. announced today that effective August 1 production of its Gary district coal mines would be cut back because of a reduction in coke requirements at the company's iron making furnaces.
>
> A U.S. Steel spokesman said the No. 6 operation would be closed and production at the No. 2 mine would be reduced slightly.[35]

U.S. Steel officials did not provide an estimate of how many miners would be affected by its action, but a UMWA spokesperson guessed the number would fall somewhere between seventy-five and eighty.[36] As it happened, the number was much higher.

Gary mines had closed before. The No. 12 mine closed in 1949, the No. 13 in 1951, and the No. 3 in 1954.[37] But low coal production at all three of these mines made their closure inevitable. Not true for No. 6, nor was it true for No. 2, where the workforce would be reduced. Of the five Gary mines in operation between 1955 and 1960—Nos. 2, 6, 9, 10, and 14—No. 2 actually produced the most coal and employed the most miners. No. 6 mine was in the middle of the pack each year in terms of employment, but the amount of coal coming from No. 6 put the mine in third place in 1955, with slightly over a million tons produced. Production declined each year until the No. 6 mine had moved into last place among the Gary five in 1960, with annual coal production for that year slightly under 250,000 tons.[38]

The decline in coal production at No. 6 was significant, but it was indicative of a trend that had been occurring at U.S. Steel's Gary operation since 1955. Combining output from both underground and surface mines, coal production in that year amounted to more than six million tons, giving U.S. Steel the distinction of being West Virginia's fourth largest coal producer. By 1960 total Gary coal production had dropped by 28 percent to slightly more than 4.5 million tons.[39] The decline in the coal mine workforce was more dramatic. Between 1955 and 1960, the number of Gary coal miners declined from 2,714 to 1,670—a drop of 38 percent. A workforce of about 65 in U.S. Steel's surface mining operation in and around Gary remained somewhat constant during the period. Of the 1,670 miners in 1960, 240 (or 15 percent of the total Gary workforce) were employed at the No. 6 mine, and 500 (or 30 percent of the total Gary workforce) were employed at the No. 2 mine.[40]

Any news of the 116-day USWA strike in 1959 no doubt caused anxiety among Gary Hollow coal miners. Ordinarily, the United Mine Workers union would have struck as well. The ties that bind steelworkers and coal miners are by nature strong, and the sympathy that one group feels toward the other is particularly powerful in labor disputes.[41] Sympathy or not, the UMWA did not strike in 1959. Gary mines remained in operation, and while the average number of workdays dropped from 196 in 1958 to 181 in 1959, the total amount of coal produced in Gary mines in 1959 actually surpassed that of the previous year.[42] Probably due to hedge buying, Gary mines produced even more coal in 1960 than in 1959.[43]

Mining productivity was not what U.S. Steel needed at the moment, however. Beginning to feel the pinch of foreign competition, the company was slow to regain its prestrike market stride. Reduced steel shipments meant that the company had to cut production. That in turn meant that less coal would be needed. Unfortunately, the last domino to fall in this industrial domino effect stood teetering in Gary Hollow. When it fell, the jobs of miners fell with it. Specific numbers of lost jobs are not available, but these are the findings from comparing employment figures for 1960 and 1961: The number of Gary Hollow coal miners in 1960 totaled 1,670. That number fell to 1,285 in 1961.[44] The difference amounted to a 23 percent loss of workforce in one year. Add that to the 38 percent workforce decline that occurred between 1955 and 1960, and the total six-year loss topped 60 percent. The loss, as the *Welch Daily News* indicated, was most severe at Gary's No. 6 mine, where 240 coal mine employees lost their job with the mine's closure. Some 70 jobs were eliminated at the No. 2 mine, dropping the workforce there from 500 to 428. But that was not all. The workforce at the No. 9 mine went from 200 to 159, and the workforce at the No. 10 mine went from 240 to 201. Only at the No. 14 mine was there a slight increase, from 490 to 497.[45]

The work situation in Gary in the 1960s was at its lowest ebb just as the decade began. But as is typical in the coal mining business, the situation improved. The need for coal increased, which buoyed employment and mining productivity. Still, the closure of the No. 6 mine had punctured the spirit of this once proud coal town. There might be jobs in the coming days, and indeed there might even be the semblance of returning prosperity, but most workers recognized a mirage when they saw one. All who lived in Gary Hollow from this point on would do so with an air of uncertainty and insecurity. Hope that something might come along tomorrow now became a subconscious mantra that carried Gary residents forward. Layoffs were followed by call backs, followed by layoffs, followed by call backs. Everyone in Gary assumed U.S. Steel was to blame for what was happening, but that was only part of the story. In reality, Gary was now in the grips of international trade. The economic health of the community was determined as much by decisions made halfway around the globe as by decisions made in Pittsburgh.

As a result, many Gary coal mine employees began looking to move their families. The so-called out-migration from Gary Hollow began in earnest in 1960, and for the next three decades families steadily moved away from the area. Many of those who left traveled far from Gary. The Goads went to Texas, the Jowers went to Alabama, the Trentadues went to California, and the Pearmans went to New Mexico. Some stayed closer to home, moving only as far as the next coal mining community in McDowell County or in bordering Virginia. Many changed occupations, choosing to leave mining behind forever.

Employment at underground Gary mines declined from 1960 through 1963. In 1960 the number stood at 1,160, and in 1963 it was down to 804. The number began to rise in 1964, and by 1968 it was back up to 1,241. The number then dipped to 1,153 in 1969 and rose to 1,290 in 1970. The number of surface mine employees averaged fifty-nine during the 1960s, with a low of forty-nine in 1965 and a high of ninety-seven in 1963. Some of the employment figures were affected by additional mine closures, new mines, and reopened mines. For example, the No. 9 mine, like its No. 6 sister mine, was closed in late 1962. The No. 10 mine was closed during the last half of 1962 but reopened the next year. The No. 1 mine, which had been closed in 1905, was reopened in 1963. A new mine, No. 17, was opened at Gary in 1964. By 1965 the No. 9 mine had reopened, and by 1967 so had the No. 6 mine. By 1969 the No. 1 mine closed again, as did the No. 17, which had been in operation for only five years. But the No. 4 mine that had been closed since before World War II was reopened. All of this is confusing, but it is important to note that in the early 1970s the lineup of U.S. Steel coal mines at Gary consisted of Nos. 2, 4, 6, 9, 10, and 14. That is one mine more (No. 4 being the addition) than had been operating in 1960.

Coal production at Gary mines during the 1960s hit its lowest point early in 1961 with 3,993,607 tons (including underground and surface production) mined. Production tonnage began to rise in 1962 and rose annually through 1967. Production figures for 1968 were below those for 1967, and annual production figures for the next three years were even lower. Generally, during the entire 1960s surface mining contributed roughly 10 percent of the total amount of coal produced. One interesting note regarding a comparison of annual employment with annual production figures: While employment numbers in 1969 were lower than in 1960 by nearly 31 percent, coal production in 1969 when compared with 1960 actually increased by nearly 22 percent. What might be concluded from this seemingly contradiction in logic is that more and more production mechanization was being introduced into the Gary mines, thus pushing up the annual per capita output. Whatever was happening, total coal production at Gary mines during the 1960s made U.S. Steel one of the leading coal producers in West Virginia and the entire country. In 1960 and 1961, U.S. Steel was ranked sixth among fellow producers, and from 1962 through 1969 it ranked in fifth place. In 1970 it fell back to sixth place.[46]

The ups and downs of Gary mine employment and coal production figures were similar to U.S. Steel's annual steel production and shipping. Nonetheless, whenever steel production and/or shipping totals fluctuated in a particular year, there was no obvious parallel in the level of coal production. U.S. Steel operated several coal mines outside of Gary, and reduced productivity at one mine might not have affected others.

Although U.S. Steel seemed well supplied with coal, the company announced in 1968 that it would be developing a new coal mine and building a coal preparation plant in the Gary coal district. The new coal mine's production capacity was estimated at four million tons per year—enough, said U.S. Steel, "to maintain an adequate supply of low-volatile washed coal for its own requirements, by replacing existing mines now nearing depletion."[47] U.S. Steel's boast in 1969 of having "some 50 years' reserves of metallurgical coal" seemed aimed at reassuring steel customers who might have doubted the company's continuing interest in the steel business.[48]

By the late 1960s, schools began to close. Company stores that for more than half a century had served practically every Gary Hollow town as combined grocery, dry goods, hardware store, and pharmacy were closed and boarded. The same was happening with theaters and recreation halls that had been around for nearly as long as the company stores. The emotional impact was tough, and it was difficult for residents to pass through Gary without experiencing some pangs of anxiety about what tomorrow might bring. And with reason. In December 1969 attorneys representing U.S. Steel petitioned the McDowell County Court seeking to incorporate Gary. In one swift move, without fanfare, the very company that had created Gary and maintained it as a company town since 1902 was asking to dissolve that relationship.

The effort to incorporate Gary officially began in mid-October, when U.S. Steel and the few noncompany property owners met to sign the petition destined for the County Clerk's office. Among the petitioners were the McDowell County Board of Education, Norfolk and Western Railroad, Pocahontas Land Company, A. N. Harris and Company, and United Methodist Churches in Filbert, Wilcoe, Thorpe, and Gary. County Court President E. L. "Tom" St. Clair set a public hearing for January 6, 1970, to allow members of the public to comment on the petition. If approved, the newly incorporated city would combine the towns of Wilcoe, Venus, Thorpe, Leslie, Ream, Elbert, Filbert, and Gary under the single corporate name "Gary." The area comprising the new city would make it McDowell County's and West Virginia's largest. Oddly, Gary also would rank as the state's longest city. The population, however, was in dispute. At least two sources put it at eight thousand. Another source dropped it to five thousand. The number finally moved to approximately three thousand after an official census required by the McDowell County Clerk. The 1960 population for all of Gary and its satellite towns was roughly 8,400.[49] The three thousand residents living in Gary in 1970 accounted for a ten-year population decline of about 64 percent.

Several steps remained before Gary would become a full-fledged city. The McDowell County Clerk had to divide the proposed city into precincts and organize an election of charter council members to create a city charter for Gary. That done, the residents of the proposed city would have to vote to approve the new charter and then elect a mayor, members of the city council, and other city officers. If all of this could be done by May 1, 1970, Gary would be officially recognized as West Virginia's newest city on July 1, 1970. "At that point," noted a reporter for the *Welch Daily News*, "a new city appears on the county and state map marking the beginning of a new taxing body, a new governing body and a new potential subdivision within the area."[50] So far, Gary's proposed incorporation meant only a transition in city management and governance. But U.S. Steel had plans for a second kind of transition, one that promised even more profound change for Gary residents. On December 12, each Gary head-of-household received a letter from U.S. Steel's corporate office in Pittsburgh notifying him or her that the company intended to sell all of the residential dwellings in Gary and its satellite towns. Company employees, widows, and pensioners were given first choice of purchase. After that the offer went to anyone wishing to buy one of the houses.[51]

U.S. Steel donated several aging company buildings to the new city of Gary, but many of its remaining structures simply were demolished.

The company sold hard-to-access dwellings to a used-lumber company in Tazewell, Virginia, for $5 per room. The lumber company was required to demolish the houses and remove all remains. All other houses were sold to a Pittsburgh company that inspected each dwelling and affixed a market value for potential buyers. Prices ranged from $1,200 for the smallest houses to $6,125 for the biggest. Most sold for $2,300 or $2,400. Duplex houses sold for $1,300 per side, but most buyers opted to pay the full $2,600 for both sides.[52] So, Gary residents, all of whom had rented houses from U.S. Steel and relied on the company for maintenance, now would become homeowners or would be forced to vacate their homes and move from Gary. Important to note is that while the residents might own their home, they would not own the land on which it sat. The land, in fact, remained in the hands of the N&W subsidiary Pocahontas Land Company, which had originally leased it to U.S. Steel.[53] Now, Gary residents themselves would become lessees of the land.

The petition seeking Gary's incorporation was approved as expected, and on July 1, 1971, a ceremony held in Gary made it official.[54] Paul E. Watson, Gary District's general superintendent, represented U.S. Steel and presented to Gary's new mayor, William S. McConnell, deeds to the water treatment and sanitation plants and the fire station and firefighting equipment. These gifts, said Mayor McConnell, "will enable the city to begin debt free and provide an immediate source of revenue." U.S. Steel also presented the mayor with a $20,000 check to provide Gary with some startup revenue to cover the kinds of things that a tax-based revenue later would be able to cover.[55] This official transition "marked the end of coal-town ownership by U.S. Steel," a liquidation that began seven years earlier when residents of Lynch, Kentucky, were given the same opportunity to purchase their homes.[56]

With the flurry of activity that surrounded what had been happening at Gary, there remained the question of exactly what U.S. Steel was up to. The *Welch Daily News* addressed the issue in a December 18, 1969, editorial, stating that the company was certainly "caught in [a] price-profit squeeze just like everybody else" and needed to cut expenses in whatever ways it could. However, continued the editorial, "it would be good for the company to outline the life expectancy of local mines under present mining conditions. After all, nobody wants to buy a house and see the town disappear."[57]

Chapter 9

The Signs Are All Around

"Rationalization" was the operative word for what was happening at U.S. Steel beginning in the 1970s. In fact, a business dictionary definition of "rationalization" illustrates precisely where U.S. Steel was headed: a "reorganization of a firm, group or industry to increase its efficiency and profitability. This may include closing some manufacturing units and expanding others .., merging different stages of the production process .., merging support units, closing units that are duplicating effort of others, etc."[1] U.S. Steel in time also would add the unique twist of cross-industry ownership diversity to its own concept of rationalization.

Practically all that happened at U.S. Steel—at least from the public's vantage point—was in one way or another connected with a push to rationalize. Change, within the realm of corporate America, certainly was nothing new. According to George P. Huber and William H. Glick, "Top managers are preoccupied by change, both the changes that they must react to, such as new and important threats and opportunities, and the changes that they initiate as a result of their beliefs and aspirations. To increase organizational effectiveness—for instance, to improve efficiency, gain market share, or simplify the organizational design—managers are constantly creating new programs, streamlining procedures, evaluating proposed courses of action, and scanning their environment for new problems or opportunities."[2]

The manner by which change is introduced into the workplace has been the subject of a small library of books.[3] Many have been written as "how-to" manuals with step-by-step suggestions for implementing change. And most contain a bounty of diagrams, charts, models, tables, and/or schematics to help analysts, advisors, consultants, and change agents apply new models, new paradigms, new theories, new dynamics, and new agendas, among other things new, to help companies improve profitability. One recommended form of change requires a company to reduce assets and/or workforce to accomplish its goals. Thus, rationalization requires that something be cut loose. The most common term for cutting loose is "downsizing." Huber and Glick have defined "organizational downsizing" as consisting "of a set of activities that are undertaken on the part of management, designed to improve organizational efficiency, productivity, and/or competitiveness. It represents a strategy that affects the size of the firm's workforce and its work processes."[4]

Since downsizing carries what Huber and Glick described as "negative connotations associated with decline . . . downsizing activities are described by managers with an amazing array of alternative terms." Compressing, consolidating, demassing, downshifting, reallocating, rebalancing, resizing, retrenching, redeploying, rightsizing, streamlining, slimming down, or even building down and leaning up are but a few of the euphemisms, according to Jack Beatty, to "act like a kind of mouthwash, sanitizing the word's grim associations."[5] Placing all of these words within the greater context of rationalization, it is obvious that many U.S. Steel employees were to understand all too well their "grim associations."

Rationalization is, conceptually, pragmatic. It is a tool used by a business to do what that business has to do to survive; it is, ultimately, protecting the financial bottom line. Whatever morality there is in rational business practices comes as a result of those who fashion and implement rationalization. The manner by which rationalization is implemented—call it applied rationalization—can be nearly surgical in its precision: A plan with its various details is accompanied by a set of instructions or orders drafted and approved at the highest level and then passed down the chain of command to mid- or low-level managers to execute. Not until the plan reaches the worker does it become personal. Here is where rationalization with its cold and calculating theoretical design takes on its human dimension.

Economic/business theory aside, U.S. Steel's presence moved front and center during the company's September 18, 1970, moving day. Its new headquarters building in Pittsburgh's Steel Triangle was nearing completion, and executives were beginning to move in. The in-house *U.S. Steel News* touted the sixty-four-story, 841-foot building as "Pittsburgh's newest, biggest, and tallest office building."[6] Among the other building projects to which U.S. Steel contributed during the 1970s were Chicago's Sears Tower, the New Orleans Superdome, the Chesapeake Bay Bridge, West Virginia's New River Gorge Bridge, and four of the forty-story buildings comprising Detroit's Renaissance Center.

Meanwhile, a U.S. Steel managerial realignment that became effective in January 1974 combined the company's oversight of domestic raw materials production with that of raw materials sales and distribution. The change placed U.S. Steel coal operations in Gary and elsewhere under a new vice-president and general manager.[7] Those associated with U.S. Steel, however, began to see cracks appearing in the company's facade—including a merger of two major Japanese steelmakers that resulted in Nippon Steel replacing U.S. Steel as the world's largest steel company.[8] In addition, U.S. Steel entered the decade with one of its most dismal economic performances in nearly twenty years. Besides the adverse effects of a sluggish economy, increased steel imports, and rising labor and plant operation costs, there was horrendous winter weather, fuel shortages, equipment failures at major plants, a trucker's strike, and a General Motors strike.

On the bright side, much of the nearly $3 billion U.S. Steel had committed to building upgrades in the mid-1960s was beginning to bear fruit as new plant facilities were either in operation or were poised to come online shortly. The company's income picture improved somewhat in 1971, bouncing upward to nearly $155 million. The trend continued with $157 million in 1972, nearly $326 million in 1973 (with a record steel shipment of some 26 million net tons), and $635 million in 1974. U.S. Steel income reached its apogee in 1974 and began curving downward to roughly $560 million in 1975, $410 million in 1976, and $138 million in 1977. Another rebound occurred in 1978 when income rose to $242 million. U.S. Steel's 1979 income was slightly under its 1978 level, although a change in company accounting practices created an anomalous loss of $293 million. The artificial loss was more than offset by U.S. Steel's 1980 income of nearly $505 million.[9] U.S. Steel's fluctuating income levels reflected what was really happening at the company. The short-lived financial gain in the mid- and late 1970s cloaked the reality of financial instability and the company's losing battle with foreign competitors. Shrouded, too, was U.S. Steel's involvement with social, environmental, and political realities that impacted the company's financial health.

Productivity also drove the fluctuation. While U.S. Steel produced a record 35.0 million tons of steel in 1973 (up from 30.7 the previous year), that number dropped to 26.4 in 1975, rose to 31.3 in 1978, and then plummeted to 23.3 in 1980. Annual shipment levels corresponded with the production levels. The company shipped a record 26.1 million tons of steel in 1973, only to see its shipment level eventually drop to 17.1 in 1980. U.S. Steel produced and shipped less steel at the end of the decade than the beginning. There also was a steadily downward trend in the percentage of steel produced and shipped by U.S. Steel when compared with the industry as a whole.[10]

The dramatic rise in U.S. Steel's income, productivity, and shipment levels during the mid- and late 1970s was due in part to the OPEC oil embargo and the Iranian oil crisis. America's efforts to become less dependent on foreign oil pushed U.S. Steel to place greater emphasis on its Oilwell Division, and the profitability of that unit became an increasingly important revenue stream for U.S. Steel throughout the 1970s. The company's 1974 annual report described the Oilwell Division as manufacturing "a wide range of oil field drilling and pumping equipment" and marketing "a complete line of products and services to the oil and gas industry."[11]

U.S. Steel's optimistic evaluation of its future contributions to the nation's energy crisis foreshadowed just how deeply involved the company
actually would become in the oil business in a few years. For now, though,
the boom that the energy crisis was bringing to the steel industry was
just beginning to reap financial rewards. U.S. Steel's Oilwell Division
field stores were providing products and services ranging from drilling
and pumping equipment to technical support; other company divisions
were building oceangoing oil tanker subassemblies, fuel storage tanks,
and even the "36,000 pipeline support assemblies for the 798-mile trans-
Alaska oil pipeline."[12] Oilwell Division production and profits reached
record levels in 1975, and new records were set in 1977, 1978, and 1979.
U.S. Steel, in fact, noted that the Oilwell Division had significantly expanded its facilities over the last four years and that its "order backlog
for drilling rig units extends into 1981."[13]

Besides the optimism engendered by U.S. Steel's success with its
oil-related manufacturing and sales, the company was fully preparing
itself at the start of the 1970s for growing steel needs in other sectors of
the economy. New or modernized steel facilities for which U.S. Steel had
dedicated nearly $3 billion five years before were now coming online,
and another $634 million had been authorized in 1970 for continued plant
expansion and modernization.[14] A portion of the modernization applied to
pollution control structures that new environmental laws—namely, the
Clean Air Act of 1970 and the Clean Water Act of 1972, both administered
by the EPA—were forcing U.S. Steel to build.[15] The company had spent
nearly $200 million in pollution control facilities between 1965 and 1970
and insisted on its commitment to effectively solve its plant's pollution
emissions problems.[16]

But keeping the air and water clean was not so easy, and within a
short time U.S. Steel was finding pollution control more and more burdensome. By 1973 the company could look to some success with cleaning
up the environment near its facilities, but the cost and what it regarded
as the unreasonable expectations of government regulators were pushing
the issue to an unrealistic degree. "In some cases," U.S. Steel reported,
"we are being asked to meet impossible standards."

> Neither U.S. Steel nor the steel industry will have the
> funds to do the job as fast as is being asked, while at the
> same time providing the modern facilities necessary to
> remain a viable domestic industry.
>
> We are convinced that what amounts to a crash
> approach to solving the problem will interfere with the
> efficient allocation of economic resources. Such an ap-
> proach would be unwise for steel, for other industries and
> for our nation."[17]

The Signs Are All Around

According to U.S. Steel, controlling coke plant emissions amounted to "the most serious and technologically difficult pollution-abatement problem facing U.S. Steel and the industry."[18] By 1972 the company operated nearly 3,500 coke ovens. The coke-making process was designed to capture certain gaseous emissions that could be used in manufacturing coke by-products. But the process also allowed certain other gases to escape into the atmosphere. Release of these waste gases was no longer acceptable. Determining how to control the emissions was a particularly vexing problem that U.S. Steel nonetheless seemed committed to solving, announcing in 1972 that it had contracted with the federal government at a cost of nearly $7 million "for development and testing of a non-polluting process for converting coal to high-grade metallurgical coke, chemicals and clean gas."[19]

By 1974 U.S. Steel was feeling even more intense pressure to increase its efforts and thus spend more money to control pollution. And company leaders grew more agitated with government regulators for applying the pressure. Certainly U.S. Steel, along with all American businesses, were responsible for protecting the environment. But, said the company in its 1974 annual report, "cleaner air and water must be achieved in harmony with the nation's economic and social goals. The benefits to be obtained must be measured against the costs to be incurred."[20] One year later, U.S. Steel Board chairman Edgar B. Speer came straight to the point of what he saw as a dilemma into which his company had been placed: "Many of the environmental standards, and time schedules for accomplishment are unrealistic. Unless these requirements are sensibly modified, construction of new facilities may be virtually brought to a halt."[21] If environmental laws were impeding construction of new facilities, their impact on existing facilities was just as significant—a point underscored by Speer in 1978: "A factor significantly restricting the Corporation's ability to invest in job-producing tools for the future is the mounting pressure for retrofitting of older facilities with sophisticated and highly expensive environmental control facilities."[22] In early 1979 he declared, "U.S. Steel is committed to improving the environment. But when the economics of expenditures under such programs make the output of the facilities unprofitable, the alternative of abandoning those facilities and their products will be weighed."[23] Speer could point to one example where "pollution abatement" efforts already had cost jobs. U.S. Steel had spent some $6 million to control emissions at its Clairton, Pennsylvania, coke ovens by the mid-1970s, but in doing so Clairton's annual coke production had been cut from roughly seven million to four million tons. As a result, steel production dropped and steelworker jobs were eliminated. Jobs were lost as well when the company decided to shut down older furnaces instead of spending anything extra on upgrading them to meet emission control standards.[24]

The Signs Are All Around

The specter of job loss and the threat that more losses could occur no doubt raised the tension level among steelworkers, but it was a convenient way for U.S. Steel to move forward with its rationalization plan that actually was more the result of foreign competition than of environmental requirements. Wage demands made by steelworkers seemed a particularly prickly issue at U.S. Steel. Board chairman Edwin Gott complained in 1970 that "steelworker wages . . . are among the highest in American manufacturing," and he went on to compare the widening gap between the wages of American steelworkers and those of foreign steelworkers. U.S. Steel even took the trouble in its 1970 annual report to provide graphs and charts to prove its point. Not only were steelworkers doing exceptionally well with regard to wages, but their wages over the years, according to U.S. Steel's figures, actually had risen by a much higher percentage than had the company's prices and thus its profits. Added to complaints over high wages were complaints over their steelworkers' productivity, or output per man-hour, which U.S. Steel officials also contended ran a poor second to foreign steelworkers.[25]

The wage/productivity assertions served as effective management propaganda that conceivably could help the company better defend its position during union contract negotiations slated for 1971. One result of those negotiations was creation of "union-management committees" at U.S. Steel sites whose purpose was "to recommend and promote productivity improvements."[26] The committees were not universally accepted with open arms by the steelworkers, but the rationale behind creating the committees had led to a "growing recognition of the relationship between productive efficiency and job security."[27]

Threats of strike and the resulting hedge-buying cycle that always accompanied steelworker contract negotiations were present in 1971, but a strike did not occur. And indeed the Experimental Negotiating Agreement (ENA) that went into effect in 1973 guaranteed that steelworkers would not strike in exchange for a 3 percent annual wage increase and a cost of living adjustment to match the current inflation rate. As a result of the ENA, the surge in steelmaking and buying that preceded potential strikes, followed by down periods, when strikes oftentimes brought steel production to a standstill, would no longer be a worry at U.S. Steel—at least as long as the ENA was in effect. If the company's customers could be assured that steel production would continue uninterrupted year after year, then there would be no need for hedge-buying.

The ENA may have ensured some wage stability among steelworkers, but coal miners were not part of the agreement, and they were determined that their wage demands be met as well. Contract negotiation loggerheads between the UMWA and the steel industry resulted in miners striking several times during the 1970s, and Gary miners participated in at least three of these strikes.[28] The third strike was the longest, stretching for 111 days from December 1977 through late March 1978. The contract that finally ended the strike contained provisions for wage increases in each of the next three years, more vacation time, and improved pension, life, and health insurance benefits that would, according to U.S. Steel, "raise average daily pay of coal miners to over $80 by the end of the contract" while at the same time increase "hourly employment costs by 37%." But the company had little choice but to agree to UMWA demands since the number of lost "man-days of production"—estimated at a combined 680,000 for 1977 and 1978—were beginning to severely affect U.S. Steel's income and productivity levels. Ironically, the coal miners began their strike only a week after U.S. Steel had settled an even longer strike at its Minnesota iron ore works. A dispute over incentive pay brought work at the iron ore pits to a standstill from August 1 to December 15, 1977, a span of 137 days.[29]

Work stoppage resulted in steel production slowdown but so did other problems associated with coal mining. U.S. Steel cited high absenteeism among its coal mining workforces and the reduced coal production that resulted as continuing concerns. Productivity in company mines also was hindered by what U.S. Steel executives claimed were excessive mine inspections made in accordance with the Federal Coal Mine Health and Safety Act, especially in view of what the company touted as its industry-leading position in mine safety. All in all, U.S. Steel was not pleased with the trouble it was having in its coalfields and made a not-so-subtle reference to its displeasure in the company's 1973 annual report: "Achievement of increased coal production, essential in a period of energy shortage, will require a greater degree of cooperation among government agencies, industry, communities and employees and their union."[30] Adding to U.S. Steel's woes was the Federal Mine Safety and Health Amendments Act of 1977, which required even greater attention to mine inspections and improving conditions to ensure coal miner safety whenever and wherever necessary. And once more U.S. Steel pointed out that its "spending for improved occupational health continues at a record pace despite our national leadership in safety and health."[31]

U.S. Steel entered 1979 with the assurance that it had managed to bring labor unrest within those subsidiary industries under its direct control to at least some degree of quiescence. But tremors still could be felt beneath the surface of the apparent labor-management tranquility. Much of the rumbling could be traced to the ENA. As satisfying as it was to have an instrument that short-circuited strikes, U.S. Steel nonetheless was paying dearly for the security. Shortly after the ENA went into effect, U.S. Steel reported that wage and pension increases and automatic cost-of-living adjustments had pushed employment costs upwards by 16 percent between May 1 and December 31, 1974.[32] Automatic increases could hardly be sustained, according to U.S. Steel officials, without a proportionate rise either in steel prices or worker productivity. Raising steel prices was not feasible, given the level of competition coming from low-cost foreign steelmakers. Even less feasible, or so it seemed, was raising the productivity of steelworkers. As a result, U.S. Steel began the process that William Scheuerman later referred to as "the deindustrialization of the nation's integrated steel corporations."[33] The company commenced closing a portion of its operations that were described as "unprofitable and offered no hope of future economic survival." To justify its action, U.S. Steel preached its "real-life economic truths" in its annual report:

> Labor cost must be competitive. Higher labor rates can be justified only if that labor is more productive and can provide a product or service which is competitive. . . .
>
> American industry and American labor must confront some new realities in the Eighties. The marketplace is international. Our standard of living must be produced in the mine, the mill, the laboratory, and on the farm by highly productive people utilizing the best tools and equipment that a favorable economic environment can foster.
>
> Guaranteed annual wage raises, compounded on top of guaranteed cost-of-living wage escalators, on top of guaranteed percent pension formulas, on top of guaranteed health and medical care benefits, can only be acceptable if productivity gains, shared with investors and customers, competitively justify such guarantees. Unfortunately, since the early Seventies, there has been little productivity improvement in steel and a decade-long decline in coal productivity.[34]

U.S. Steel had closed down plants before. In 1977 the company experienced "constant weeding-out of facilities" due to inefficiency or obsolescence.[35] But, the decision of U.S. Steel CEO David Roderick to close certain manufacturing and fabricating plants in 1979 was regarded less as part of an inevitable industrial evolution than as part of the deindustrialization process that U.S. Steel already had put in place. Plant workers who lost their jobs as a result of this process were understandably distressed.[36] And even more so, it would seem, when the company laid much of the blame for its current plight on workers' wage and benefit demands, which seemed hardly justified in view of their productivity. Underlying all the changes was the same industrial thorn that had been poking the steel industry's side since the 1960s—foreign competition.

The "problem of steel imports is growing more serious month by month," reported Edwin H. Gott, chair of the U.S. Steel board in 1971.[37]

The remark followed comments about the number of recently completed steel fabrication projects built using foreign steel. "Every ton of foreign steel bought by an American customer—every foreign car or other consumer product made of steel that is bought by Americans—every piece of fabricated foreign steel that goes into a construction project in this country—means there was an order, somewhere that we might have gotten, but didn't," continued Gott. "And every possible order we lose means that many fewer hours of work, that many fewer dollars in pay for the people who might have produced or fabricated that steel."[38]

The problem of imports was only worsening, though. Less than a year after making the above comments, Gott lamented the irony of increased steel consumption in the United States that was satisfied not by American steelmakers but by foreign companies whose workers earned "from one third to one half" the hourly pay and benefits paid to steelworkers in this country. Added to this were the government subsidies and tax preferences that foreign steel producers received as incentives for exporting steel while American steelmakers were hampered by restrictions that many countries placed on steel imports.[39]

U.S. Steel zeroed in on the government subsidy matter in a special *U.S. Steel News* issue in November 1975. Only once before had U.S. Steel published a special issue, but now the company devoted considerable space to explaining that rebates paid to domestic steelmakers by several European Common Market nations for steel shipped to the United States amounted to "unfair trade practices." The intent of the special edition was to persuade readers to pressure the U.S. Treasury Department into placing import duties (or countervailing duties) on steel arriving at American ports from European Common Market nations that would force the steelmakers to bring the cost of their steel back to a level more competitive with the cost of American steel. Some of the seven European countries whose subsidy practices were targeted—France, Italy, Belgium, Netherlands, Luxembourg, Great Britain, and West Germany—were receiving rebates of up to 30 percent of the sales value of their particular steel products.[40]

The subsidy issue carried its own set of problems for U.S. Steel. But then there was the simultaneous problem of dumping that was centered in Japan. The dumping occurred when Japanese steel was sold in America for less than what the same steel product cost in Japan. Evidence that Japanese steelmakers were flooding the American market with steel products whose prices domestic steelmakers could not meet led U.S. Steel in 1977 to seek redress from the U.S. Treasury Department. The result was trigger price mechanisms (TPM), which seemed to work for the moment, but too much damage already had been done. Unfair trade practices attributed to European Common Market nations, as well as to Japan, already had led to inevitable "depressed domestic steel prices and profits."

Even worse, though, were what Edgar B. Speer called the "corollary results" that "included shutdown of certain operations in the industry, with an attendant unfortunate loss of thousands of steelworker and related jobs, and economic chaos in many steel-based communities."[41]

U.S. Steel made a strong case for its opposition to foreign competition. However, the company owned extensive overseas properties crucial to its business, and it was constantly scouring the world for new sources of raw material, particularly iron ore. It also joined with foreign partners to produce steel in Spain and Italy; steel products in Brazil, Nicaragua, and Germany; and chemicals in India. And U.S. Steel held total or partial ownership in manganese mines in Gabon, copper mines in South Africa, and zinc mines in Bolivia.[42]

By every measure U.S. Steel had become a multinational company by the mid-1970s. It was multifaceted, too, with a branch to fabricate buildings and bridges, a branch to mine and ship ores, and a branch to produce plastics, resins, chemicals, and cement.[43] Size ordinarily would be a sign of strength, but for U.S. Steel the various elements that made it as big as it was were contributing to its inevitable decline. The role of steel in America—once the symbol of its economic strength—was changing in the 1970s. The need for steel in building and manufacturing was declining. And what need there was could be more easily filled by foreign steel producers and more streamlined minimills.[44] The energy crisis of the early 1970s had given a spurt of optimism to U.S. Steel's oil field drilling business, but the spurt was short lived.[45] What had become all too apparent to U.S. Steel executives was the need to push the company's rationalization in another direction. The company could no longer rely on steel entirely as its primary income source.

In 1975 the company declared its intention: "U.S. Steel has had as one of its major objectives the establishment of significant nonsteel, but related, lines of business to lessen the cyclical effects of the basic Steel Manufacturing business," said Speer.[46] The nonsteel investment search that Speer initiated was continued by his successor, David M. Roderick. Roderick was determined that the rational approach to searching for a new business investment would pivot on two objectives. First, he wanted a business so different from steelmaking that there was little chance that both would suffer simultaneously from the whims of the marketplace or the economy. The ideal would be for all of U.S. Steel's holdings always to prosper. But at the very least Roderick intended to invest company money in a business that theoretically could prosper whenever steel was caught in one of its cyclical downturns. Roderick's second objective was to search for a business that "would not be energy—or labor—intensive, or a constant victim of low cost, foreign competition."[47]

A decision on the type of business to buy was helped immensely, or so it appeared, when upheavals in Iran once more threatened the world's oil supply. U.S. Steel again benefited by the second boom in less than a decade in oil field exploration. Providing pipes and drilling rigs for the oil industry meant profits, but anyone with an ounce of sense and a dollar to invest would have seen immediately that the oil business was a potential investment gusher. And Roderick was not interested in owning just a part of any business; he wanted it all. So, as the 1970s came to an end, U.S. Steel began searching for an oil company to buy.

First, however, U.S. Steel had to streamline itself by cost-cutting wherever possible. Plant closings that already had begun were accelerated. The company created a strategic planning group to engage in capital starving. Steel plants were analyzed for their long-term potential. Those that had potential remained open; those that did not closed. No longer would U.S. Steel invest money in shoring up plants whose future was murky at best. Also on the chopping block were subsidiary units of the company whose operations were costly and whose sale would produce needed income. Even if something could not be sold, its closure meant company savings in the long run. And as long as money could be made or saved, there seemed little sentiment in what part of its vast holdings U.S. Steel was willing to divest.

The very concept of an integrated steel company that had applied to U.S. Steel from its very beginning was starting to unravel. The unraveling meant that U.S. Steel no longer saw the need to own the transportation system that for so long had carried to company plants the raw material to make steel. More important, though, U.S. Steel no longer saw the need to control its own source of raw materials.[48] Whatever was needed to produce steel could be purchased more cheaply from independent sources, maybe even—ironically—from overseas. The company's iron ore operation was too much a financial drain, and so it had to go. Even more a drain, however, were U.S. Steel's coal mines. In time they, too, would have to go.

The Signs Are All Around

Chapter 10

Tough but Hopeful Times

Charles Davis noted in his well-researched study of McDowell County coal mining that "the 1970s began with a generally downward trending of coal production in southern West Virginia." However, several factors had combined by the end of the decade "to make the coal production picture look rather consistently good."[1] Three events were significant in boosting the fortunes of McDowell County coal. Two of these—the 1973–74 oil embargo and the uncertainty about America's oil supply resulting from the Iranian political upheavals of the late 1970s—were of foreign origin. The third event—the lengthy 1977–78 coal miner's strike—was entirely domestic.[2]

Federal laws intended to make coal mining safer and less destructive to the environment were discouraging to the industry. The EPA, created in 1970 to make certain that clean air and water standards were enforced,[3] introduced laws that added to the cost of doing business. All of the new environmental legislation was designed to force the coal mining industry to become more aware of the consequences of its actions. The clash between environmentalists and strip-mining operations is a case in point. Surface mining was never a major part of U.S. Steel's coal mining operation at Gary, although for several years in the 1970s surface-mined coal contributed to the overall tonnage of coal produced at Gary's underground mines. Nonetheless, surface mining was a major issue in other parts of McDowell County, and state laws regulating the surface mining industry were among some of the most hotly debated pieces of legislation ever to come before the West Virginia legislature.[4] The federal government joined the fray when Congress passed The Surface Mining Control and Reclamation Act of 1977.[5]

Meanwhile, McDowell County entered the 1970s in its accustomed position as the leading coal producing county in West Virginia. McDowell County yielded its first-place ranking to Monongalia County in 1973, and in subsequent years Boone, Logan, and Kanawha counties also surpassed McDowell County as West Virginia's leading coal producers. McDowell County, in fact, was in third place by 1979, just behind Monongalia and Boone, respectively. McDowell County's decline in coal production ranking emphasized the county's steady decline in coal tonnage production.

From approximately 16.5 million tons of coal mined in 1970 (accounting for 12 percent of West Virginia's total coal production) production figures fell to approximately 10.3 million tons (or 9 percent of the state's total) mined in 1979. While actually a marked improvement over coal production totals from the previous two years, when the 111-day UMWA strike dropped production to approximately 8.2 million tons in 1977 and even lower to approximately 6.4 million tons in 1978, the figures for 1979 reveal the eroding position of prominence McDowell County had held among West Virginia's coal producing counties since the beginning of the century.[6]

Gary coal mines continued to play a key role in their contribution to McDowell County's total coal production. Throughout the 1970s, in fact, Gary's coal production ranked U.S. Steel as one of West Virginia's leading coal producers. But that ranking dropped steadily with McDowell County coal production figures in general. Even more telling was the steady erosion in the commanding lead Gary mines held in McDowell County's total coal output. From approximately 5.1 million tons of coal (accounting for 31 percent of the county's total) produced in 1970, Gary mines produced slightly less than 2.3 million tons (or about 22 percent of the county's total) by 1979. Similar to what happened countywide, the 1979 production number was up from the approximately 1.5 million tons produced by the strike-shortened work year at Gary mines in 1978.

Production totals during the 1970s certainly were headed downward. The consistency was undeniable. Even so, employment figures were rising. There were 1,290 employees working the Gary mines in 1970, and 1,454 working the mines in 1979. So, in some odd sort of imbalance, the year-by-year rise in employment numbers was just as consistent as the year-by-year drop in coal production. Added to the employment figures were the approximately 60 surface mine personnel employed by U.S. Steel from 1970 through 1973, and the number of Alpheus preparation plant employees that averaged about 190 from 1970 through 1979. Employment at Gary mines seemed on the upswing. And five U.S. Steel mines—Nos. 2, 4, 9, 10, and 14—were in operation throughout the decade. The No. 6 mine, which was closed and later reopened during the 1960s, was closed once more in 1972 when the amount of coal mined there during the year dropped to approximately 49,000 tons in 1972.[7]

Employment figures for Gary mines during the 1970s were better—and more encouraging—than the 1960s, and so were the number of working days. The average 229 workdays for Gary's three most productive coal mines during the 1970s were greater than the average 221 workdays during the 1960s. UMWA strikes during 1971 and 1974, and especially the lengthy strike that stretched from late 1977 into 1978, shortened the average workdays. The strikes undoubtedly contributed to lower production figures, even though production was on a downward slide anyway.

Nonetheless, had there been more workdays, more coal presumably would have been mined.

Everyone living in coal country knew strikes cut into productivity and lowered the number of workdays for miners. But to local residents, the important thing was that the downward spiraling employment figures of the 1960s had been reversed. Miners were working during the 1970s, and that was without doubt a sign of hope and stability to many Gary residents. In reality, though, the signs hardly pointed toward hope and stability. Gary mines during the 1970s operated on a very fragile foundation. Fundamental changes in the steel industry, due in part to foreign competition but in greater part to the steelmaking process itself, had lessened U.S. Steel's interest in and need for Gary coal. New mining and environmental regulations also directed U.S. Steel's interest to its newer mining operations, where the regulations could be more easily implemented than at the older Gary mines.

Another problem concerned geology. The Pocahontas No. 3 and No. 4 seams, which were among the richest and most abundant sources of high grade metallurgical coal in the country, had been mined by U.S. Steel for most of the twentieth century. While the mountains of McDowell County still contained plenty of the Pocahontas coal, the mountains in and around Gary had been mined so extensively over the years that the recoverable level of coal reserves had dropped considerably. "Recoverable" pertains to that portion of coal that can be mined in the most cost-effective manner. Substantial amounts of coal still might exist in a coal bed or seam once the recoverable portion has been removed, but mining what remains would demand extraordinary means at astronomical expense.[8] U.S. Steel had too many other sources of coal to sink money into developing more mines at Gary.

U.S. Steel, in fact, operated numerous other coal mines and preparation facilities throughout Appalachia and beyond. Clustered in what the company classified as mining districts were seven mines and one preparation plant in the Frick District of southwestern Pennsylvania, five mines and one preparation plant in the Lynch District of southeastern Kentucky, one mine and one preparation plant in the Southern District of northern Alabama, and two mines and one preparation plant in the Western District of eastern Utah and western Colorado.[9] U.S. Steel spent considerable money throughout the 1970s constructing new coal mines and expanding or rehabilitating several others in each of the above districts. Some of these were predicted to eventually yield several million tons of coal annually.[10]

One of these new mines was located in the Gary District but at some distance from Gary proper. The Gary No. 50 mine was in Wyoming County, just to the north of McDowell County, and situated near the town of Pineville. The No. 50 mine began operation in late 1970 and was joined a year later by construction of a nearby coal preparation plant. Both mine and preparation plant were said to "incorporate the very latest mining techniques, and safety devices known" and to be "equipped with the most modern air and water treating facilities." Expectations were that the No. 50 mine eventually would produce four million tons of coal annually.[11] By 1979 the No. 50 mine cleared the 1 million ton mark, producing nearly 1.6 million tons of coal from the Pocahontas No. 3 seam.[12] Not since 1975 had any of the original cluster of Gary coal mines produced in excess of a million tons. The No. 14 mine was the last to do it in 1975 at just over that mark. Even so, the No. 14 mine total comprised coal from both the Pocahontas No. 3 and No. 4 seams. The success of Gary No. 50 was such that U.S. Steel opened a second Wyoming County mine in 1979.[13]

The construction and operation of the No. 50 mine and preparation plant were light years ahead of the original Gary mines and the Alpheus preparation plant. Different, too, was the absence of any residential community attached to the No. 50 mine. U.S. Steel was holding to its decision to depart from the real estate business once the company divested itself of holdings in Gary. If mine employee housing or service facilities developed around the No. 50 mine, none of it would be furnished by U.S. Steel. The idea for the No. 50 mine to eventually develop into a mega-mine was in keeping with U.S. Steel's coal mining plans in the early 1970s. Already, the company's Frick District Robena mine in Greene County, Pennsylvania, was producing upwards of three million tons of coal annually. Robena was one of U.S. Steel's consistently biggest producers—having yielded in excess of five million tons annually at its production peak. But Robena's reserves, like those in the Gary mines, were declining, and the mine's life span was limited. To take its place U.S. Steel developed the nearby Dilwirth mine, which went online in 1973 and was intended eventually to produce three million tons of coal annually.[14] Yet another potential three million ton-producing U.S. Steel coal mine became operational at Cumberland in Greene County in 1977.[15]

U.S. Steel's coal reserves during the 1970s actually provided more coal than needed at the company's steel plants. The long-range coal production plan initiated during the 1960s called for expanding U.S. Steel's coal producing capabilities in order to be totally self-sufficient and not have to rely on any amount of coal from outside sources. Rather than regulate its rate of coal mining to its rate of need as the 1970s progressed, U.S. Steel was happy to generate a surplus supply of coal. The extra coal was a valuable commodity that U.S. Steel could sell both domestically and overseas.[16] International events occurring during the 1970s would prove just how important—and profitable—coal could be.

Coal had supplied much of America's energy needs from the mid-1800s until the 1950s. Oil and natural gas, however, had rapidly replaced coal and by the 1970s had taken the lead as the country's major energy producers. Railroads by then had turned from coal to diesel fuel to power locomotives; homeowners had turned from coal to fuel oil to supply residential needs; and electric utility companies were increasingly turning to natural gas to run their power plants. Oil and natural gas were much cleaner fuels and easier to transport than coal. The major downside to using oil and natural gas, however, was that domestic resources of both were limited. American oil companies in particular were relying more and more on oil imported from the vast oil fields of the Middle East to help bolster their own supplies.

The 1973–74 oil embargo proved the precarious nature of such dependence. Suddenly, American oil suppliers could not guarantee oil's availability, nor could they control oil's escalating price. There was little choice but for energy users who could make the conversion to consider moving back to coal. Burning coal would produce more pollution for certain, but coal now had become the most inexpensive fuel. Perhaps even more important, the vast American coal reserves meant that plenty of coal would be available whenever and wherever needed for a long, long time.[17]

A 1978 U.S. Senate report on the coal industry noted that "opportunity has been an infrequent visitor to this beleaguered industry for most of the past half century." Now, as a result of the Arab oil embargo, opportunity had come knocking. The report went on to make an especially important observation: "The Clean Air Act of 1970, heightening the level of permissible sulfur emissions from utility coal combustion, has enhanced the desirability of coal with high heat value and low percentage of sulfur by weight because the upper limits of allowable emissions have been based on the amount of sulfur compounds produced-per-million-Btu's."[18] The report's technical language clearly implied something very important. The kind of high carbon (and thus high heat) value and low sulfur content described the properties of metallurgical bituminous coal. And the highest quality coal of this kind was confined to the coalfields of eastern Kentucky and southern West Virginia.[19]

The high heat value of this coal meant that it could be used to convert water into the steam necessary to drive power plant turbines in their production of electricity. Steam coal, as it came to be called, had proved its value many years before as the principle steam-producing fuel for U.S. naval vessels. And railroad locomotives had used steam coal for the same purpose for years. In fact, an earlier chapter noted that Norfolk & Western, the major coal-hauling railroad in the country and the railroad that had carried coal from the Gary Hollow mines from their first day of operation, did not fully convert to diesel locomotives until 1960.

One important point should be understood about utility company conversion to fuel other than coal. While the conversion was under way, the growing need for electrical energy throughout America was such that the use of steam coal never diminished. Quite to the contrary, electric utilities consumed approximately 92 million tons of coal in 1950, and by 1969 that number had increased to nearly 311 million tons. Only once during that period (in 1958) were there fewer tons consumed than during the previous year. Statistics from the 1970s, though, clearly showed how dramatically the coal consumption rates increased. In 1970 electric utility companies consumed slightly over 320 million tons of coal. By the end of the decade coal consumption had jumped to nearly 530 million tons.[20]

Gary coal, however, was not marketed as steam coal. The cost of transporting Gary coal to end-user utility companies was high and became even higher following the Arab oil embargo. In addition, the cost of mining coal underground was becoming more expensive due to the 1969 Federal Coal Mine Health and Safety Act. The cost of Gary coal could not compete with coal coming from the less expensive surface mining operations in nearby eastern Kentucky, or even from Wyoming and Montana, where low sulfur, high Btu coal comparable to that of southern West Virginia was available. Geological conditions presented certain obstacles and possible costs to surface mining operations, but those conditions aside, the surface mining operators' initial investment requires little more than the cost of a "leased bulldozer, front loader, and truck." Add to these the minimal number of employees necessary to work the operation, and the surface coal mine operator is in business. Such an investment is a far cry from the $30 to $40 million (in 1980) required to construct an underground mine capable of producing a minimum of one million tons per year. The lower cost of surface mining, in fact, allowed coal produced in western states to be transported great distances to end-user utility companies at lower costs than could be charged for coal coming from the closer underground mines.[21] The cost advantage of surface mining over underground mining disappeared with the enactment of the 1977 Surface Mining Control and Reclamation Act. The law required that "surface-mined lands were to be returned to their previous use capabilities and their original contours restored as much as possible. Hydrological conditions were to be reclaimed and erosion damage minimized through vegetation."[22]

Another reason Gary Hollow coal was not considered for the steam coal market can be traced back to the Clean Air Act of 1970. The law did two things that actually reduced the need for utility companies to burn the lowest sulfur content coal available. One of these was approval of scrubbing methods whereby end product gases produced at coal-burning power plants could be cleansed of a certain percentage of sulfur dioxide before their emission into the atmosphere. Added to this was the Clean Air Act provision that empowered individual states to determine their own acceptable level of sulfur dioxide emissions. This provision meant that some states could allow utility companies to burn coal whose sulfur content was higher than would be allowed in other states. The provision also meant that coal from northern West Virginia, Ohio, and Pennsylvania could be just as valuable in the steam coal market as the higher quality coal from southern West Virginia.

Even though, as its Cumberland mine development clearly illustrated, U.S. Steel saw the value in producing steam coal, it needed Gary coal for the company's steel production. So, Gary coal continued to be transported to U.S. Steel plants in Gary, Indiana; Duluth, Minnesota; and Lorain, Ohio; and the Clairton and Fairless plants in Pennsylvania.[23] U.S. Steel had been fortunate from its very beginning to have unimpeded access to such a premium grade of metallurgical coal as was mined in Gary Hollow. The coal's coking qualities were superior. But environmental laws in the 1970s that required U.S. Steel to install expensive emission control devices at coking facilities had created a challenge for the company.[24]

In its efforts to find ways to decrease coke-making emissions as much as possible, U.S. Steel announced in 1972 that it had "entered into a $6.6 million contract with the Federal Government for development and testing of a non-polluting process for converting coal to high-grade metallurgical coke, chemicals and clean gas."[25] Throughout the latter years of the 1970s, U.S. Steel announced newly opened and rehabilitated coke oven batteries at its plants in Gary, Indiana; Fairfield, Alabama; Clairton, Pennsylvania; Lorain, Ohio; Fairless Hills, Pennsylvania; and Provo, Utah.[26] In 1978, U.S. Steel announced that "since 1974, three new giant coke oven batteries have become operational. Each of these batteries produces as much coke as approximately three smaller, older batteries. Ten other batteries were completely rebuilt and improved. By the end of 1980, nine additional batteries will be completely rebuilt and improved." The company especially noted that "effective, modern environmental controls are embodied in these facilities."[27]

But inasmuch as "cokemaking presented perhaps the greatest engineering and cost challenges in seeking compliance with air pollution standards," as Christopher Hall noted, upgrading coke-making facilities was proving to be expensive. As a result, the production of coke fell dramatically. The percentage decline in coke production, in fact, surpassed the percentage decline in steelmaking in the U.S. overall.[28] In 1970 coke plants consumed roughly 96 million tons of coal. By 1975 that number had dropped to a little more than 83 million tons. And by 1979, coke plants consumed just over 77 million tons of coal.[29] All told, the 1970s saw a nearly 20 percent decline in the production of coke.

While the decline in American steel production in general during the 1970s accounted for a portion of the decline in coke production, a more significant factor contributing to the drop was development of steel producing methods that required less coke. Blast furnaces were becoming more efficient and electric furnaces used scrap metal rather than coke.[30] Perhaps conditioned by high energy costs or environmental regulations, or maybe in deference to changes industrywide, U.S. Steel executives near the end of the 1970s announced their intention "to use the most efficient manufacturing practices to convert coal and ore economically into iron for steelmaking." Efforts already under way, according to the executives, had reduced the number of blast furnaces operated by the company and as a result had increased the efficiency of those that remained in operation. Most important, though, noted the executives, was the company's declining use of coke. Statistics showed that while U.S. Steel's annual production fluctuated during the 1970s, the company's total production of 29.7 million tons in 1979 was only a little more than 5 percent under its 31.4 million ton production of 1970. On the other hand, U.S. Steel's coke production dropped by more than 21 percent, from 17.6 million tons in 1970 to 14.5 million tons in 1979.[31] Coke production in 1979 actually was higher than in 1978, due presumably to the prolonged UMWA strike of 1977–78.

The decline in coke production carried enormous implications for the Gary Hollow mines. U.S. Steel already had earmarked coal from the mines exclusively for conversion to coke. And yet at the same time company efforts were under way to discover and implement steelmaking methods that would lessen the need for metallurgical coal. What was occurring here in retrospect is clear. Gary's role in U.S. Steel's bigger plans was growing smaller and smaller. The company was moving on. The move would be gradual, nearly imperceptible, but it was happening. Whether obsolescence by design or circumstance, Gary Hollow mines were undergoing industrial suffocation.

U.S. Steel, of course, had ultimate control over how far it chose to reduce its need for Gary Hollow coal. But economic forces and the not-to-be-ignored technological imperative resulting from steelmaking innovation had begun in the 1970s to remold the company's paternal connection with Gary. There were other factors that contributed to the fissures that began to characterize U.S. Steel's relationship with Gary. The time, effort, and expense of accommodating mine safety and inspection requirements mandated by the Federal Coal Mine Health and Safety Act and enforced by the U.S. Bureau of Mines was a primary concern. U.S. Steel executives complained that while "the Bureau's own statistics show our mine safety record to be the finest by far in the entire coal industry," bureau safety inspectors nonetheless "made more than 4,000 visits to our coal mines during 1972—an average of 16 every working day. Each visit consumed management time and reduced their ability to devote maximum attention to daily production problems."[32] The complaints continued throughout the decade, and in 1978 U.S. Steel once more drew attention to the financial burden imposed by federal law and the fact that its "spending for improved occupational health continues at a record pace despite our national leadership in safety and health."[33] "Safety is our first consideration" had been a company mantra since its earliest days, and there were plenty of awards, citations, and plaques attesting to U.S. Steel's attention to the safety of its employees. One might also conclude that the company took particular notice of the safety record at its Gary Hollow mines, since Woods G. Talman, formerly the general superintendent of the Gary District, had been promoted by the 1970s to U.S. Steel's chief inspector of its entire coal operations.[34] But that did not diminish the cost, nor the time, nor the bother of complying with Bureau of Mines' requirements. And however safety conscious the miners might have been, Gary Hollow mines were ancient by mining standards. Not only were they rapidly being worked out; they were also being worn out. Sustaining the Gary mines' safety required more time, attention, and money than was required at U.S. Steel's more modern mining operations.

Another troubling component of U.S. Steel's relationship with its coal miners was the labor disputes that became more and more common during the 1970s. To U.S. Steel executives, work slowdown and stoppage while contract talks or grievances of one kind or another were negotiated meant lowered productivity and higher operating costs. To miners and their families, the decision to walk off the job in protest of management decisions carried an entirely different meaning. However the miners might have justified their position, chances were that such disputes did little to improve U.S. Steel's attitude toward its Gary works. Wildcat strikes, erupting on short notice and usually without union sanction, popped up like smoldering embers throughout the 1970s. But this would be a decade of the sanctioned strike, a decade of coal miner unrest, agitation, and general disquietude more reminiscent of struggles from the distant past.

There were three notable UMWA strikes during the 1970s, all in response to contract disputes. The first industrywide strike began October 1, 1971, at precisely 12:01 a.m., when roughly 80,000 bituminous coal miners in the Appalachian region walked off the job. Gary Hollow miners, along with 29,000 miners from southern West Virginia and southeastern Virginia, joined the strike. UMWA President W. A. (Tony) Boyle actually never formally issued a call to strike, but when the UMWA-BCOA (Bituminous Coal Operators Association) contract expired with nothing as yet to replace it, all union miners invoked what had become coalfield tradition since the days of John L. Lewis: "no contract, no work!" The most contentious contract items between Boyle and BCOA chairman R. Heath Larry, who happened coincidentally also to be U.S. Steel's vice-chairman, were the following: a wage increase from thirty-seven to fifty dollars per day, doubling of BCOA's contribution to the UMWA Welfare and Retirement Fund from forty cents to eighty cents for each ton of coal mined, and greater fringe benefits for miners suffering from black lung disease. The pay-raise issue was particularly important to the UMWA, since better wages seemed to be the one incentive above all others that the mine industry could use to attract new workers and to persuade older and more highly skilled workers to stay put.[35]

By the third week, the strike's effects were felt not only in the coal-fields themselves, where tightened belts from lost wages caused businesses to suffer, but also outside the coalfields. Coal-hauling railroads such as the N&W began laying off workers, and power plants began curtailing their customers' energy supplies. U.S. Steel announced soon after the strike began that the company's coal supply was sufficient enough not to force any curtailment of steel production. However, U.S. Steel was eventually forced to close some of its coke ovens as coal supplies continued to dwindle.[36]

A contract was finally signed on November 14, 1971, bringing an end to a coal strike that had stretched forty-four days, the longest UMWA walk-out since the nine-month strike of 1949–50. By all appearances, the union achieved practically everything it was seeking. Daily wages for most bituminous miners would rise to about forty-six dollars and to fifty dollars for skilled workers, and BCOA contributions toward the UMWA's welfare fund would rise incrementally. These were the most important items, but miners also won important leave, vacation, and health benefit concessions. The BCOA appeared to have given much more than it received in settling its contract dispute with the UMWA. However, there was one specific stipulation agreed to by the UMWA that became very important in years to come. That was the miners' promise to increase productivity.[37]

In 1974 there were two strikes in the West Virginia coalfields. The first, a wildcat strike that had no input from the UMWA whatsoever, began on February 24, 1974. Unlike the higher wages/better benefits issues that ignited most strikes, the motivations behind this one were quite unique. Miners were protesting their inability to purchase gasoline. The energy crisis arising from the oil embargo was in full force by then, and as a result less and less gasoline was being delivered to service stations across the country. The shortage had forced West Virginia Governor Arch Moore to order service station attendants in his state to limit customers to no more than a quarter tank of gasoline. A number of miners claimed that the quarter-tank limit simply was not enough for them to make the long drives that many had to make to and from the coal mine. A group of McDowell County miners meeting in Welch on February 24 concluded that their most effective means of dealing with the situation was to strike. Their "no gas—no work" position quickly spread throughout the county and then into neighboring counties both in West Virginia and Virginia. By the evening of the twenty-fourth, practically every mine in the region, including those in Gary Hollow, had shut down, and within a short time some 26,000 miners had joined the strike.[38]

As the wildcat strike stretched into March, Governor Moore tried to ease matters somewhat by ordering that gasoline purchase restrictions be lifted for miners whose work-related travel exceeded 250 miles per week. When that failed to move the miners back to work, accusations began surfacing about possible reasons other than the gasoline shortage that were behind the strike. A U.S. Steel official who noted that the company soon would begin layoffs at its steel plants if the strike continued, charged that coal miners were refusing to work as a result of "terrorist tactics by roving pickets."[39] The situation came to a head on March 13, 1974, when Judge H. Emory Widener of the U.S. Court of Appeals for the Fourth Circuit issued a temporary injunction against UMWA locals ordering that members cease their work stoppage. The injunction came at the request of U.S. Steel and several other mine operators. A decision by Governor Moore to suspend his quarter-tank gasoline ban for thirty days also helped puncture any more reason for prolonging the strike. Miners began returning to work almost immediately, and by March 15, 1974, practically all mines that had been closed due to the strike had reopened.[40]

There was suspicion that the motivation behind the strike had less to do about gasoline than about reducing coal stockpiles in anticipation of upcoming UMWA contract negotiations. Whether or not the suspicion carried any merit, there was no secret about the better than fifty-fifty chance that the UMWA contract talks that loomed just seven months away would be accompanied by a strike. Sure enough, when the talks that began in September 1974 did not reach agreement on a new contract by the 12:01 a.m., November 12, deadline, 120,000 bituminous coal miners walked off the job. UMWA president Arnold Miller, who recently had succeeded Tony Boyle, noted that negotiations with the BCOA were near settlement, but contract provisions involving miners' rights to strike over mine safety issues, as well as sick pay, increased wage, health, pension, and vacation benefits, and a "cost-of-living escalator clause" remained unresolved. Added to the mix was the BCOA's continuing concern over lowered miner productivity resulting from, among other things, absenteeism and wildcat strikes.[41]

As it happened, a settlement was announced on November 24. Government representatives, including U.S. Treasury Secretary William E. Simon, eventually were called in to help conclude negotiations and to fashion an agreement. The UMWA strike, however, would continue for at least two more weeks while the union rank-and-file studied the new contract. In the meantime, U.S. Steel announced layoffs that eventually numbered nearly 18,000 steelworkers and a shutdown of nearly 35 percent of its production capabilities. By December 5, 1974, the UMWA-BCOA contract had been ratified, and mines began to reopen on December 9.[42] The 1974 strike was only half as long as the 1971 strike. Failure once more to settle contract differences during the next triennial negotiation in 1977 would result in the longest strike of the 1970s and one of the longest UMWA walk-outs in history.

These were the big headline-grabbing strikes whose consequences spread throughout America's industrial heartland. Unobserved for the most part, but nonetheless causing headaches to the immediate industries affected—steel in particular—were the wildcat strikes that continued to flare. Grievance and arbitration procedures put in place by the 1974 UMWA-BCOA contract and meant to quell arbitrary strikes appeared ineffective from the start. Usually, too, it was small, seemingly insignificant issues, such as disagreement over a changed work assignment, that would spark a strike at one mine that soon spread to other mines in other states as one grievance piled on top of another. One such wildcat strike began at a northern West Virginia mine in July 1976 and eventually spread to six other states. Miners did not return to work for more than a month.

One year later, miners in the major bituminous coal region walked away from their jobs once more. This time the cause was more universal—depletion of union medical and pension benefits and the announcement by Arnold Miller in June 1977 that union members would have to contribute up to five hundred dollars per year to offset the depletion. The irony of this particular strike was that the pool from which medical and pension benefits were paid, as noted above, was funded by the BCOA based on a royalty formula of coal tonnage produced and man hours worked. Every time coal miners struck they were contributing to the very depletion with which they now were confronted. The strike was temporarily suspended in late August when miners agreed to return to work for a sixty-day period to give UMWA and BCOA officials time to resolve the benefits issue. For those miners who had been first to walk away from their jobs in June, this particular wildcat strike had stretched to more than ten weeks by the time they finally returned to work.[43]

The next strike began precisely at 12:01 a.m. on December 6, 1977. Once more, UMWA-BCOA contract talks had bogged down. The issues had not changed appreciably in the intervening years since the last contract negotiations, although in the union's case, priorities had shifted somewhat in its list of demands. Higher wages and the right to strike over grievance disputes rather than submit to binding arbitration were on the list, but both were in secondary position to restoration of all medical and pension benefits. The BCOA list was unchanged. Productivity decline, exacerbated by losses resulting from wildcat strikes, and absenteeism were problems that the BCOA demanded be addressed and fixed. Coal operators also wanted some form of legal penalty that could be applied to miners engaged in wildcat strikes.

Money, of course, was at the core of the contract dispute. Both sides wanted more of it. Deciding how to resolve the several issues that radiated from this core issue would take time. And that is one thing that the BCOA now felt it had plenty of. In preparation for this potential strike, coal operators had made certain that they and their customers had a stockpile of coal that would last for up to 160 days. In addition, coal needs could be more readily supplied by western strip and surface mines, which were less unionized than the eastern mines. In fact, although 70 percent of the coal produced in 1974 had come from UMWA mines, that percentage had declined to 50 percent by 1977. Such a decline in addition to the alternative coal supply clearly gave the UMWA less bargaining power in 1977 than it possessed in 1974.

The BCOA had managed to batten down the hatches for the 1977 strike, but the UMWA had not. Union members had much to lose when they walked away from their jobs on December 6. At that moment their wages (then averaging some sixty dollars per day) would cease, as would their medical and pension benefits. Blue Cross eventually devised an emergency coverage plan that retired miners could buy to supplement basic Medicare coverage. A total of 160,000 UMWA miners nationwide, nearly 64,000 of them in West Virginia alone, were doing what so many had done before. The 1977 strike was, after all, the tenth nationwide UMWA strike in thirty-five years and the third in the last six years. The fact that this one left so many miners with no income just two weeks before Christmas and no health insurance in the dead of winter seemed not to blunt their resolve, nor did the strike's predicted length of several months. The miners and their families had done this before. And emotionally, if not financially, they were prepared to repeat the coalfield ritual.[44]

True to the predictions, the strike wore on into the first months of the new year. The stakes were high. Medical benefits that the UMWA had won for coal miners during another lengthy strike in 1946 now were threatened, and the union rank and file were pushing their leaders to stand firm until the other guys blinked. The BCOA was just as determined in its position, bolstered by the coal operators' wise preparation for this strike. The strike had become a contest of will and endurance, and the stand-off appeared heavily in the BCOA's favor. Nonetheless, the coal miners had plenty of resources to help them hold their own. Many had been conditioned by previous strikes to set aside a portion of their income for a strike fund. Government food stamps helped keep food on the table, and the UMWA's Miners Relief Fund dispersed money to union members in particularly dire straits financially. Other labor unions even came to the coal miners' assistance by providing an infusion of money contributed by laborers from around the country. Merchants and business owners who lived nearby were also supportive, extending credit and assisting with bill payments.[45]

So, even though coal miners and their families were no doubt financially squeezed, sustenance of a material sort, albeit on a limited basis, nonetheless was available. Available, too, was sustenance of the emotional sort. Coal mining towns possess many of the same collective traits as other small communities in America. Neighbors usually mind their own business, tend to their own affairs, and sometimes even have spats with one another. But unlike other communities, most of the adult male population of a coal mining town is engaged in the singular occupation of coal mining. And when something like a strike threatens that livelihood, there is a unity of purpose and determination—a closing of the ranks, as it were—that draws the folks together. "Strength in numbers" is not a cliché to coal miners and their families; it is a way of life.

There is yet one more kind of reserve that coal miners can resort to in difficult times. For a coal miner, there is always the immediate threat to life and limb, not to mention the long-term threat from such hazards as black lung disease. The ordeal of staring the odds of survival squarely in the face on a day-to-day basis builds into the coal miner a fearless nature. The miner is tough—tough in body, mind, and spirit. While toughness gave miners the will and strength to succeed, the miners also possessed a level-headedness that made them very aware that resolution of the strike issues under consideration in 1977 and 1978 would require some give and take. Standing firm with a will to succeed was one thing, but that had to be tempered by a degree of logic as to which of the issues were most worth fighting for and which were expendable.

Three Gary Hollow miners spoke very clearly about issue priority in the *Welch Daily News*. William Puskar, a veteran coal miner of twenty-eight years, treasurer of UMWA Local 7905, and employee of the Alpheus preparation plant, stated flatly that restoration of medical benefits was at the top of the list of contract issues, followed closely by equalizing pensions. As it happened, miners who retired after the 1974 contract became effective received a higher pension than miners who retired prior to implementation of the 1974 contract. In Puskar's opinion, this imbalance would have to be corrected and pensions for coal miners would have to be equalized by the 1977 contract. "The right-to-strike clause in our local is way down on the list," said Puskar. "In fact, it's immaterial whether or not we get it." And if contract talks came down to a trade-off between health benefits and the right to strike, Puskar felt certain that Arnold Miller would give up the latter.

Nathaniel Bell, who had worked at the plant for the past seven years and was nearly half Puskar's age, agreed with his colleague that medical benefits were the most important contract issue on the table. He also ranked pension equalization as a high priority. However, the right to strike, in Bell's view, was important, but only because the grievance mechanism was inadequate. Other priority items for younger miners, said Bell, were "more vacation, personal days, accumulative leave [and] a 5-day work week, with Saturdays optional."

Ernest Moore, a retired coal miner of twenty-seven years who soon would take office as vice-president of UMWA District 29, agreed with Puskar and Bell about the importance of medical benefits to contract negotiations. And while the right to strike was further down Moore's list of priorities, he nonetheless felt that such a right on a limited scale carried merit as a "deterrent to the outburst of wildcat strikes." "A lot of wildcats are provoked by coal operators who aren't willing to sit down and communicate in good faith," Moore said. "It's a new day in the coal industry. There are more young people who read and understand the contract. They're not going to stand idle by and be talked to and abused like it has been in the past."

Addressing BCOA's complaint about falling productivity, Moore cited the "faulty equipment and breakdown" that accompanied more mining mechanization. Puskar and Bell, perhaps owing to their closer and more current proximity to the workplace, were in virtual agreement as to why production had dropped. According to Puskar, "Your older miner, like my father, worked in hazardous conditions, took more chances, and got more coal. Younger people aren't going to do that." When questioned about the future of the coal mining industry in southern West Virginia, each of the three Gary Hollow miners was optimistic. Nathaniel Bell perhaps best summed up the feelings of his colleagues, saying, "There's plenty of coal down here, and if the coal industry is willing to give up some of its profits to the miners, I think it has a great chance to make it."[46]

At day eighty-two of the UMWA strike, there at last appeared to be a breakthrough. President Jimmy Carter announced on February 24, 1978, that the union had reached a contract settlement with the BCOA. The settlement came after Carter threatened government intervention to end the strike. But UMWA and BCOA officials failed to account for how the contract would be received by the rank and file. In this regard, the new contract appeared doomed from the start. Even union officials dispatched to explain contract details to members of union locals showed little enthusiasm for the contract and little hope for its success.

The contract's contentious provisions centered on the same issues that had caused the strike in the first place: medical benefits, pensions, and productivity. Higher wages were nearly a nonissue, as both sides agreed to a 37 percent wage and benefits increase to be added incrementally over the next three years. Medical benefits, however, would change drastically. Private insurers, rather than the joint union/management funding system that had been in place for so long, would provide coverage under the new agreement. Plus, the miners now would be responsible for deductibles that could amount to $50 for drugs, $150 for doctors' fees, and $500 for hospital fees. In addition, the post- and pre-1974 pension imbalance remained unchanged. The contract also included penalties for instigating and/or participating in wildcat strikes.

UMWA members began voting on the new contract on Friday, March 3. On Sunday, March 5, the union locals rejected the pact by a nearly two-to-one margin (69.7 percent opposed to ratification and 30.3 percent in favor). On March 6, President Carter, responding to pressure from utility companies whose coal stockpiles now were becoming depleted and by industries that were having to lay off employees and suspend operations as a result of the UMWA strike, began the process of invoking the Taft-Hartley Act. The law's provisions allowed the president to seek a court injunction to order striking miners to return to work under the 1974 UMWA-BCOA contract for an eighty-day cooling-off period. During that time, the UMWA and BCOA would resume contract negotiations under government supervision. The two sides would have to produce a new contract within two months, submit it to a vote by the union members, and allow the National Labor Relations Board to count the votes. Failure of the new contract to win approval would mean resuming the strike.

There was no assurance that the power accompanying Taft-Hartley would induce miners to end their strike, even if only temporarily. Since the law's passage in 1947, it had been invoked three times against the UMWA—twice in 1948 and once in 1950—by President Harry Truman. In all three cases UMWA members refused to budge. The more effective route of actually seizing the bituminous coal mines had been tried by Presidents Roosevelt and Truman during and immediately following World War II. Although coal miners had gone back to work under government seizure, the process raised troubling implications. The strike situation in 1978 presumably bore conditions that made invoking Taft-Hartley the more palatable course of action.

In compliance with President Carter's request, UMWA and BCOA negotiators returned to the bargaining table on March 10, 1978, while U.S. District Judge Aubry Robinson Jr. issued a temporary restraining order requiring UMWA members to cease their strike activities by 7 a.m. on March 11. In forcing discontinuance of all formal strike activity such as picketing, the order did not, and in fact could not, force miners to return to work. Phrasing of the order was very clear on that point: "nothing in this paragraph shall be construed to require an individual employee to render labor without his consent nor to make the quitting of his labor or service by an individual employee an illegal act." Failure to abide by Judge Robinson's order in matters that did apply, however, could result in contempt citations against the miners and union officials. The attitude in the coalfields, however, remained defiant.[47]

A few miners reportedly returned to work, but most continued striking. Whether in reaction to the miners' determined stand or government pressure, UMWA and BCOA negotiators fashioned another agreement within a week of their resuming contract talks. Rank-and-file union members voted to approve the contract on Friday, March 24, 1978, by a margin of 57 to 43 percent. While the vote to approve had a comfortable lead, the 43 percent disapproval indicated significant disenchantment with concessions that UMWA leaders had managed to win from the BCOA. In its final form, the new contract increased miners' $7.80 hourly wage by $2.40 over the next three years. With the exception of a provision that would require union members to pay up to $200 per year of their medical expenses, all medical benefits that had been part of the 1974 contract were restored and would be administered as before. The imbalance in pre- and post-1974 pension pay remained unchanged, although pre-1974 retirees received a slight boost in monthly pension pay. Deleted from the new contract was a provision that would have allowed coal operators to fire any employee for instigating a wildcat strike.

Thus, the 109-day strike came to an end. By the time the coal mines had undergone safety inspections and were actually ready for mining to resume on Monday, March 27, at least two more nonwork days could be added to the 109-day record. And as the first shift arrived for work, there seemed to be relief that the strike had ended. Bills had stacked up and needed to be paid, and there were few notches remaining on all the belts that had been tightened for nearly four months. But with the relief was a feeling that the new UMWA contract fell far short of what union negotiators should have demanded. Miners now were working because they needed the income, but disillusionment spread across America's unionized bituminous coalfields.[48]

Bituminous coal production statistics left little doubt as to the striking miners' impact. About 14.5 million tons of coal had been mined during the week preceding the start of the UMWA strike in December 1977. One week later, that number was down to about 5.3 million tons. Nonunion bituminous coal mines, particularly the surface mines, were producing most of the coal during the strike and actually accelerated their pace to supply hard-pressed utility companies. As soon as miners returned to work, production climbed to more than 15 million tons per week.[49] Meanwhile, the loss to U.S. Steel was substantial: 245,000 coal miner man days and roughly 2.1 million tons of coal in 1977 and 435,000 man days and nearly 3.8 million tons of coal in 1978.[50]

U.S. Steel's displeasure over the string of work stoppages, increasing absenteeism, and declining productivity shone through in the company's annual reports. The company noted in 1971 that "financial results from steel producing operations were at an unsatisfactory level for the second half of the year," due primarily to the "44-day coal strike and a substantial cost increase resulting from the new labor contract with the United Mine Workers of America."[51] One report gave a detailed account of the UMWA contract ratified after the twenty-four-day strike in 1974 and added that, "with the coal mine workers' settlement behind us, we hope that, working with our employees and the union, we can find ways of returning at least to the prior level of output per man-day, which has declined by 25% from the level of five years ago."[52] U.S. Steel continued complaining about the deteriorating "productivity or output per man-shift . . . in the Corporation's coal mines and for the coal industry generally" in its 1977 annual report.[53]

According to the U.S. Department of Energy, the amount of coal (both bituminous and anthracite) produced daily at underground mines peaked at 15.61 tons per miner in 1969. That number was down to 7.8 tons per miner by 1977 and had shown a steady decline during the intervening years.[54] For Gary Hollow coal miners, rough calculations show a similar trend for daily output throughout much of the 1970s. Daily output in 1970 was approximately 15.9 tons per miner. Output dropped steadily and precipitously until 1978, when it stood at 5.7 tons per miner, or only about a third of what it was eight years earlier. Economist Curtis E. Harvey's analysis of the trend zeroed in on likely reasons. "The new safety regulations [resulting from enactment of the Federal Coal Mine Health and Safety Act of 1969] altered work procedures," and thus "a greater share of a miner's workday was required to be spent on safety-related procedures," Harvey explained. He also noted the influx of younger and less experienced coal miners to the industry as a reason for productivity declines.[55] There were also the issues raised by the Gary Hollow miners: time-consuming equipment breakdowns and refusal of young miners to take the risks older miners once took.

U.S. Steel's concern with productivity appeared not to be directed so much toward Gary Hollow as to its other mining interests.[56] The matter of productivity in and of itself seemed less a focus of the company's complaints and more a sign of its general uneasiness with its far-flung raw materials empire. Maintaining reasonable profitability while dealing with mounting labor and workplace problems was beginning to call into question the whole idea of the integrated steel company. Was the concept's survival worth the trouble, considering that the UMWA strike failed to eclipse the 137-day strike at U.S. Steel's iron ore works in Minnesota?[57]

U.S. Steel could not have been pleased with what it saw during the 1978 UMWA-BCOA contract negotiations either. The union was able to hold out for a better contract, but the widespread unhappiness among the miners over the way UMWA president Arnold Miller had represented the union did not bode well for contract talks in 1981. Rumblings in the UMWA showed U.S. Steel that union membership was becoming younger, better educated, more militant, and certainly more aggressive in demanding that they be well represented by their UMWA leaders. And there were union leaders at the local level who shared the feelings and attitudes of the miners they represented and who were poised to take control of the union at first opportunity.[58] Obviously, there was much for U.S. Steel officials to think about in the coming years.

In the meantime, the bump in coal production that usually follows a strike was slow to develop in most bituminous coalfields. Utility companies were buying less coal, due in part to more imports of foreign coal and conversions to nuclear power. Less demand meant lower prices for domestic coal. Since the cost of mining had escalated as a result of mine safety and environmental laws and increased pay and benefits flowing from the new UMWA-BCOA contract, some mine operators closed their mines. Quite a few of the smaller operators simply went out of business.[59] Gary Hollow mines were slow to come back as well. The production total for 1978 was nearly a million tons less than in 1976 (the last nonstrike year). Less need for coke and the continuing malaise in the steel industry also contributed to the less-than-optimistic outlook for Gary Hollow coal.

But then came 1979 and a turnaround. The most immediate reason for improving work conditions seemed most closely connected to the steel needs of the American oil industry. Continuing uncertainty over foreign oil supplies pushed American producers to increase their level of oilfield exploration. U.S. Steel was in a unique position to take advantage of the situation. The company was poised to make up for lost time with a vengeance, and Gary Hollow reaped the rewards. Its coal suddenly was in great demand. Guarded optimism and a tinge of prosperity not experienced in many years began returning to Gary. In fact, the *Bluefield Daily Telegraph* dispatched a reporter in September 1979 to look into what was happening. The resulting story, written by Garret Mathews, was headlined "Gary Is an Oasis, Employment-Wise." Mathews explained the oasis reference, stating, "While many other coal companies in southwest Virginia and southern West Virginia are forced to juggle their manpower needs to cover less than a five-day work week, the personnel people at U.S. Steel frequently are having to deal with an almost unheard of situation these days—overtime." A U.S. Steel spokesperson in Pittsburgh said that all Gary Hollow mines had been working five days a week for several months and that this schedule likely would "remain in effect in the near future, depending of course on the steel demand situation." Adding to Gary's good fortune was U.S. Steel's decision to use 100 percent Gary coal to meet its steelmaking needs. Since 1972, only about 70 percent of Gary coal had been used, with the remaining 30 percent purchased from other suppliers. The U.S. Steel spokesperson also noted the value of Gary's captive mine status to the level of current coal mining activity. "Various other companies operating in the Gary area export much of their coal and recently the export market has declined as has the demand for metallurgical coal domestically."[60]

Imagine a Gary native who moved away in 1969 and returned in late 1979. What would he see, or not see, and what would his impressions be about changes that have occurred during his absence? First, standing in the middle of Gary, he would notice how quiet the place is. There would be the sounds of an occasional automobile or truck and maybe a chirping bird. The stillness of the place would be almost haunting. Next he would see the rectangular concrete slabs with their attached steps leading to what used to be company stores, pharmacies, post offices, barber shops, theaters, and the like. All are gone now, save for their foundations, which likely will remain for centuries. Schools that he and his friends once attended still stand, but they are locked and their windows are boarded. Houses—those that remain, at least—are noticeably different. No longer company houses, these once uniform structures have been remodeled and painted to look more individual. The N&W diesel locomotives continue to snake through Gary Hollow, making their way to coal tipples here and there and exchanging strings of empty coal cars for cars full of coal. At shift change, there are more miners than in the 1960s, and some of them are women. All seem animated and happy. And there seems to be cause for optimism. Gary has survived the worst of the steel slump, and U.S. Steel has brought some measure of prosperity to the town.

Chapter 11

U.S. Steel, Marathon Oil, and Depression

U.S. Steel's 1989 annual report was crafted as a ten-year retrospective of a decade of change. One of the most obvious was the company's 1986 name change to USX Corporation. But that cosmetic makeover did not even approach the significance of other changes. Over the span of ten years, noted the annual report, "USX acquired about $10 billion in assets, primarily energy; sold close to $7 billion of assets and businesses; and wrote off approximately $3.5 billion, primarily in steel." All of this carried obvious implications for the USX workforce. "In 1979, there were 171,654 on the [USX] payroll—all in steel and related businesses. In 1989, that number had decreased to about 53,000, including employees in the energy sector."[1]

U.S. Steel's corporate evolution during the 1980s left the company "leaner and more sharply focused," but achieving these results "would prove to be a bumpy ride."[2] Numerous trends—in steelmaking technology, in market economics, in labor relations, in coal and coke production, and in the very nature of the integrated steel company—all began to reach the point of finality where trends invariably lead. Such trends had played significant roles in U.S. Steel's efforts to rationalize. The company's rationalization effort already had resulted in major changes—some more economically beneficial than others. By the start of the 1980s, though, rationalization had taken on a more intentional and in some respects a more radical demeanor. Rationalization now would expand from downsizing into dismemberment. But at the same time U.S. Steel was looking to merge its traditional corporate interests with new ventures, primarily in what the company's 1989 annual report described as the energy sector. All of this seemed directed toward a concerted effort for U.S. Steel to reinvent itself, the results of which would be treated by corporate America as a classic story of resilience and survival. To coal miners in Gary Hollow, though, the story was much different.

The optimism that spread throughout Gary Hollow in 1979 as work began to pick up had proved illusory. By 1980 optimism had turned to pessimism. Demonstrating just how quickly things could change in the coalfields, U.S. Steel announced a layoff of some 170 miners from Gary's No.

14 mine in June 1980. More layoffs and reduced workdays were to follow.[3] By year's end the number of Gary Hollow coal miners had dropped from 1979's total of 1,454 to 1,271.[4] The 183 person reduction accounted for nearly 13 percent of the mining workforce. The *Bluefield Daily Telegraph* carried news of the Gary Hollow layoffs on the first page of its June 18, 1980, edition.[5] Less than a year before, the paper had carried a page 1 story titled "Gary Is an Oasis, Employment-Wise." That story, noted in the previous chapter, was accompanied by the same two photographs of Gary houses and the Alpheus preparation plant that now accompanied the June 18 layoff story. The current story's positioning and photographs so similar to the earlier story may have been coincidental (if not someone's dark sense of humor), but the two *Daily Telegraph* first pages viewed side by side underscored the coalfield's version of a rags-to-riches-to-rags saga. And as disheartening as the layoffs were, they were but the first in a series of blows that left folks in Gary Hollow reeling.

One of those blows happened somewhat imperceptibly, but when census figures for 1980 were released in 1982, they revealed that Gary's population continued to slide downward. The census listed Gary's population as 2,233, with 791 households, a 26 percent decline from the time of its incorporation.[6]

As for the blow occasioned by U.S. Steel's June announcement, Gary Hollow coal miners interviewed for the *Bluefield Daily Telegraph* story were somewhat philosophical about their plight. Most knew that layoffs were coming, and most expressed resentment toward government foot-dragging in its failure to force more utility companies to convert from oil-burning to coal-burning power plants. According to Stewart Preseley, employed at the No. 14 mine for six years, "I think the company had a choice to make and they made what they thought to be the best one. With coal production at the low level it is there wasn't much they could have done other than lay off some workers. The leaders of our country need to get up off their golf carts and get the coal conversion plan to work." Arnold Walters, who at age twenty-two was a nearly five-year employee at the No. 14 mine, gave a slightly different perspective on his and his fellow miners' situation. He cited the falling demand for the kind of metallurgical coal being mined in Gary Hollow as a major reason for the No. 14 layoffs. Even more important and more insightful, though, was Walters' comment about the cost of operating the No. 14 mine. "The cost of production at No. 14 is overwhelming because we have such bad top," said Walters. "Everything available has to be used to support the roof, and none of it is inexpensive."[7]

UMWA President Sam Church Jr. reported in early 1980 that some 20,000 miners nationwide now were without work. The West Virginia Coal Association estimated that over 10,000 coal miners in West Virginia alone had been laid off from late 1978 through early 1980. West Virginia's northern region was most affected by the layoffs, since higher sulfur content of coal coming from the region made its use as steam coal less desirable and more likely to cause emission problems.[8] Emission problems, of course, had to do with standards set by the EPA for releasing pollutants into the atmosphere. While burning high sulfur coal generally leads to a more highly polluted by-product than burning low-sulfur coal, the by-product of both are problematical. Nonetheless, the oil shortages and threat to America's oil supplies during the 1970s suggested the need for a pragmatic approach to solving the nation's energy situation. And such an approach would require not only a nationwide conversion from oil- to coal-burning power plants but a simultaneous reduction in EPA emission standards. President Jimmy Carter had promised some resolution to the situation when he entered the White House. However, after three years in office President Carter had yet to commit to an energy policy that would benefit coal miners. Mine industry leaders and coal miners alike were complaining about the president's slow response.[9]

President Carter created the President's Commission on Coal on May 26, 1978, with the intention of conducting "a comprehensive and independent review of the coal industry with particular emphasis on four areas: the future of the coal industry, labor-management relations, living conditions of coal miners, and the effects of government regulations on the production and utilization of coal." West Virginia Governor John D. (Jay) Rockefeller chaired the commission, which concluded its work and issued a report in March 1980.[10] Its recommendations for setting requirements and deadlines for converting from oil- and natural gas–burning power plants suggested that all could be done without loosening EPA standards. The plan for accomplishing the conversion was to become part of a bill that President Carter shortly would send to Congress.[11]

Political efforts might have been under way by 1980 that eventually assisted coal miners, but long-term solutions meant nothing to those miners and their families whose needs were more immediate. And realistically, the conversion issue was less central to the needs of the coal industry in McDowell County, where most of the coal was headed not to power plants but to steel plants. Under the circumstances, McDowell County miners might have wished that utility plants instead of steel plants had been their coal's destination. Reports from the American Iron and Steel Institute (AISI) were giving a rather grim picture for steel production and steel industry unemployment for the coming decade. And as always, much of the bad news was predicated on the impact that foreign steel imports were predicted to have on American steel production and sales.[12]

The decline in steel production and shipping at U.S. Steel suggested that the AISI-predicted downturn in steelmaking nationwide was right on target. U.S. Steel's production of raw steel was down from 29.7 million tons in 1979 to 23.3 million tons in 1980, the company's lowest output

U.S. Steel, Marathon Oil, and Depression

since 1946. Likewise, the company's steel shipments were down from 21.0 million tons shipped in 1979 to 17.1 million tons shipped in 1980. Little wonder, then, that U.S. Steel's coke making also fell from 14.5 million tons of coke produced in 1979 to 12.0 million tons produced in 1980.[13] That 17 percent difference was even more pronounced when compared with the 14 percent drop in coke making nationwide.[14] Not surprisingly, U.S. Steel's coal production also fell from 16.1 million tons in 1979 to 14.6 million tons in 1980.[15] The reduced working days and employee layoffs in Gary and the total Gary mines' 1.9 million tons production—down from the previous year's 2.3 million tons—were, of course, all part of the bigger picture reported by U.S. Steel.[16]

Lumping U.S. Steel's situation with that of its American competitors shows an industry on the ropes. The one bit of good news was that the 1980 steel exports actually had nearly doubled from the previous year, while steel imports had fallen somewhat. This reversal of the steel export/import trend was only momentary, though; the situation returned to a more normal pattern in 1981. In terms of international production figures, American steelmakers fell from a 16.5 percent contribution to total world steel production in 1979 to a 14.1 percent level in 1980. U.S. Steel's contribution to America's total steel production dropped from 22 percent in 1979 to 21 percent in 1980. The company's percentage of shipments when compared with total American steel shipments dropped from 21 percent to 20 percent.[17] Besides representing declines in steel production and shipping, these numbers also represented a continuation of U.S. Steel's downward slide in steelmaking. The company remained the major steel producer in America, but its influence within the steelmaking community appeared on the wane.

All of this might have led to the logical conclusion that U.S. Steel's fiscal condition for 1980 was rather grim. Not so. In fact, conditions were remarkably good and even more remarkably, the attitude of company executives was upbeat. The company's after-tax income for 1980 was $504.5 million as compared to its 1979 loss of $293 million, despite lower sales and a sluggish economy. The trick in turning U.S. Steel around came not from blue smoke and mirrors but rather from CEO David Roderick's decision to ratchet up the rationalization plan already in motion. Various steel and nonsteel plant operations were closed in 1979, and even more were closed in 1980. The money saved from the cost of running these operations was directed toward U.S. Steel's more profitable units. Income from the sale of the company's Universal Atlas Cement Division, as well as the sale of a New York City office building, also pumped up the company's 1980 earnings. Ironically, much of the 1979 income loss was attributed to expenses associated with the shutdown of fifteen facilities and the layoff of some 11,000 workers. The additional funds now available to U.S. Steel "permitted management to concentrate on other business opportunities." The oblique reference to "other business opportunities" gave notice that while steel production would remain U.S. Steel's primary business for the foreseeable future, the company nonetheless was exploring a "diversification strategy" to bring other business ventures into the U.S. Steel fold.[18]

U.S. Steel's investments in its steel producing facilities now focused on product improvement, higher productivity, and better use of energy. The key was efficiency. Particular attention was given to upgrading operations at the Gary Works, South Works, Fairfield Works, and Texas Works. U.S. Steel's annual report made particular note of the steady profitability of the Texas Works, "which primarily serves energy markets with its plate and pipe products."

The oil sector was becoming a bigger and bigger part of U.S. Steel's overall business. Sales of pipe and tubing, for example, that had comprised 11 percent of the company's steel product sales in 1976 had climbed to 15 percent by 1978, and by 1980 they reached 20 percent. The company attributed much of its earnings increase for 1980 to the "continued strong demand for drilling rigs, pumps, tubular products and other oilfield-related products." U.S. Steel's attention to serving the oil and gas industry through its Oilwell Division, in fact, was pushing one of the company's few efforts to expand facilities and production. Its sucker rod plant in Oil City, Pennsylvania, was upgraded in 1980 to produce more and better quality oilwell pumping tubes and rods. A company plant in McAlester, Oklahoma, was opened to produce pumps for use in the oil business. And a U.S. Steel plant in Orange, Texas, was "utilized to fabricate and assemble machinery and equipment for discovery and recovery of oil and gas." "Barge hulls" and "marine drilling units" also were being manufactured and assembled at the Orange, Texas, plant.

U.S. Steel's construction projects continued apace in 1980, with plans announced for new office buildings in Houston and Pittsburgh and new bridges in Chicago and Sewickley, Pennsylvania. Labor issues, taken from U.S. Steel's management perspective, appeared to be minimal in 1980. A new USWA three-year contract became effective with base level wage, insurance, and benefits increases as well as a union agreement to divert some of its active workers' cost-of-living increases to help cover promised increases for USWA pensioners. The new contract also included provisions to create so-called labor-management participation teams that allowed representatives from both sides to discuss conflicts or disagreements related to productivity or working conditions.

U.S. Steel was strongly supportive of the government's reinstatement of the TPM as a way to prevent foreign steel producers from dumping their underpriced steel in America and was even willing to withdraw its formal dumping complaints in anticipation of the strengthened TPM. The company's decidedly upbeat assessment of its 1980 progress reached into its coal mining sector, where performance improvements were said to have lowered the cost of mining. And at least three new longwall mining units became operational during the year with two more on the way. Longwall mining has been described as a "highly productive" technique that "employs a steel plow or rotating drum, which is pulled mechanically back-and-forth across a face of coal that is usually several hundred feet long. The loosened coal falls onto a conveyor for removal from the mine." Longwall mining systems also "include a hydraulic roof support system that advances as mining proceeds allowing the roof to fall in a controlled manner."[19]

Another bit of news that signaled optimism for U.S. Steel but that otherwise should have caused discomfort within the company's coal mining community was the negotiation for disposal of certain coal properties. One of the properties in southwestern Pennsylvania was sold to Conoco, while talks to sell a second property to Standard Oil Company of Ohio (Sohio) had only begun in late 1980. Much of the coal property already sold or under negotiation for sale contained steam coal. Disposing of these two properties would drop U.S. Steel's recoverable coal reserve by nearly a third—from approximately 3.4 billion to about 2.4 billion tons. Even so, the company contended that it was continuing to explore for new coal properties and to expand its current properties.[20]

Administrative and management changes that began at U.S. Steel headquarters in Pittsburgh and moved downward to the company's Gary District offices in 1980 were in place by 1981. One of the major corporate changes was transfer of U.S. Steel's coal mining operations into a new subsidiary unit known as U.S. Steel Mining Co. John L. Schroder Jr. was named president of the new company, and A. E. Moran was elevated from his position as Gary District general superintendent to U.S. Steel Mining's new general manager. Replacing Moran at Gary was Robert E. Yourston. Moving former Gary District general superintendents to executive positions at U.S. Steel's Pittsburgh office was almost routine. And, generally, newly appointed general superintendents arrived at Gary after a long stint with the company. Yourston, for example, had worked at various U.S. Steel coal mine operations and most recently had served as general superintendent for the Lynch District in Kentucky. Yourston became only the seventh person to serve in Gary District's chief management position since World War II. His predecessors included T. J. McParland, who served as general superintendent during the war and left the position in 1950; W. R. Stedman, 1950–54; Woods G. Talman, 1954–59; C. W. Connor Jr., 1959–70; P. E. Watson, 1970–72; and A. E. Moran, 1972–80.[21]

Robert Yourston's first full year as general superintendent was accompanied at first by a general stability in the Gary Hollow mines. The mine employment level remained roughly the same from 1980 through 1981. Official numbers show only a loss of four jobs from one year to the next—from 1,271 to 1,267. While the total number remained nearly the same, there was a shifting of employment numbers at the individual mines. Employment at the No. 2 mine went from 255 to 225, at the No. 4 mine from 184 to 174, at the No. 9 mine from 436 to 424, and at the No. 10 mine from 147 to 146. Employee figures at the No. 14 mine where so many jobs recently had been eliminated actually rose from 249 to 298. Even with the positive employment numbers there were two bothersome statistics that overshadowed all else. The number of days worked per mine in 1981 were far below those for 1980. And the 1,683,644 total tons of coal produced at Gary Hollow mines in 1981 fell below the 1,902,068 tons produced in 1980.[22] The reason for both drops had less to do with productivity than with yet another UMWA strike—and another long one at that.

The strike began on March 27, 1981, when 160,000 UMWA members, citing the expiration of their previous contract with the BCOA without agreement on a new one, refused to enter the mines. UMWA President Sam Church had forged a tentative settlement with the BCOA, but it had come too late to head off the March 27 strike deadline. Church, a former mine electrician elected to the union presidency only the year before, had agreed to several contract provisions that many among the UMWA rank and file claimed would doom the document's approval. Among the new contract's benefits were a 36 percent wage and benefits hike and a $100 monthly pension for roughly 45,000 spouses of miners who retired before 1974. But the contract's most controversial provision appeared to trump these two benefits. The provision allowed for processing nonunion coal at preparation plants located at union mines. Additionally, BCOA members would not be required to pay the $1.90 per ton royalty into the UMWA pension fund for the processed nonunion coal, as they presently paid for coal mined by union members. This provision was the deal-breaker that most UMWA members claimed led them to reject the new contract by more than a two-to-one margin during a March 31 ratification vote.[23]

Processing nonunion coal was irksome enough, but the BCOA's decision not to pay royalties on the processed coal made matters even worse. The situation also underscored major changes beginning to take hold in the coal mining industry. One change was the UMWA's waning influence. Only 44 percent of the nation's coal was now mined by UMWA members. Thus, the current issue of actually processing nonunion coal was less important than making certain that the union could take advantage of that coal by standing pat on the $1.90 royalty payment. The abundance of so much coal from nonunion sources, however, removed one of the UMWA's strongest and most traditional bargaining chips—the declining coal supply. Coal customers had become accustomed to stockpiling a reasonable supply of coal in anticipation of another triennial UMWA strike. And at times, as happened during the previous 111-day strike, stockpiles had run dangerously low before the strike ended. Now there was less chance of

that happening, since nonunion suppliers were able to keep most customers reasonably well stocked with coal throughout the strike period.

Elimination of the coal scarcity factor diminished but did not entirely eliminate the UMWA bargaining power. Still left was the memory
of disruptions caused by past UMWA strikes and the image of labor unrest that had little appeal to coal company executives. B. R. Brown, chief
negotiator for the BCOA, made note of that point following the March 31
nonratification vote, saying, "The rejection is a serious setback in the
achievement of the goals sought by both union leadership and the industry to demonstrate labor-management stability to prospective domestic
and worldwide customers."[24] Worldwide customers were especially important, and by all appearances and projections the foreign markets, particularly in Europe and Japan, were looking more to the United States to
supply their coal needs. The American coal export business had risen
by a dramatic 85 percent in 1979, and the level of exports continued to
rise in 1980 and 1981. American ports where coal must be stored, sorted,
blended, and eventually loaded into cargo holds of ships were caught unprepared for what they were suddenly having to deal with.

Political unrest in Poland and labor union problems in Australia—
two countries that heretofore had supplied most of Europe's and Japan's
coal—were the reasons that foreign buyers now turned to the United
States. And even while domestic coal was more expensive than coal purchased in other countries, the reliability of the American coal supply,
according to Curtis Harvey, outranked cost as a reason for buying coal
from domestic suppliers.[25] So, not only was the image of labor/manage-
ment solidarity important, the reality of that solidarity in order to assure
European and Japanese coal customers of a reliable supply was equally
of concern.

There was much to lose both domestically and internationally if the
current strike dragged on. The UMWA also appeared to have the upper
hand in seeing that union demands were met. Church announced on
May 29, 1981, a settlement whose contract provisions he planned on immediately submitting to the union's bargaining council and then, assuming council approval, to the rank and file. The UMWA contract would
require payment of the $1.90 royalty on processed nonunion coal as well
as the pension payment to widows. Also included was a 37.5 percent wage-
benefit increase over a forty-month period that would boost the hourly
wages of most of the highest paid coal miners from $10.56 to $14.16.
The miners voted to approve the new contract and to end their strike
officially on June 8, 1981. The strike, lasting officially for seventy-two
days, became the nation's second longest UMWA-sanctioned coal strike.
However, the miners' return to work immediately was complicated by the
strike of the Association of Bituminous Contractors (ABC), representing
mine construction workers. Some 95,000 coal miners nationwide, includ-

ing those in Gary Hollow, decided not to work until the ABC strike was settled. Finally, after prolonging the end of their own strike by another ten days, UMWA members returned to their jobs on June 18, 1981, following settlement of the ABC strike.[26]

The UMWA strike purportedly cost U.S. Steel more than $100 million and was cited as a reason for the company's operating income not being higher than it obviously could have been. Even so, its $1.1 billion dollar net income more than doubled the company's previous year's income. A feat like this would seem nearly impossible since U.S. Steel's 1981 production of raw steel, coal, and coke fell below 1980 figures, and the company's steel shipments dropped from 17.1 million tons in 1980 to 16.5 million tons in 1981. A major portion of U.S. Steel's remarkable 1981 income was attributable to the successful revival of coal property transfer negotiations begun in 1980 with Sohio.[27]

The Sohio deal alone would transfer nearly 900 million tons of coal reserves to the oil company for an estimated $750 million. Two of the coal mines that were part of the transaction were the Cumberland and Robena in Greene County, Pennsylvania—two of U.S. Steel's largest mines. U.S. Steel's 2.4 billion ton coal reserve that would remain after its Sohio sale would, according to analysts, provide the company all the coal it would need for the next three hundred years. What was most important to U.S. Steel, though, was that money coming from the transaction, in CEO David Roderick's words, would be used not only for "modernization and expansion," but also to "respond to diversification opportunities into allied fields."[28]

Disagreement over the $750 million price tag brought a momentary delay in talks between U.S. Steel and Sohio in March 1981, but a final deal was struck between the two the following month. For $700 million, Sohio would take control of nearly the same amount of U.S. Steel's coal reserves, but instead of taking ownership of U.S. Steel's Robena mine, Sohio instead would receive mine properties in Utah and Illinois.[29] The sale added immensely to Sohio's existing billion ton coal reserve and helped the company expand on its effort to provide public utility companies with steam coal. Sohio also intended to use its newly acquired coal to increase its coal export business to Europe and Japan.[30]

Sohio's purchase of such a large portion of U.S. Steel's coal reserve was in step with two significant trends that had begun in the 1960s. One was the venture into coal mining as a complement to the oil production business that had come to characterize so many major oil companies by the 1980s. The soaring price of oil during the 1970s, and the transition from oil to coal by public utility companies, had accelerated such oil and coal combinations. The other trend was the divestiture of excess coal reserves owned by integrated steel companies such as U.S. Steel. A slump in the steel business meant not only that the steel companies needed less coal, but that ready cash could be realized by selling underutilized or totally unnecessary reserves. In time these transactions would turn some of the biggest American oil companies into some of the biggest coal producers as well.[31]

A logical question about these oil/steel company transactions is why the steel companies did not compete with oil companies by selling their coal directly to public utility companies. However, several of them, including U.S. Steel, did just that. Some of U.S. Steel's coal mine improvements and expansions, in fact, were undertaken with an eye to servicing the same steam coal customers, both domestic and foreign, that oil companies now were servicing. U.S. Steel also was busily looking for customers to sign long-term contracts for supplying coal by the end of 1980. And in anticipation of what analysts saw as a growing foreign market for American coal, U.S. Steel also began upgrading its coal-loading port facilities at Mobile, Alabama; Baton Rouge, Louisiana; and its Fairless plant on the Delaware River.[32]

Whether by long-term contract or spot sales, U.S. Steel was moving aggressively to market its coal wherever it could. The company nearly doubled the 1.1 million tons of coal sold in 1980 to some 2.1 million tons sold in 1981.[33] And coal from Gary Hollow mines by now had been included in the mix. General superintendent Yourston even noted how the ability of Gary District "to produce coal competitively in the outside market will go a long way toward keeping people working."[34] This new destination for Gary Hollow coal no doubt was responsible for keeping Gary's mine employment at a reasonably steady level from 1980 through 1981. But U.S. Steel's message to Gary Hollow that its coal was no longer necessary for steelmaking carried enormous implications. Coal miners probably gave little heed to where the coal they mined was destined or how it would be used. As long as U.S. Steel was willing to pay a decent wage, a coal miner was willing to dig the company's coal. The simplicity of this arrangement had been in place from the first days of Gary's existence. Not until now, though, did the Gary Hollow coal miner's job rely so heavily—actually, entirely—on a precarious domestic energy market where coal, for the moment at least, was favored over oil and natural gas to fuel power plants, and on a precarious international marketplace where American coal was valued only so long as coal from other countries was not so reliably available.

What might happen tomorrow was of little concern in 1981. The situation that existed then was one of hustle and bustle as U.S. Steel moved ever more swiftly into the coal marketing business. In view of this commercial scenario, though, there remains the question of why the company was so willing to sell big chunks of its coal reserves that it could easily be marketing directly to customers? The situation appeared irrational, but U.S. Steel saw it as just the opposite. It was a perfect fit with the company's strategic plan to downsize and divest. And the money realized from the Sohio sale fit the plan perfectly. The money provided some monetary grease to U.S. Steel's cash flow pump. More important, the money created an opportunity for U.S. Steel to realize a new phase of its plan—diversity.

Diversity of a very major sort was on its way. By year's end the public would know of what new direction U.S. Steel executives would be taking the company. In the meantime downsizing continued. Sales of assets, including coal reserves, had brought more than a billion dollars into U.S. Steel's coffers. Chemical production and uranium mining facilities that no longer were profitable for the company were shut down. The shutdowns were costly, but the closures eventually would save U.S. Steel considerable money.

There were other operating expenses that company executives griped about. Certain of the EPA's environmental policies were a continuing complaint, as was the inexpensive foreign steel that was subsidized by foreign governments and dumped in America. The availability of such steel raised another issue that troubled U.S. Steel executives: the cost of labor. "American steelworkers, along with workers in other basic industries [read: coal mining] have attained wage costs which may be self-defeating," noted U.S. Steel CEO David Roderick in the company's annual report. If foreign steel produced by workers whose wage demands were much lower than American workers continued to flood the market, then, as Roderick clearly insinuated, jobs of the higher paid American workers would begin to disappear. Roderick had only to point to the decline in steel production and shipments in 1981 to emphasize the logic of what he was saying.[35Δ1i90]

Steel workers and coal miners countered Roderick's none-too-subtle criticism of their wage demands. No steel worker or coal miner was getting rich on what he earned from U.S. Steel, but he certainly deserved to earn a wage that allowed him to live comfortably. And that meant a paycheck that would keep pace with the basic cost of living. Moreover, steel workers and coal miners could not be blamed for the country's recession-driven general economic sluggishness. The recession had caused a domino effect whereby companies such as automobile manufacturers were selling fewer cars, and therefore building fewer cars, and therefore buying less steel.

The recession equation adversely affected steel production in all of U.S. Steel's product lines with only one exception. Energy-related products, those pipes and tubes and other equipment needed for oil exploration, were selling at an astonishing rate. In fact, sales of pipe and tubing that had accounted for 15 percent of the total dollar income for all steel products manufactured in 1979, and for 20 percent in 1980, now were up to 26 percent in 1981. The demand for these products and the high price that U.S. Steel could charge for them were cited as the major reason that steel product sales for 1981 surpassed 1980 sales by 38 percent, pulling in the highest product sales income—$386 million—since 1974.

Besides the manufacture of tubes and pipes, U.S. Steel also expanded its manufacturing capabilities for other oil and gas exploration and production equipment. Drilling barge fabrication began at the company's Orange, Texas, facility, and manufacture of pumping and drilling equipment at both the Garland, Texas, and McAlester, Oklahoma, plants were in high gear by the end of 1981. The importance of this aspect of U.S. Steel's operation was underscored in its 1981 annual report: "Plants manufacturing oilfield equipment experienced peak operations during 1981. . . . The long-term outlook is strong for demand and profitability of oilfield services and equipment, especially replacement parts."[36]

The financial rewards for so much attention to the oil industry proved the importance of that industry to U.S. Steel. Little wonder, then, that when the company began searching for ways to implement the diversification component of its rationalization plan the oil business came into sharp focus. Diversity had shone on David Roderick's radar screen nearly as soon as he had become U.S. Steel's CEO. He had named a strategic planning group headed by Charles A. Corry to examine acquisition possibilities for a company whose product would complement steel but whose product need and use would not parallel the same marketplace ups and downs as steel. Corry had finalized a list of about ten such companies by early 1981. Most prominent on the list were several middle-tier oil companies that appeared ripe for acquisition.

As it happened, Marathon Oil Company, based in Findley, Ohio, was in the takeover sights of Mobil Oil. Marathon at the time was the nation's seventeenth largest oil and gas company, owning four refineries capable of producing more than half a million barrels of gasoline daily. Mobil was aiming to purchase Marathon stock at bargain rates in order to gain access to Marathon's badly needed American oil reserves. Marathon executives, unhappy at the thought of being consumed by Mobil, successfully filed suit against the company on November 1, 1981, charging violation of antitrust laws, and then began searching for a white knight to buy Marathon. U.S. Steel immediately stepped forward as the potential buyer.

The two companies began negotiating a purchase price and arrangements in November 1981. A deal was struck for U.S. Steel to acquire a 51 percent controlling interest in Marathon by purchasing thirty million shares of Marathon's common stock at $125 per share. Once Marathon shareholders approved the deal, U.S. Steel would acquire the remaining 49 percent interest in Marathon via twelve-year notes valued at $86 per share. U.S. Steel would pay a total purchase price for Marathon Oil

Company of approximately $6.4 billion. On November 18, 1981, U.S. Steel CEO David Roderick and Marathon Oil president Harold Hoopman appeared jointly to announce that a merger deal had been struck.[37]

U.S. Steel was exceedingly upbeat about the merger's benefits in its 1981 annual report. David Roderick said that company executives "are convinced that acquisition of Marathon Oil—an increasingly profitable producer, refiner, and marketer of petroleum products—will substantially benefit all of U.S. Steel's shareholders." Roderick added, "Marathon's exploration and development programs and production management expertise have enabled it to maintain the level of its oil and gas reserves extremely well in recent years. Its impressive growth in sales and income, substantial reserves and plans for continued growth will contribute to U.S. Steel's profitability and growth in the future."[38] Roderick noted in particular the 49 percent ownership that Marathon held in the Yates Field of West Texas, whose 125,000 barrel per day yield of oil made it the "second largest producing reserve in the United States." Yates Field reserves were predicted to last for at least another twenty years. In addition, a daily 40,000 barrel yield of oil was predicted for Marathon's Brae Field site in the North Sea near the Scotland coast when the field began scheduled production in 1983. Roderick assured U.S. Steel shareholders that the company's financial ability to purchase Marathon was in good order. Cash reserves had been strengthened through sale of "underutilized assets," such as its coal reserves, and by the company's "stringent cash management program." "We are confident the added debt can be successfully managed in both the short- and long-term," said Roderick.[39]

Marathon shareholders approved the Marathon–U.S. Steel merger on March 11, 1982.[40] The deal had tremendous implications for the parent company. It brought to U.S. Steel, according to William T. Hogan, "the single most significant change in terms of diversification and restructuring that [had] taken place since the foundation of the corporation."[41] Roderick described U.S. Steel as a new company during the annual stockholders meeting in May 1982. Oil and gas now accounted for 38 percent of U.S. Steel's asset base, equal to that of steel. An assortment of other subsidiary businesses such as chemical, real estate, transportation, etc., accounted for the remaining 24 percent.[42]

The new U.S. Steel was reflected prominently in the company's annual report where readers now found detailed descriptions of oil field and refinery operations, in addition to the more traditional steel-related information. The number of offshore oil rig platforms and land-based rigs, the amount of oil and gas produced per day, and the development of exploration projects around the globe—from the North Sea Brae area to Tunisia, Australia, and Brazil—were all described in language meant to impress and excite.[43] But couched within the hype was a series of red flags that almost as soon as U.S. Steel took possession of Marathon challenged the wisdom not only of the transaction's cost, but also of the kind of business to which U.S. Steel had staked its future.

The $6 billion Marathon purchase left U.S. Steel with an $8 billion long-term debt. A portion of the debt pay-down was predicated on the income derived from oil. Marathon had estimated that crude oil prices would continue to rise from their current level by "about 8% annually in nominal terms, through 1986. That escalation would push the price of crude from $33 per bbl. [barrel] to about $48 in five years and—by Marathon's own estimate—would help the company double its operating cash flow by 1984."[44] However, instead of reaching Marathon's estimated $33 per barrel, the price actually declined from 1981's high of $31.8 to $28.5 per barrel by the end of 1982.[45] Unbeknownst to U.S. Steel executives this was year one of a downward spiral in crude oil prices that would continue for several years to come. Pushing that trend was a "severe recession in the national economy" that would strain the economic foundations of industrial America to the core.[46] Recession aside, U.S. Steel had fallen victim to the kind of oil business speculation that the company's highly touted "sophistication in analyzing and forecasting" should have warned it to avoid.[47] Now the company was stuck.

Unable to rely on projected income from higher priced oil, U.S. Steel was forced to resume at a more aggressive pace its asset redeployment as the company continued to downsize the more traditional parts of its operation. Asset redeployment euphemistically meant "converting underutilized assets into assets generating more profits and possessing brighter long-term potential." In real terms, though, asset redeployment meant a range of things from curtailing work at some plants and operations to completely closing others. And steel plants and coal mines continued to be the hardest hit. Even the assets of newly acquired Marathon were not off limits. The company had sold its Canadian oil, gas, and mineral interests by year's end. Also phased out were all of Marathon's mineral explorations worldwide—with the exception of, ironically, coal properties in Colombia and Australia.[48] Marathon also had reduced its spending projections for oil and gas exploration, as well as "field development and production outlays" during the first quarter of 1982.[49]

U.S. Steel's need to improve cash flow put asset redeployment to work overtime. Among the assets placed on the selling block were U.S. Steel's ocean-shipping subsidiary, its barge company, huge tracts of timberland, its Percy Wilson Mortgage and Finance Corporation, and a number of real estate holdings, most notable of which were the William Penn Place Building in Pittsburgh and the U.S. Steel Building itself. U.S. Steel now would pay rent for office space that it once owned.[50]

As difficult as things were in the oil and gas business, matters were far worse in the steel business. A severe depression in the steel industry, exacerbated by the national recession, made 1982 the worst year for steel since before World War II. The ten million tons of steel shipped by U.S. Steel in 1982 accounted for the company's smallest shipment since 1938. Shipment of tubular steel in particular was at a forty-year low.[51] The depressed tubular steel market was a direct result of the sluggish oil and gas industry, despite a predicted growth in the manufacture of pipes, based on unofficial data from Hughes Tool Company. Hughes, the manufacturer of drill bits used by practically all American oil companies, had projected a 15 percent increase in the number of oil rigs operating or preparing to operate in 1982. Steel companies estimated how much drilling pipe would be needed based on Hughes's rig count. Instead of climbing, however, the number of rigs began to decline early in 1982. Week after week the numbers dropped, yet orders for drilling pipe nonetheless continued arriving at U.S. Steel. When surplus pipe began stacking up in storage areas around the country, the orders stopped. The reversal began in March, the same month U.S. Steel assumed full ownership of Marathon. Little more than a week after the Marathon deal was closed, on March 20, 1982, U.S. Steel—largely because of what was occurring in the oil industry—began laying off steelworkers in massive numbers.[52]

Sluggishness in the oil business also contributed to a slowdown in the fabricating sector of U.S. Steel's Oilwell Division. The slowdown in construction projects associated with oil and gas exploration contributed substantially to a reversal in U.S. Steel's manufacturing income that in 1981 had been roughly $84 million. By 1982 that income level had vanished, only to be replaced by an $18 million operating loss. The result of this bleak economic landscape was an $852 million total operating loss in steel that followed 1981's $382 million operating gain. That helped push U.S. Steel's total 1982 net loss to approximately $361 million. Add to that the company's billion dollar annual interest expense and a drop in company stock market value from $32.75 per share in 1981 to $17.65 per share in 1982.[53]

All of this disappearing income probably should have caused U.S. Steel executives to be a bit uneasy about their decision to buy Marathon. Company executives like CEO David Roderick might have second-guessed what was happening with the idea of product balance—that is, when oil is down, steel is up and vice-versa—that had been the cornerstone of U.S. Steel's decision to even consider buying Marathon. The company's financial statement proved the fallacy of that reasoning. When oil and gas were down, they brought steel with them. And the reverse probably was true, although this particular business cycle was hard to discern, since the steel industry now seemed locked in a perpetual down mode. But U.S. Steel executives could take heart in not being completely wrong about the Marathon purchase. America, after all, is oil dependent. Steel needs in 1982 were nowhere near the need for oil and gas. And so,

Marathon made money—probably only a fraction of what it would have made had the worldwide recession not slowed oil consumption and caused a glut in the oil and gas marketplace. Nonetheless, the hedge that U.S. Steel intended that Marathon would provide against the vagaries of the steel business and the resulting economic vulnerability with which steel producers were forced to contend had proved a qualified success.[54]

There was little for U.S. Steel to celebrate about the wisdom of its Marathon decision, though. The recession had created too great a climate of doubt within the steel industry about where it was headed and what, besides the economy, was to blame for its predicament. U.S. Steel executives certainly could be blamed for shortsightedness, poor planning, and overly optimistic forecasts that proved wildly off-target, but they were prepared to deflect any and all criticism for poor judgment. There were, after all, other reasons they could cite for the doldrums affecting America's steel business. And once again the unfair trade practices of European and Japanese steel producers took center stage. U.S. Steel, along with several other American steel producers, joined forces in January 1982 to file "extensive antidumping and countervailing duty petitions" against a number of European countries, including the United Kingdom, West Germany, France, and Italy. The American companies were successful in convincing the International Trade Commission of the merits of their charges, and the matter appeared to be moving toward resolution by late 1982. Unresolved by year's end was a similar unfair trade practices complaint filed against Japanese steelmakers.[55]

Trade statistics helped bolster the American steel producers' case. Steel imports and exports both were down in 1982—imports by 16 percent and exports by 36 percent. However, the total amount of 1982 imports—16.7 million tons—far surpassed the 1.8 million tons of exported steel. In addition, the 9-to-1 ratio of imported to exported steel tonnage in 1982 actually surpassed the 7-to-1 import-to-export ratio of 1981. Another troubling statistic was the steady decline in the percentage of steel that American steel producers had been contributing to the world market. One of the biggest drops in years occurred between 1981 and 1982, when the percentage of steel produced in America, when compared with the rest of the world's steel producers, dropped from 15.5 percent to 10.5 percent. And while the worldwide economic recession had caused steel production declines in every major industrialized nation (except South Korea), the decline was most pronounced in the United States, where total domestic production fell from 1981's 121 million tons to 1982's 75 million tons—a difference of some 38 percent.[56] Clearly, American steel producers were in a battle that they appeared to be losing.

More troublesome to U.S. Steel than the prolonged battle with foreign steel producers was the cost of labor. In order to get a better grasp of how such costs impacted U.S. Steel's overall finances, the company undertook in 1982 "the most comprehensive analysis" of the subject "in the steel industry's history."[57] U.S. Steel's objective here was to gather data that would help the company position itself to negotiate for labor concessions with the USWA. The labor cost analysis actually was a collective effort of eight Coordinating Committee Steel Companies (CCSC) that served as the steel industry's bargaining unit. The results of the analysis was publicized by U.S. Steel in a special edition of *U.S. Steel News* in July 1982.

The analysis indicated that the automatic wage and cost-of-living (COLA) increases implemented by the Experimental Negotiating Agreement (ENA) in the 1970s had pushed steelworker wages to the top of the chart among pay levels for all U.S. manufacturing workers. In February 1982, steelworkers were paid an average $22.69 hourly wage—some 95 percent above the average for hourly wages in all manufacturing jobs in the United States. These wage gains were made, according to the analysis, while steelworker productivity actually decreased. Moreover, a comparison of wages and productivity levels of American steelworkers with their counterparts overseas showed that European and Japanese steelworkers generally were paid less and produced more. Unless labor costs could be brought under control, according to the analysis, more American steel plants would close and more steelworker jobs would be lost.

In a letter written to USWA president Lloyd McBride by CCSC chairman J. Bruce Johnston on May 28, 1982, Johnston summarized the data from the above analysis and the bleak future awaiting everyone associated with the American steel industry unless labor and management leaders could arrive at some method of bringing labor costs under control. Within that context, Johnston concluded his letter by proposing that, effective June 14, 1982, the CCSC and USWA begin negotiating a new labor agreement that would replace the ENA.[58] Under that ominous cloud, negotiations began in July. Steel industry management refused to renew the ENA, choosing instead to offer a three-year contract that called for substantial COLA reductions to virtually nothing. What management wanted had all the markings of a wage freeze. And there appeared no room for compromise; management had chosen to stand firm. Such a drastic proposal was certain not only to fail but also to encourage talk of a USWA strike when the current contract expired in August 1983. However, given the union's weakened position, with so many plant closures and so many steelworkers laid off, threat of a strike did not generate the kind of foreboding among steel industry executives that it had in years past.

U.S. Steel was willing to take a calculated risk that the USWA would not strike. Its risk was leveraged as much by the very real examples to steelworkers that management was willing to close even more plants than it already had. Worker attitudes, though, were buoyed by hard feelings toward U.S. Steel management, particularly over the Marathon purchase. U.S. Steel officials had made a concerted effort over the last few years to convince USWA rank and file that economic conditions prevented major expenditures to modernize steel plants. Money simply was not available—not available, that is, until Marathon came along. "The union guys must feel as if they've been duped," said one former U.S. Steel employee. Indeed, such feelings seemed to permeate company worker gatherings. As a result, the USWA local presidents, gathered in the ballroom of Pittsburgh's William Penn Hotel on July 30, resoundingly rejected the contract offered by steel company management. Another try at forging an agreement met with similar rejection the following November.[59]

U.S. Steel CEO David Roderick was determined to push ahead as aggressively as possible with his downsizing and reorganization. "Salaried workforces and base salaries were reduced, cost-of-living allowances were frozen, and management overtime and holiday premiums were suspended." Employee health insurance plans were modified by chopping off some types of coverage and by raising deductibles on others.[60] Tradition and company loyalty seemed irrelevant to Roderick's cost cutting as sights were set on "administrative and operational reorganization of five Pittsburgh area plants that make up one of [U.S. Steel's] oldest and largest concentrations of steelmaking capacity." The move, according to *Business Week* magazine, was "certain to lead to the closing of even more steel-producing or processing facilities." Targeted were Monongahela (or "Mon" as known locally) Valley plants at Homestead, Braddock, Duquesne, McKeesport, and Clairton, all within twenty miles of Pittsburgh. The five Mon Valley plants were to be "combined into a consolidated steelmaking complex" that Roderick insisted would "cut costs and improve quality and productivity." Following the consolidation, 95 foremen at the Homestead plant were either furloughed, retired, or terminated, and 210 of the 450 foremen at the Clairton plant and 82 of the 680 supervisors at the combined McKeesport-Duquesne operation were laid off. Those U.S. Steel employees in supervisory positions who thus far had been unaffected now had to compete with one another for their jobs.[61] A mixture of anger, resentment, and fear spread throughout the Mon Valley communities. There was surprise as well at the abrupt manner by which so many loyal U.S. Steel employees, particularly those at the supervisory level, had been told to pack up their belongings and vacate the premises. Such demeanor, according to U.S. Steel plant employees, was indicative of the way communication from top to bottom—and very rarely from bottom to top—had come to be.[62]

Things were bad and getting worse. By April 1982, unemployment in the Mon Valley had reached a Depression-era level.[63] By October, half of U.S. Steel's 99,300 unionized steelworkers were laid off.[64] It was during this time that John Hoerr, a native of McKeesport, traveled through the area compiling material for a book he would write later about the steel industry's troubles. What he saw in 1982 clashed sharply with his childhood memories. Then the Mon Valley communities had been alive with the hustle and bustle of an industrial mecca. All of that had disappeared by 1982. Here is how John Hoerr described the scene: "The industrial detritus of a fading culture stretches for mile upon unrelieved mile on these riverbanks: abandoned furnaces, mill buildings, railroad tracks and bridges, storage yards, pumping stations, pipelines, transmission towers. The American steel industry lies dying in its cradle."[65]

Bleak conditions in the Mon Valley would eventually find their way into the coalfields of West Virginia and into the heart of Gary Hollow. However, neither a cursory nor a careful reading of U.S. Steel's 1982 annual report gave the impression that its steel problems were spreading to other parts of the company. Indeed, the report was rather upbeat, noting, for instance, that "U.S. Steel Mining Company is the fourth largest underground coal producer and one of the largest metallurgical coal producers in the United States"; that U.S. Steel Mining Company, "through aggressive sales efforts," had "become a successful commercial marketer," growing the amount of coal sold "from 2.5 million tons in 1980 to 6.1 million tons in 1982"; and that the "nine longwall mining systems" in place in 1982, with one more to begin operation in 1983, "accounted for 23 percent of total production."

Less conspicuous among such high points of U.S. Steel coal mining were production statistics showing that the company had produced only 10.2 million tons of coal in 1982, as compared to 12.2 million tons the year before, and 14.8 million tons in 1980. Nearly at the end of the annual report was this statement: "The trend of reduced coal . . . shipments to corporate steel operations continued in 1982, similar to the decline in 1981 from 1980."[66]

The reduced coal production figures, as well as the reduced shipments to U.S. Steel plants, should have come as no surprise. After all, with steel plants shutting down left and right, what need was there for coal and coke. But the declining need for coke would have occurred anyway. Newer methods of reducing iron ore in the steel-making process meant that technology had begun pushing coke to the side. Government statistics clearly showed a trend in the drop-off of coke production. And a 1982 government report asserting that "the amount of coking coal required per ton of steel produced should continue to decline" sent an unambiguous message to the metallurgical coal industry. Little wonder that integrated steelmakers nationwide were beginning to sell or otherwise divest their raw material property and mining operations. They were holding on to their iron ore,[67] but everything else—coal included—was becoming an unnecessary burden to future company plans. Just how much of a burden might U.S. Steel's Gary Hollow coal operation prove to be? The answer was not long in coming.

U.S. Steel, Marathon Oil, and Depression

Chapter 12

A Bleak Year

New Year's Day 1982 in Gary Hollow probably was like New Year's Day in many places across America. Folks were sleeping late, having stayed up the night before, partying, drinking a little too much of the stiff brew, popping firecrackers, and hugging and kissing to welcome the New Year. The day quite likely was filled with football games on television and a meal of traditional food meant to assure good fortune for the coming year. Children were still enjoying their toys from Christmas and no doubt regretting the end to their holidays. Gary Hollow mine workers would return to work the next day, probably negotiating icy roads to do so but nevertheless happy to be employed. Last year's long strike was a faded memory by now, and the hope for better days boosted the spirits of everyone in Gary Hollow.

That would have been the ideal, of course. But just like pristine snow melts to reveal dirt and grime beneath, so did those hopeful thoughts of better times hide doubts about what really lay in the future. After all, the miners had been reduced to a three-day workweek since September.[1] Less work resulted in less pay. But they at least were working. They realized how fortunate they were when compared with their steelworker colleagues in the Mon Valley. What was happening there was of particular concern to Gary Hollow. Mon Valley steelworkers and Gary Hollow coal miners all worked for the same company and were subject to the same economic and market forces that now moved the company in uncertain directions.

How the slowdown in steel production might affect Gary Hollow coal mines was the subject of more and more talk in Gary, and rumors of mine closures were becoming more persistent.[2] Whatever might happen, the Gary Hollow mines—Nos. 2, 4, 9, 10, and 14—at the moment were all operating, although official records show a decrease in coal miner employment, from 1,267 in 1981 to 1,149 in 1982.[3] Fewer miners and fewer workdays, but still the mines stayed open. Then came March 11. Reports of U.S. Steel's massive layoffs at its Mon Valley plants quickly filtered through Gary Hollow. While there was apprehension, hope prevailed that what was happening at the steel plants would not automatically affect the coal mines. Such hopes were buoyed by what one observer said was steel's cyclical business. "Historically, even when the steel orders are down, we keep producing coke so that when we get new orders, we'll have coke on hand and won't have to wait to start making steel."[4]

It was an interesting bit of history and an interesting theory as well. Neither, unfortunately, applied to the present situation. Things were different now. Downturns and subsequent recoveries had always meant recovering to what had existed prior to the downturn. But U.S. Steel, from this point on, would never be the same company. Forces from both inside and outside U.S. Steel were causing changes that were so fundamental that recovery, if and when it did occur, would find a company shed of much of its former self. So many of the steel plants and the persons who worked there now were gone, and under no circumstances would either plants or persons be returning. U.S. Steel's purge of what company officials saw as excess industrial baggage had only begun.

So, under the circumstances, the announcement that U.S. Steel official Michael Koff made on March 26, 1982, should not have been so much a surprise as it presumably was. Effective that date, said Koff, several company mining sites in southern West Virginia's Gary District would be closed indefinitely. The No. 10 mine was idled completely, while the Nos. 2, 4, and 9 mines would operate on a reduced basis. The No. 14 mine would not be affected. The Gary District now included the Shawnee mine in Wyoming County, which would be idled, and the No. 50 near Pineville in Wyoming County, which would not be affected. Employee numbers at the Alpheus preparation plant and District Maintenance Operations would be reduced, but the Pinnacle preparation plant in Wyoming County would be unaffected. In all, 550 Gary District employees would be laid off.[5]

The news was bad, but the worst was yet to come. Little more than two weeks after the March 26 announcement, U.S. Steel, effective April 19, 1982, closed its Gary Hollow operations completely. No additional cuts were made at the Wyoming County mines, but adding the layoffs at the Shawnee mine to those at the Gary Hollow mines brought the grand total to roughly 1,250 out-of-work coal miners. Only persons in salaried management positions, their office staff, and about thirteen persons at the maintenance shop remained on the job. There had been mine closures and layoffs before in Gary Hollow, but this was the first time since Gary's founding, nearly eighty years before, that U.S. Steel had shut down completely all of its Gary Hollow mining operations. U.S. Steel's official reason for closing the mines was a "continuing depressed order level in the steel industry which has reduced demand for metallurgical coal for coking purposes and a reduction in outside sales because of adverse business conditions."[6] While this explanation gave the broad parameters of the problems now besetting the metallurgical coal industry, it failed to give the details. And that, so the saying goes, is where the devil resides.

Once more, and to a much greater extent than ever before, Gary Hollow inhabitants were caught up in the uncertain momentum of international trade. Now that U.S. Steel was forced to sell Gary Hollow coal on the open market, miners there no longer had the security of knowing that coal they had mined always would have a customer. And customers, unfortunately, were becoming fewer in number and less dependable. A number of factors—economic, political, and technological—all intermingled with one another to reduce to nearly nothing what heretofore had been a reasonably strong overseas metallurgical market. First came the worldwide recession that affected the amount of steel that European and Japanese steelmakers could sell. Many of these steelmakers purchased coking coal from America, probably a lot of it mined in Gary Hollow. But less of that coal now was needed because less steel was being produced. A note of irony here is that part of the problem faced by foreign steelmakers was the sluggish demand for their steel by American buyers.

Coal sales abroad were also diminished by the overvalued American dollar. The unrealistically high value in comparison with other world currency resulted in higher prices for American coal. European and Japanese steelmakers had willingly, if grudgingly, paid the inflated prices as long as they needed the coal. By 1982, that need had dropped significantly.

Additionally, political and labor problems that had slowed coal production in Australia and Poland had come to an end. As a result, coal production in these two countries was back to normal. This meant that European and Japanese steelmakers now had a more convenient and less expensive supply of coal from Poland and Australia, respectively. No longer would they have to buy expensive coal from the United States. Meanwhile, just as in America, European and Japanese steelmakers were using production processes that required less and less coke. Of all the other factors, this one held the greatest potential to permanently damage the metallurgical coal industry.[7]

These conditions affected Gary Hollow mines probably more severely than other mines, but their impact on America's metallurgical coal business nonetheless spread across the country. Besides the roughly 1,250 idled Gary Hollow miners, which included nearly one-half of all West Virginia coal miners employed by U.S. Steel, the company also laid off about 1,300 miners from its Robena District in southwestern Pennsylvania, and about 250 miners from its Lynch District in Harlan County, Kentucky. In all, nearly 3,000 of the 7,000 coal miners employed by U.S. Steel were without jobs as of late April 1982. According to a company spokesperson, this 43 percent unemployment level among coal miners nearly equaled the unemployment rate among the company's steelworkers. In terms of facilities, U.S. Steel had closed seventeen mines and two preparation plants and had reduced operations at another nine mines and three preparation plants.

Other steel producers—Bethlehem, Armco, and National among them—were closing mines as well. By July, coal miners were being laid off throughout Appalachia. The state of the industry at that point led one official of the National Coal Association (NCA) to claim, "The metallurgical coal business domestically is dead, gone and almost buried." The steam coal industry was having its problems, too. Domestic utility companies simply had more coal than they needed. When many of these companies had converted from oil, natural gas, or nuclear energy to coal, the steam coal industry accommodated with what amounted to an oversupply. Part of the oversupply also resulted from reduced energy usage by consumers. As such, utility companies in 1982, with their stockpiles of coal, were in a position to demand a bottom dollar price when they purchased steam coal. Overseas steam coal buyers were in the same position, and a warmer-than-normal winter had required less coal than expected. In addition, oil and natural gas began to make a comeback when the price of these two energy sources dropped low enough to make them once more affordable to utility companies. All of the stockpiling, lower usage, and bottom dollar demands left many steam coal producers unable to earn enough money for their product to keep their mines operating. So, the mines were closed and the miners, just like their brethren from the metallurgical mines, queued up at the unemployment office.[8]

Although this situation appeared to be happening in steamroller fashion, the coal industry in general was not in panic mode. There no doubt were problems—big, big problems—but the NCA optimistically projected that U.S. mines would produce more coal in 1982 than in the previous strike-shortened year or in 1980.[9] Even in West Virginia, where miners were most affected by the coal mine closures, the situation did not appear so bleak when considering coal production statistics alone. The nearly 129 million tons of combined underground and surface coal mined in West Virginia in 1982 far exceeded the nearly 113 million tons of coal mined during the strike-shortened 1981, but, more important, it exceeded even the 121.6 million tons mined during the nonstrike year of 1980.

By zeroing in on McDowell County, however, a sense of what was happening with respect to the skidding fortunes of at least a portion of the coal industry sharpens considerably. Total coal production there for 1982 was 7.6 million tons—nearly 1.5 million tons (or 16 percent) less than production in 1981 (again, due in large part to the UMWA strike) and nearly 2.6 million tons (or 25 percent) less than production in 1980. Keep in mind, too, that nearly 500,000 tons of McDowell County's total for 1982 comprised coal mined in Gary Hollow in the three months before U.S. Steel brought production to a halt.[10]

Lower coal production from 1980 to 1982 still did not tell the whole story for McDowell County. Mine technology, after all, now allowed miners to produce more coal per person than before. For that reason, mine employment figures—and not coal production figures—for the county really told the most precise story of what was happening. And the story was dismal. Even though representatives from a number of other coal companies operating in McDowell County claimed at the time of the Gary Hollow mine closures that their companies were not considering closures or even layoffs, employment records proved otherwise. In fact, the West Virginia Department of Employment Security showed that McDowell County lost 1,840 coal mining jobs between August 1981 and June 1982. This accounted for the greatest loss of coal mining jobs in the entire state for that period.[11] The job loss among coal miners becomes even more significant when West Virginia Department of Mines statistics are considered. McDowell County miners, both surface and underground, totaled 5,814 in 1980, 5,465 in 1981, and 5,005 in 1982.[12] However, the 1982 total did not factor in the 1,250 mining jobs lost in Gary Hollow. Subtract that number from 5,005, and the 1982 coal mine employment totaled 3,755. These numbers represent a 31 percent job loss from 1981 to 1982, and a 35 percent job loss from 1980 to 1982.

Unemployment statistics highlight one side of the story, but they fail to shed much light on the human side, which could be seen daily as Gary Hollow miners prepared to cope with the uncertainty of what lay ahead and as miners gathered at Welch to apply for unemployment compensation. Peggy Hearl of the West Virginia Department of Employment Security's Unemployment Compensation Division had scheduled three days for taking claims at the Welch armory on April 12, 13, and 14. The number of anticipated claimants had prompted a move from Hearl's regular office to the bigger armory facility, as well as a request for additional help from the Beckley and Charleston unemployment offices. And this was only for round one of the Gary Hollow closures. When round two occurred the following week, Hearl scheduled another three days for the balance of miners seeking unemployment compensation.[13]

As miners descended on the armory, Peggy Hearl became accustomed to hearing the same story of surprise from miners who felt broadsided by what U.S. Steel had done. "It's unbelievable," said Hearl. "Everybody thought it would never happen, that they'd completely close their operation." "If you had a job with U.S. Steel," she added, "you thought you had a job for a lifetime." Arnold Walters, president of UMWA Local 9534 and an employee for thirty-seven years, twenty-five of them at Gary Hollow's No. 14 mine, said, "We were shocked. . . . It came up so quick. The week before, they had told us that our mine would keep on working. Then, on Monday when we went to work, the superintendent called me and the Mine Committee in and told us the mine would be shutting down on Wednesday." Walters was willing to forgive U.S. Steel for the abrupt mine closures and instead blame his and his fellow miners' current plight on foreign steel imports. Other miners were less forgiving. Earl Adair, a forty-two-year employee at Gary Hollow's No. 9 mine who had never been unemployed until now said, "The company will tell you we paid you for your work. . . . They don't feel like they owe you nothing." W. C. Wooldridge, another No. 9 miner, echoed similar sentiments: "Those people up there in Pittsburgh, sitting in those air-conditioned offices, they don't know you. They don't even care about you."[14]

The manner by which U.S. Steel had carried out its Gary Hollow mine closures also was on the mind of West Virginia Governor Jay Rockefeller, who visited McDowell County on May 3. During a meeting with county representatives, including several persons from Gary, Rockefeller spoke of how U.S. Steel president David Roderick had not extended the governor the courtesy of notifying him in advance that the mine closures were about to happen. Only after the fact, and after Rockefeller had communicated his displeasure to Roderick, was there a delegation sent from Pittsburgh to Charleston to explain the situation. What the U.S. Steel officials could not tell Governor Rockefeller was anything about the possible length of the mine closures. Other than listening to and commiserating with attendees at the May 3 meeting, there was little more the governor could do. He did note, however, his satisfaction in having called a special legislative session recently to approve extending the unemployment compensation period from twenty-eight to thirty-nine weeks.[15]

Stretching the unemployment compensation safety net by eleven weeks offered a temporary solace, but it would be barely enough to pay bills and buy food. For miners who qualified for the maximum unemployment benefit, they could count on receiving about $194 per week, tax free. This was for longtime employees, though. For those miners who had not been with U.S. Steel as long, the minimum unemployment benefit was around $25 per week.[16] This was not the kind of pay that most miners were accustomed to receiving, but most could make do when savings and government-issued food stamps were added to the unemployment check. A few Gary Hollow miners opted out of the mining business altogether, choosing to retire. Quite a few moved, and some were lucky enough to find jobs at the other U.S. Steel mines that remained open in Wyoming and Kanawha counties.

Those who elected to stay the course in Gary Hollow were just as apt to be planning fishing trips or gardening projects for the short term. There was little else to do but to settle in, take matters in stride, and hope that the mines soon would reopen. "If we allow ourselves to give up hope, then we have nothing to cling onto," said Mildred Landers, wife of James Landers, a seven-year veteran of the Gary Hollow mines. "Right now that is what we need most—the thought that things can't be like this always."

James and Mildred both had been born and raised in Gary Hollow, as had their two children whom the Landers were hoping to raise there as well. Spending more time with his family was one of the few benefits of being laid off, according to James Landers. "But as the days and weeks go on that's even going to get rough," he said. Echoing his wife's comments, James added, "There is only the hope the mines will re-open, but we haven't been shown any proof that it is a realistic hope. Nonetheless, all we have to hold on to is that hope."[17]

Unfortunately, there seemed to be little hope as spring moved toward summer. No one from U.S. Steel was willing to venture a guess on how much longer the Gary Hollow mines would remain closed. Everything seemed to pivot on the economy improving and the American steel industry turning around. But, as a company official told Gary Mayor Charles Hodge in mid-April, the situation "looks bad for the remainder of this year." By early May, rumors were beginning to circulate that the Gary Hollow mines would never reopen and that U.S. Steel was planning to obtain necessary coal from independent coal companies via contract mining rather than from the company's owned and operated mines.[18]

Less money coming into most Gary Hollow households affected more than just the individual families. The entire economic base of Gary and surrounding areas was hard hit by the mine closures. Much of Gary's tax base came from business and occupation taxes paid by U.S. Steel. That was now gone. Even the small income derived from selling treated mine water back to U.S. Steel now was at zero. Under such pressure to cope with existing conditions, Mayor Hodge announced in mid-June that five city employees would have to be furloughed. In addition, two of Gary's six member police force could not be paid and had volunteered to work for free. "People must start doing more things for themselves and the quicker they learn that the better off we'll be," said Hodge.[19]

Welch, where so many Gary Hollow dollars were spent, was pounded by the closures. "It is an unusual business that will not be hurt by the shutdown," reported the *Bluefield Daily Telegraph* in mid-April. Welch restaurants closed early because of the dwindling number of customers; clothing stores laid off their own workers because so few customers were buying new clothes; and car dealers were hitting new lows in sales. Some dealers, in fact, were showing their anger at what they saw as the root cause of the mine closures by admonishing customers not to buy foreign cars. Perhaps worse than the actual loss of dollars Welch merchants suffered was the psychological impact that filtered through not only the business community but all of McDowell County. A Welch grocery store owner put it this way: "When a company with the stature of U.S. Steel takes such a drastic step things are bound to be pretty bad."[20]

Amidst all the problems that now beset Gary Hollow, U.S. Steel decided to implement a major management shift, sending Gary District general superintendent Robert Yourston to the company's Western Coal

Operations and replacing him with John Dickinson. Dickinson held the distinction of being the first Gary native to hold the company's general superintendent position in his hometown. He had grown up in Munson, graduated from Gary High School in 1967, earned a mine engineering degree from Virginia Tech in 1972, and since then had held several U.S. Steel management positions in the Gary District as he rose steadily through the ranks. His last stop before ascending to the top position was a three-year stint as Gary District's assistant general superintendent. Dickinson's other distinction—a dubious one at best—was his arrival in the top spot during what was without doubt Gary Hollow's lowest point to date. Had it not been for the miners still working at the Gary District's No. 50 Mine in Wyoming County, Dickinson would have been a superintendent without much to supervise.[21]

As summer turned to fall there were signs that the mines would reopen. Cable repairs at the Alpheus preparation plant were taken as one such sign. But hopes were dashed when word came that the repairs had been scheduled long in advance of the mine closures and had nothing to do with their reopening. However, the fact that U.S. Steel had delivered $15 million worth of longwall mining equipment to No. 9 and No. 14 mines for eventual installation suggested that, at the very least, these two mines might someday reopen. Why else would the company, now so stingy with its mine operation money, invest so much in the new equipment? Actually, according to Dickinson, each Gary Hollow mine was maintained on a stand-by basis for quick return to service.[22]

Financial woes stacked on top of one another for Gary. The city budget was slashed from $152,000 to $90,000, and in late September Mayor Hodge traveled to Welch with hat in hand to request some financial relief from the McDowell County Commission. His request for $30,000 fell not on deaf ears but on ears hearing the same request from other county municipalities. The county's own budgetary problems left little money for the commission to hand out. Commenting on the money shortage, commission president R. E. Blair said bluntly, "This is the real world. . . . There is a day of reckoning . . . and it is here."[23]

October marked six months since the Gary Hollow mine closures. Normally, it is the month when the air begins to cool and the leaves begin to change color. The fall grandeur of the southern West Virginia mountains is every bit the equal of that found in the more famous New England region. Fall in Gary Hollow normally is a time to worry about the upcoming Friday night football game or some other mundane matter. But October 1982 in Gary Hollow brought more serious worries, such as how to pay the heating bills, spend less on groceries, postpone the car payment, and find health insurance. The Gary Hollow unemployment rate now stood at 90 percent—unchanged since the previous April. Salaried U.S. Steel employees, several city employees, schoolteachers, and retailers remained on the job. U.S. Steel miners collectively were the hardest hit at first, but one by one other McDowell County mines closed. The county's 25.5 percent August unemployment rate was the highest in the state, and that level was certain to climb as 1,400 more area miners were laid off in early October.[24]

Word of McDowell County's unemployment predicament by now had reached Washington. Certain members of the U.S. House Committee on Banking, Finance and Urban Affairs became interested enough about what was happening in the county to travel there on October 12, 1982, to observe conditions for themselves. According to subcommittee chair Representative Walter E. Fauntroy of Washington, D.C., the stated reason for the subcommittee's visit was "to understand at first hand the pain and suffering which those who work in our basic industries are presently experiencing." Besides Fauntroy, the subcommittee comprised representatives Steny H. Hoyer of Maryland and Nick Joe Rahall, who represented West Virginia's Fourth Congressional District, which included McDowell County. They convened their one-day hearing in the Welch armory at 10:55 a.m.[25]

What the panel of congressmen heard could best be described as a litany of distress. Many of those appearing before the panel were angry at their plight, and they reserved some harsh comments not so much for the overseas steelmakers but for President Ronald Reagan, whose trickledown economic policy, or Reaganomics, as it was called, was criticized for not doing enough to help coal miners. If foreign trade was to blame for the American steel industry's economic trouble, then why did the White House sit idly by and not do something? In one form or another, this particular question was posed repeatedly during the October 12 hearing.

Coming under particularly sharp criticism was the Reagan administration's position on the trade adjustment assistance (TAA) program. TAA had been set up as a means to assist American workers who had lost jobs as a result of foreign competition. Once application was made to receive TAA benefits, a Department of Labor investigator then would review the applicant's eligibility for the program. According to UMWA executive board member Joe Davidson, some 4,700 UMWA members in southern West Virginia had been certified as eligible for TAA benefits from 1978 through 1980. "Once the current [Reagan] administration came into office, as far as I know there hasn't been the first benefit paid under trade readjustment to those unemployed miners whose job was displaced because of foreign imports," commented Davidson. Even worse, according to Davidson, was a ruling that the 1,250 laid-off Gary Hollow coal miners were ineligible for TAA benefits because they were not steelworkers and thus were only indirectly the victims of foreign competition.[26]

Lashing out at the Reagan administration, whether or not absolutely justified, at least gave hearing participants a means to vent some of their frustration. There was plenty else to tell the visiting congressmen, though. Mayor Hodge was there to describe Gary's budgetary troubles. While doing so, he alluded to personal troubles of Gary Hollow coal miners who soon would be losing hospitalization as well as unemployment benefits. "I just do not know what our people will do, or how they will exist," Mayor Hodge said.[27] Most of the October 12 hearing participants, like Mayor Hodge, attempted to cut directly to the heart of what was happening in McDowell County. The situation in Gary Hollow was bad—no doubt about that—but just where folks there fell on the county's misery scale, as if such a thing existed, was hard to determine. What was obvious to everyone was that in the context of whatever other conditions existed, the human condition was taking a beating. Coal miners generally have too much pride to admit it, but anyone experiencing the kind of long-term unemployment that Gary Hollow miners and their families were experiencing have to deal with a range of emotions. Anxiety, frustration, fear, loss of dignity, anger, despair, depression, and outright boredom, each in various ways and at various times bubble up from the subconscious to manifest themselves in what often is very uncharacteristic behavior. The result can be anything from a spat with the spouse, to grousing at the kids, or just a general surliness with friends and relatives alike. But there were more serious behaviors that local physicians and mental health workers were noticing in McDowell County miners. Looking to those times in the not-too-distant future with no prospects for a job, unemployment benefits running out, health insurance gone, meals made with government hand-out cheese, and the real possibility of having to stand in the welfare line, a number of miners were giving up the hope that had sustained them thus far and either turning to alcohol or simply giving up on life altogether.[28] The subcommittee concluded its October 12 hearing at about 3:30 p.m., after listening to roughly four and a half hours of testimony.[29] Once the subcommittee packed up and departed, there probably was little expectation on anyone's part that much could be done for the county.

Winter finally arrived, and Christmas was just around the corner. The Christmas season in Gary Hollow had once been a festive time. Houses were decorated, company stores were festooned with everything that made Christmas shopping such fun, and U.S. Steel provided displays in lights perched upon a Gary hillside and gifts for Gary Hollow children. Christmas 1982 was a bit different. The company stores had long ceased to exist. Those that had not been torn down or burned down were boarded up. Individual homes were decorated, but there were no city Christmas lights. In fact, Gary's budget woes were such that Mayor Hodge had been forced to turn off the street lights. The six-member police force—which once had two volunteers—now was down to a two-member paid police force with four volunteers. And U.S. Steel, so patronizing of its coal miners in the past, was nowhere to be found. Since the day the company closed all the Gary Hollow mines, it had made no effort to help the town, according to Mayor Hodge.

Lay aside thoughts about material things and celebrate the true meaning of Christmas, the ministers would say. A good thought, but easier for some than for others in Gary Hollow in 1982. Mike Krajc was one who could take the minister's suggestion to heart. "We've been through this so many times I think we'll survive," he said. Krajc, his wife, and four children, had lived frugally and had spent wisely through the years and now were seeing the benefits of both. "We never got in so deep that we couldn't see our way through for a year or two.... You have to cut back; we don't go out as much as we used to. The savings days are gone, but we've always managed to make it through hard times and good times," Krajc said. Even so, he added, there would not be as many presents under the Christmas tree this year as in past years, "but we'll have food on the table and friends around us."[30] Krajc also was confident that the mines would reopen. That confidence was not shared universally in Gary Hollow, nor was his contentment to make do with less.

Archie and Carolyn Hairston and their five children were struggling. Archie had worked for U.S. Steel only a short time before the mines were closed, and he was earning minimal unemployment income. Their children wanted things that Archie and Carolyn would not be able to provide. Conversations about their finances too often had ended in arguments, and their children were choosing to avoid their father more and more rather than saying something in his presence that might add to a household tension that increased daily.

Francis Martin, union leader and Gary Hollow coal miner of many years, was in a much better financial situation than the Hairstons, but he, too, could muster little Christmas joy. "People are downhearted about what's happening here," said Martin. "It's different from the '50s and '60s. You don't see anyone. Then, men would congregate on the side of the road. Now, I don't know where people are except maybe in their homes."[31] Gary Hollow once had a congregational tradition. It was a place of gatherings, a place of small neighborhoods set within the bigger neighborhood of Gary. But no more. Coal miners coming to the end of the worst year in Gary Hollow history simply had nothing they cared to talk about. What they least could talk about and what none of them likely would even admit to was the feeling of helplessness that gradually permeated life there.

Gary Hollow coal mines had closed before, but in a more limited way. The miners took the closings in stride, made adjustments, and went on. And the miners had been out of work before. During strikes, the most recent one not more than a year before, coal miners had walked off the job. But they remained, at least, in partial control of the situation. Their UMWA representatives negotiated deals, contracts were signed, and the miners returned to work. Even when they had to endure hardships as part of the strike, they were steadfast behind their cause. Their defiance had a purpose. It symbolized a contest of willpower to see who would have the greatest resolve to win the struggle. And besides, the miners were certain they would return to the worksite and that U.S. Steel would take them back, pay them well, and appreciate the fruit of their labor.

Now, there was no certainty. As days had stretched into weeks, and weeks into months, there seemed to be no one doing anything at all on their behalf. The coal miners of Gary Hollow were for the first time ever totally at the mercy of a complicated set of circumstances over which they had no control. They could pick up stakes and leave Gary Hollow. But they were coal miners, and the likelihood of their finding employment at another mine, given the current state of affairs in the industry, was limited at best. Besides, Gary Hollow was home for many. Their roots ran deep; leaving would be hard. And what if the day after leaving, U.S. Steel suddenly reopened the mines and called everyone back to work? Best to stay and not run the risk of that happening.

Uncertainties and no control. The only sure thing in Gary Hollow as 1982 came to a welcomed end was that things were about as bad as they could be. What had begun as an economic recession earlier in the year now had been kicked to a whole new level, a full-blown depression.[32]

Chapter 13

U.S. Steel and Asset Redeployment

"Rationalizing" was one of U.S. Steel's favorite euphemisms for several years. Of late, U.S. Steel's rationalization program as part of the company's strategic plan had evolved into its asset redeployment program. And by 1983 the company's euphemism lexicon included a facility reconfiguration program as part of its asset redeployment program, which, of course, was all part of its rationalization program. Responsibility for fine-tuning and implementing the facility reconfiguration program's objectives was placed in the hands of Thomas C. Graham, U.S. Steel's newly hired vice-chairman and chief operating officer for steel and related resources. Most recently, Graham had served as president and chief executive officer for Jones and Laughlin Steel Company.[1]

Thomas Graham had been recruited by U.S. Steel CEO David Roderick and was highly regarded for his abilities as a steel company executive. He also was regarded as ruthless. Roger Ahlbrandt characterized Graham's management style as "both combative and irreverent. He had a vision, communicated it throughout the organization, and saw to it that it was implemented. He had little patience for bureaucracy and saw himself as an agent of change."[2] In time, Graham's fellow U.S. Steel executives, along with U.S. Steel stockholders, would come to regard him as the right man arriving at precisely the right time. Steelworkers and coal miners, on the other hand, would come to regard Thomas Graham's facility reconfiguration game plan with far less enthusiasm.

What Graham saw in U.S. Steel's profit-and-loss situation helped set his plan in motion. His focus was on that part of the business that was weakening U.S. Steel's overall performance: the company's steel sector. The downward trend in company finances that had been bleak in 1982 continued in 1983. The company generated sales of $17.5 billion by the end of 1983, a drop of nearly $1.5 billion from 1982 sales. But the big drop came in 1983's net income loss of almost $1.2 billion—more than three times 1982's loss. Costs associated with shutting down plant facilities accounted for most of the loss, although a $634 million loss in steel sales alone contributed immensely to U.S. Steel's red ink. The $634 million loss actually was an improvement over the previous year's $852 million loss. A 10 percent increase in tons of steel shipped helped to somewhat reduce the 1983 loss. Even so, the amount of raw steel produced at U.S. Steel plants remained at 50 percent below the company's capacity.

U.S. Steel continued to attribute its income and sales problems to foreign steel imports. Overall, 1983 imports were down only slightly from the previous year, although trade negotiations with the European Economic Community and Japan had resulted in a considerable steel import decline from producers in these two parts of the world. Taking their place were Third World countries eager to enter the American market with inexpensive, government-subsidized steel. Optimism that might have occurred over U.S. Steel's increased steel shipments in 1983 was muted by the substantial decline in the amount of pipe and tubular steel included in these shipments. Tubular steel accounted for only 5 percent of the company's total steel shipments in 1983—a sizable drop from 1982's 11 percent and 1981's 16 percent. The drop in shipments reflected a weakening in the oil business, since much of the tubular steel was destined for oil drilling use. Steep declines in drilling activity also affected U.S. Steel's engineering and fabricating sector that manufactured oil well drilling platforms and related equipment. The sector, in fact, lost $137 million in 1983 on sales of $674 million. It had incurred an $18 million loss on sales of $1.3 billion in 1982 to compare with its $84 million income on sales of $1.8 billion in 1981.[3] The remarkable swing from 1981's gain to 1983's loss reflected troubling times in the oil business. Driving the slowdown in exploration and drilling activity was the drop in the price for a barrel of crude oil.[4]

The direction in which oil was headed ordinarily would not have inspired much confidence among oil industry leaders. For U.S. Steel, though, income from its oil sector—however much it may have been reduced from previous years—was probably all that was saving the company from financial collapse. So much of the American economy was based on oil that it remained a more reliable source of income than steel. To underscore oil's current and future importance to U.S. Steel the company announced in 1983 that oil had begun flowing to its Marathon Oil platform in the North Sea's South Brae Field. The field was expected to produce a daily yield of approximately 100,000 barrels of crude oil and 12,000 barrels of natural gas liquids by 1984. In August 1983, a Marathon tanker, the *Garyville*, carried the first South Brae oil to the United States, where it offloaded to a pipeline near the Louisiana coast and pumped to a Marathon refinery in Illinois. Gasoline produced from the South Brae oil was available to motorists by the end of the year.[5]

Conventional wisdom suggests that gasoline from South Brae oil would fuel more and more automobiles as the South Brae Field reached its maximum output. In truth, the demand for gasoline and for oil products in general—resulting from national economic conditions—was decreasing in 1983 while the amount of oil available worldwide was increasing. Nonetheless, U.S. Steel was forecasting that improved economic conditions in 1984 would favor increased oil sales and a reversal in the downward trend of crude oil prices. Such optimism from U.S. Steel's oil sector executives was not shared by executives in the company's steel sector. Thomas Graham in particular saw little to cheer him about the company's steel business when he arrived in May 1983. Graham's immediate assessment of U.S. Steel's plight was that the company was losing cash in practically every facet of its steelmaking operation. The reasons, according to Graham, were simple. U.S. Steel was failing to respond to the most obvious needs of the marketplace, was producing product lines that competitors such as minimills could produce more efficiently, and was operating without a strategy providing for a long-term view of where the company should be directing its resources. In effect, U.S. Steel had too many inefficient and costly facilities producing too little that would benefit the company's bottom line.

Thomas Graham's perspective on U.S. Steel's steel sector problems and ways to resolve these problems came from someone who did not have the same stake in the company's corporate history as his fellow executives. He was also a person who was fully capable of implementing changes that he regarded as necessary for the company's survival.[6] On December 27, 1983, U.S. Steel announced its Thomas Graham devised blueprint for further reversing its declining steel fortunes. *Time* magazine commented that U.S. Steel was carrying on a "grim yuletide tradition" begun the previous year by Bethlehem Steel. Bethlehem had chosen the days between Christmas and New Year's Day to announce major plant closings and job losses.[7] Graham's plan included "the permanent total or partial shutdown of a number of non-competitive steelmaking facilities and the consolidation of certain other operations. . . . Production capabilities [would] be concentrated on more profitable product lines, such as flat-rolled steels, seamless pipe and heavy plates and beams. Long-term profit and market potential were the criteria for deciding which facilities would continue to operate and which must close."[8]

Facilities tagged for shutdown in accordance with Graham's facility reconfiguration plan included blast furnaces, rail mills, rod mills, bloom mills, wire mills, structural mills, billet mills, forge shops, and others in traditional U.S. Steel locations, including Mon Valley (the Clairton, Homestead, Duquesne, Edgar Thomson, Irvin-Vandergrift, and National plants all would be affected); Gary Works in Gary, Indiana; Gary Works South in Chicago; Fairfield Works in Alabama; Fairless Works in Pennsylvania; Geneva-Pittsburg Works in Utah; and Lorain-Cuyahoga Works in Ohio. A number of these facilities already had been partially closed. Now the closures would become permanent.[9]

Of those affected facilities that had continued operating through 1983, all had produced at less than a quarter of their capacity during the previous two years. Their closure would reduce U.S. Steel's raw steel production capability from approximately 31.3 million tons to 26.2 million tons and reduce steel shipments by about 4 percent. With the exception of rail and wire products, all other product lines produced by facilities destined for closure would be produced at other U.S. Steel facilities deemed more efficient. Besides steelmaking facilities, U.S. Steel also planned to close several of its chemical and fertilizer plants, fabrication plants, and inactive coal mines. In all, some seventy-three operations spread over thirteen states were to be shut down partially or entirely.[10]

Shut down of these facilities carried significant cost, both in personnel and money. U.S. Steel estimated that at least 15,000 workers (only a third of whom were active employees; the rest already having been laid off) would be affected—essentially, unemployed—once all the closures were complete.[11] Severance pay, continued insurance coverage, supplemental unemployment, and pensions that would apply in various degrees to the soon-to-be-released 15,000 workers would account for a majority of the estimated billion dollars that U.S. Steel would spend to complete Thomas Graham's facility reconfiguration plan. Eventually, though, the company hoped to improve its income by nearly $2 million annually in its more streamlined operation.

The only thing that could hinder full implementation of Graham's plan was strenuous labor union objection. As it happened, U.S. Steel executives were contractually bound to at least discuss facility closures with officials of the various unions that represented company workers affected by the closures.[12] What the unions might or could do to prevent the closures was limited at best. Evidence of the USWA's inability to do much about the situation came as well in the union's finally giving in to U.S. Steel's efforts begun in 1982 to renegotiate contractual guarantees of future wage and COLA hikes. Local union presidents had refused to budge on the company's request to renegotiate in order to show their disapproval of U.S. Steel spending $6 billion to purchase Marathon Oil rather than investing that amount into improving the company's existing steel facilities. But by March 1, 1983, the USWA finally had agreed to a new contract that effectively cut steelworker wages by 9 percent. COLA payments also were reduced, as were vacation days and pay.[13] For those steelworkers who now would be among the 15,000 U.S. Steel employees destined to lose their job, their concessions at the bargaining table had gained them absolutely nothing.

The coal mines that U.S. Steel had slated for permanent closure did not include the Gary Hollow mines. Temporary closure still seemed to apply to those mines, and temporary as opposed to permanent likely provided some consolation to Gary Hollow miners. But when 1983 began, every mine in Gary Hollow remained closed and practically all the miners there remained idled. About twenty-five salaried employees continued on the job at the Gary District's main office, and about seventy other employees were assigned to keep the mines in working order. Several Gary miners also commuted to U.S. Steel's Wyoming County mines, although a limited three-day workweek put the miners just above the lay-off level themselves. In addition, an employment inventory compiled by *Bluefield Daily Telegraph* reporter Garret Mathews in early February 1983 revealed that the Gary Hollow employment list included several teachers, about six postal workers, six Wilcoe Health Center employees, a combined twenty-five employees at the Wilcoe Board of Education Office and Tug Valley Health Clinic, four workers at the First National Bank of Keystone's Gary branch bank, and twelve employees at Gary's two convenience stores. Three City Hall employees were working a reduced schedule at a reduced salary, and both the street department and water and sewage departments each were operating with staffs cut from six to two. Two policemen remained on salary, while five others volunteered their services.[14]

Those working in Gary Hollow counted their blessings. Unemployment remained at about 90 percent, while the unemployment rate for McDowell County hovered around 35 percent. Gary's unemployment rate, in fact, was said to be the highest in the nation as of March 1983.[15] The plight of Gary Hollow miners continued to attract national media attention, with articles about the miners' condition appearing in *Time* magazine and the *New York Times* newspaper.[16] Both articles' April 1983 publication, whether by coincidence or by design, helped commemorate the sad fact that one year earlier, this longest of all Gary Hollow mine shutdowns had begun. Only in March 1983 had there appeared any glimmer of hope that matters might be changing. U.S. Steel president Thomas J. Usher told reporters during a Bluefield press conference that there was a chance that some Gary mines might reopen and that some Gary Hollow coal miners might be called back to work by July if coal orders continued to arrive at U.S. Steel as anticipated. If a callback did occur—and Usher was cautious not to arouse any premature hopes about that happening—the size and number of orders would determine how many mines would reopen and how many miners would be recalled. Less encouraging in Usher's remarks was his prediction for the value of the kind of metallurgical coal that steelmakers had prized for so long and that Gary Hollow coal mines had supplied in such abundance. Steelmakers now were quite capable of producing high quality steel using a coke blended from about 80 percent high-volatile and about 20 percent low-volatile metallurgical coals. This likely meant, according to Usher, that U.S. Steel would be placing greater emphasis on its mine operations in other parts of the country.[17]

July arrived, and as the muggy days of summer moved from one day to the next, the Gary Hollow mines remained closed. The coal orders that Thomas J. Usher said U.S. Steel was anticipating for the summer of

1983 simply had not materialized, according to a mid-July statement by company spokesman Michael Koff. No further predictions were made as to when or if the mines might resume operation. In the meantime, most unemployed Gary Hollow miners now had exhausted both their health insurance coverage and their unemployment benefits.[18] Then, with under a week remaining in July, a break finally came. Superintendent John Dickinson said in February that he would be the first person to let Gary Hollow miners know that mines would resume operation.[19] He remained true to his word, calling the *Welch Daily News* as soon as the story was confirmed to ask that the newspaper help spread word that indeed the miners soon would be returning to work. Thomas Usher later said that U.S. Steel had been very concerned about conditions in Gary and had worked hard to find markets for Gary Hollow coal. As good as the news was, it was tempered by U.S. Steel's decision to open only the Nos. 2 and 4 mines and the Alpheus preparation plant. And even these would not be fully reopened. The No. 4 mine was scheduled for partial reactivation on August 8, to be followed on August 15 by partial reactivation of the No. 2 mine and the preparation plant. An estimated three hundred miners were slated to return to the mines. Thomas Usher noted that the mines would operate at least through the end of the year and expressed hope that the other Gary Hollow mines would reopen soon and that all mines eventually would be at full operation.[20]

Partial or not, the reopening gave a boost to everyone in or connected with Gary Hollow. *Welch Daily News* publisher David H. Corcoran delivered his reaction and best wishes to U.S. Steel Mining in a page 1 editorial in the July 26 edition. Noting that news of the development came as a "dramatic surprise" to everyone, particularly in view of U.S. Steel's announcement only two weeks before that any Gary Hollow mine reopening likely would not happen until early 1984, Corcoran repeated the "100 percent turnaround" explanation given him by U.S. Steel's Michael Koff: "This shows the dynamics of the marketplace (for metallurgical coal)—it's a day-to-day thing. But, we're pleased that the orders have come in during these past two weeks from nearly all of our existing customers."[21]

As time approached for the first group of miners to return to work, more reporters from the national media—CNN, the *Washington Times,* and *USA Today,* among them—traveled to Gary Hollow. The page 1 story about the miners' plight appearing in *USA Today* was representative of what the media were after. The story captured the miners' excitement and optimism, but it carried some cautionary comments as well. UMWA District 29 vice-president Ernest Moore, who represented the Gary Hollow miners, shared the happiness of fellow Gary residents in what now was happening there, but he nonetheless was a bit skeptical of just why U.S. Steel had decided to reopen the mines. He suggested that the decision was tied more to the company's wanting to help President Reagan's image by showing an improving economy than to any long-term commitment to Gary Hollow's employment needs. Gary mayor Ron Estep was not as willing to attach a similar motive to U.S. Steel's decision. Estep instead gave a more pragmatic and certainly more diplomatic spin to the situation. "This, at best, is going to be an up and down business from here out," remarked Estep.[22] Even more pragmatic was preparation plant worker Ernest Day's assessment. He saw U.S. Steel's mining efforts in southern West Virginia focused more and more on the company's mines near Pineville. "Anybody can figure out that Gary Hollow will be secondary instead of a primary coal source. Gary is about mined out," Day said. "We used to support U.S. Steel but not any more," he added. "We have good people down here though and I think we can compete. If we can run some cheap coal and mine some cheap coal, we can probably keep working."[23]

Shortly before operations resumed at the No. 2 and No. 4 mines in August, U.S. Steel Mining announced an additional partial resumption of mining at the No. 14 mine to begin on August 15. This added another 85 employees to the previously announced 385 who would be recalled.[24] The list of partially reopened Gary Hollow mines grew once more in early December when U.S. Steel announced that the No. 9 mine would reopen in early January. Thomas Usher noted that demand for Gary Hollow's grade of metallurgical coal had made it possible to reopen the mine and to recall an additional 130 employees.[25] By year's end, the total number of Gary Hollow miners who were back on the job or would be working by the end of January numbered approximately 600. Those miners on the job at the Nos. 2, 4, and 14 mines lost little time in picking up where they had left off. Working five-day workweeks for the remainder of 1983, the miners managed to produce nearly 450,000 tons of coal.[26]

The absence of Gary Hollow coal during much of 1982 and 1983 brought McDowell County's total annual production from 1981's 9.0 million tons to 1983's 6.2 million tons. In 1973 McDowell County had accounted for 11 percent of all the coal mined in West Virginia during the year, ranking the county as the state's leading coal producer. By 1983 McDowell County accounted for only 5 percent of the state's total and ranked as West Virginia's eighth leading coal producer.[27] Even more telling than the dramatic fall that McDowell County had taken in ten years was the decline in coal contributed by Gary Hollow mines to the county's total. In 1973 Gary Hollow mines accounted for 27 percent of all coal mined in McDowell County; in 1983 Gary Hollow's contribution stood at 6 percent. While annual production levels for Gary Hollow mines stood to possibly rise appreciably in 1984, thus improving McDowell County's overall production figures, everything depended on just how long U.S. Steel intended for Gary Hollow miners to work. Even if the miners worked at full tilt, however, the sad truth was that Gary's contribution to McDowell County's total coal production had been declining over the years while the county's total coal production also had been in decline. That trend was unlikely to change.

To underscore the uncertain conditions that existed in Gary Hollow during the fall and winter of 1983, U.S. Steel's public affairs officer Michael Koff announced that the No. 10 mine would be closed permanently. Given the age of the mine and the current state of the marketplace, Koff said that U.S. Steel simply found it economically unfeasible to reopen the mine. Miners who worked there, said Koff, would be eligible for transfer to other Gary District mines whenever positions became available. When questioned about the prospects for Gary Hollow coal in the coming year, Koff noted that improvement in costly transportation rates and increased numbers of purchasing contracts were the two major factors that could move coal from what currently was a flat market. He added that competition in the world marketplace for coal came not just from other area coal mines but rather from mines stretching from Europe to South Africa to China.[28] And since Gary District coal not only was sold to domestic customers, but also to customers in Canada, Italy, and Spain, Gary Hollow coal mines were competing with mines located in their international customers' backyards.[29]

The closing of the No. 10 mine was not a good omen. It served notice that the folks at U.S. Steel who managed the company's rationalization plan now had their sights set on Gary Hollow. The reopened mines there easily could go the way of No. 10. All but the No. 14 mine were close in age to No. 10 and nearing depletion at roughly the same rate. As if the probability that more Gary Hollow mines could be closed at moment's notice was not troubling enough, even more discomforting was the fact that output from other U.S. Steel mines had managed to increase the company's total 1983 coal production by more than a million tons over 1982's production total. Part of the reason for the rising productivity was the longwall mining systems that now were in place in many of U.S. Steel's newer mines. The longwall systems not only increased production; they also operated in a more cost effective manner.[30] However it was done, though, the increased production occurred while the Gary Hollow mines were for the most part closed. For a mining community that had contributed so much to U.S. Steel in the past and that had taken such pride in the commanding position among the company's other coal mines that Gary Hollow mines once had held, there was little happiness in now occupying a secondary, peripheral position. The reality that Gary Hollow mines were operating once more, even though at a reduced level, was nevertheless a positive indication that they remained in U.S. Steel's mining plans at least for the short term. Any long-term role for Gary Hollow seemed to pivot on the answer to two questions: Would the need for coal overseas or for the domestic steel industry rise to the point where the value of Gary Hollow coal would outweigh the cost of mining and transporting it? And, would U.S. Steel remain dedicated to the idea of an integrated steel company, or would its asset redeployment or rationalization plan continue to disengage the company from the coal mining business altogether?

Chapter 14

The New U.S. Steel

U.S. Steel had a good year—not a great year—in 1984. The company reversed its $1 billion loss from the previous year into a nearly $500 million income. The downward trend in overall sales also was reversed, as was income recorded for each of U.S. Steel's industry sectors. The steel sector rebounded from its $610 million loss in 1983 to earnings of $142 million in 1984. But oil and gas income continued to outpace steel by a wide margin. The nearly $1.3 billion oil and gas earnings topped both the 1983 and 1982 income levels for that sector. U.S. Steel crowed about its accomplishments in its 1984 annual report, remarking that a *"New* U.S. Steel came into its own in 1984." Noting how the transformation had occurred, the report went on to say that "our Oil and Gas segment [or sector] is now our major line of business in terms of both revenues and earnings," but that steel "remains a substantial part of our profile."

The long-range strategic plan that had brought U.S. Steel to this point and that now would move it into the future had been disclosed in bits and pieces over the last few years, but not until 1984 was the plan stated publicly in such succinct, point-by-point fashion. Several of the items in the company's ninefold plan had particular bearing on the future of steel and coal production. Among the company's stated objectives were the following:

> We intend to achieve optimum performance from all operations;
>
> When we identify obsolescence, we will shrink operations accordingly. What can be modernized will be, and what is not process-competitive will be closed;
>
> We will be a highly selective steel producer. Our emphasis is on what sells—and what sells better because of our special expertise. We will only produce what is economically justifiable;
>
> When assets are not considered part of our long-range plan and are worth more to others than they are to us, we will divest them—to our ultimate benefit. We have

done so successfully, and we will continue to do so as opportunities arise. We are also open to future acquisitions when business conditions are favorable and we identify opportunities;

We will treat each of our lines of business as a business—and as the very kind of business it is, deriving the most advantage from our diversity within corporate unity.[1]

U.S. Steel's top-heavy reliance on its oil and gas sector continued paying off in 1984. While the price of a barrel of crude oil declined slightly from 1983, the drop was far less dramatic than the more than two dollar drop from 1982 to 1983.[2] Countering that drop was the income produced by oil that now had been pumped from Marathon's South Brae field for an entire year. Some cost-cutting moves and improved sales of oilfield equipment also helped boost the oil and gas sector's overall bottom line.[3]

The asset redeployment component of U.S. Steel's strategic plan was lumbering on unabated. By 1984 the company operated only two of its twenty-five Mon Valley blast furnaces that were in operation shortly after World War II.[4] Plant closures were among the most significant reasons that U.S. Steel had returned to profitability in 1984. However upbeat the profit-and-loss statement might have been, though, the loss of steelworker jobs that had contributed to the economic turnaround had taken its toll. Protests that had become more vocal in 1983 turned ugly in 1984. Protestors said to be representing steelworkers interrupted church services to publicize the plight of the unemployed and even reportedly phoned death threats to U.S. Steel executives and their families.[5]

Protestors who often acted alone began to organize in 1984. Two groups in particular emerged during the year. One was the Network to Save the Mon/Ohio Valley, comprised of about five hundred unemployed steelworkers and militant union leaders. The other consisted of about twenty-five clergymen organized into what they called the Denominational Ministry Strategy. Both groups aimed their protests at U.S. Steel and the Mellon Bank. Neither of these two, according to group spokespersons, was doing enough to assist the nearly 20,000 steel plant workers who had lost their jobs since U.S. Steel began closing its Mon Valley plants.[6]

Unemployment statistics were grim, but numbers alone failed to capture the personal dramas and agonies of job loss. When the Rev. D. Douglas Roth used the pulpit of the Trinity Lutheran Church in Clairton, Pennsylvania, to preach in support of the unemployed steelworkers' protests, several members of his congregation opposed his views and his use of church money to support protest group activity. When Reverend Roth refused his bishop's court order to cease and desist his activities, Roth was removed from his pulpit and sentenced to a ninety-day contempt-of-court jail term.[7]

The unemployment situation was just as bleak at U.S. Steel's Gary Works in Indiana, where the jobless count reached nearly 6,000 by August 1984. Lake County Sheriff Rudy Bartolomei, whose jurisdiction included Gary, ordered his deputies not to evict persons from their homes during the winter months, citing the inability of unemployed homeowners to pay their mortgage fees as a primary reason for so many foreclosures. Sheriff Bartolomei's gesture reportedly was met with criticism from a local mortgage company official who felt that mortgage loan investors would be adversely affected.[8]

Steelworker jobs were disappearing left and right. What the workers and their families were experiencing became part of a series of parallel universes in one town after another. U.S. Steel's American Bridge Company in Ambridge, Pennsylvania, closed its gates for good in 1984. It was here that steel was fabricated for the Empire State Building, the United Nations Building, the Houston Astrodome, the Louisiana Superdome, and the Gateway Arch in St. Louis. Suspension bridges such as the George Washington Bridge and Verrazano-Narrows Bridge in New York City, the Mackinac Straits Bridge in Michigan, and the New River Gorge Bridge in West Virginia also were fabricated at the Ambridge plant. How ironic it was that many of these structures that so symbolized American progress and prosperity were largely created by persons no longer working and in a plant now closed.

Employees of U.S. Steel's Johnstown, Pennsylvania, operation actually voted themselves out of their jobs by refusing to accept the company's demand for wage concessions (dropping the average hourly wage from about eleven dollars to roughly eight dollars) as a means to profitability. Failure to win concessions meant that U.S. Steel now would follow through with its decision, announced in December 1983, to close the Johnstown plant along with twelve others at a cost of over 15,000 jobs.[9] U.S. Steel plants that lined the Mon Valley for nearly twenty miles to the southeast of Pittsburgh were closing. From Homestead, at the center of what once was U.S. Steel's vast array of steel mill sites, to McKeesport and beyond, unemployment was rampant. The close-knit families of mostly Eastern European descent who had settled in these communities and whose fathers and grandfathers had spent their working lives in U.S. Steel plants now were part of the last steelmaking generation in these parts.[10]

The unemployed steelworkers probably were shocked when in February 1984 U.S. Steel announced its intentions to purchase National Steel, America's seventh largest steel company. The purchase would cost U.S. Steel nearly $1 billion—$575 million in cash and stock in addition to absorption of National's nearly $400 million in long-term debt.[11] Closing its own steel operations only to buy the steel operations of another company seemed to make little sense on the surface. In reality, though, the move was in keeping with U.S. Steel's strategic plan. Not only would the purchase affirm the company's commitment to remain in the steel business, but it also would replace the nearly obsolete plants that had been closed with some of the most modern and efficient plants (plants whose $575 million purchase price would be only 10 percent of what it would cost to build comparable facilities) then in operation. National Steel also specialized in producing flat-rolled steel that was highly profitable because of its use in building automobiles and manufacturing home appliances. National's single most prominent deficiency was its lack of ready access to coke—a commodity that U.S. Steel obviously had plenty of.

U.S. Steel's purchase of National Steel fit the growing mergers-and-acquisitions trend that was becoming commonplace in the American steel industry. Even so, the deal had to pass muster with the U.S. Justice Department's Antitrust Division before it could be finalized.[12] As it happened, the Justice Department was not favorably inclined toward the U.S. Steel–National Steel merger. However, Antitrust Division personnel agreed to approve the deal if the two companies would divest themselves of part of their operations, namely U.S. Steel's Fairless Works near Philadelphia and National's Granite City Steel Division near St. Louis. The combined six million ton steel capacity that the merged companies would lose would be more than National Steel by itself produced annually. The loss was too great for either company to absorb, and the merger plan was dropped in late March 1984.[13]

U.S. Steel now was back to where it had been at the beginning of the year. Ahead would be the seeming never-to-end bouts with steel imports. The company continued filing antidumping and countervailing duty petitions, although not with the same urgency as in past years.[14] Climbing back to profitability apparently took some of the sting from having to compete with foreign steelmakers. Adding to what seemed to be brighter days ahead was the first strike-free contract settlement with the UMWA in twenty years. The contract took effect on October 1, 1984, and was to run for forty months.[15] Brighter days for U.S. Steel's corporate office, however, did not necessarily filter down to the company's coal mines. Circumstances surrounding the UMWA contract negotiations, as positive as they appeared to be for U.S. Steel in general, would have some unforeseen and potentially devastating consequences on Gary Hollow coal miners during the latter part of 1984.

Actually, the notion that miners in Gary Hollow who were returning to work after so long a layoff would then turn around and strike seemed preposterous. Would any of them have supported the strike had UMWA officials actually called one? It is a moot issue in light of the subsequent contract negotiations; nonetheless, in the weeks preceding the start of contract talks UMWA president Richard Trumka claimed that union members were preparing to strike in the event that coal mine operators sought to reverse wage and benefit gains that were part of the existing contract.[16] UMWA District 29 president Dennis Saunders, whose district included Gary Hollow, advocated a more "business-like" and "smarter" approach to negotiating a new contract. He regarded the 1977 and 1981 strikes as creating more harm than good in the manner by which they opened doors to overseas coal suppliers able to enter markets that ordinarily would have relied on American coal suppliers.[17]

U.S. Steel president Thomas J. Usher agreed with Dennis Saunders that a strike-free contract negotiation and settlement would be to everyone's advantage. And given the hedge-buying that traditionally preceded UMWA contract talks, Usher suggested that the earlier a new contract could be ironed out, the more beneficial it would be. Usher's remarks came during a very candid interview with *Welch Daily News* publisher David H. Corcoran in February 1984. Usher's appraisal of metallurgical coal's future in general and Gary Hollow's coal mining future in particular was less than optimistic. In what was becoming a U.S. Steel mantra with respect to its coal properties, Usher repeated the importance of increased productivity and reasonable operating costs as two very important factors in keeping the Gary Hollow mines up and running. However, Usher cited other factors over which neither U.S. Steel executives nor coal miners had any control with regard to the future of Gary Hollow mining operations. One of these factors was the technological advances in producing high quality steel that required less coal than before. In addition, lower grades of coal now could substitute for high quality metallurgical coal in steel production. The Pocahontas coal that Gary Hollow mines produced simply did not meet the same need, nor did it command the same premium prices as in the past. Another factor was that Gary Hollow coal was the competitive and, for the moment, declining overseas customer base on which Gary coal marketers had come to rely. U.S. Steel Mining was having to compete with coal suppliers in other countries who could mine and transport coal at less cost than American coal producers. Added to this was the slowdown in purchase of coal from any supplier, American or otherwise, by overseas steel producers who were suffering from the same economic recession that had infected the American steel industry. For these reasons, Usher could muster scant optimism about the future of Gary Hollow coal mining.[18]

Credit Usher for his honesty. He made no promises for the future. Instead he laid down the twin challenges: produce more coal and produce it for less. And while you are at it, do not forget that the coal you mine today carries less value than in years past. Chances for meeting the production and efficiency challenges were not good. Just how much more productive could the Gary Hollow mines be? And the example that U.S. Steel already had made when it closed the No. 10 mine could not have made a stronger statement about the health of the other company mines. They all were on life support, and U.S. Steel seemed no longer to be concerned about pulling the plug.

Signs of just how frail Gary Hollow's condition happened to be were all around. For example, besides the No. 10 mine, U.S. Steel's 1984 mine closure plans included two other West Virginia coal mines as well as one in Kentucky and one in Utah. All were characterized by the company as "non-productive, non-competitive facilities" that nonetheless held a total of about 18 million tons of coal reserves that conceivably never would be mined.[19] Added to the closures was the sale of all three of U.S. Steel's coal mines in the company's Lynch Coal District in Kentucky, a coal preparation plant in Corbin, Kentucky, the Dilworth and Robena mines, and the Robena preparation plant in southwestern Pennsylvania.[20]

The downward trend in coke production that had been occurring since 1979 gave every reason for U.S. Steel to jettison even more coal mines in the near future. Coke production dropped from 77.4 million tons in 1979 to roughly 37 million tons in 1983. That number would rise to 44 million tons in 1984 but then resume its downward track to 41.1 million tons in 1985 and then to 36 million tons by 1986.[21] Declining coke production naturally translated to a declining price of coal. Cost for a ton of coal in the United States in 1984 was approximately $39.37. That price marked a nearly three-dollar drop from 1983's price.[22] Presumably, the falling price of coal combined the price for steam coal and coking or metallurgical coal. It appeared that neither of the two was having overwhelming success in the marketplace. Nonetheless, U.S. Steel was growing more committed by the day to selling as much coal as possible on the open market. At least half the coal produced at company mines in 1983 was sold commercially, and nearly 40 percent of what was sold went overseas.[23] Most of the coal sold domestically was steam coal destined to fuel power plants. The exported coal was mostly metallurgical.

U.S. Steel had done a good job transitioning from coal user to coal marketer over the last few years, but it was only one among several other major steel companies—for example, Bethlehem, National, Inland—that owned significant coal reserves and that also had entered the business of commercial coal sales. And then there were the many non-steel connected independent coal companies that sold commercially. Even though U.S. Steel had developed considerable expertise in commercial coal sales in just a short time and obviously possessed some advantages over its competitors, such as ownership of barge and rail lines and oceangoing vessels, competition was fierce.[24] And competition was even greater from other coal producing countries. Poland, Australia, and South Africa posed major competitive threats to American coal producers, but perhaps the biggest threat of all was the People's Republic of China.[25]

All of this meant very little to the six hundred or so Gary Hollow coal miners who had been called back to work in late 1983. It meant even less to the other six hundred miners who were still unemployed. Some had given up and left Gary Hollow for good. Others, like Robert "Bear" Presley, seemed for whatever reason too attached to the place ever to leave. He and his father had ventured to New Mexico searching for work, but having found little there, both returned to Gary. Bear was at least able to find some odd jobs cutting wood, digging ditches, loading coal, or doing repair work at Gary Elementary School. The work had kept him busy, but the pay was barely adequate. He had lost his truck, was now driving a car with a "wobbly front end on it," and he and his family were surviving on food stamps. When a *Pittsburgh Press* reporter asked Bear if he still liked Gary Hollow, he replied, "It's just a place to live. No, not live, exist."[26]

Meanwhile, those Gary Hollow miners who were lucky to be working were pushing ahead, filling production demands at an above average rate in order to supply buyers stockpiling coal in anticipation of what many assumed would be a UMWA strike in the fall. BCOA and UMWA leaders alike realized that they were in weakened positions, yet their rhetoric during the spring and summer months of 1984 suggested that a strike indeed might happen.[27] Just as contract negotiations were moving to a critical stage, U.S. Steel announced a major restructuring of its West Virginia and Pennsylvania coal mining operations. The company's Gary District would be merged with its Decota District in Kanawha County into what would become U.S. Steel's Central Division. In Pennsylvania the Frick District in Washington County would merge with the Cumberland District in Greene County to form the Northern Division. C. W. Connor, U.S. Steel Mining's vice-president and general manager, noted of the new structure, "The administrative and operating efficiencies that will result from the merger will enable the company to become even more competitive in the international coal market place."[28]

Catching many observers off guard, Richard Trumka emerged from negotiation talks with BCOA representatives on September 21 to announce that a contract agreement had been reached. The agreement now would be submitted to miners at UMWA's eight hundred locals for ratification. Chances for success appeared good, given that nearly a third (about 55,000) of the rank and file presently were laid off. They probably would have voted their approval had the new contract been nothing more than a rewrite of the previous one. In fact, Trumka, in office for a little under two years, had been given no long list of demands such as had taxed the negotiating skills of previous UMWA presidents. Trumka's only mandate was "No backward steps." As it happened, he managed to improve on the old contract by adding a 10 percent pay raise that would be paid incrementally over the next forty months. Miners earning the top pay of about $113 per day would be earning $124 per day by the end of the contract. Along with several other items, the new contract would also increase pensions for UMWA retirees and widows, as well as provide more job security and mine safety inspections.[29]

On September 27, Trumka happily announced that UMWA members were overwhelmingly approving the new UMWA-BCOA contract. Voting was incomplete, but the roughly 5-to-1 margin of approval at 484 of the union's 800 locals meant that it was statistically impossible for the new contract to fail. As noted earlier, this marked the first time in twenty years that the UMWA rank and file had approved a new labor contract without striking. Trumka announced that he and BCOA contract negotiator Bobby R. Brown would meet in Trumka's Washington office on Friday, September 28, to formally sign the agreement.[30]

Any relief from having avoided a strike not only was short lived but reached the peak of irony in view of what happened to the miners now working the Gary Hollow mines. For on the same day that Trumka and Brown were signing the UMWA-BCOA agreement, Gary Hollow miners and their families all were staggering from the punch U.S. Steel Mining had delivered the day before. In a curious choice of timing the company announced on September 27 that it was shutting down operations in the entire Gary District. Miners would be laid off at Nos. 2, 4, 9, and 14 mines, and the Alpheus preparation plant in Gary Hollow, and the No. 50 and Shawnee mines and the Pinnacle preparation plant in Wyoming County. All maintenance facilities also were to be closed.

Announcement of the closures was made by U.S. Steel public affairs representative Gus Tremer, who said that the Gary District operations would "be suspended indefinitely as of 12:01 a.m. Friday, September 28th . . . due to a lack of orders on hand and sales expected in the foreseeable future." In all, about 1,500 U.S. Steel Mining Company employees would be laid off, with only about forty employees remaining on the payroll to maintain the mines and other facilities on a stand-by basis in the event that conditions improved to the point that mines could be reopened on short notice.[31]

U.S. Steel also had suspended operations at other West Virginia mines in Boone and Kanawha counties, as well as three of its Pennsylvania mines, bringing the grand total of laid-off company miners to 2,300. An industry official predicted that more mine closures nationwide probably would occur soon, as the many coal customers that had stockpiled coal in anticipation of a UMWA strike now would have to "burn down those stockpiles" before placing new orders for more coal. The official felt that it might take the rest of the year and maybe even the early part of 1985 before existing stockpiles were completely exhausted.[32] Gary District Superintendent John Dickinson said that the company indeed did have orders for coal shipments in 1984's first quarter, but even he was unprepared to say for certain when the Gary Hollow mines might reopen.[33] And while some local union officials expressed shock over U.S. Steel's decision, other officials said they had heard rumors for more than three weeks of the coming mine closures. In fact, rumors began to fly immediately that Gary District mines were destined to be sold. U.S. Steel denied the rumors, but the company's September 28 announcement that it was selling its Lynch District coal mines in Kentucky only helped fuel speculation even more about what might be in store for the Gary Hollow mines.

The Unemployment Compensation Office at Welch once more published special sign-up dates and times to accommodate laid-off Gary Hollow miners.[34] All who appeared could take special solace in that brother and sister miners from throughout the nation's coal mining regions were doing the same thing. Whether a particular region specialized in metallurgical or steam coal made absolutely no difference. Stockpiles of coal were forcing one coal company after another to suspend operations. Coal miners affected by the shutdowns had only the assumption that the mines once more would return to full operation during the spring months when coal supplies would need replenishing.[35]

For some Gary Hollow coal miners this latest layoff was the last straw. "Gary's going to look like a ghost town," said one laid-off miner in reference to the anticipated departure of Gary residents in search of work. Tom Anderson Jr. was one such soon-to-be departee. "I've had my fill of the whole thing," he said. "I'll start in Western Virginia and work my way East. I'll take any job I can get. I don't care if it's a mechanic, a police officer or a ditch digger." Anderson not only had lost his mining job, but he had also quit his volunteer police job after working seventeen months for virtually no pay.

Leaving was easier for some than for others. Young persons had little vested in Gary Hollow and saw few reasons to stay. Others, however, owned homes there and were less able to just up and leave. And Gary Hollow was by no means a seller's market when it came to real estate. Gary's mayor, Ron Estep, understood the point, noting, "There are more houses available than I've seen in my lifetime." Those who stayed put were mostly veteran miners who had been aware of the rumors circulating about the mine closures. Jerry Hairston worked for U.S. Steel for thirty-four years and had heard the rumors, "but we didn't think much of it. You hear a lot of rumors when you work in the coal mines. The rumors got more and more serious and as it turned out they weren't rumors at all." So now Hairston was out of work and playing the waiting game, hoping optimistically that his indefinite layoff, as U.S. Steel called it, would be short. But Hairston had been around long enough to know "'indefinite' could mean anything from next week until doomsday."[36]

The New U.S. Steel

How many departed during this most recent coalfield exodus probably never was known with any degree of certainty. Gary's population in 1984 was estimated at the same 2,300 as had been shown in the 1980 census.[37] Chances were, given recent events, that the actual population had dropped far below that. And now those numbers were going to drop even more. Likely, too, is that the persons most motivated to leave Gary were young. Young men in particular by now should have seen that little future remained in Gary Hollow. Those who had families had the most reason to leave. And children in Gary Hollow old enough to understand what was happening received a valuable lesson in why coal mining should be struck from their list of career choices.

Population and jobs were not the only thing in decline in Gary Hollow. The community's physical infrastructure was rapidly decaying. Richard Trumka, who had recently visited Gary, compared the place to a "cadaver, just waiting for its bones to be picked." Half of Gary's twenty-five municipal employees were laid off. Street lights that had just been turned back on after being turned off the year before might once more go dark. And the estimated $3 million needed to repair the fifty-seven miles of leaking water pipes simply was not to be found.[38] Gary Hollow residents, whose lives seemed not the least bit interesting to the rest of the world when conditions were good, once more became the subjects of reporters from national media organizations ranging from the *Washington Post* to NBC.[39] The local media had reported Gary Hollow's story on a regular basis, but the national media seemed drawn only to the scent of distress. In the fall of 1984, that was an odor that even the tall mountains of McDowell County could not contain.

Once more, as week blended into week and month into month, the Christmas season began with practically everyone in Gary Hollow out of work. The situation was nearly a repeat of the previous Christmas. The one difference was that miners who had worked for nine months of the year had managed to save some money and were actually better off financially than the year before. But then there was the other half of the Gary Hollow labor force who had not worked since April 1982. They were worse off. A few of the laid-off miners' wives had found jobs at fast food restaurants in Welch, but wages were low. A group representing all the Gary Hollow churches collected and repaired toys for distribution to families with young children. And the UMWA Local 7906 distributed free cheese, butter, honey, flour, and cornmeal.

The Christmas spirit would have been dismal had it not been for a persistent rumor now on everyone's mind that U.S. Steel would reopen the Gary Hollow mines in January. As one miner put it, "A lot of guys listen to the rumors to keep going. It's good to sit around with your friends and speculate. But when [the mines] open back up it will be a surprise to everyone."[40]

The New U.S. Steel

Chapter 15

Muted Optimism

Storms always signal their approach. Winds increase, temperatures fall, and dark clouds gather on the horizon. When all of these occur at the same time and in the same place, there is no mistaking what is on the way. If changing business and economic conditions carried the same kind of forewarnings as nature, then U.S. Steel executives certainly would have been aware that something big—and potentially destructive—was approaching in 1985. The company was careful in how it communicated troubling news to stockholders, but the pattern of events that began to emerge during the year showed beyond any doubt that uncertain times were fast approaching.

U.S. Steel's 1985 annual report spoke of the company's success in debt reduction, its capital expenditures, the strategic plan it continued to implement, and the diversification and restructuring that were part of its asset redeployment program. With regard to its diversification efforts, U.S. Steel made note of a merger agreement with Texas Oil and Gas (TXO) that was announced in October 1985. TXO, based in Dallas, was primarily in the natural gas exploration and drilling business and was viewed as adding a needed balance to Marathon's oil business. TXO's growth rate during the last few years and the company's profit potential within the energy market were seen as good reasons for U.S. Steel to make its purchase. Final stockholder approval of the $1.3 billion merger would be announced on February 11, 1986.

U.S. Steel once more touted its wise decision to purchase Marathon, both for the income it generated as well as the shield that the company provided against profit downturns in the steel business. Marathon had aggressively and successfully explored for oil throughout the world during 1985, and recently constructed oil platforms were just beginning to produce. All of this was good news. But readers of U.S. Steel's annual report were jolted by some not-so-good news about oil. "World oil prices began to slide in 1985, and continued to slump in early 1986," said the report. And the text continued with commentary on how such a slump, if not reversed, could severely slice into U.S. Steel profits. Oil consumers would be the beneficiaries of such a slide; oil producers and stockholders of oil producing companies would be hit hard.

U.S. Steel's 1985 sales and income figures already reflected what was happening in the marketplace. The company's sales of $19.3 billion were up nearly $200 million from 1984. However, 1985's net income had dropped from $493 million in 1984 to $409 million in 1985. What is even more revealing was the comparison between 1984 and 1985 income for U.S. Steel's various industry segments. Oil and gas sales, which accounted for 54 percent of the company's total sales for 1985, managed only to break even with 1984 income. Both years netted the same $1.274 billion. Income in the steel and related resources sector, accounting for 33 percent of total company sales in 1985, was abysmal. Income declined from $142 million in 1984 to only $27 million in 1985. Worse even were declines in U.S. Steel's chemical and manufacturing/engineering sectors. Both accounted for a combined 12 percent of 1985 sales, and both recorded negative earnings for the year.[1] Regardless of the failure of the 1985 oil and gas sector income to exceed the previous year's income level, there was no denying that had U.S. Steel not had Marathon's earnings to rely on but instead was forced to rely only on its steel sector earnings, the company would have been in dire straits. That fact alone helped to underscore the wisdom of U.S. Steel's decision to purchase Marathon.

Not to be denied either was the depression now affecting the entire American steel industry. And it was that depression that continued fueling U.S. Steel's decision to rid itself of unproductive steel facilities. Productivity indeed was becoming a wedge issue in 1985 as the company readied USWA contract negotiations, set to begin in 1986 in advance of the current contract's July 31 expiration. U.S. Steel asserted in its 1985 annual report the company's determination "to remain the nation's premier steelmaker," but the company pointed to such hurdles in maintaining that status as "steel employment costs, plainly not supported by today's steel market, and work arrangements too restrictive to permit competitive productivity standards."[2] Three months prior to the labor contract's expiration the five major integrated American steel companies that remained in operation agreed to end the thirty-year practice of coordinated bargaining with the USWA. The advantage to ending the arrangement fell entirely to the companies who now would be able to negotiate wage reductions independent of what their competitors intended to do.[3]

Things of a more troubling nature also began happening as contract talks were set to begin. Labor activists who earlier had taken their protests to Pittsburgh area churches resumed their activities in 1985. Lutheran, Presbyterian, and Roman Catholic churches where U.S. Steel and Mellon Bank executives were members or where the clergy failed to more strongly support steel workers once more became the targets of picketing or other disruptive activities. Protesters claimed that U.S. Steel had failed to put adequate funds into upgrading and modernizing the company's steel facilities and that bankers were withholding funds from heavy industry and instead investing those funds in more high-tech, service-oriented industries.[4] At one point in late January, activists and former workers at U.S. Steel's "Dorothy" blast furnace in Duquesne, Pennsylvania—a plant slated for demolition the following month—made a direct appeal to the company to reconsider its decision. A USWA study suggested that the plant could be renovated and operated profitably with a reduced workforce. The intervention won a delay in the demolition, but by April the company had rejected the appeal to save the blast furnace.[5]

Plant closures were devastating enough to steelworkers and their families, but there was devastation as well to the communities—once the booming Mon Valley steel towns—where so many of the now unemployed workers lived. Reminiscent of what had been happening in Gary Hollow, the steel towns were having to lay off city workers, turn off the streetlights, and look very seriously at filing for bankruptcy. The town of Clairton had laid off its police force of fourteen, its fire department of ten, and its clerical staff of five in September 1985. Officials also were busy at the time selling city property in order to raise money to pay creditors. The only bright spot in Clairton's otherwise dismal financial outlook was the continuing operation for now of U.S. Steel's major coke works in the town. The situation with regard to McKeesport's and Homestead's bank accounts was not so drastic yet, but both communities were headed down the same financial slope as Clairton. Chances that city officials had taken by borrowing money in the hopes that the steel industry would pick up from its sluggishness over the years now had come back to haunt them. The industry had not picked up, and the area economy had worsened.

U.S. Steel had furnished much of the municipal revenue for communities up and down the Mon Valley via hefty property taxes. Loss of much, if not all, of that money was devastating, but added to that were the additional property tax losses that resulted from a declining population. As one financial source after another began drying up, Mon Valley steel towns had fewer and fewer means to support services.[6] The sometimes abstract notion of a declining steel industry, certainly a behemoth like U.S. Steel, now was being felt in a very realistic—a very visceral—way by persons in steelmaking communities throughout America. But perhaps nowhere else was the pain of that decline being experienced in such a concentrated area as in the Mon Valley.

What folks in the Mon Valley were forced to confront was a changing way of life that was as much emotional as it was economic. The Humpty Dumpty that was U.S. Steel had fallen from its perch, and no matter how hard the Mon Valley communities tried to put the broken pieces back together, their task simply could not be done. The steel industry to which so many workers and their families in these communities had grown accustomed simply no longer existed and quite likely never would again. Coal miners and their families in Gary Hollow shared much in common with their Mon Valley counterparts. But in one ironic sense, if the steelworkers of Mon Valley saw foreign steel imports as one of the major causes of their pain, Gary Hollow coal miners saw foreign steel perhaps as their salvation. After all, who else was to use Gary Hollow's metallurgical coal but the steelmakers overseas?

Coal orders from overseas customers with the hope of more to come succeeded in bringing Gary Hollow coal miners and their families out of their very dismal last few months of 1984 into a more encouraging new year. Rumors that had circulated in December 1984 that mines soon would be back in operation proved true. U.S. Steel announced that as of January 1, 1985, roughly 1,000 of the 1,500 laid-off Gary District miners would be returning to work. What's more, the company seemed certain enough about the future to announce at the end of January that sales projections for Gary Hollow coal suggested that mines would be operating at "100 percent capacity" through the rest of 1985 and 1986. The customers were in France, primarily, although some of Gary Hollow's coal also would be heading to Belgium, Spain, and Italy.[7]

Not all of the Gary District miners were called back, and only three mines—Nos. 4, 9, and 14—were reopened. The number of miners working each of these mines—146 at No. 4, 220 at No. 9, and 114 at No. 14—surpassed the numbers that had worked the three mines before they were closed in 1984. Added to these were the 149 workers at the Alpheus preparation plant.[8] U.S. Steel public affairs executive Michael Koff stated that productivity would be key to Gary Hollow's long-range prospects. The mines would have to produce enough coal to justify U.S. Steel Mining's continued support.[9] If Koff's remarks were intended as a challenge, then Gary Hollow coal miners appeared to have met it in a very impressive way. Gary Hollow mines produced a reported 1,324,852 tons of coal in 1985.[10] Such output was ample evidence that Gary Hollow miners had both the will and the ability to outpace all previous production levels.

For all their effort, though, the miners likely were not aware of the economic forces with which they were competing. Essentially, they were fighting an uphill battle, because the coal that they mined was steadily decreasing in value. The average market price per ton of coal (both metallurgical and steam combined) had dropped every year since 1981, when the price was $45.04. By 1985 the price was down to $34.95 per ton, a 22 percent difference in only four years.[11] Pricing declines aside, there were positive signs that U.S. Steel Mining indeed had turned a corner and was now including the Gary District Works as part of its future plans. A newly installed longwall mining unit at the No. 14 mine became operational in 1985,[12] and plans for upgrading the Alpheus preparation plant in order to improve the facility's ability to recover fine particles of coal were well under way by midyear. The plans proved newsworthy enough to warrant a lengthy story in *Coal Age* magazine describing the significance of the plant upgrade and how the improved facility would operate.[13]

As 1985 wore on, the situation in Gary Hollow improved. Unemployment still was too high, but a majority of the miners in the community were back at work and earning money. And while there appears to have been no scheduled events to commemorate the moment, March 16, 1985, marked the fifteenth anniversary of Gary's incorporation as an independent municipality. A *Bluefield Daily Telegraph* article noted the anniversary and included a brief history of Gary's founding in 1902.[14] Embedded within the article was a subtext about industrial paternalism—the force, both visible and invisible, subtle and pervasive, benevolent and overbearing, that had connected Gary Hollow with U.S. Steel since the town's very beginning. And once more that paternalistic connection had led U.S. Steel to resuscitate the spirit if not the very life of the place. But the connection was growing weaker. The numerous mine closures and loss of so many jobs, in fact, were just the more recent examples of how thin the connection had become. In little more than a year the connection would dissolve entirely.

Chapter 16

Disengagement

In 1986 conditions aligned to create the perfect storm. Foreign trade, labor unrest, industrial retrenchment, transport costs, and consumer demands all managed to converge at once, and U.S. Steel was at the center of the resulting economic deluge. Ironically, while U.S. Steel felt the brunt of this economic perfect storm, the company had played a major role in seeding the storm. It used a struggling economy as a convenient way to make one last thrust to rid the company of all that its executives considered irrelevant, unnecessary, and generally burdensome. U.S. Steel's perfect storm was actually a perfect opportunity for the company to sustain short-term financial loss while at the same time putting all the final pieces in place to complete its restructuring plan and assure a quick return to economic prosperity.

Storm clouds gathered almost as soon as the new year began. When leaders of the United Steelworkers of America met in mid-January 1986 to discuss strategy for upcoming contract negotiations, their collective position was to call workers off the job before yielding to steelmakers on any pay or benefit concessions. Holding that line would not be easy, though. And even USWA president Lynn R. Williams conceded that he and other union executives would be more understanding toward steelmakers who could make a reasonable case for just how severe their financial condition might be.

Both the USWA and the steelmakers found themselves in a peculiar position in 1986. For the first time since 1956, the union would be negotiating contracts with individual steel companies and not with a single representative of all the companies. Thus, separate deals would be struck between the USWA and each of the "Big Six" steel companies: U.S. Steel, Bethlehem Steel, LTV Steel, National Steel, Inland, and Armco. All six companies employed a combined 125,000 (or roughly 20 percent) of the 700,000 USWA members nationwide. Labor costs were certain to be an issue at each negotiation site. Such costs represented about one-third of a steelmaker's operating costs. So working either to cut labor costs or at the very least to hold them in check would be the management objective. The USWA, on the other hand, had a pay increase and improved benefits in its sight. Backing that up was the reminder that a 116-day strike had driven home the point in 1959 and that a similar strike might do the same in 1986. The USWA leadership nonetheless was aware of how much conditions in the steel industry had changed since 1959. The union in 1986 was in a position to push steelmakers only so far with its demands.

To better ascertain its bargaining position, the USWA commissioned a study of the steel industry's financial status. The study presented some sobering conclusions, showing for instance that in eight years America's steel consumption had declined by nearly 19 percent. On the other hand, the study showed that steelmakers had made significant savings in recent years by cutting labor-related expenses. The bottom line seemed clear: the USWA was perfectly aware of how the steel industry had been declining, but if the industry intended to survive at all, then steelworkers, whose numbers also were in decline, should receive a decent wage.[1] Any leveraging argument that the USWA hoped to propose suffered a major blow when U.S. Steel's second quarter 1986 earnings figures were released. The news could have been worse but not much worse. U.S. Steel income for the period was $14 million as compared to $180 million in second quarter earnings the previous year. Second quarter sales also had declined from $5.44 billion in 1985 to $4.17 billion in 1986. The steel sector accounted for the company's biggest financial hit, sustaining a second quarter operating income loss of $42 million as compared to an operating income of $85 million in 1985. But income from oil and gas dropped precipitously as well. Marathon Oil, for example, generated a 1986 second quarter income of $163 million as compared to $322 million for the same period in 1985.[2] The bad news reflecting from the second quarter figures did not improve by year's end. As it happened, U.S. Steel reported a net income loss of $1.83 billion for 1986. The steel sector accounted for the most significant portion of that loss: $1.37 billion. But while U.S. Steel's oil and gas sector contributed a $42 million operating income to company coffers, that amount was far, far below 1985's oil and gas income.

Much of the diminished income from U.S. Steel's oil and gas sector came from restructuring costs attributed to the company's TXO acquisition earlier in the year. Nonetheless both TXO and Marathon Oil income suffered from lower crude oil prices resulting from decisions by OPEC to flood the world market with cheap oil.[3] As noted earlier, crude oil prices that had been dropping steadily during the 1980s to reach an average $24.09 per barrel in 1985 now plunged by nearly 50 percent to $12.51 per barrel in 1986.[4] The volatility of the oil and gas business was revealing its ugly side to a U.S. Steel executive team that heretofore had been so positive about its good sense in moving the company into the energy business. Now, though, these same executives were not optimistic that crude oil prices would rebound anytime soon. The amount of surplus oil was such that drilling and oil exploration either would cease altogether or would be considerably diminished until conditions returned to a more profitable level.[5]

As it happened, U.S. Steel's oil and gas business, as much as that business might now be struggling, probably was the single reason the company had not fallen into bankruptcy. The nation's second biggest steel producer, LTV Corporation, had no similar subsidiary business to which it could turn and as a result had filed for Chapter 11 bankruptcy protection in July 1986. There were fears that other steel companies, Bethlehem being one of them, might soon follow suit. Foreign steel imports were still seen as the chief source of American steel company woes. Company executives continued pleading with President Ronald Reagan to implement foreign steel import quotas, but the White House balked. Retaliatory measures by foreign governments' setting import quotas on American goods could hurt a broad spectrum of domestic manufacturers who depended heavily on export sells. Moreover, American manufacturers also would be penalized for logically seeking out the lowest costing steel, even though that steel might be coming from foreign producers. Perhaps even more important was the overall reduction in the amount of steel that American manufacturers needed as they began using less expensive metals and plastics in place of steel. And in an ironic twist, even those companies who remained loyal customers of domestic steelmakers might find themselves eventually competing with foreign manufacturers who exported a variety of finished steel products, such as automobiles, for sale in the United States.

Apart from the competition posed by the flow of foreign steel, either in raw or finished form, the big integrated steel companies like U.S. Steel found themselves also having to compete with the smaller, more productive and more cost efficient minimill steel producers that were popping up in every part of the country. The minimills took advantage of the newest production technology and techniques, and they focused on producing only a narrow range of steel products for which there was a known market. Companies such as U.S. Steel were slowly transitioning to the newer production technologies, but they had invested so heavily in older production methods that moving from one to the other required considerable time and expense. Rather than make such an investment U.S. Steel chose to restructure.[6]

Restructuring in the manner undertaken by U.S. Steel was as symbolic as it was a practical solution to a vexing problem. It was tacit acknowledgment that the age of the integrated steel company was over. U.S. Steel, as the biggest of all integrated steelmakers, was, according to the blueprint it had drawn years before, responding in rational fashion to what it felt needed to be achieved as far as disassembling the parts that for so long had comprised the integrated whole of its business. "Disassembly" was only one more euphemism to add to the lexicon of what otherwise had become the routine of closures and sell-offs by 1986. By year's end U.S. Steel had liquidated USS Chemicals, United States Steel Supply Division, and most of its U.S. Agri-Chemicals subsidiaries.[7] In late July 1986, U.S. Steel temporarily closed a number of steelmaking facilities as orders for steel dwindled due to the anticipated USWA strike. Affected sites included a major coke making plant at the company's Clairton, Pennsylvania, works and coke making batteries, blast furnaces, and tin and sheet mills at the Gary, Indiana, works.[8]

Another closure occurred on July 25, 1986, that definitely was permanent. The Homestead Works had last operated in May 1986, but it had taken the intervening two months to remove the hardware that once had made Homestead a giant among giants in steelmaking. The 500-acre plant, located just a few miles southeast of downtown Pittsburgh on the banks of the Monongahela River, once employed as many as 20,000 workers. From Homestead's massive mills had come rails, pipes, tubes, armor plates, and beams used to construct the Empire State Building, Chicago's Sears Tower, and other landmark structures across the length and breadth of America. The Homestead Works had been built in 1879 by the Pittsburgh-Bessemer Steel Company and purchased four years later by Andrew Carnegie. Homestead changed hands once more when a group of investors led by J. P. Morgan purchased Carnegie's company and turned it into the United States Steel Corporation in 1901. From that time Homestead had served as a symbol of U.S. Steel's strength and dominance in the steelmaking industry. By the 1980s, though, the company no longer found it economically feasible to continue Homestead's operation.[9]

Homestead, as mentioned earlier, had been the scene of one of the most violent confrontations between organized labor and management in American industrial history. How ironic that at the very time when doors to the Homestead Works were closing for good, steelworkers were poised to strike U.S. Steel. And again pay would be the issue. Unlike the 1892 confrontation, though, labor and management would battle one another with words and not weapons. However, labor once more would end up on the losing side. Closing the Homestead Works, for so long the very heart of U.S. Steel, represented the company's concerted effort to physically disengage itself from its past. Homestead stood as a massive, outdated, and rusting behemoth that visually shouted out to anyone within eyesight of what U.S. Steel had been and where its roots were firmly placed. But there apparently was no rational reason that company executives could see for U.S. Steel to hang on to any part of what seemed to be regarded as its irrelevant past. And so Homestead was rationalized out of existence.

Disengagement from the past occurred as well in 1986 when U.S. Steel changed its name. Taking its new name, "USX Corporation" from the New York Stock Exchange symbol of "X" that had identified U.S. Steel since 1924, CEO David Roderick announced on July 8, 1986, that a corporate restructuring would accompany the new name. USX essentially would become a holding or parent company under which four separate units would operate: USS, Marathon Oil Company, Texas Oil and Gas Corporation, and U.S. Diversified Group. USS would comprise USX's steel business with U.S. Steel Mining as a distant appendage, and U.S. Diversified Group would comprise the company's other businesses, such as real estate and engineering. Roderick explained that the new structure "provided increased flexibility at the corporate level to manage our individual companies more effectively and to expand into the new and profitable areas of business in the future which meet our goals of financial strength and stability."

The name change and restructuring were characterized in the *New York Times* as "a move that ratifies the fall from dominance of the American steel industry" and an acknowledgment that "steel has lost its clout" at the now restructured company. Indeed, with nearly 70 percent of company sales now attributed to its nonsteel businesses, there was speculation that the new USX was only a step or two away from a departure from steelmaking altogether. Roderick, however, affirmed that USX was "committed to remaining the nation's premier steel organization."[10] Even so, the new USS steel division was given an enormous burden to shoulder. As an independent company, USS now would have to manage a $1.8 billion debt and pay for any future plant construction or modernization from its own cash flow. And with cash flow all but dried up at present, USS apparently was left with only two options to succeed: cut costs (meaning workers' pay and benefits) or close more steel plants. Just how well USS would function in its new guise soon would be tested.[11]

A midnight July 31 deadline was set for the USWA and USX representatives to settle on a contract. With no agreement in sight when midnight arrived, USWA members struck. Agreements already had been reached with other major steel producers, so only the roughly 22,000 union employees working for USX walked off the job. Reaching contract agreements with other companies had been part of a USWA strategy in dealing with USX. Since USX's competitors were up and running and selling steel, the USWA presumed that USX would feel the pressure to settle contract disputes and reopen its steel plants as quickly as possible. USWA negotiators were aware, however, that if USX were pushed too far that the company might close more plants. In fact, as noted above, rumors were rampant that USX might decide to close its entire steel operation, sell what it could, and be done with making steel forever. That did not happen, but the threat of it totally nullified USWA's leveraging strategy. USX clearly held the upper hand, and what USX wanted were wage, benefit, and work rule concessions.[12]

The USWA strike stretched from summer into fall, and on November 24, 1986, reached a milestone when it tied the 116-day steelworkers' strike record set in 1959. Ironically, steel companies that continued operating in USX's absence did not experience any substantial increase in orders. The need for steel by such big users as automobile companies had dwindled so much that whatever steel needs remained were being easily met with existing steel inventories. And in view of how much money USX had lost in its steel sector prior to the strike, the company probably was experiencing significant savings by not having to pay steelworker wages as the strike stretched on into winter.[13] USWA and USX negotiators finally reached agreement on a new contract on January 17, 1987. The rank-and-file USWA members' overwhelming approval of the new contract brought the six-month strike to its conclusion on January 31. By every count, USX had scored a lopsided victory, having won practically every contract provision it was demanding. The contract would extend to four rather than the usual three years, USWA granted significant wage concessions, and cost-of-living allowances were eliminated along with redundant job positions.[14]

Restructuring, reorganizing, rationalizing, downsizing, disassembling, disengaging—regardless of what the process was called, it was all part of a plan. Unfortunately, nowhere in that plan was there space for considering the emotional turmoil and upended lives of thousands of laid-off steelworkers and their families, not to mention towns that for so long had depended on the steel industry and whose very existence now was threatened. U.S. Steel's and now USX's plan would have none of that. It was, after all, not intended to be sentimental. The plan was all business. And by the looks of it in 1986, the plan was progressing without a hitch.

In Gary Hollow there was no awareness of U.S. Steel's plan, and if anyone knew just how the town and its coal operations fit into the company's grand scheme of things, that knowledge appeared to be well concealed. Indeed, signs that had carried over from 1985 gave hope to Gary Hollow coal miners and their families as they awoke on New Year's Day that work conditions might be stabilizing if not improving. The signs were deceptive, though. Far from improving, conditions soon began deteriorating. So much so, in fact, that Gary Hollow would be a far different place at the end of 1986 than at its beginning.

Operations at Gary's Nos. 4, 9, and 14 mines and Alpheus preparation plant were as near normal as could be expected in early 1986. Economic, industrial, and marketplace forces that had been gnawing away at Gary Hollow for years were temporarily at rest, but only temporarily. These same forces were causing fundamental change in the steel industry, and in due time they would do the same in the hills of southern West Virginia.

The unusual slowdown in steel production that U.S. Steel experienced in 1986 indeed was a problem. Less steel meant less need for coke and thus coal. Even without the slowdown, though, continuous casting methods and the growth of electric arc technology for steelmaking translated to less need for coal. Add to the mix the lower than expected demand for U.S. coal overseas due to increased competition from other coal producing countries. The bottom line was that annual demand for U.S. metallurgical coal had dropped from 1976 to 1986, from 85 million tons to 36 million tons.[15] Just what this meant for Gary Hollow was stated in unusually blunt terms in *Coal Age* magazine in its April 1986 issue: "The metallurgical coal industry, which once built entire mining regions in Appalachia, soon may be no more."[16]

None of what currently was happening in the metallurgical coal industry or predictions for the industry's demise was good news for Gary Hollow miners. To a great extent they already had been victimized by these slowdowns and changes through recent mine closures and miner layoffs. Overseas orders did not materialize to anywhere near the same extent as in 1985. The blame partially lay in the ability of foreign coal suppliers to outmaneuver U.S. Steel in their deal making. But even the foreign suppliers were having limited success due to an oversupply of steelmaker inventories (estimated at almost 200 million tons). Foreign steelmakers, like their American counterparts, also were suffering from a sluggish buying market and as a result were needing less coal in 1986.

Even if coal orders had materialized as expected, the price would have been too low to produce a profit for the company. Export coal prices in 1986 were down 5 percent from 1985. And prices in 1985 were down as much as 20 percent from 1984. These prices were particularly onerous for Gary Hollow coal mines because of the high cost of transporting coal by rail. Gary's location right in the middle of the great Pocahontas coalfield had been an advantage for many years. Now the distance that had to be covered in taking that coal to market became a liability. Worse still, rail transportation costs continued to climb.

There appeared to be few directions now for U.S. Steel to turn. Thought was given once more to selling Gary Hollow coal for use as steam coal. But in order to do that the coal would have to be blended with coal coming from U.S. Steel mines in northern West Virginia and southwestern Pennsylvania. Costs for transporting Gary Hollow coal to the location where it could be blended would be too high, and besides, the whole effort seemed illogical. If U.S. Steel already had steam coal from its other mines that was perfectly suitable for the utility market, then why go to the unnecessary trouble and expense of transporting metallurgical coal, regardless of its origin, for the purpose of blending?[17]

Everything that U.S. Steel tried in spring 1986 to find some market for Gary Hollow coal seemed useless. Times were bad for steel, but times were worse for coal. *Coal Age*'s bleak assessment for the metallurgical coal industry might not have applied universally, but it most certainly applied in every respect to the Gary Hollow coal mines. Signs of what was coming first appeared in May when 225 Gary Hollow miners were laid off and all area mines were put on a week-to-week operating schedule.[18] Within a month, 235 more miners were laid off. By August the number of laid-off miners in Gary Hollow rose by another 290. Added to this list were 45 layoffs at what now was USX's No. 50 mine in Wyoming County and 210 more layoffs at the company's Morton Mine in Kanawha County.[19]

Mine closures in Gary Hollow had become commonplace by now. Since 1982 a miner could have been laid off as many as three different times.[20] How long the layoffs would last and whether the mines would reopen at all were questions for which answers had grown more uncertain and more cautious recently. Now, with the latest August layoffs, USX mining operations in Gary Hollow had all but ceased. The all-too-familiar routines once more began to unfold among households scattered throughout Gary's far-flung town. Thoughts of looking for a new job, but where to look and what to do? Thoughts of moving, but where to go? And if moving required selling a house, just exactly who would be buying anything in Gary and for how much? What about city services? Would more municipal jobs have to be eliminated, and would streetlights have to be turned off once more? Could city officials even provide the bare essentials of what is required of a municipality? Or would city hall have to close entirely?

Amidst all of the emotional and economic strains that Gary Hollow coal miners and their families now faced, USX issued a terse and less-than-reassuring statement of the obvious as it addressed current conditions in Gary: "The continuing depressed market for met-grade coal and the current strike against USX ... are having a very detrimental effect on mining operations in McDowell County. No relief in this depressed market is evident. However, U.S. Steel Mining Company intends to position itself to take advantage of all opportunities that may be available. Unfortunately, employment at Gary operations during this period continues at the lowest level in many years."[21]

Then, on Thursday, November 6, 1986, things hit rock bottom. U.S. Steel announced an indefinite layoff of all Alpheus operation employees. Everything that now was idled—the Gary Hollow mines and the Alpheus preparation plant included—would remain so. Factors that had convinced U.S. Steel to make its shutdown decision were as dire as at any time in the past. Market conditions, according to U.S. Steel Mining Company president Charles C. Gedeon, were so poor that chances for the Gary mines to become once more competitive looked to be at least three to five years away at best. On top of that, said Gedeon, the company could not continue operating the mines and preparation plant while absorbing financial losses that between January 1985 and July 1986, were estimated at nearly $12 million.[22]

The company's decision had not surprised many.[23] And it really required very little reading between the lines to understand the real message that U.S. Steel was delivering. For all intents and purposes, the company was finished in Gary Hollow. Gedeon's words said as much. Expecting miners to wait even three years for mines to reopen was unrealistic, and he knew it. But he was straight-up in delivering the unvarnished, no sugar-coated truth. U.S. Steel would never again run a coal mining operation in Gary, West Virginia.

To its credit, U.S. Steel Mining immediately hired a professional job counseling firm from Michigan to assist unemployed miners in job searches, interviewing, and résumé preparation. The company reportedly budgeted some $500,000 for this purpose. The transition team set up shop in Gary alongside the Job Search Assistance Center on November 17. One possible hope for laid-off Gary Hollow miners was a company transfer to the Pinnacle operations mines in nearby Wyoming County. But while these mines remained open, there were some forty-five laid-off miners there as well who would have first choice of returning to work if a call-back occurred.[24]

The one chance that Gary Hollow miners now saw for reopening the mines was to do it themselves, to purchase U.S. Steel Mining's assets and to set up an employee owned and operated business. All of the reasons why U.S. Steel had closed the mines in the first place remained unchanged, but talk of operating the mines on their own provided miners an ever-so-slight glimmer of optimism in what otherwise was a depressing and potentially desperate situation. Some forty unemployed Gary Hollow miners met with government and U.S. Steel representatives on November 21, 1986, at Gary United Methodist Church in what was termed an "informational and instructional meeting." The employees were looking at the feasibility either of creating an employee stock ownership plan or of leasing U.S. Steel Mining Company property and equipment. U.S. Steel official Gary Gadley announced to the group that while the company had no immediate plans to sell or lease the Gary facilities, U.S. Steel nonetheless would take a serious look at any plan for doing so. Dennis Altizer, a representative from now U.S. Senator Jay Rockefeller's office, said that any chances for financing an employee-owned operation like the one being discussed rested with a feasibility study showing the competitive potential for marketing the operation's coal.[25] The meeting ended on that note, and the year ended with the matter still in limbo, the mines closed, and the miners not working. Meanwhile, U.S. Steel Mining Company ended the year with company coal shipments down by almost two million tons from the previous year's level. The continuing USWA strike and the coal glut resulting from worldwide production were taking their toll. With only one exception, U.S. Steel had had to reduce its workforce or suspend operations altogether at its coal mines. The one exception was the company's Cumberland Mine in Pennsylvania, whose total coal output was contracted to a Canadian utility company.[26]

Like so many times in recent years, Gary Hollow coal miners—all unemployed now—were facing a bleak winter. There were family needs to take care of, and Christmas was just around the corner. This was supposed to be a season of joy, but joy in Gary Hollow was in short supply. For all of its starts and stops and its hope-raising and hope-dashing moves in recent years, U.S. Steel had continued to offer Gary Hollow miners the one best chance that when all else failed, the company would come through in the end. No more. The company remained visible and physically present for the moment, but in spirit it was gone. As 1986 groaned to an end, citizens of Gary were facing a far different future than they had faced at any time in the town's nearly eighty-five-year history. Its survival, quite literally, was on the line.

Chapter 17

Prosperity and Uncertainty

The year 1987 would be good for U.S. Steel—in fact, *very* good. Company management would carefully and successfully exploit U.S. Steel's strongest assets while continuing to rein in and divest its weakest liabilities. Company executives and stockholders alike would be happy to see the word "profit" describe U.S. Steel's financial performance. The company's net income for the year—$219 million—would be little more than a third of its net income of two year's before. But considering a nearly $2 billion loss in 1986, anything in the plus column was welcomed.[1]

The year began on an upbeat note when USWA officials voted on January 18 to ratify a new four-year contract with U.S. Steel. The contract, if approved by union rank and file, would take effect on February 1, thus ending USWA's six-month strike, the longest in the union's history. Historical, too, were the contract concessions that would not only cut steelworker wages and benefits but also eliminate some 1,300 jobs. The wage cut of $1.13 an hour from the average $12.50 per hour was calculated to save U.S. Steel about $300 million throughout the life of the new contract. In return for these reductions the company agreed to implement a profit-sharing plan and to pay $37 million in pension or severance pay to steelworkers who previously had worked at the now closed U.S. Steel plants. Those plants would be closed permanently, although the company did agree to invest upwards of $500 million to modernize plants that remained open.[2] The USWA-USX contract was approved by union members on January 31. The five-to-one margin of approval was significant. Only one of the forty-seven union locals rejected the pact.[3]

U.S. Steel moved aggressively to resume steel production and to regain lost sales momentum with its customers. Such efforts paid off. By year's end steel sales income had rebounded from a 1986 operating loss of nearly $1.4 million to a 1987 operating income of $125 million.[4] And while company executives were anticipating a drop in domestic steel sales for the coming year, they were projecting an increase in export sales. Better yet, the percentage of imported steel had been dropping for three straight years. The amount of foreign steel that accounted for 25 percent of the American steel market in 1985 was down to 21 percent in 1987.[5] This presumably would bode well for U.S. Steel in coming years.

The company was not nearly as vociferous in its denunciation of steel imports as in years past. And for good reason. The company recently had completed a major transaction with the People's Republic of China (PRC) for purchase of U.S. Steel's Fairless Works steel rod mill. The mill was dismantled and moved piece by piece to the PRC's Anshan plant, and by April 1987 it was up and running. The moving process was impressive. First there was the coding, cataloging, and photographing (18,000 pictures in all) of every piece of the Fairless rod mill destined for disassembly. Then came the "262 truckloads and 86 railroad carloads" of disassembled parts that were carried twenty-two miles from the Fairless plant to the Port of Philadelphia, where they traveled 10,650 nautical miles to Dalian, China, and then 125 miles overland to the Anshan Iron and Steel Company. Reassembly of the rod mill began in October 1986 and was completed by April 1987.[6]

If U.S. Steel's deal with the PRC meant future marketplace competition with the industrial behemoth that the PRC was becoming, there appeared little of the angst, trepidation, and protest over foreign imports that had until so recently become nearly an annual ritual at U.S. Steel. The arrangement with the PRC appeared to be good for the company, and money from the Fairless sale certainly helped significantly in shaping U.S. Steel's steel segment income turnaround for the year. But the company's attitudinal turnaround regarding the threat of overseas steelmakers and its decision to actually assist one of the largest in such dramatic fashion was, at the very least, bewildering.

U.S. Steel's energy sector rebound in 1987 equaled that of the steel sector's. Operating income for the energy sector ended 1987 at $447 million, up considerably from its $52 million 1986 operating income. All but $2 million of the $447 million was attributed to Marathon Oil Company. Texas Oil and Gas Corporation kicked in the additional $2 million. Much of Marathon Oil's improved performance reflected higher crude oil prices. A barrel of crude oil that sold for as little as $11.25 in 1986 was selling for $16.50 by the end of 1987. The potential for future North Sea oil drilling and natural gas drilling in the American Southwest put U.S. Steel in excellent position for continued financial improvement in its energy properties.[7]

U.S. Steel reported to stockholders the company's continued restructuring program in 1987. Properties sold during the year included the Geneva, Utah, steelworks and the American Bridge Division. Stockholders also learned of U.S. Steel Mining Company's improved income picture for 1987 as a result of restructuring in that division. Higher productivity was reported from the company's Oak Grove Coal Mine in Bessemer, Alabama, where a recently installed longwall mining unit was beginning to pay off. A report of mineral reserves showed that U.S. Steel continued to control, by ownership or lease, property that contained roughly 1.86 billion tons of coal.[8] In general, U.S. Steel appeared upbeat about its coal mining prospects. Not surprisingly, nothing about the coal mining situation in Gary, West Virginia, appeared in the company's 1987 annual report.

Folks in Gary Hollow would not have the same success as U.S. Steel in 1987. Even so, there were a few signs early in the year that something positive might be happening there. And just as U.S. Steel seemed to have forgotten about Gary, Gary Hollow residents were thinking less and less about the town's industrial patriarch. Not to be ignored, though, was U.S. Steel's continuing physical presence. Mining hardware and structures remained in place, chief among them the now rusting hulk of the Alpheus preparation plant that had for so long symbolized Gary's central position in U.S. Steel's coal mining empire. The mammoth cluster of buildings, sitting in total silence, came to symbolize something altogether different now.

Also remaining was the two-story stone building in the center of Gary that continued to house U.S. Steel Mining Company's Central Division Operations Office and the company's general superintendent. John Dickinson, who as general superintendent had presided over some of Gary Hollow's toughest years, left in 1987.[9] From the earliest days of the U.S. Coal and Coke Company, the main office, sitting imposingly high above the banks of the Tug River, had served as U.S. Steel's command center in Gary. Tentacles from that building had reached into every facet of life in Gary's satellite towns. Now, a new general superintendent—the last to occupy that position in Gary—replaced John Dickinson with nothing more relative to do in Gary Hollow than to oversee closing down what remained of U.S. Steel's McDowell County coal mining operation. In military parlance the assignment amounted to mop-up duty.

Gary Hollow's employment troubles had attracted national media coverage in the past, and it returned in 1987. In January the *Atlanta Journal and Constitution* gave an account of the situation as "Gary Becomes an 'Old Folks' Town as Younger Generations Vanish." The *Fort Lauderdale News* gave a more ominous bent with "When a Town Dies." The *Fort Lauderdale News* ran its story with a photograph of Gary houses that looked similar to typical middle-income American homes. The *Atlanta Journal and Constitution,* on the other hand, ran photographs showing substandard housing often associated with coal mining communities. The houses were from an area near Gary, but none were located in Gary proper, and none had been built by U.S. Steel. Most of the U.S. Steel houses built in Gary Hollow appeared in the early part of the century. Specifications for the houses—available for public inspection at the Eastern Regional Coal Archives in Bluefield, West Virginia—show that the company had every intention of building sturdy structures that were meant to last. They may not have won any prizes from *Architectural Digest* for their aesthetic appeal, but U.S. Steel nonetheless had cared for them through the years, making necessary repairs and applying fresh coats of paint on a regular basis. Occupants of these houses who now (since the early 1970s) owned them had done even more to improve their appearance and livability. To now represent the houses as substandard was an indignant slap in the face.

The *Atlanta Journal* updated the ongoing saga of travail that centered on Gary's crumbling infrastructure and the departure of the unemployed to find better opportunities elsewhere. There was nothing new either in Mayor Estep's assessment of the town's future: "We'll be down to about 1,600 people next year when some who plan to leave have left. After that, who knows? It's pitiful. Some of our families have lived in Gary for generations. It's hard for some to leave for that reason. Their people are buried here. It's even harder for a middle-aged man who has no skill except mining coal to find another job somewhere else. Face it. The town has been on its deathbed since last July."[10]

Talk that had begun in late 1986 of reopening one or more of the Gary Hollow mines continued into early 1987. Two approaches to reopening were on the table. One was for former mine employees to create a company to buy the mines outright from U.S. Steel. Another was to lease rather than purchase the mines. The lease idea was favored by a group of unemployed miners, Gary officials, and former Welch mayor and coal mine operator W. B. Swope. Swope claimed that it would take up to three years to purchase the Gary Hollow mines, whereas a leasing agreement could be accomplished much faster.

The Swope group remained cautious in making any move and decided to solicit Marshall University's Center for Regional Progress to conduct a feasibility study of any marketing potential for Gary coal. The $32,000 study was funded by money coming equally from the West Virginia governor's office and the state legislature. Marketability was one question to be examined, but there were others. For example, how would expensive machinery needed to operate the mines be financed? What sort of rail shipping fees might new mine operators expect to pay? And what kind of royalty rates might the Pocahontas Land Company, owner of all the land in Gary, demand? The Center for Regional Progress was given a June 29 deadline for finding answers to these and other questions.[11]

Meanwhile, a third group, composed of Gary Enterprises and Iaegar Construction Company, also showed interest in reopening the Gary Hollow mines. Gary Enterprises president Ted Osborne was aggressive in negotiating with U.S. Steel. On July 28, 1987, Osborne announced that he not only had signed an agreement with U.S. Steel to purchase some of the company's mine machinery and other equipment, but also had leased mineral rights from the Pocahontas Land Company that would enable Gary Enterprises to reopen and operate up to four Gary Hollow mines.[12] Arrangements were made to process Gary Enterprise coal at the Soho preparation plant in nearby Premier and to sell the processed coal on the spot market.[13] The No. 2 mine would be the first to reopen—scheduled for early August—followed at two- to three-month intervals by the Nos. 4, 14, and 9 mines. Roughly 300 laid-off miners would be recalled initially to work the mines, with the intention to recall up to 700 miners in all. This would fall short of the 1,100 miners who had been laid off by U.S. Steel the year before, but Ted Osborne suggested that retirement and relocation of many of the 1,100 actually had left only about 700 available miners to work the reopened mines. Of those who would be recalled, seniority and job qualifications would determine the recall order.

West Virginia Governor Arch Moore expressed satisfaction with developments in Gary, and he felt confident that the ability thus far shown by Gary Enterprises in operating nine other coal mines in McDowell and Wyoming Counties was a good sign that the Gary Hollow mines might be operated successfully. Moore helped matters by approving a state grant that accompanied a federal grant of nearly $173,000 to help retrain the returning miners as well as subsidize construction workers who would be bringing the mines back to operational status.[14]

In early August 1987 Gary Enterprises hired about fifteen miners, all of whom had worked for U.S. Steel for many years, to begin the tedious and very important process of pulling the No. 2 mine back to working order. Electrical power had to be restored, along with replacing some equipment and repairing tracks. By early September more recalled miners brought the workforce to about thirty. All had held some level of seniority with U.S. Steel, and all were familiar with the No. 2 mine. Most senior was newly hired mine superintendent Harry Harman. Harman had retired from U.S. Steel after working at the Gary Hollow mines for thirty-five years. Gary Enterprise owners Ted Osbourne and Homer Hopkins had persuaded Harman to come out of retirement to help get the No. 2 mine up and running.

Finally, on September 8, 1987, the No. 2 mine once more was open for business.[15] The occasion was historic. For the first time since the mine became operational in 1902, its ownership fell to a company other than U.S. Steel. The No. 2 mine also had been the first Gary Hollow mine that U.S. Steel had operated on a continuous basis. A 1937 survey of U.S. Coal & Coke Co. mines indicated that the No. 2 mine still was yielding nearly 3,600 tons of coal per day after thirty-five years and that more than 20 million tons of coal remained to be mined there. Assuming normal working conditions and a 300-day work year, the No. 2 mine was estimated to have a remaining lifespan of about nineteen years.[16]

The lifespan estimate obviously missed the mark. The No. 2 mine continued for the next several decades to be one of U.S. Steel's most productive. From 1971 through 1980 alone, West Virginia Department of Mines data showed that the No. 2 mine yielded over 8 million tons of coal.

Even during the erratic years of the 1980s when U.S. Steel was closing, reopening, and closing again so many of its mines, the No. 2 Gary Hollow mine still managed to yield nearly 875,000 tons of coal. Now, after a longer than usual shutdown, coal once more would flow from the mine. Predictions, in fact, placed daily coal production at about three thousand tons, once additional miners were hired and extra shifts were added to the workday. U.S. Steel was estimating that the amount of coal remaining in the No. 2 mine would give it at least a five-year lifespan.[17]

The miners returning to work at the No. 2 mine seemed confident that the operation would be a success. Some were so confident that they had left positions at U.S. Steel mines in Wyoming County to return to jobs with Gary Enterprises. Morale obviously was high, but almost to a person the miners who now were working at No. 2—several of whom were third-generation miners—felt that they would be the last in their families to mine coal. The abundant, good-paying jobs that had persuaded so many young people to enter the mines in times past simply no longer existed. In addition, problems and uncertainties affecting coal mining in general were reasons enough to avoid the business altogether. Among those who were happy to be returning to work at the No. 2 mine, none seemed particularly anxious to have a son or daughter follow in their footsteps.[18]

U.S. Steel's formula for making money was in its stride by 1988 and doing even better in 1989. The company's net income nearly quadrupled from 1987's $219 million to 1988's $756 million and bounced upward again in 1989 to $965 million. The 1988 and 1989 income figures followed sales of roughly $16.9 billion and $18.7 billion, respectively. U.S. Steel's $1.6 billion operating income in 1989, in fact, was noted by USX board chairman and CEO Charles Corry as "the highest ever earned by the Corporation, capping a decade of tumultuous change for [the company] and presaging a period of promise in the 1990s." Corry went on to note that U.S. Steel's energy sector accounted for two-thirds of the company's gross revenues. Even so, the steel sector continued to maintain "its leadership position in the domestic industry." With regard to restructuring, Corry remarked that U.S. Steel's strategic plan carried out during the 1980s had allowed the company to improve its financial health substantially.[19]

Restructuring had resulted in a decade-long series of radical change at U.S. Steel, much of it engineered by David Roderick, whose ten-year tenure at the company's helm ended in 1989. Just how radical these changes were—assets acquired, assets sold or written off, and reduction in payroll employees from 171,654 in 1979 to 53,000 in 1989—was emphasized earlier. Roderick took delight in his accomplishments, particularly with regard to his company's steel business. He addressed the subject before shareholders at U.S. Steel's annual meeting in May 1989: "Our steel sector has been rationalized, with unprofitable lines eliminated and redundant capacity pared. Yet, while reducing our dependence on steel, we have certainly not abandoned nor de-emphasized that sector of our business. We remain America's largest steel producer."[20]

Outside observers and industry analysts also took note of U.S. Steel's "successful restructuring" and reviewed precisely how the company had engineered its turnaround and at what cost: "It eliminated inefficient mills or whole plants, got rid of unprofitable businesses, cut out layers of unneeded management, invested strategically in new technologies, and found the resources to carry out these needed investments. By the early to mid-1990s, this firm and a few other industry giants had been recast. Their gains were achieved at a tremendous cost to both workers and communities. But while the decisions involved were difficult and costly, they were necessary to the survival of the companies."[21]

Roderick had reinvented U.S. Steel, helping to create a steel industry model that would remain in place for some time to come. He had managed to refashion and redirect an industrial giant whose mode of operation had become so firmly entrenched as to defy change. But Roderick had done the nearly impossible. And in doing so, according to *Forbes* magazine, he had succeeded in dismantling J. P. Morgan's and Elbert Gary's "rounded proposition" legacy of "a fully integrated steel giant with seemingly inexhaustible supplies of iron ore, limestone, and coal, which were mined and transported to the mills by the company's large shipping fleet and its own rail lines."[22]

Nowhere more so than in Gary, West Virginia, was the dissolution of the Morgan-Gary "rounded proposition" legacy more apparent. There were few tangible links between U.S. Steel and Gary Hollow that remained as of 1988. Most mine equipment and machinery were transferred to the company's Pineville mine in Wyoming County. What remained was stored in part of the same warehouse that also served as Gary City Hall.[23] One of the most visible artifacts of U.S. Steel days that had yet to be removed was the main office building with its staff of about twenty employees at Gary. But plans were already in place to pack up the Central Division Operations Office and move it to Pineville by mid-April. Staff administrator Gary Gadley said that U.S. Steel had decided on the move in order to place the office closer to the only working coal mine it continued to operate in the area. All but about ten staff employees would be making the move to Pineville immediately. The ten remaining in Gary would handle not only employee benefits for the few former U.S. Steel miners who continued to live in Gary, but also any sublease negotiations for coal companies like Gary Enterprises that wanted to reopen any of the company's remaining Gary Hollow mines or perhaps open a new mine within the area that continued under control of U.S. Steel's original lease.[24]

Within a short time a number of coal companies arranged subleases, hoping to eke out whatever profits they could from what coal remained accessible in the Gary Hollow mines. One of these operators, West

Virginia–Tennessee Coal, was notable for what it agreed to do as part of its sublease arrangement—dismantle the Alpheus preparation plant.[25] Ironically, U.S. Steel had spent nearly a million dollars to update and expand the plant just before the decision to abandon its Gary operation altogether.[26] The expenditure had been a costly error and one that had given false hope to Gary Hollow residents as to U.S. Steel's real intentions. Demolition of the plant would take time, since much of the structure would be salvaged and sold for scrap or for use at other preparation plants. But piece by piece, the steel plates, beams, and other components of the massive building complex began coming down in early 1990. All of the steel that had been used to construct the plant no doubt had come from U.S. Steel itself. Now, as the Alpheus plant began slowly to disappear, the act of its removal became a perfect metaphor for what had been happening in Gary Hollow. As the plant disappeared, so did the last semblance of U.S. Steel's dominance in McDowell County. When the structure was completely gone, the bare foundation that remained was a monument to an era of coal mining prosperity that likely never will be equaled.

Postscript

U.S. Steel's departure from Gary Hollow was not a departure from the company's coal mining business. The company, after all, continued to maintain coal mines, like the ones in Wyoming County, whose reserves amounted to a roughly 400-year supply of coal. Even so, U.S. Steel was mining less and less of that coal each year while continuing to pay heavy taxes on what remained in the ground.[1] Given this scenario, support among U.S. Steel officials for maintaining the company's coal mining interests began to erode.

By the early 1990s U.S. Steel was rumored to be negotiating with potential buyers to divest itself of more mining properties and perhaps of the company's entire mining operation.[2] The rumors proved true, but a deal to sell U.S. Steel's mines was not finalized until July 2003, when the company announced that PinnOak Resources would acquire all U.S. Steel Mining Company assets for a total purchase price to be determined in the future. U.S. Steel received $50 million as an advance payment, but more would be added to that amount once final asset inventory was completed.[3]

The number of mining jobs that remained in Gary Hollow in 1990 was estimated at 180. There were only 1,250 estimated for all of McDowell County. Young persons were encouraged to leave the place once they completed high school, since there obviously was little future for those who remained.[4] And leave they did. Gary's 1990 population was estimated at 1,355, a 39 percent drop from 1980. Among that population, 458 were males, twenty years of age and older. Of the 458 males, 53 percent were fifty-five years of age or older.[5] Clearly, Gary's male population had skewed toward the older crowd. More discouraging yet were numbers from the 2000 U.S. Census that revealed a Gary population estimate of 920—a near 32 percent decline from 1990. Of the 920 residents, age sixteen and over, 340 were males; 424 were females. Little more than a third (37.3 percent) of the Gary population was estimated to be in the labor force. And only 421 of the 543 housing units then existing in Gary were occupied.[6]

Many of those who elected to remain in Gary Hollow were retired. Maybe they could have moved elsewhere, but they owned their home in Gary, they probably had spent much of their life there, and they were content to stay. Some also were content to use their seniority to put them at the head of any recall list. And some, it might be assumed, stayed because they simply had nowhere else to go.

What also was clear was that Gary had come to resemble other McDowell County towns in ways that for so long had kept it apart. All the big coal companies, U.S. Steel being the biggest, now had departed the county. Small operators had moved in to scavenge what coal remained. But the "wagon mines" that these operators opened had about twenty employees per mine. And many of the miners, like the operators themselves, lived in Virginia or perhaps no closer than Bluefield.[7] Oddly, coal mining in Gary Hollow had become a kind of commuter enterprise. Coal production in general migrated toward the western part of the county and away from the once-vaunted Pocahontas Field, which now was capable of yielding far less coal with far less metallurgical quality.[8]

The year 2002 marked Gary's centennial. One hundred years before Gary Hollow was bursting with activity. Trees were falling to make way for mines and communities. Houses and other structures were beginning to appear. Mining engineers were plotting the best spots to begin opening portals to the rich and abundant veins of Pocahontas coal. And the folks who would work the mines and inhabit this place—in some cases for generations to come—began arriving. One hundred years later, there would be no parades, no speeches, no pageants, no celebration of any sort to mark the occasion of Gary's birth. Most Gary Hollow residents probably had no idea that Gary had been around so long. Quite likely, few cared.

The trucks and trains that so seldom moved along Gary Hollow's roads and railroad tracks in 2002 were a constant presence in year's past. Such a buzz of activity as existed in Gary was common for what arguably was the coal capital of the country. Life was good, and money was plentiful. All that a hard-working man had to do to live a good life and earn a decent wage was sign on to work the mines. Then he had to disappear in a hole in the earth for an eight-hour shift (sometimes longer) and do whatever his particular job required. It was well for him not to dwell on the fact that his occupation topped the chart of the most dangerous in America. Moreover, if he could stand the back-breaking work, the cold, the damp, the mud, and the grime of the coal mine, then he might succeed as a miner. Thousands did.

In 2002 Gary was eerily quiet. Activity of any sort was hard to find. Talk, if it was to be heard, often centered on what nearby mine operation was still working and the chance for things to pick up, maybe even some of the local mines, long closed, to reopen. The talk, however, carried little optimism. Down deep, anyone who remained in Gary knew that the community's life was dangling by a thread. And once those few Gary residents who remained were gone, Gary might indeed become the ghost town that it already so closely resembled.

Postscript

Gary, West Virginia, for all that it gave the world, is known to few now. It is a symbol of industrial obsolescence. Coal was Gary's heart and soul. The mineral wealth of all the coal that was carried from Gary was enormous. But coal mining was Gary's singular industry and the economic foundation on which the livelihood of everyone who ever lived in Gary depended. The town literally had nothing else going for it. Gary's geographical boundaries would have prevented it from becoming much else than what it was. Fact is, had there been no coal, there would have been no Gary.

Notes

Introduction

1. John P. Hoerr, *And the Wolf Finally Came: The Decline of the American Steel Industry* (Pittsburgh: Univ. of Pittsburgh Press, 1988), 88.
2. Ibid.
3. Ibid., 88; James H. Bridge, *The Inside Story of the Carnegie Steel Company* (New York: Aldine Book Co., 1903), 169; Christopher G. L. Hall, *Steel Phoenix: The Fall and Rise of the U.S. Steel Industry* (New York: St. Martin's Press, 1997), xiv.
4. Charles H. Ambler and Festus P. Summers, *West Virginia, the Mountain State*, 2d ed. (Englewood Cliffs, NJ: Prentice-Hall, 1958), 336.
5. Stuart McGehee, "Bramwell: 100 Years in the W.Va. Coalfields!" *Coal People*, May 1988, 10–13.
6. George L. Fowler, "Coals and Coal-Mining Methods of the Pocahontas Field," *Engineering Magazine* (May 1904): 217–18; Jack M. Jones, *Early Coal Mining in Pocahontas, Virginia* (Lynchburg, VA: Jack M. Jones, 1983), 3–18.
7. Joseph T. Lambie, *From Mine to Market* (New York: New York Univ. Press, 1954), 39.
8. Houston Kermit Hunter, "The Story of McDowell County," *West Virginia Review* 17 (Apr. 1940): 166.
9. Stephen and Stacy Soltis, *West Virginia: Off the Beaten Path* (Old Saybrook, MA: Globe Pequot Press, 1995), 68.
10. Harry M. Caudill, *Night Comes to the Cumberlands* (Boston: Little, Brown and Co., 1963), xi.
11. Ibid., 342–43.
12. Crandall A. Shifflett, *Coal Towns: Life, Work, and Culture in Company Towns of Southern Appalachia, 1880–1960* (Knoxville: Univ. of Tennessee Press, 1991).
13. See, for instance, Charles Buxton Going, "Village Communities of the Factory, Machine Works, and Mine," *Engineering Magazine* (Apr. 1901): 59–74; F. W. Parsons, "A Modern Coal-Mining Town," *Engineering and Mining Journal* (Nov. 3, 1906): 830–32; Joseph H. White, "Houses for Mining Towns," *Bulletin* (U.S. Dept. of the Interior, Bureau of Mines), vol. 87 (1914): 1–64; Karl B. Lohmann, "A New Era for Mining Towns," *Coal Age* (Nov. 13, 1915): 799-800; Leifur Magnusson, "Company Housing in the Bituminous Coal Fields," *Monthly Labor Review* (U.S. Dept. of Labor, Bureau of Labor Statistics), vol. 10 (Apr. 1920): 215–22; Thomas F. Downing Jr., "Where to

Build Our Mining Towns and What to Build," *Proceedings of the West Virginia Coal Mining Institute* (1923): 41–51; Edward T. Devine, *Coal: Economic Problems of the Mining, Marketing and Consumption of Anthracite and Soft Coal in the United States* (Bloomington, IN: American Review Service Press, 1925), 248–60; C. A. Cabell, "Building a Mining Community," *West Virginia Review* 4 (Apr. 1927): 208–10; and Raymond E. Murphy, "A Southern West Virginia Mining Community," *Economic Geography* 9 (Jan. 1933): 51–59.

14. Gladys Tolleen Ahrenhols, "Factors Affecting Social Participation in Coal Communities" (master's thesis, West Virginia Univ., 1951), 4.

15. Shifflett, *Coal Towns*, 2–3, 9; Mack Henry Gillenwater, "Cultural and Historical Geography of Mining Settlements in the Pocahontas Coal Field of Southern West Virginia, 1880 to 1930," Ph.D. diss., Univ. of Tennessee, 1972, 38–42.

16. Cabell, "Building a Mining Community," 209.

17. Shifflett, *Coal Towns*, xiv.

18. Murphy, "A Southern West Virginia Mining Community," 51.

19. Michael Hornick, interview with author, July 1992.

20. Malcolm Keir, *The Pageant of America: The Epic of Industry* (New Haven, CT: Yale Univ. Press, 1926), 54.

21. Winthrop D. Lane, *Civil War in West Virginia: The Story of the Industrial Conflict in the Coal Mines* (New York: Oriole Chapbooks, 1979), 43.

22. See, for instance, Thomas Condit Miller and Hu Maxwell, *West Virginia and Its People*, vol. 1 (New York: Lewis Historical Publishing Co., 1913); James Morton Callahan, *Semi-Centennial History of West Virginia* (Charleston, WV: Semi-Centennial Commission of West Virginia, 1913); George Byrne, ed., *1915 Hand-Book of West Virginia* (Charleston: West Virginia Panama-Pacific Exposition Commission, 1915); James Morton Callahan, *History of West Virginia, Old and New*, vol. 1 (New York: American Historical Society, 1923); Morris Purdy Shawkey, *West Virginia: In History, Life, Literature and Industry*, vol. 1 (New York: Lewis Publishing Co., 1928); Phil Conley, *The West Virginia Encyclopedia* (Charleston: West Virginia Publishing Co., 1929); and Maude A. Rucker, *West Virginia: Her Land, Her People, Her Traditions, Her Resources* (New York: Walter Neale, 1930).

23. George O. Torok, *A Guide to Historical Coal Towns of the Big Sandy River Valley* (Knoxville: Univ. of Tennessee Press, 2004).

24. Thomas E. Wagner and Phillip J. Obermiller, *African American Miners and Migrants: The Eastern Kentucky Social Club* (Urbana: Univ. of Illinois Press, 2004).

25. Alex P. Schust, *Gary Hollow: A History of the Largest Coal Mining Operation in the World* (Harwood, MD: Two Mule Publishing, 2005).

Chapter 1

1. McDowell County Centennial Committee, *McDowell County Centennial, 1858–1958* (Welch, WV: McDowell County Centennial Committee, 1958), 45–48.

2. Ibid., 9, 44, 94.

3. "More Than Billion Tons of Coal Mined in McDowell," *Welch Daily News*, June 3, 1958.

4. "Train of Gary Produced Coal Would Encircle Earth," *Welch Daily News*, June 3, 1958.

5. Peter J. Smith, ed., *Hutchinson Encyclopedia of the Earth* (London: Century Hutchinson, 1986), 78–79.

6. Dudley H. Cardwell, *Geologic History of West Virginia* (Morgantown: West Virginia Geological and Economic Survey, 1975), 43–44.

7. Sheldon Judson, Marvin E. Kauffman, and L. Don Leet, *Physical Geology*, 7th ed. (Englewood Cliffs, NJ: Prentice Hall, 1987), 366.

8. Cardwell, *Geologic History of West Virginia*, 43–44.

9. Smith, *Hutchinson Encyclopedia of the Earth*, 13, 91; Carla W. Montgomery, *Physical Geology* (Dubuque: Wm. C. Brown, 1987), 227.

10. Cardwell, *Geologic History of West Virginia*, 51–52, 57.

11. Mrs. Samuel Solins and Mrs. Paul W. Jones, *McDowell County History* (Fort Worth: University Supply & Equipment Co., 1959), 9.

12. Anna R. Stratton, "History of McDowell County," *Welch Daily News*, Oct. 7, 1932; Oct. 11, 1932; Oct. 14, 1932; Oct. 18, 1932.

13. William C. Pendleton, *History of Tazewell County and Southwest Virginia, 1748–1920* (Richmond, VA: W. C. Hill Printing Co., 1920), 443–47; William Frederick Neal, "The Indians of Tazewell County," in *History of the Settlement and Indian Wars of Tazewell County, Virginia*, ed. George W. L. Bickley (Parsons, WV: McClain Printing Co., 1974), 71; Ernest M. Howerton, "Logan, the Shawnee Indian Capital of West Virginia—1760 to 1780," *West Virginia History* 16 (July 1955): 328–29.

14. Pendleton, *History of Tazewell County and Southwest Virginia*, 164–65, 167, 171–73, 179.

15. J. Stoddard Johnston, *First Explorations of Kentucky: Doctor Thomas Walker's Journal*, Filson Club Publications No. 13 (Louisville, KY: John P. Morton and Co., 1898), xv–xix, 1–27, 70–71.

16. Ibid., 71n1.

17. Pendleton, *History of Tazewell County and Southwest Virginia*, 237.

18. Stratton, "History of McDowell County," Dec. 16, 1932; Dec. 20, 1932; Dec. 23, 1932.

19. James Webb, *Born Fighting: How the Scots-Irish Shaped America* (New York: Broadway Books, 2004), 9–10, 12–13.

20. Pendleton, *History of Tazewell County and Southwest Virginia*, 486–87, 551–52; Norma Pontiff Evans, *First Families of McDowell County (West) Virginia* (N.p.: Self-published, 1981), v.

21. Edgar B. Sims, *Making a State* (Charleston: State of West Virginia, 1956), 35–36.

22. Callahan, *Semi-Centennial History of West Virginia*, 2–3, 141–51; Elizabeth Cometti and Festus P. Summers, eds., *The Thirty-Fifth State: A Documentary History of West Virginia* (Morgantown: West Virginia Univ. Library, 1966), 337, 376–77; Ambler and Summers, *West Virginia*, 229–48.

23. Stuart McGehee, "Jordan Nelson's Coalbank," *Coal People Magazine* (Sept. 1988), 11–12.

Chapter 2

1. Phyllis Deane, *The First Industrial Revolution* (London: Cambridge Univ. Press, 1965), vii; Gavin Weightman, *The Industrial Revolutionaries: The Making of the Modern World, 1776–1914* (New York: Grove Press, 2007), 1–9.
2. Deane, *The First Industrial Revolution*, 75–76.
3. Thomas Southcliffe Ashton, *Iron and Steel in the Industrial Revolution*, 2d ed. (Great Britain: Manchester Univ. Press, 1951), 3–5.
4. Ibid., 5–7.
5. Barbara Freese, *Coal: A Human History* (Cambridge, MA: Perseus Books, 2003), 6.
6. Ibid., 65.
7. T. S. Ashton, *The Industrial Revolution, 1760–1830* (New York: Oxford Univ. Press, 1972), 29; Ashton, *Iron and Steel in the Industrial Revolution*, 8–9.
8. Ashton, *Iron and Steel in the Industrial Revolution*, 9.
9. Ibid., 65; Weightman, *The Industrial Revolutionaries*, 25.
10. Deane, *The First Industrial Revolution*, 104.
11. Ibid., 74–76; Freese, *Coal*, 22.
12. Deane, *The First Industrial Revolution*, 75–76, 111.
13. Weightman, *The Industrial Revolutionaries*, 25.
14. Ibid., 48–56; Deane, *The First Industrial Revolution*, 106.
15. Deane, *The First Industrial Revolution*, 109.
16. Weightman, *The Industrial Revolutionaries*, 58–60, 118–35; Deane, *The First Industrial Revolution*, 113, 156–57; Freese, *Coal*, 87–95; Ashton, *The Industrial Revolution, 1760–1830*, 60.
17. Weightman, *The Industrial Revolutionaries*, 93–103, 139–40.
18. Ibid., 140–50.
19. Ibid., 140–41.
20. Victor S. Clark, *History of Manufactures in the United States, 1860–1914* (Washington, DC: Carnegie Institution of Washington, 1928), 73.
21. William T. Hogan, *Economic History of the Iron and Steel Industry in the United States* (Lexington, MA: Lexington Books, 1971), 1: 1–2.
22. Ibid., 2.
23. Paul Paskoff, "Charcoal Fuel," in *Iron and Steel in the Nineteenth Century*, ed. Paul Paskoff (New York: Facts on File, 1989), 84; Hogan, *Economic History* 1: 1.
24. Hogan, *Economic History* 1: 3.
25. Weightman, *The Industrial Revolutionaries*, 40–47, 141.
26. Freese, *Coal*, 13, 106–13; Quincy Bent, *Early Days of Iron and Steel* (New York: Newcomen Society in North America, 1950), 11–12.
27. Peter Temin, *Iron and Steel in Nineteenth-Century America* (Cambridge, MA: MIT Press, 1964), 83–85.
28. Hogan, *Economic History* 1: 23–25.
29. Freese, *Coal*, 121–23.
30. Hogan, *Economic History* 1: 38.
31. William McKinley Merrill, "Economics of the Southern Smokeless Coals," Ph.D. diss., Univ. of Illinois, 1953, 57.
32. Temin, *Iron and Steel in Nineteenth-Century America*, 200–201; Clark, *History of Manufactures*, 514.

33. Temin, *Iron and Steel in Nineteenth-Century America*, 200–201; Clark, *History of Manufactures*, 204; Hogan, *Economic History* 1: 25.
34. Clark, *History of Manufactures*, 515–16.
35. Ibid., 514–16.
36. David Nasaw, *Andrew Carnegie* (New York: Penguin Press, 2006), 209–10; Stewart H. Holbrook, *The Age of Moguls* (Garden City, NY: Doubleday & Co., 1954), 80–83; Matthew Josephson, *The Robber Barons: The Great American Capitalists, 1861–1901* (New York: Harcourt Brace Jovanovich, 1934), 261–64.
37. Freese, *Coal*, 137–38.
38. Nasaw, *Andrew Carnegie*, 209–10, 290.
39. Ibid., 141; Josephson, *The Robber Barons*, 107.
40. Weightman, *The Industrial Revolutionaries*, 270–79; Temin, *Iron and Steel in Nineteenth-Century America*, 125; Thomas J. Misa, *A Nation of Steel: The Making of Modern America, 1865–1925* (Baltimore: Johns Hopkins Univ. Press, 1995), 5–14.
41. Clark, *History of Manufactures*, 62, 514; Hogan, *Economic History* 1: 17–22.
42. Nasaw, *Andrew Carnegie*, 513–17.
43. Ibid., 141–43; Josephson, *The Robber Barons*, 254.
44. Nasaw, *Andrew Carnegie*, 399.
45. Ibid.
46. Misa, *A Nation of Steel*, xx; Clark, *History of Manufactures*, 655, 692–93; Ray Ginger, *Age of Excess: The United States from 1877 to 1914*, 2d ed. (New York: Macmillan Publishing Co., 1975), 39–40.
47. Nasaw, *Andrew Carnegie*, 517.
48. Ibid., 400–401; Hogan, *Economic History* 1: 238; Clark, *History of Manufactures*, 590–91.
49. Clark, *History of Manufactures*, 540–41.
50. Ibid., 235–36.
51. Ibid., 237.
52. Kenneth Warren, *Triumphant Capitalism: Henry Clay Frick and the Industrial Transformation of America* (Pittsburgh: Univ. of Pittsburgh Press, 1996), 49–51; Nasaw, *Andrew Carnegie*, 289; Hogan, *Economic History* 1: 270.
53. Ida M. Tarbell, *The Life of Elbert H. Gary: The Story of Steel* (New York: D. Appleton and Co., 1925), 18–21, 46–49, 68–69, 76–77, 86–89.
54. Ibid., 90–95.
55. Clark, *History of Manufactures*, 580–81.
56. Nasaw, *Andrew Carnegie*, 553.
57. Josephson, *The Robber Barons*, 290–314, 404–7, 409, 411, 413–14.
58. Nasaw, *Andrew Carnegie*, 585.
59. Jean Strouse, *Morgan: American Financier* (New York: Harper Collins, 1999), 395–403; Nasaw, *Andrew Carnegie*, 560–65, 579–87; Holbrook, *The Age of Moguls*, 144–56; Josephson, *The Robber Barons*, 417–28.
60. Nasaw, *Andrew Carnegie*, 585; Hogan, *Economic History* 2: 471; Holbrook, *The Age of Moguls*, 151; Clark, *History of Manufactures*, 591; Josephson, *The Robber Barons*, 425.
61. Clark, *History of Manufactures*, 591.

62. Hogan, *Economic History* 2: 470–72; Lambie, *From Mine to Market*, 238.
63. Strouse, *Morgan*, 404.
64. Clark, *History of Manufactures*, 593; Misa, *A Nation of Steel*, 170.
65. Hogan, *Economic History* 2: 472–73; Clark, *History of Manufactures*, 591–92.
66. Clark, *History of Manufactures*, 591–94.

Chapter 3

1. Thomas Jefferson, *Notes on the State of Virginia*, ed. William Peden (Chapel Hill: Univ. of North Carolina Press, 1955), 28–29.
2. William Barton Rogers, *A Reprint of Annual Reports and Other Papers, on the Geology of the Virginias* (New York: Appleton and Co., 1884), 28, 113–14; Jerry B. Thomas, "Jedediah Hotchkiss, Gilded-Age Propagandist of Industrialism," *Virginia Magazine of History and Biography* 84 (Apr. 1976): 191.
3. J. R. Dodge, *West Virginia: Its Farms and Forests, Mines and Oil-Wells* (Philadelphia: J. B. Lippincott & Co., 1865), 160–67; James Macfarlane, *The Coal-Regions of America: Their Topography, Geology, and Development* (New York: D. Appleton & Co., 1873), 263–302.
4. M. F. Maury and William M. Fontaine, *Resources of West Virginia* (Wheeling, WV: Register Co., 1876), 193, 392.
5. Thomas, "Jedediah Hotchkiss," 189, 200.
6. Ibid., 189–90, 192–93.
7. Peter L. Bernstein, *Wedding of the Waters: The Erie Canal and the Making of a Great Nation* (New York: W. W. Norton & Co., 2005), 41.
8. Mark Twain and Charles Dudley Warner, *The Gilded Age: A Tale of To-Day* (Hartford, CT: American Publishing Co., 1880), 567.
9. Lambie, *From Mine to Market*, 40; W. P. Tams Jr., *The Smokeless Coal Fields of West Virginia: A Brief History* (Morgantown: West Virginia Univ. Press, 1983), 16.
10. Ronald D. Eller, *Miners, Millhands, and Mountaineers: Industrialization of the Appalachian South, 1880–1930* (Knoxville: Univ. of Tennessee Press, 1982), 44–64; David Alan Corbin, *Life, Work, and Rebellion in the Coal Fields: The Southern West Virginia Miners, 1880–1922* (Urbana: Univ. of Illinois Press, 1981), 3–4.
11. Randall Lawrence, "Appalachian Metamorphosis: Industrializing Society on the Central Appalachian Plateau, 1860–1913 (West Virginia, Kentucky, Tennessee, Virginia)," Ph.D. diss., Duke Univ., 1983, 65–68.
12. General Assembly of Virginia, "An Act, to Authorize the Formation of the New River Railroad, Mining and Manufacturing Company," Mar. 7, 1872, in Norfolk and Western R.R. Company, Corporate History, *General Railroad Laws*, 689–91, Norfolk & Western Archives, Virginia Tech Library, Blacksburg, VA [hereafter N&W Archives, Virginia Tech]; Pendleton, *History of Tazewell County and Southwest Virginia*, 660–61; David E. Johnston, *A History of Middle New River Settlements and Contiguous Territory* (Huntington, WV: Standard Printing & Publishing Co., 1906), 350–51.
13. Thomas, "Jedediah Hotchkiss," 194.
14. Pendleton, *History of Tazewell County and Southwest Virginia*, 661–62.
15. Thomas, "Jedediah Hotchkiss," 194.

16. General Assembly of Virginia, "An Act to Amend and Re-enact Section First of the Act to Authorize the Formation of the New River Railroad, Mining and Manufacturing Company as Amended by Acts Approved 2d Apr., 1873, and 15th March, 1875, and to Change the Name of Said Company to the New River Railroad Company," March 4, 1880, in Norfolk and Western R.R. Company, Corporate History, *General Railroad Laws*, 698–99, N&W Archives, Virginia Tech.

17. Lambie, *From Mine to Market*, 31, 32.

18. Ibid., 19; Thomas, "Jedediah Hotchkiss," 197–98; Allen W. Moger, "Railroad Practices and Policies in Virginia after the Civil War," *Virginia Magazine* 59 (Oct. 1951): 434, 436; Robert H. Smith, *General William Mahone, Frederick J. Kimball and Others—A Short History of the Norfolk & Western Railway* (New York: Newcomen Society in North America, 1949), 22–24; Lawrence, "Appalachian Metamorphosis," 41.

19. Lambie, *From Mine to Market*, 32–34; Smith, *General William Mahone*, 24.

20. Lambie, *From Mine to Market*, 35, 38–39; Flat Top Land Trust, *First Annual Report*, 1887, 23.

21. Lambie, *From Mine to Market*, 39; Tams, *The Smokeless Coal Fields of West Virginia*, 20.

22. Norfolk and Western Railroad Co., *First Annual Report*, Dec. 31, 1881, 15; *Second Annual Report*, Dec. 31, 1882, 13.

23. Jed Hotchkiss to F. J. Kimball, Apr. 14, 1881, File: NW RR Co., Hotchkiss, Jed—Report on extension to coal basin, Box: Norfolk & Western Railroad Co., 1.82, N&W Archives, Virginia Tech.

24. W. W. Coe to F. J. Kimball, Apr. 17, 1885, File: NW RR Co., Line to the Ohio River—Reports and Estimates, 1885–86, Box: Norfolk & Western Railroad Co., 1.85, N&W Archives, Virginia Tech.

25. E. F. Pat Striplin, *The Norfolk & Western: A History*, rev. ed. (Forest, VA: Norfolk & Western Historical Society, 1997), 53; Eugene L. Huddleston, *Appalachian Crossing: The Pocahontas Roads* (Sterling, VA: TLC Publishing, 1989), 29–40.

26. Lambie, *From Mine to Market*, 120–33; W. W. Coe to F. J. Kimball, May 3, 1886, and June 10, 1886, File: NW RR Co. Line to the Ohio River—Reports and Estimates, 1885–86, Box: Norfolk & Western Railroad Co., 1.85; Harvey Linton, letter to W. W. Coe, February, 1888, File: NW RR Co., Ohio Extension Line to Ohio R. Via Big Sandy—Reports, etc., 1888, Box: Norfolk and Western Railroad Co., 1.88, N&W Archives, Virginia Tech.

27. Lambie, *From Mine to Market*, 237; E. W. Clark to F. J. Kimball, Jan. 4, 1888, Norfolk & Western Railroad, letters referring to the projected completion of the Norfolk and Western Railroad Co., with lines centering on the Ohio River, File: NW RR Co., Ohio Extension Line to Ohio R. Via Big Sandy—reports, etc., 1888, Box: Norfolk and Western Railroad Co., 1.88, N&W Archives, Virginia Tech.

28. See, for instance, J. C. McClenathan et al., *Centennial History of the Borough of Connellsville* (Connellsville, PA: Connellsville Area Historical Society, 1982), 263–91; Howard N. Eavenson, "The Connellsville Region," *Mines and Minerals* (Aug. 1902): 26–29; C. S. Wardley, "The Early Development of the H. C. Frick Coke Company," *West Pennsylvania Historical Magazine* 32

(1949): 79–86; Kenneth Warren, *Wealth, Waste, and Alienation: Growth and Decline in the Connellsville Coke Industry* (Pittsburgh: Univ. of Pittsburgh Press, 2001); Kenneth Warren, *Triumphant Capitalism: Henry Clay Frick and the Industrial Transformation of America* (Pittsburgh: Univ. of Pittsburgh Press, 1996); "The Connellsville Coke Regions: Their Past, Present and Future," Special Historical and Statistical Number, *(Connellsville) Weekly Courier,* May 1914, clipping in Coal and Coke Heritage Center, Pennsylvania State Univ., Fayette.

29. Charles Kenneth Sullivan, "Coal Men and Coal Towns: Development of the Smokeless Coalfields of Southern West Virginia, 1873–1923," Ph.D. diss., Univ. of Pittsburgh, 1979, 1, 19, 41–42.

30. *Coal and the Norfolk and Western Railway* (Roanoke, VA: N&W Historical Society, 1996), 6.

31. Merrill, "Economics of the Southern Smokeless Coals," 8–10.

32. Jerry Bruce Thomas, "Coal Country: The Rise of the Southern Smokeless Coal Industry and Its Effect on Area Development, 1872–1910," Ph.D. diss., Univ. of North Carolina at Chapel Hill, 1971, 8.

33. As quoted in Gillenwater, "Cultural and Historical Geography," 3–4.

34. Jed Hotchkiss, "The Great Flat-Top Coal-Field," *Virginias* (June 1882): 88.

35. Jed Hotchkiss, "The Bluestone—Flat-Top Coal-Field," *Virginias* (June 1882): 93.

36. Andrew S. McCreath, *The Mineral Wealth of Virginia* (Harrisburg, PA: Lane S. Hart, 1884), iv, 110–11.

37. Jed Hotchkiss, "The Coke Question," *Virginias* (April 1883): 49–51; McClenathan et al., *Centennial History of the Borough of Connellsville,* 164.

38. Editorial, *(Connellsville) Weekly Courier,* Special Historical and Statistical Number, May 1914.

39. "A Brief Outline of the development of the Great Connellsville Coke Region, located in Fayette and Westmoreland Counties, State of Pennsylvania," for distribution at the Chicago World's Fair, 1893, Coal and Coke Heritage Center, Pennsylvania State Univ., Fayette, 2.

40. F. E. Saward, "The Connellsville Coke Region," *Engineering Magazine* (Oct. 1900): 28.

41. Sullivan, "Coal Men and Coal Towns," 18, 20.

42. Christopher H. Marston and Elizabeth Fairbanks, "Connellsville Coal and Coke Region," Southwestern Pennsylvania Recording Project, Connellsville Historical Society, Connellsville, Pennsylvania, 1–2.

43. "The Industrial Wars of the Connellsville Coke Region," in "The Connellsville Coke Regions: Their Past, Present and Future," 28.

44. Frank Helvestine, "The Building of the 'Ohio Extension,'" *Norfolk and Western Magazine,* Oct. 1924, 8, 75–76.

45. William Seymour Edwards, *Coals and Cokes in West Virginia* (Cincinnati: Robert Clarke & Co., 1892), 116.

46. McGehee, "Bramwell: 100 Years in the W.Va. Coalfields," 10–11.

47. Sullivan, "Coal Men and Coal Towns," 141–44; Ken Sullivan, "Coal Men of the Smokeless Coalfields," *West Virginia History* 41 (Winter 1980): 160–62.

48. Tarbell, *The Life of Elbert H. Gary,* 88–89.

49. Flat Top Land Trust, *First Annual Report,* 1887, 20.

50. Schust, *Gary Hollow*, 39.
51. Flat Top Land Trust, *First Annual Report*, 20; E. W. Clark to F. J. Kimball, 2; Lambie, *From Mine to Market*, 241.
52. Warren, *Triumphant Capitalism*, 324–27.
53. George W. Summers, *The Mountain State: A Description of the Natural Resources of West Virginia* (Charleston: Board of World's Fair Managers for West Virginia, 1893), 201.
54. Lambie, *From Mine to Market*, 237–39.
55. Ibid., 237, 239–41, 243–51; Ronald L. Lewis, "Railroads, Deforestation, and the Transformation of Agriculture in the West Virginia Back Counties, 1880–1920," in *Appalachia in the Making: The Mountain South in the Nineteenth Century*, ed. Mary Beth Pudup, Dwight B. Billings, and Altina L. Waller (Chapel Hill: Univ. of North Carolina Press, 1995), 299.
56. Lambie, *From Mine to Market*, 241, 247, 249–50.
57. Ibid., 187, 240–41.

Chapter 4

1. Schust, *Gary Hollow*, 41; "A Trip to the West Virginia Coal Mines," *U.S. Steel News*, July 1944, 13.
2. Corporate Agreement, United States Coal and Coke Company, June 13, 1902, draft copy available at Eastern Regional Coal Archives, Bluefield, WV (hereafter ERCA).
3. Schust, *Gary Hollow*, 41–46.
4. "Steel Trust Lets Local Contracts," *Bluefield Daily Telegraph*, June 15, 1902, emphasis added.
5. Schust, *Gary Hollow*, 286, 312.
6. "The United States Steel Corportation in the Pocahontas Field," *The Coal Trade Journal* (Feb. 12, 1902): 100.
7. "United States Coal and Coke Company," *Engineering and Mining Journal* (Feb. 15, 1902): 254.
8. Ibid. (May 10, 1902): 676.
9. Ibid. (June 28, 1902): 908.
10. Schust, *Gary Hollow*, 267–69.
11. Norfolk and Western Railway Co., *Seventh Annual Report*, Aug. 11, 1903; *Eighth Annual Report*, 1904, 13; Richard E. Prince, *Norfolk & Western Railway, Pocahontas Coal Carrier* (Millard, NE: R. E. Prince, 1980), 68.
12. George R. Wood, "United States C. & C. Company's Operations in W.Va.," *Mines and Minerals* (Nov. 1903): 153, emphasis added.
13. Ibid.
14. Schust, *Gary Hollow*, 149.
15. Robert F. Munn, "The Development of Model Towns in the Bituminous Coal Fields," *West Virginia History* 40 (Spring 1979): 243–45.
16. Donald R. Beeson to Michael Hornick, Dec. 31, 1975, Mike Hornick Collection, ERCA.
17. Ibid.
18. Robert Hundt, as quoted in S. H. F. Hickey, *Workers in Imperial Germany: The Miners of the Ruhr* (Oxford, UK: Clarendon Press, 1985), 63–64.

19. Beeson to Hornick, Dec. 31, 1975.
20. Howard N. Eavenson, "Labor Problems in Southern West Virginia," *Mining and Metallurgy* (Mar. 1923): 129; William Z. Price, "Steel Corporation Mines at Gary," *Colliery Engineer* (Mar. 1914): 471.
21. Price, "Steel Corporation Mines at Gary," 471.
22. Schust, *Gary Hollow*, 313.
23. W. W. Coe to F. J. Kimball, July 13, 1888, File: NW RR Co., Ohio Extension to Ohio R. Via Big Sandy—maps, profiles, etc., 1888, Box: Norfolk and Western Railroad Co. 1.88, N&W Archives, Virginia Tech.
24. "County's Hills Once Echoed Stroke of the Woodman's Axe," *Welch Daily News*, Sept. 21, 1926; Anna R. Stratton, "History of McDowell County: Industrial Development—Chapter IX, Timber Resources," *Welch Daily News*, Feb. 7, 1933.
25. Photograph, "No. 6 Works: Nunar & Carr Sawmill at the Mouth of Mont Murphy Branch Near Present Little League Field," ERCA.
26. Gillenwater, "Cultural and Historical Geography," 70–86.
27. Schust, *Gary Hollow*, 157–60, 165–69.
28. Plan No. 26, Superintendent's House, United States Coal and Coke Company, Inc., Gary, W.Va., Engineer's Office, Feb. 14, 1910; Details, Plan No. 26, Superintendent's House, United States Coal and Coke Company, Inc., Gary, W.Va., Feb. 23, 1910, ERCA.
29. Schust, *Gary Hollow*, 185, 195, 219–25, 240–42, 251–64, 271, 273, 311, 317.
30. E. F. Ketter, "History of United States Coal and Coke Company," June 15, 1945, ERCA, 6.
31. Edward O'Toole, "Power Use in Mining," *Proceedings* (West Virginia Coal Mining Institute) (1910): 29.
32. Norfolk & Western Railway Co., Pocahontas Division, Time Table No. 24, Effective 5:00 a.m., Sunday, January 18th 1903, N&W Archives, Virginia Tech.
33. "Busy Scenes on the Banks of the Tug," *Bluefield Daily Telegraph*, July 14, 1903.
34. See, for instance, Charles Buxton Going, "Village Communities of the Factory, Machine Works, and Mine," *Engineering Magazine* (Apr. 1901): 59–74; F. W. Parsons, "A Modern Coal-Mining Town," *Engineering and Mining Journal* (Nov. 3, 1906): 830–32; W. M. Judd, "Miners' Houses and Mining Towns," *Proceedings* (Coal Mining Institute of America) (1910): 109–33; Leifur Magnusson, "Housing by Employers in the United States," *Bulletin* (U.S. Dept. of Labor, Bureau of Labor Statistics), no. 263 (Oct. 1920): 1–283; Joseph H. White, *Houses for Mining Towns* (Washington, DC: U.S. Dept. of the Interior, Bureau of Mines, 1914); Karl B. Lohmann, "A New Era for Mining Towns," *Coal Age* (Nov. 13, 1915): 799–800; R. H. Hamill, "Design of Buildings in Mining Towns," *Coal Age* (June 16, 1917): 1045–1048; A. F. Huebner, "Houses for Mine Villages," *Coal Age* (Oct. 27, 1917): 717–20; Leifur Magnusson, "Employers' Housing in the United States," *Monthly Review* (U.S. Dept. of Labor, Bureau of Labor Statistics), vol. 5 (Nov. 1917): 869–94; George H. Miller, "Plan Your Town as Carefully as You Would Your Plant," *Coal Age* (June 20, 1918): 130–32; Leifur Magnusson, "Housing: Sanitary Aspects of Company Housing," *Monthly Labor Review* (U.S. Dept. of Labor, Bureau of Labor Statistics), vol. 8 (Jan. 1919): 289–99; Leifur Magnusson, "Housing: Company Housing in the Bituminous Coal Fields,"

Monthly Labor Review (U.S. Dept. of Labor, Bureau of Labor Statistics), vol. 10 (Apr. 1920): 1045–52; Thomas F. Downing Jr., "Where to Build Our Mining Towns and What to Build"; L. Brandt, "Housing the Coal Industry," *Proceedings of the West Virginia Coal Mining Institute*, (1923): 51–64.

35. "Gardens and Playgrounds in Mining Towns," *Coal Age* (Sept. 7, 1912): 336–37.

36. C. E. Owen, "A Successful Centralization of Township Schools," *Coal Age* (Apr. 1, 1916): 601–4; C. H. Archer, "School Consolidation at Gary, McDowell County, W.Va.," *Coal Age* (May 6, 1916): 807–8.

37. "Company Schools at Gary, W.Va.," *Coal Age* (July 12, 1913): 61; "Coal Company Makes an Exhibit of Practical Housekeeping," *Coal Age* (May 2, 1914): 738.

38. U.S. Congress, Committee on Mines and Mining, "Bituminous Coal—Detailed Labor and Engineering Studies," pt. 3, *Report of the United States Coal Commission* (Washington, DC: Government Printing Office, 1925), 1411–1602; Harold U. Faulkner and Mark Starr, *Labor in America*, rev. ed. (New York: Oxford Book, Co., 1957), 169–70.

39. See, for instance, George R. Wood, "Electrical Equipment," *Mines and Minerals* (Dec. 1906): 193–97; John S. Walker, "Coal Mining Methods at Gary, West Virginia," *Engineering and Mining Journal* (July 3, 1909): 6–10; George R. Wood, "Electricity in Mines," *Proceedings of the American Institute of Electrical Engineers* (Aug. 1909): 1095–1105; O'Toole, "Power Use in Mining," 26–35; Howard N. Eavenson, "Construction Engineering of Modern Coal Plants," *Proceedings of the West Virginia Coal Mining Institute* (1910): 76–87; Howard N. Eavenson, "Engineering of Modern Coal Plants," *Mines and Minerals* (Aug. 1910): 57–59; Vitus Klier, "Mine Laboratory Work at Gary, W.Va.," *Mines and Minerals* (Nov. 1910): 217–18; "Electricity in a Group of Mines," *Coal Age* (Mar. 29, 1913): 485–87; Price, "Steel Corporation Mines at Gary," 463–72; W. H. Grady, "The System of Mining in the Pocahontas Region," *Coal Age* (Jan. 24, 1914): 156–59; William H. Grady, "Cost Factors in Coal Production," *Transactions* (American Institute of Mining Engineers), vol. 51 (1916): 138–76; Edward O'Toole, "Pocahontas Coal Field and Operating Methods of the United States Coal and Coke Company," *Coal Age* (Mar. 8, 1923): 399–407; "Pathways in the Hills," *West Virginia Review* (July 1943): 5–10.

40. Walker, "Coal Mining Methods at Gary, West Virginia," 10.

41. Elbert Gary, "Human Life—Worth Saving," *Coal Age* (Sept. 1927): 124; Raynel C. Bolling, "Rendering Labor Safe in Mine and Mill," *Year Book* (American Iron and Steel Institute) (1912): 107.

42. Peter Westleigh, "Safety the First Consideration," *Coal Age* (Mar. 1, 1913): 347–49; Frank H. Kneeland, "Safety in West Virginia," *Coal Age* (Feb. 7, 1914): 243–47; (Feb. 21, 1914): 314–18.

43. Howard Eavenson, "Safety Methods and Organizations of United States Coal and Coke Company," *Transactions* (American Institute of Mining Engineers) (1916): 319–64; Maltby Shipp, "Report of the Secretary of the Committee on Safety and Sanitation," *Transactions* (American Institute of Mining Engineers) (1918): 260–62.

44. "Moving Pictures," *Colliery Engineer* (Sept. 1913): 97–98, (Mar. 1914): 495–97; Frank H. Kneeland, "The Moving Picture in Coal Mining," *Coal Age* (June 27, 1914): 1036–40.

45. "Thomas Lynch," *Coal Age* (Jan. 16, 1915): 130.

46. "William Glyde Wilkins," *History of Pittsburgh and Environs* (New York: American Historical Society, 1922), 175; "Engineer and Author Succumbs," *Pittsburgh Dispatch,* Apr. 13, 1921.

47. "United States Coal and Coke Company," 254; advertisement, W. G. Wilkins Co., *Coal Field Directory and Mining Catalog,* 1915, 71; advertisement, Coal Mining Institute of America, *Proceedings,* 1907, 1908, 1910.

48. Beeson to Hornick; "Howard Nicholas Eavenson," in *Western Pennsylvanians,* ed. Charles Alexander Rook (Pittsburgh: Western Pennsylvania Biographical Association, 1923), 192, 366.

49. "In Memoriam," *Carnegie Magazine,* Mar. 1953, 101; "Howard Nicholas Eavenson," *History of Pittsburgh and Environs* (New York: American Historical Society, 1922), 313; "Memorial Resolution in Honor of Howard N. Eavenson," *Mining Engineering* (July 1953): 729; "Howard Nicholas Eavenson," *National Cyclopaedia of American Biography* 39 (1954): 554–55.

50. See, for example, "Safety Methods and Organization of United States Coal and Coke Company"; "Construction Engineering of Modern Coal Plants"; "Engineering of Modern Coal Plants"; "Labor Problems in Southern West Virginia"; "The Connellsville Region"; and "Beehive Oven Construction," *Mines and Minerals* (Sept. 1906): 80–82; "Building Complete Thousand-Dwelling Town for a Mine Population of 7,000 at Lynch, Kentucky," *Coal Age* (Oct. 6, 1921): 532–36; "Bathhouse, Hospital and Heating Arrangements Provided for Employees of Lynch Mine in Kentucky," *Coal Age* (Oct. 27, 1921): 676–78; "Mining an Upper Bituminous Seam after a Lower Seam Has Been Extracted," *Transactions* (American Institute of Mining and Metallurgical Engineers) (1923): 398–405; "Data about Labor Employed in Various Bituminous Coal Mines," *Transactions* (American Institute of Mining and Metallurgical Engineers) (1924): 805–25; "Seventy-five Years of Progress in Bituminous Coal Mining," in *Seventy-five Years of Progress in the Mineral Industry, 1871–1946,* ed. A. B. Parsons (New York: American Institute of Mining and Metallurgical Engineers, 1947), 223–46; and "The Low-Volatile Coal Field of Southern West Virginia," *Transactions* (American Institute of Mining and Metallurgical Engineers) (1932): 74–99.

51. Beeson to Hornick.

52. "E. O. O'Toole," in Fred R. Toothman, *Great Coal Leaders of West Virginia* (Huntington, WV: Vandalia Book Co., 1988), 200–205; Keith Dixon, *What's a Coal Miner to Do? The Mechanization of Coal Mining* (Pittsburgh: Univ. of Pittsburgh Press, 1988), 37–38; Frank Kneeland, "O'Toole Machine Is a Combined Cutter and Loader," *Coal Age* (May 28, 1925): 783–87.

53. Schust, *Gary Hollow,* 169.

54. Stuart McGehee, "Gary, A First Class Mining Operation," in *The History of McDowell County, West Virginia, 1858–1999,* ed. Thomas C. Hatcher et al. (War, WV: McDowell County Historical Society, n.d.), 106–7.

55. L. Edward Purcell, *Immigration* (Phoenix: Oryx Press, 1995), xiii, 43, 53.

56. The Immigration Commission, *Immigrants in Industries* 1, pt. 1, *Bituminous Coal Mining* (Washington, DC: U.S. Government Printing Office, 1911), 23, 43; Hoerr, *And the Wolf Finally Came,* 84–85, 169–71.

57. Peter Roberts, *The New Immigration* (New York: Macmillan Co., 1912), 54–57.

58. "Directory of Coal Companies in the Pocahontas–Flat Top Field," *Bluefield Daily Telegraph*, Nov. 3, 1896; N&W map, Pocahontas Coal District, *Coal and the Norfolk and Western Railway*, back page insert.

59. USCC Payroll, No. 2 Works, Mar. 1–15, 1910, ERCA.

60. O'Toole, "Power Use in Mining," 28.

61. USCC Payroll, No. 1 Works, Jan. 16–31, 1904, ERCA.

62. Ibid.

63. USCC Engineers Pay Roll for Month ending Jan. 31, 1904, ERCA.

64. Stan Cohen, *King Coal: A Pictorial Heritage of West Virginia Coal Mining* (Charleston, WV: Pictorial Histories Publishing Co., 1984), 11; O'Toole, "Pocahontas Coal Field," 402; Westleigh, "Safety the First Consideration," 347; Eller, *Miners, Millhands, and Mountaineers*, 176.

65. Westleigh, "Safety the First Consideration," 347; O'Toole, "Pocahontas Coal Field," 400, 402; Eavenson, "Mining an Upper Bituminous Seam," 398.

66. Eavenson, "Engineering of Modern Coal Plants," 57.

67. "Electricity in a Group of Mines," *Coal Age* (Mar. 29, 1913): 487.

68. West Virginia, U.S.A., Dept. of Mines, *Annual Report*, June 30, 1920, 101; July 1, 1924, to Dec. 31, 1925, 68.

69. Warren, *Wealth, Waste, and Alienation*, 157–94, 229.

70. Coal Mines in the State of West Virginia, U.S.A., *Twenty-second Annual Report*, June 30, 1904, 27, 75; *Twenty-third Annual Report*, June 30, 1905, 32, 81; *Twenty-fourth Annual Report*, June 30, 1906, 40, 94; *Annual Report*, June 30, 1907, 25–26, 84; June 30, 1908, 25, 89; June 30, 1909, 25, 89–90; June 30, 1910, 29, 101; June 30, 1911, 33, 115.

71. Kenneth Warren, *Big Steel: The First Century of the United States Steel Corporation, 1901–2001* (Pittsburgh: Univ. of Pittsburgh Press, 2001), 83–85, 363; Brian Apelt, *The Corporation: A Centennial Biography of United States Steel Corporation, 1901–2001* (Pittsburgh: Cathedral Publishing, 2000), 68, 85–88; Clark, *History of Manufacturers*, 596, 639.

72. Warren, *Big Steel*, 64, 86–103, 124.

73. Ibid., 363–64; Schust, *Gary Hollow*, 115, 117.

Chapter 5

1. Josephson, *The Robber Barons*, 372.

2. Ibid., 368–72.

3. Warren, *Wealth, Waste, and Alienation*, 77–105.

4. Nasaw, *Andrew Carnegie*, 363, 386, 390–93, 409–27, 456, 469–71.

5. Gerald G. Eggert, *Steelmasters and Labor Reform, 1886–1923* (Pittsburgh: Univ. of Pittsburgh Press, 1981), 33.

6. Paul A. Tiffany, *The Decline of American Steel: How Management, Labor, and Government Went Wrong* (New York: Oxford Univ. Press, 1988), 7; Henry W. Broude, *Steel Decisions and the National Economy* (New Haven, CT: Yale Univ. Press, 1963), 162; Gertrude G. Schroeder, *The Growth of Major Steel Companies, 1900–1950* (Baltimore: Johns Hopkins Press, 1953), 44.

7. Schroeder, *The Growth of Major Steel Companies*, 44–45, 100; Tiffany, *The Decline of American Steel*, 8; Eggert, *Steel Masters and Labor Reform*, 31.

8. Eggert, *Steel Masters and Labor Reform*, 6–9, 11, 14–15; Tarbell, *The Life of Elbert H. Gary*, 286–90; Warren, *Big Steel*, 110, 112.

9. Eggert, *Steelmasters and Labor Reform*, 92–93, 112.

10. David Brody, *Labor in Crisis: The Steel Strike of 1919* (Urbana: Univ. of Illinois Press, 1987), 62–174.

11. Eggert, *Steelmasters and Labor Reform*, 150–60; Charles Hill, "Fighting the Twelve-Hour Day in the American Steel Industry," *Labor History* 15 (Winter 1974): 19–35; John A. Fitch, *The Steel Workers* (New York: Charities Publication Committee, 1911); William Z. Foster, *The Great Steel Strike and Its Lessons* (New York: Da Capo Press, 1971); Committee on Work-Periods in Continuous-Industry of the Federated American Engineering Societies, *The Twelve-Hour Shift in Industry* (New York: E. P. Dutton & Co., 1922); Horace B. Drury, "The Three-Shift System in the Steel Industry," *Bulletin of the Taylor Society* 6 (Feb. 1921): 1–49; Commission of Inquiry, Interchurch World Movement, *Report on the Steel Strike of 1919* (New York: Da Capo Press, 1971).

12. Eggert, *Steelmasters and Labor Reform*, 172.

13. Brody, *Labor in Crisis*, 183–84.

14. Ibid., 179–87; Warren, *Big Steel*, 167.

15. Robert Asher, "Painful Memories: The Historical Consciousness of Steelworkers and the Steel Strike of 1919," *Pennsylvania History* 45 (Jan. 1978): 61–86.

16. Lon Savage, *Thunder in the Mountains: The West Virginia Mine War, 1920–21* (Pittsburgh: Univ. of Pittsburgh Press, 1990); Howard B. Lee, *Bloodletting in Appalachia* (Parsons, WV: McClain Printing Co., 1969); Richard D. Lunt, *Law and Order vs The Miners, West Virginia, 1907–1933* (Hamden, CT: Archon Books, 1979); Corbin, *Life, Work, and Rebellion in the Coal Fields*.

17. Lunt, *Law and Order vs. The Miners*, 11–13; David J. McDonald and Edward A. Lynch, *Coal and Unionism: A History of the American Coal Miners' Unions* (Silver Springs, MD: Cornelius Printing Co., 1939), 17–23.

18. Lunt, *Law and Order vs. The Miners*, 14–15.

19. Lane, *Civil War in West Virginia*, 44.

20. Thomas, "Coal Country," 232–70.

21. Edward Eyre Hunt, F. G. Tryon, and Joseph H. Willits, eds., *What the Coal Commission Found* (Baltimore: Williams & Wilkins Co., 1925), 60–62.

22. Lee, *Bloodletting in Appalachia*, 65–72.

23. Thomas, "Coal Country," 89–92, 262–67, 289–91; Corbin, *Life, Work, and Rebellion in the Coal Fields*, 12, 212–13; Eller, *Miners, Millhands, and Mountaineers*, 210–19; Harold E. West, "Civil War in the West Virginia Coal Mines," *Survey*, Apr. 5, 1913, 43.

24. Bituminous Operators' Special Committee to the United States Coal Commission, *The United Mine Workers in West Virginia* (Bituminous Operators' Special Committee, 1923), 81–82.

25. Lane, *Civil War in West Virginia*, 125–26.

26. Corbin, *Life, Work, and Rebellion in the Coal Fields*, 43.

27. Lawrence, "Appalachian Metamorphosis," 217–18.

28. Broude, *Steel Decisions and the National Economy*,164.
29. Thomas, "Coal Country," 89–92, 289–91; Lane, *Civil War in West Virginia*, 122–23; Arthur E. Suffern, *Conciliation and Arbitration in the Coal Industry of America* (Boston: Houghton Mifflin Co., 1915), 91.
30. "Welfare Work for Employees in Industrial Establishments in the United States," *Bulletin* (U.S. Bureau of Labor Statistics), no. 250 (Feb. 1919): 8.
31. Morrell Heald, *The Social Responsibilities of Business: Company and Community, 1900–1960* (Cleveland: Press of Case Western Reserve Univ., 1970), 3–5.
32. Ibid., 15, 20–34.
33. G. W. W. Hanger, "Housing of the Working People in the United States by Employers," *Bulletin* (U.S. Bureau of Labor Statistics), no. 54 (Sept. 1904): 969–71, 1191–1243.
34. Heald, *The Social Responsibilities of Business*, 5.
35. Stuart D. Brandes, *American Welfare Capitalism, 1880–1940* (Chicago: Univ. of Chicago Press, 1976), 1–7, 10–37; Eller, *Miners, Millhands, and Mountaineers*, 220–21.
36. Brandes, *American Welfare Capitalism*, 32.
37. As quoted in Joe William Trotter Jr., *Coal, Class, and Color: Blacks in Southern West Virginia, 1915–32* (Urbana: Univ. of Illinois Press, 1990), 131.
38. Corbin, *Life, Work, and Rebellion in the Coal Fields*, 184, 196; Lunt, *Law and Order vs. The Miner*, 80–90.
39. Schust, *Gary Hollow*, 110.
40. Bituminous Operators' Special Committee, *The United Mine Workers*, 5–6.
41. Caudill, *Night Comes to the Cumberlands*, 193–99.
42. Schust, *Gary Hollow*, 87–97.
43. Ibid.
44. Lane, *Civil War in West Virginia*, 17.
45. "Pathways in the Hills," 5–10.

Chapter 6

1. "Train of Gary Produced Coal Would Encircle Earth"; "More Than Billion Tons of Coal Mined in McDowell"; U.S. Steel Corp., *Annual Report*, 1945, 26.
2. U.S. Steel Corp., *Annual Report*, 1945, 3, 6.
3. Ibid., 5, 9–11.
4. Ibid., 1943, 18–19.
5. Alan J. Singer, "'Something of a Man,' John L. Lewis, the UMWA, and the CIO, 1919–1943," in *The United Mine Workers of America: A Model of Industrial Solidarity?* ed. John M. Laslett (University Park: Pennsylvania State Univ. Press, 1996), 140–44.
6. U.S. Steel Corp., *Annual Report*, 1943, 18–19.
7. U.S. Coal and Coke Co., West Virginia Division, "Central Coal Cleaning Plant, Alpheus, W.Va.," TS, Dec. 26, 1945, 1–2.
8. Bituminous Coal Institute, *Bituminous Coal, 1949* (Washington, D.C.: Bituminous Coal Institute, 1949): 149. The conversion from hand-loaded to machine-loaded coal was not a simple one. Later chapters of this book will

examine the hand-loading era and its relevance to miner productivity and security in greater detail, but the appearance of coal-loading machines in the mines was revolutionary and caused an immediate loss of jobs by thousands of miners who heretofore had determined how much coal they would load in a coal car and how quickly it would be loaded. In addition, "The skilled hand-loader had always prided himself on sending clean coal to the surface, which he did by picking out the impurities and setting them aside before loading his coal. And some hand-loaders believed that their skill in mining clean coal would protect their jobs against competition from the machines." But they were wrong. The coal-loading machines meant speed and efficiency—both achieved with fewer miners, and whatever impurities remained in coal thus loaded could be removed outside the mine at the preparation plant. Keith Dix, "Mechanization, Workplace Control, and the End of the Hand-Loading Era," in Laslett, *The United Mine Workers of America*, 167–76.

9. U.S. Coal and Coke Co., "Central Coal Cleaning Plant."

10. U.S. Steel Corp., *Annual Report*, 1946, 15; 1947, 15–17; 1948, 17–18; 1949, 15–16; 1950, 18.

11. "U.S. Steel Plans to Merge 4 Units," *New York Times*, Nov. 7, 1950. The U.S. Steel Corporation of New Jersey was the parent company of this monolithic organization. Since a number of subsidiary companies existed within the U.S. Steel corporate fold, the U.S. Steel Corporation of New Jersey had been created originally as a "holding" company with essentially no management or operational responsibilities over its subsidiaries, most of which existed as fairly autonomous units. As a result, a new corporation called the U.S. Steel Corporation of Delaware was created in 1938 as its parent company's management arm. The 1951 reorganization, however, merged the Delaware corporation into the new U.S. Steel Company. And, if matters were not confusing enough, the U.S. Steel Company was merged into the U.S. Steel Corporation of New Jersey in 1952. As a result, the U.S. Steel Corporation of New Jersey became, for the first time in the company's history, an "operating" rather than a "holding" company. William T. Hogan, *Economic History of the Iron and Steel Industry in the United States* (Lexington, MA: Lexington Books, 1971), vol. 4: 1677–79.

12. "Big Steel Streamlines Itself," *Business Week*, Nov. 11, 1950, 23.

13. "Train of Gary Produced Coal Would Encircle Earth."

14. "John Munson, U.S. Steel Raw Materials Officer, Retires," *Iron Age* (Jan. 18, 1951): 76–77.

15. U.S. Steel Corp., press release, June 4, 1952, 1–2.

16. "'Big Steel' Capacity 32% of Total; Taft Proposes Congress Inquiry," *New York Times*, Mar. 16, 1950.

17. "Big Steel's Coal Needs Prompt New Mine Plan," *Business Week*, Sept. 16, 1950, 76.

18. "Train of Gary Produced Coal Would Encircle Earth."

19. Ibid.

20. "Kennedy in Gary," *Goldenseal* 26 (Winter 2000): 6.

21. U.S. Bureau of Mines, "Production, value, employment, days active, man-days, and output per man per day at bituminous-coal and lignite mines in

the United States . . . ," *Minerals Yearbook, 1950* (Washington, DC: U.S. Bureau of Mines, 1951), 321; *1951,* 373. U.S. Bureau of Mines, "Coal production . . . by counties, in short tons," *Minerals Yearbook, 1952,* vol. 3, *Area Reports,* 970; *1953,* 1085; *1955,* 1169; *1956,* 1235; *1957,* 1188; *1958,* 1013; *1959,* 1077; *1960,* 1106.

22. U.S. Bureau of Mines, *Minerals Yearbook,1952,* 979; *1953,* 1092; *1954,* 1140–41; *1955,* 1178; *1956,* 1243; *1960,* 1118.
23. National Coal Association, "50 Largest Bituminous Coal Mines in the U.S. Rated According to Tonnage Produced in 1956," *Bituminous Coal Facts 1958* (Washington, DC: NCA), 58; National Coal Association, "50 Largest Bituminous Coal Mines in the U.S. Rated According to Tonnage Produced in 1958," *Bituminous Coal Facts 1960* (Washington, DC: NCA), 85; National Coal Association, "50 Largest Bituminous Coal Mines in the U.S. Rated According to Tonnage Produced in 1961," *Bituminous Coal Facts 1962* (Washington, DC: NCA), 73.
24. U.S. Bureau of Mines, *Minerals Yearbook, 1957,* 1199.
25. Ibid., *1952,* 970–71.
26. "Production by Method of Mining," *Bituminous Coal Facts 1960,* 83.
27. National Coal Association, *Bituminous Coal Facts 1958,* 14–15.
28. Schust, *Gary Hollow,* 287, 298, 328–29, 339, 348, 377, 403, 410, 412, 429, 434.
29. Ibid., 168.
30. Michael Hornick, interview with author, July 1992.
31. Tam Park Vannoy, *Along the Norfolk and Western Olden Days and New Ways: People, Places, Events* (Bedford, VA: B & B Printing-Advertising, 1992), 28.
32. William E. Warden, *Norfolk & Western: Diesel's Last Conquest* (Lynchburg, VA: TLC Publishing, 1991), 2–7.
33. Alice E. Carter, "Segregation and Integration in the Appalachian Coalfields: McDowell County Responds to the *Brown* Decision," *West Virginia History* 54 (1995): 1–8, 12–17, http:// www.wvculture.org/history/journal_wvh/wvh54-5.html.
34. Ibid., 1.
35. See, for instance, Darold T. Barnum, "The Negro in the Bituminous Coal Mining Industry," in *Negro Employment in Southern Industry,* ed. Herbert R. Northrup and Richard L. Rowan (Philadelphia: Univ. of Pennsylvania, 1970), 1-72; Corbin, *Life, Work, and Rebellion in the Coal Fields;* Eller, *Miners, Millhands, and Mountaineers;* James T. Laing, "The Negro Miner in West Virginia," *Social Forces* 14 (Oct. 1935–May 1936): 416–22; Ralph D. Minard, "Race Relationships in the Pocahontas Coal Field," *Journal of Social Issues* 8 (1952): 29–44; Herbert R. Northrup, *Organized Labor and the Negro* (New York: Harper & Brothers, 1976); Sterling D. Spero and Abram L. Harris, *The Black Worker: The Negro and the Labor Movement* (New York: Columbia Univ. Press, 1931); Trotter, *Coal, Class, and Color;* Wagner and Obermiller, *African American Miners and Migrants.*
36. Thomas, "Coal Country," 178.
37. Trotter, *Coal, Class, and Color,* 68–70.
38. Thomas, "Coal Country," 173, 198.
39. O'Toole, "Pocahontas Coal Field," 406–7.

40. Schust, *Gary Hollow*, 169.
41. Northrup, *Organized Labor and the Negro*, 154–71.

Chapter 7

1. Apelt, *The Corporation*, 227.
2. Warren, *Big Steel*, 231.
3. Hall, *Steel Phoenix*, 61–63, 66–67.
4. Roger S. Ahlbrandt et al., *The Renaissance of American Steel: Lessons for Managers in Competitive Industries* (New York: Oxford Univ. Press, 1996), 12–19.
5. Donald F. Barnett and Louis Schorsch, *Steel: Upheaval in a Basic Industry* (Cambridge, MA: Ballinger Publishing, 1983), 4–5.
6. Hall, *Steel Phoenix*, 61–63, 66–67.
7. Ibid., 36–37; William T. Hogan, *Minimills and Integrated Mills* (Lexington, MA: Lexington Books, 1987), 3–5.
8. Warren, *Big Steel*, 281–82.
9. Ibid., 214–15.
10. Ibid.
11. G. J. McManns, "World Steelmaking Heads into an Era of Major Change," *Iron Age* (Dec. 31, 1959): 17–19.
12. Apelt, *The Corporation*, 272.
13. Tiffany, *The Decline of American Steel*, vii.
14. Hogan, *Economic History* 5: 2033–37, 2040–47; Barnett and Schorsch, *Steel*, 47–50.
15. Hall, *Steel Phoenix*, 44–45; Warren, *Big Steel*, 235–36.
16. Hall, *Steel Phoenix*, 40.
17. McManns, "World Steelmaking Heads into an Era of Major Change," 18–19.
18. Ahlbrandt et al., *The Renaissance of American Steel*, 33.
19. Barnett and Schorsch, *Steel*, 54–56; Hall, *Steel Phoenix*, 40–41; Luc Kiers, *The American Steel Industry: Problems, Challenges, Perspectives* (Boulder, CO: Worldview Press, 1980), 68–73; McManns, "World Steelmaking Heads into an Era of Major Changes," 18–19; Warren, *Big Steel*, 249.
20. William Scheuerman, *The Steel Crisis: The Economics and Politics of a Declining Industry* (New York: Praeger, 1986), 51–52.
21. Ibid., 250.
22. Ibid., 233–34.
23. American Iron and Steel Institute, *Annual Statistical Report*, 1965, 106–7; 1970, 74–75; 1975, 92–93; 1980, 92–93; 1985, 102–3.
24. Ahlbrandt et al., *The Renaissance of American Steel*, 12–13.
25. Barnett and Schorsch, *Steel*, 43–47, 51, 231–32.
26. Scheuerman, *The Steel Crisis*, 55–61.
27. Hogan, *Economic History* 5: 2038–39; Scheuerman, *The Steel Crisis*, 64.
28. American Iron and Steel Institute, *Annual Statistical Report*, 1969, 36–37; 1970, 36–37; 1971, 36–37.
29. Scheuerman, *The Steel Crisis*, 64–69. Only one integrated steel producer, Armco, "had significant manufacturing interests overseas" prior to the early 1960s. Bethlehem and U.S. Steel were the only two American steel

companies that "had raw materials properties outside the United States and Canada." Hall, *Steel Phoenix*, 109–10.

30. Scheuerman, *The Steel Crisis*, 71; Barnett and Schorsch, *Steel*, 239; Hall, *Steel Phoenix*, 112–13, 115–20.
31. Scheuerman, *The Steel Crisis*, 71–73.
32. Barnett and Schorsch, *Steel*, 238–42; Hall, *Steel Phoenix*, 113–14.
33. Hall, *Steel Phoenix*, 129–32.
34. American Iron and Steel Institute, *Annual Statistical Report*, 1965, 106–7; 1970, 74–75; 1975, 92–93; 1980, 92–93; 1985, 40, 50, 53, 102–3; 1990, 6.
35. Barnett and Schorsch, *Steel*, 40–42; Hoerr, *And the Wolf Finally Came*, 100.
36. Barnett and Schorsch, *Steel*, 83–84; Hall, *Steel Phoenix*, 145–49.
37. Hogan, *Minimills and Integrated Mills*, 87–121; Donald F. Barnett and Robert W. Crandall, *Up from the Ashes: The Rise of the Steel Minimill in the United States* (Washington, DC: Brookings Institution, 1986), 20–29.
38. Barnett and Crandall, *Up from the Ashes*, 7–9, 18–19. Christopher Hall noted also that in the "if you can't beat them, join them" fashion, many integrated steel companies by the 1990s "had adopted minimill practices even if they retained the traditional integrated steelmaking process" (Hall, *Steel Phoenix*, 148–49).
39. Hall, *Steel Phoenix*, 86–88.
40. American Iron and Steel Institute, *Annual Statistical Report*, 1980, 10.
41. Todd Brewster and Peter Jennings, *The Century* (New York: Doubleday, 1998), 431.
42. David Reynolds, *One World Divisible: A Global History Since 1945* (New York: W. W. Norton, 2000), 155.
43. Brewster and Jennings, *The Century*, 431.
44. Richard Holt, *The Reluctant Superpower: A History of America's Global Economic Reach* (New York: Kodansha America, 1995), 189.
45. Brewster and Jennings, *The Century*, 431.
46. Anthony Sampson, *The Seven Sisters: The Great Oil Companies and the World They Shaped* (New York: Viking Press, 1975), 5–7, 13–14, 59.
47. Holt, *The Reluctant Superpower*, 188–89; Sampson, *The Seven Sisters*, 249.
48. Reynolds, *One World Divisible*, 370.
49. Sampson, *The Seven Sisters*, 174–75; Holt, *The Reluctant Superpower*, 190.
50. Holt, *The Reluctant Superpower*, 189–91.
51. Reynolds, *One World Divisible*, 382–83.
52. Ibid., 373.
53. Ibid., 373–75.
54. Clifton Daniel, ed., *Twentieth Century Day by Day* (London: Dorling Kindersley, 2000), 1070.
55. Reynolds, *One World Divisible*, 382–83.
56. Daniel, *Twentieth Century Day by Day*, 1071–72, 1075–76.
57. Reynolds, *One World Divisible*, 369–70.
58. Holt, *The Reluctant Superpower*, 202–3.
59. Ibid., 192–94.
60. Sampson, *The Seven Sisters*, 267–69; Brewster and Jennings, *The Century*, 431.

61. Reynolds, *One World Divisible*, 407.
62. Daniel, *Twentieth Century Day by Day*, 1074.
63. Ibid., 1126; Reynolds, *One World Divisible*, 460.
64. Hoerr, *And the Wolf Finally Came*, 137.
65. Hall, *Steel Phoenix*, 67.
66. Hoerr, *And the Wolf Finally Came*, 137–38.
67. American Iron and Steel Institute, *Annual Statistical Report*, 1975, 32–33; 1985, 34–35.
68. Drilling counts include oil wells, gas wells, dry holes, and service wells. Data from the American Petroleum Institute and the American Association of Petroleum Geologists, "Statistical Summary," *The Oil and Natural Gas Producing Industry in Your State*, Sept. 1989, 16.
69. Data from the American Petroleum Institute and the Energy Information Administration, "Statistical Summary," 14.
70. Hoerr, *And the Wolf Finally Came*, 137–43.
71. American Iron and Steel Institute, *Annual Statistical Report*, 1985, 34–35.
72. Hoerr, *And the Wolf Finally Came*, 137–43.
73. Ibid., 101.
74. Hogan, *Economic History* 4: 1621.
75. Ibid., 1611–41; Hall, *Steel Phoenix*, 46.
76. Hogan, *Economic History* 4: 1637.
77. Ibid., 1637–38.
78. Hoerr, *And the Wolf Finally Came*, 105–6.
79. Warren, *Big Steel*, 225–26.
80. Ibid., 227.
81. Hoerr, *And the Wolf Finally Came*, 107.
82. Ibid., 15.
83. Ibid., 16.
84. American Iron and Steel Institute, *Annual Statistical Report*, 1970, 16.
85. Barnett and Schorsch, *Steel*, 233–38.
86. Barnett and Crandall, *Up from the Ashes*, 40–41.
87. Hall, *Steel Phoenix*, 48–49.
88. Ibid., 69–72, 74–79; Hoerr, *And the Wolf Finally Came*, 20.
89. Hoerr, *And the Wolf Finally Came*, 15–23.
90. Hall, *Steel Phoenix*, 120.
91. Scheuerman, *The Steel Crisis*, 73–86.
92. Warren, *Big Steel*, 235–36.
93. American Iron and Steel Institute, *Annual Statistical Report*, 1975, 67; 1985, 78.
94. Hall, *Steel Phoenix*, 73.
95. Ibid.
96. American Iron and Steel Institute, *Annual Statistical Report*, 1985, 8.
97. Hoerr, *And the Wolf Finally Came*, 19.
98. Scheuerman, *The Steel Crisis*, 22.
99. Hall, *Steel Phoenix*, 335–37; Ahlbrandt, *The Renaissance of American Steel*, 3–6, 24–28; Hoerr, *And the Wolf Finally Came*, 297; Scheuerman, *The Steel Crisis*, 7–11.
100. Ahlbrandt, *The Renaissance of American Steel*, 6.

Chapter 8

1. Schroeder, *The Growth of Major Steel Companies, 1900–1950*, 198. An "ingot" is defined as "a mass of metal cast in a convenient form for shaping, remelting, or refining." *Random House Webster's College Dictionary* (New York: Random House, 1992).
2. Schroeder, *The Growth of Major Steel Companies*, 36. U.S. Steel's "rated annual steel ingot capacity" in 1950 was nearly 34 million tons compared to Bethlehem Steel's 16 million tons. Ibid., 16–17.
3. Ibid., 86–87.
4. Ibid.
5. Ibid., 120.
6. Ibid., 130–31.
7. Hoerr, *And the Wolf Finally Came*, 86.
8. U.S. Steel Corp., *Annual Report*, 1950, 4.
9. Hogan, *Economic History* 4: 1652–56.
10. Apelt, *The Corporation*, 216.
11. Hogan, *Economic History* 4: 1649–50.
12. U.S. Steel Corp., *Annual Report*, 1951, 3, 9; 1952, 6.
13. Ibid., 1951, 3.
14. Ibid., 3–4; 1952, 3–4; 1953, 3–4; 1954, 3–4; 1955, 3–4; 1956, 3–4; 1957, 3–4.
15. Ibid., 1958, 3–4.
16. Ibid., 1959, 3–4.
17. Ibid., 1961, 20; 1964, 4, 17.
18. Apelt, *The Corporation*, 296–97, 321–22.
19. U.S. Steel Corp., *Annual Report*, 1962, 13; 1965, 3, 7.
20. Broude, *Steel Decisions and the National Economy*, 165.
21. Warren, *Big Steel*, 245.
22. Ibid., 216.
23. Ibid., 253, as quoted from *U.S. Steel Quarterly*, Feb. 1968.
24. Warren, *Big Steel*, 254.
25. U.S. Steel Corp., *Annual Report*, 1960, 4; 1959, 4; 1958, 4; 1961, 4; 1962, 4; 1963, 4; 1964, 3; 1965, 4; 1967, 3; 1968, 3; 1969, 2; 1970, 2; American Iron and Steel Institute, *Annual Statistical Report*, 1970, 16; U.S. Steel Corp., *Annual Report*, 1952, 3–4.
26. Hoerr, *And the Wolf Finally Came*, 296–97.
27. Ibid.
28. U.S. Steel Corp., *Annual Report*, 1960, 21.
29. Ibid., 1961, 3.
30. Ibid., 1962, 8–14, 21.
31. Ibid., 1964, 3.
32. Ibid., 1967, 33–34.
33. Apelt, *The Corporation*, 317.
34. U.S. Steel Corp., *Annual Report*, 1962, 5–7; 1963, 18–19; 1967, 15.
35. "U.S. Steel to Close Gary No. 6 Operation," *Welch Daily News*, July 21, 1960.
36. Ibid.
37. State of West Virginia, *Annual Report of the Department of Mines*, 1950, 50; 1952, 36; 1955, 31.
38. Ibid., 1955, 31; 1956, 27; 1957, 48; 1958, 52; 1959, 58–60; 1960, 66.

39. Ibid., 1955, 10; 1960, 14. A comparison of data from U.S. Steel Corporation *Annual Reports* and West Virginia Department of Mines *Annual Reports* during the 1950s shows that Gary mines consistently provided annually about one-quarter of U.S. Steel's total coal needs. Moreover, individual mines operated by U.S. Steel in Pennsylvania and Kentucky yielded higher production levels than the company's Gary mines. For example, U.S. Steel's Robena mine in southwestern Pennsylvania produced about 3.14 million tons of coal in 1950 as compared with the little less than 500,000 tons produced by Gary's No. 14 mine. In 1960, the Robena mine produced about 3.83 million tons of coal, U.S. Steel's Lynch No. 32 mine in eastern Kentucky produced nearly 2.1 million tons, and Gary's No. 14 mine produced nearly 1.35 million tons. National Coal Association, *Bituminous Coal Facts 1962*, 73.
40. State of West Virginia, *Annual Report of the Department of Mines*, 1955, 30–31; 1960, 66–67; *Keystone Coal Buyers Manual*, 1956, 688; 1961, 633.
41. Hoerr, *And the Wolf Finally Came*, 101–2.
42. State of West Virginia, *Annual Report of the Department of Mines*, 1958, 52–53; 1959, 58–61; *Keystone Coal Buyers Manual*, 1959, 584; 1960, 644.
43. State of West Virginia, *Annual Report of the Department of Mines*, 1960, 66–67; *Keystone Coal Buyers Manual*, 1961, 633.
44. State of West Virginia, *Annual Report of the Department of Mines*, 1960, 66–67; 1961, 74–75; *Keystone Coal Buyers Manual*, 1961, 633; 1962, 580–81.
45. State of West Virginia, *Annual Report of the Department of Mines*, 1961, 74–75; *Keystone Coal Buyers Manual*, 1962, 580–81.
46. State of West Virginia, *Annual Report of the Department of Mines*, 1960, 14, 66–67; 1961, 15, 74–75; 1962, 15, 62–65, 72–73; 1963, 15, 66–67, 74–75; 1964, 15, 64–65, 74–75; 1965, 15, 66–67, 76–79; 1966, 12, 26–29, 96–97, 110–11; 1967, 13, 50–51, 56–59; 1968, 13, 54–55, 66–67; 1969, 8; 1970, 8, 39; *Keystone Coal Buyers Manual*, 1961, 633; 1962, 580–81; 1963, 591–94; 1964, 597; 1965, 594; 1966, 593; 1967, 569–72; 1968, 557; 1969, 580; 1970, 633–34; 1971, 659–60; U.S. Dept. of the Interior, Bureau of Mines, *Minerals Yearbook, 1962*, 1154; *1963*, 1181; *1964*, 1099.
47. U.S. Steel Corp., *Annual Report*, 1968, 17.
48. Ibid., 1969, 5.
49. Schust, *Gary Hollow*, 287, 298, 328–29, 339, 348, 377, 403, 410, 412, 429, 434.
50. "Incorporation of Gary Proposed; Petition Filed," *Welch Daily News*, Dec. 10, 1969; "Petition to Incorporate Gary Presented to Court," *Bluefield Daily Telegraph*, Dec. 11, 1969; "Birth of a City: Process Outlined for Incorporation of Gary," *Welch Daily News*, Dec. 15, 1969; "Gary, W.Va.—from Coal Town to City," *U.S. Steel News*, Sept.–Oct. 1971, 20–21.
51. "U.S. Steel to Offer Houses for Sale," *Welch Daily News*, Dec. 11, 1969; "U.S. Steel Coal Also Is Involved," *Coal Age* (Oct. 1973): 96.
52. Hornick, interview with author, July 1992.
53. Stuart McGehee and Eva McGuire, *A Century of Stewardship: The History of Pocahontas Land Corporation* (Bluefield, WV: Pocahontas Land Corp., 2001), 43–44.
54. Charter of the City of Gary, West Virginia, *Deed Book No. 288*, County Court of McDowell County, WV, Clerk's Office, June 15, 1970, 573–610.
55. "Gary, W.Va.—from Coal Town to City," 20.

56. Ibid., 20–21.
57. "The Town of Gary . . . Some Questions," *Welch Daily News*, Dec. 18, 1969.

Chapter 9

1. *A Dictionary of Business and Management*, 4th ed. (New York: Oxford Univ. Press, 2006), 439.
2. George P. Huber and William H. Glick, eds., *Organizational Change and Redesign: Ideas and Insights for Improving Performance* (New York: Oxford Univ. Press, 1993), preface.
3. See, for instance, Eric Abrahamson, *Change without Pain: How Managers Can Overcome Initiative Overload, Organizational Chaos, and Employee Burnout* (Boston: Harvard Business School Press, 2004); David K. Carr, Kelvin J. Hard, William J. Trahant, *Managing the Change Process: A Field Book for Change Agents, Consultants, Team Leaders, and Reengineering Managers* (New York: McGraw-Hill, 1996); Patrick Dawson, *Understanding Organizational Change: The Contemporary Experience of People at Work* (Thousand Oaks, CA: Sage Publications, 2003); M. David Dealy, *Change or Die: How to Transform Your Organization from the Inside Out* (Westport, CT: Praeger, 2006); Timothy J. Galpin, *The Human Side of Change: A Practical Guide to Organizational Redesign* (San Francisco: Jossey-Bass Publishers, 1996); Linda Holbeche, *Understanding Change: Theory, Implementation and Success* (Boston: Elsevier, 2006); Huber and Glick, *Organizational Change and Redesign;* David K. Hurst, *Crisis and Renewal: Meeting the Challenge of Organizational Change* (Boston: Harvard Business School Press, 1995); Donald L. Kirkpatrick, *How to Manage Change Effectively* (San Francisco: Jossey-Bass Publishers, 1985); Gordon L. Lippitt, Peter Langseth, and Jack Mossop, *Implementing Organizational Change* (San Francisco: Jossey-Bass Publishers, 1985); John L. Mariotti, *The Shape Shifters: Continuous Change for Competitive Advantage* (New York: Van Nostrand Reinhold, 1997); David A. Nadler, *Champions of Change: How CEOs and Their Companies Are Mastering the Skills of Radical Change* (San Francisco: Jossey-Bass Publishers, 1998).
4. Huber and Glick, *Organizational Change and Redesign*, 24.
5. Ibid., 25; Jack Beatty, *Colossus: How the Corporation Changed America* (New York: Broadway Books, 2001), 403.
6. "Big Move-In," *U.S. Steel News*, Dec. 1970, 8–9.
7. U.S. Steel Corp., *Annual Report*, 1973, 6,17; 1974, 14; 1976, 17.
8. Warren, *Big Steel*, 241.
9. U.S. Steel Corp., *Annual Report*, 1970, 2; 1971, 2; 1972, 2; 1973, 2, 4; 1974, 2; 1975, 2; 1976, 2; 1977, 2; 1978, 2; 1979, 2; 1980, 2.
10. U.S. Steel Corp., *Annual Report*, 1971–80; American Iron and Steel Institute, *Annual Statistical Report*, 1971–80.
11. U.S. Steel Corp., *Annual Report*, 1974, 14.
12. Ibid., 1975, 13–14.
13. Ibid., 1975, 13; 1977, 28; 1978, 27; 1979, 11.
14. Ibid., 1970, 2.
15. Apelt, *The Corporation*, 325–48.

16. U.S. Steel Corp., *Annual Report*, 1970, 3.
17. Ibid., 1972, 16.
18. Ibid., 17.
19. Ibid.
20. Ibid., 1974, 5.
21. Ibid., 1975, 3.
22. Ibid., 1977, 3.
23. Ibid., 1978, 3.
24. Warren, *Big Steel*, 307.
25. U.S. Steel Corp., *Annual Report*, 1970, 2–3, 24–25; 1971, 3.
26. Ibid., 1972, 6.
27. Ibid.
28. Donald Phillips, "Mine Strike Starts; Negotiations Fail," *Welch Daily News*, Oct. 1, 1971; Craig Ammerman, "Appalachian Coal Miners Return to Jobs," *Bluefield Daily Telegraph*, Nov. 15, 1971; "Mine Strike Begins," *Bluefield Daily Telegraph*, Nov. 12, 1974; Charles E. Flinner, "Miners to Return to Work after Approving Contract," *Welch Daily News*, Dec. 5, 1974; Karen Stouthwick, "Arnold Miller Orders Miners onto Picket Lines," *Welch Daily News*, Dec. 6 1977; "Strike Is Over," *Bluefield Daily Telegraph*, Mar. 25, 1978.
29. U.S. Steel Corp., *Annual Report*, 1977, 31; 1978, 5.
30. Ibid., 1973, 12.
31. Ibid., 1978, 5.
32. Ibid., 1974, 6–8.
33. Scheuerman, *The Steel Crisis*, 15.
34. U.S. Steel Corp., *Annual Report*, 1979, 4–5, 14.
35. Ibid., 1977, 2, 4.
36. Apelt, *The Corporation*, 372–73.
37. "Between us," *U.S. Steel News*, May/June 1971, frontispiece.
38. Ibid.
39. U.S. Steel Corp., *Annual Report*, 1972, 3.
40. *U.S. Steel News*, Special Issue, Nov. 1975, 1–4.
41. U.S. Steel Corp., *Annual Report*, 1977, 2, 31; 1978, 6; 1980, 18.
42. Ibid., 1972, 12–13; 1973, 9–11; 1975, 9; Scheuerman, *The Steel Crisis*, 85–86.
43. Apelt, *The Corporation*, 365–66.
44. Warren, *Big Steel*, 4.
45. Apelt, *The Corporation*, 351–55, 489.
46. U.S. Steel Corp., *Annual Report*, 1975, 2.
47. Apelt, *The Corporation*, 381–82.
48. Warren, *Big Steel*, 310, 315.

Chapter 10

1. Charles Peter Davis, "The Impact of the Coal Industry on McDowell County, West Virginia," master's thesis, San Jose State Univ., 1997, 91–92.
2. Ibid.
3. For example, the Federal Coal Mine Health and Safety Act of 1969, P.L. 91-173, 83 Stat. 742; the Federal Mine Safety and Health Act of 1977, P.L. 95-

164, 91 Stat. 1290; and the Black Lung Benefits Reform Act of 1977, P.L. 95-239, 92 Stat. 95. A number of laws and amendments were passed during the 1970s that strengthened the original Clean Air Act passed in 1955, P.L. 84-159, 69 Stat. 322, 42 USC 1857; and the two subsequent air pollution control laws passed in the 1960s: the Clean Air Act, P.L. 88-206, 77 Stat. 392 (1963); and the Air Quality Act of 1967, P.L. 90-148, 81 Stat. 485. Related laws enacted during the 1970s included the Clean Air Amendments of 1970, P.L. 91-604, 84 Stat. 1676; the Energy Supply and Environmental Coordination Act of 1974, P.L. 93-319, 88 Stat. 246; and the Clean Air Act Amendments of 1977, P.L. 95-95, 91 Stat. 685. Water pollution problems also had come under federal scrutiny as early as 1948, when Congress passed the Water Pollution Control Act, P.L. 80-845, 62 Stat. 1155. This law was further strengthened in the 1970s by enactment of the Water Quality Improvement Act of 1970, P.L. 91-224, 84 Stat. 91; Federal Water Pollution Control Act Amendments of 1972, P.L. 92-500, 86 Stat. 816; and the Clean Water Act of 1977, P.L. 95-217, 91 Stat. 1566. The Environmental Protection Agency was created by Reorganization Plan No. 3 of 1970, 84 Stat. 2086.

4. "Strip Mining? How Would You Vote?" *Welch Daily News*, Ninth Annual Coal Edition, Feb. 12, 1972.

5. P.L. 95-87, 91 Stat. 445, 30 USC 1201.

6. State of West Virginia, *Annual Report of the Department of Mines*, 1970, 11; 1971, 12; 1972, 12; 1973, 12; 1974, 12; 1975, 12; 1976, 12; 1977, 15; 1978, 18; 1979, 18.

7. Ibid., 1970, 8, 39; 1971, 9, 39; 1972, 9, 34; 1973, 9, 29; 1974, 9, 37; 1975, 9, 45; 1976, 9, 54; 1977, 14, 114; 1978, 17, 141; 1979, 17, 165. Coal production figures are for underground or drift mines and do not include coal production figures for surface or contour mines. U.S. Steel actually engaged in surface mining to a minimal degree in the Gary area. The approximately 461,000 tons of coal produced by U.S. Steel's surface mining operation in 1970 accounted for about 9 percent of the production total for Gary mines that year. The production percentage contributed by surface mining dropped to about 6 percent in 1971, 4 percent in 1972, and 1 percent in 1973. There is no record of U.S. Steel surface mining activity in 1974, but in 1975 and 1976 the approximately 12,000 tons and 11,000 tons coming from surface mining operations during the two respective years accounted for less than 1 percent of the total coal produced by Gary mines. U.S. Steel apparently ceased its surface mining operations in Gary altogether after 1976. *1971 Keystone Coal Industry Manual*, 659–60; *1972*, 723; *1973*, 770–71; *1974*, 800–801; *1975*, 949–50; *1976*, 1024–25; *1977*, 1099–1100.

8. Davis, *The Impact of the Coal Industry*, 81.

9. "U.S. Steel Coal Operations—Five Districts, Six States," *Coal Age* (Oct. 1973): 93.

10. U.S. Steel Corp., *Annual Report*, 1971, 18; 1972, 12, 14; 1975, 7; 1976, 9; 1977, 10; 1978, 29; 1979, 35.

11. Advertisement, Gary District, U.S. Steel Corp., *Welch Daily News*, Seventh Annual Coal Edition, Feb. 14, 1970; "U.S. Steel Opens Environment Study," *Welch Daily News*, Eighth Annual Coal Edition, Feb. 13, 1971.

12. *1980 Keystone Coal Industry Manual*, 1145.

13. U.S. Steel Corp., *Annual Report*, 1979, 35.
14. "U.S. Steel . . . A Quiet Giant in America's Coal Industry," *Coal Age* 78 (Oct. 1973): 105.
15. U.S. Steel Corp., *Annual Report*, 1977, 10.
16. Ibid., 1970, 2; 1977, 4.
17. Ercan Tukenmez and Mary K. Paull, *Outlook for U.S. Coal* (U.S. Dept. of Energy), Aug. 1982, 3–8.
18. Congressional Research Service, Environmental and Natural Resources Policy Division, *The Coal Industry: Problems and Prospects, A Background Study,* prepared for Senate Committee on Governmental Affairs, Permanent Subcommittee on Investigations, Committee Print, 95th Cong., 2d sess., 1978, 1, 8. The release of sulfur compounds into the atmosphere as a result of burning coal can be quite harmful to the environment. Sulfur dioxide, along with carbon dioxide, carbon monoxide, nitrogen oxides, hydrocarbons, and water vapor are among the by-product elements produced when coal is burned. Among all of these, sulfur dioxide is the most problematical. It alone can affect human health and plant life and can even corrode metal, marble, limestone, and concrete structures. Sulfur dioxide comes from sources other than coal, but scientists say that "at least 62% of the sulfur emitted into the atmosphere has its source in coal combustion." Curtis E. Harvey, *Coal in Appalachia: An Economic Analysis* (Lexington: Univ. Press of Kentucky, 1986), 104–5.
19. Harvey, *Coal in Appalachia,* 31; Davis, "The Impact of the Coal Industry on McDowell County, West Virginia," 51–52.
20. Eugene R. Slatjck, U.S. Dept. of Energy, *Coal Data: A Reference,* July 1980, 11; Energy Information Administration, *Historical Monthly Energy Review,* 1973–88, 169–70.
21. Harvey, *Coal in Appalachia,* 13, 26, 124.
22. Davis, "The Impact of the Coal Industry on McDowell County, West Virginia," 50–51.
23. "Production Detailed for U.S. Steel Gary District," *Welch Daily News,* 1976 Coal Edition, Feb. 28, 1976; "Coal—Major Part of U.S. Steel Energy Base," *Welch Daily News,* 1977 Coal Edition, Feb. 26, 1977.
24. Hall, *Steel Phoenix,* 23.
25. U.S. Steel Corp., *Annual Report*, 1972, 17.
26. Ibid., 1975, 7; 1976, 9; 1977, 10; 1978, 29; 1979, 35.
27. Ibid., 1978, 23.
28. Hall, *Steel Phoenix,* 90–91.
29. Slatjck, *Coal Data,* 33; Energy Information Administration, *Historical Monthly Energy Review,* 169–70.
30. Harvey, *Coal in Appalachia,* 52–53; Hogan, *Minimills and Integrated Mills,* 102.
31. U.S. Steel Corp., *Annual Report,* 1974, 12; 1979, 7.
32. "At U.S. Steel's Coal Mines, 'Safety' Is an On-Line Concept," *Coal Age* (Oct. 1973): 99.
33. U.S. Steel Corp., *Annual Report,* 1978, 5.
34. "At U.S. Steel's Coal Mines, 'Safety' Is An On-Line Concept," 97.

35. Phillips, "Mine Strike Starts"; Philip Shaberoff, "Some Coal Miners Are Walking Out," *New York Times*, Oct. 1, 1971; Mike Stater, "29,000 Area Miners Join Industry Strike," *Bluefield Daily Telegraph*, Oct. 2, 1971; Neil Gilbride, "Strike On; Quick Accord Sought," *Bluefield Daily News*, Oct. 2, 1971; Philip Shabecoff, "Soft-Coal Mines Are Shut Down as 80,000 Strike," *New York Times*, Oct. 2, 1971.

36. "Coal Strike Hurts Rails; UMW Editor Hits Nixon," *Welch Daily News*, Oct. 5, 1971; "C&O, B&O to Lay Off More Men," *Welch Daily News*, Oct. 13, 1971; Rudy Cernkovic, "Railroad Industry Being Hard Hit by Coal Strike," *Welch Daily News*, Nov. 12, 1971; "Steel Layoffs Mount," *New York Times*, Nov. 13, 1971.

37. Emanuel Perlmutter, "Coal Miners Sign Pact, Ending Strike of 44 Days," *New York Times*, Nov. 14, 1971; Craig Ammerman, "Appalachian Coal Miners Return to Jobs," *Bluefield Daily Telegraph*, Nov. 15, 1971.

38. Wayne Scarberry and Ronnie Briggs, "McDowell County Miners Fail to Report for Work," *Welch Daily News*, Feb. 25, 1974; "Miners Still out Due to Gas Trouble," *Welch Daily News*, Feb. 26, 1974; Wayne Scarberry, "Area Miners Vote at Two Meetings to Stay Off Job," *Welch Daily News*, Mar. 4, 1974; "Coal Miners Vote Not to End Strike," *New York Times*, Mar. 11, 1974.

39. "Coal Miners Vote Not to End Strike"; "Steel Makers Cut Output and Jobs on Coal Shortage," *New York Times*, Mar. 13, 1974.

40. Wayne Scarberry, "Two Mine Pickets and One Woman Shot at Keystone," *Welch Daily News*, Mar. 13, 1974; "Editorial: No Wonder People Get Shot," *Welch Daily News*, Mar. 13, 1974; "West Virginia Lifts 'Gas' Curb; 3 Mine Pickets Shot by Snipers," *New York Times*, Mar. 14, 1974; "Back-to-Work Move on in Area Coal Mines," *Welch Daily News*, Mar. 14, 1974; "Back-to-Work Movement Continues Gain Today," *Welch Daily News*, Mar. 15, 1974.

41. "Slow but Steady Progress Reported in Negotiations," *Bluefield Daily Telegraph*, Nov. 10, 1974; Reginald Stuart, "Opinion Is Mixed on Coal Effects," *New York Times*, Nov. 11, 1974; Charles E. Flinner, "Coal Mine Strike Begins at Midnight," *Welch Daily News*, Nov. 11, 1974; Ben A. Franklin, "Coal Pact Delay to Extend Strike," *New York Times*, Nov. 12, 1974; "Issues in Mine Strike," *New York Times*, Nov. 12, 1974; "Mine Strike Begins," *Bluefield Daily Telegraph*, Nov. 12, 1974; Charles E. Flinner, "120,000 Miners on Strike; Still Talk," *Welch Daily News*, Nov. 12, 1974.

42. Reginald Stuart, "Coal Strike Curbs Steelmakers; Texas Instruments Closings Set," *New York Times*, Nov. 23, 1974; Ben A. Franklin, "Miners Council to Be Exhorted to Accept Offer," *New York Times*, Nov. 26, 1974; Charles E. Flinner, "Miners to Return to Work after Approving Contract," *Welch Daily News*, Dec. 5, 1974; "Pact Becomes Effective Today," *Bluefield Daily Telegraph*, Dec. 6, 1974; George Vecsey, "Picketing Mars Coal-Strike End," *New York Times*, Dec. 7, 1974.

43. A. H. Raskin, "The Labor Scene: Mine Workers and the Grievance Process," *New York Times*, Aug. 6, 1976; "Striking Miners Going Back on Job," *New York Times*, Aug. 13, 1976; Steven Rattner, "Economy Unharmed by Mine Strike; Coal Industry Faces Investment Lag," *New York Times*, Aug. 16, 1976; James F. Clarity, "Wildcat Strikes by Miners Spread amid Fears of

Dwindling Benefits," *New York Times*, Aug. 3, 1977; "8-Week Coal Strike Apparently Ending," *New York Times*, Aug. 23, 1977; "10-Week Miners' Strike Appears Near an End," *New York Times*, Sept. 3, 1977.

44. Ben A. Franklin, "Years of Conflict in Coal Fields Set Stage for a Strike," *New York Times*, Nov. 27, 1977; "Coalfields Set for Strike as Bargaining Continues," *Bluefield Daily Telegraph*, Dec. 4, 1977; "Labor Problem in the Coal Mines: Industry, Union Share Blame," *Bluefield Daily Telegraph*, Dec. 4, 1977; Karen Southwick, "Arnold Miller Orders Miners onto Picket Lines," *Welch Daily News*, Dec. 6, 1977; "Half of Nation's Mines Closed as Strike Begins," *Bluefield Daily Telegraph*, Dec. 7, 1977.

45. Ben A. Franklin, "Coal Strikers: Mountain Men Are Clannish, Combative," *New York Times*, Mar. 5, 1978; William Robbins, "Miners' Ability to Weather a Long Strike Aided by Merchants' Support and Patience," *New York Times*, Mar. 10, 1978.

46. Heidi Weckwert, "Veteran Viewpoint: Area Miner Says Right-to-Strike Clause Is Not Top Priority in New Contract, "*Welch Daily News*, Dec. 16, 1977; Heidi Weckwert, "Younger Miners Favoring Options for Time Off," *Welch Daily News*, Dec. 17, 1977; Heidi Weckwert, "Moore Says 'It's a New Day' in Coal Industry . . . Young Miners Won't Be Abused," *Welch Daily News*, Dec. 22, 1977.

47. Ben A. Franklin, "Pact to End Coal Strike Is Announced by Carter; Miners Urged to Back It," *New York Times*, Feb. 26, 1978; "For Coal, This Is the Weekend That Counts," *New York Times*, Mar. 5, 1978; "Operators Cave-In: 82-Day Walkout Yields Nearly All Miners Wanted," *New York Times*, Feb. 25, 1978; "President Invokes Taft-Hartley," *Welch Daily News*, Mar. 6, 1978; Ben A. Franklin, "Miners Reject Contact, 2 to 1; Carter to Announce Plan Today for Compelling Return to Work," *New York Times*, Mar. 6, 1978; Robert D. McFadden, "U.S. Options after Rejections: Taft-Hartley Act," *New York Times*, Mar. 6, 1978; Peter Kihss, "U.S. Options after Rejections: Seizure of Mines," *New York Times*, Mar. 6, 1978; "3 Main Issues in Dispute," *New York Times*, Mar. 7, 1978; Drew Von Bergen, "Striking Miners Now under Court Order," *Welch Daily News*, Mar. 10, 1978; Ben A. Franklin, "U.S. Court Orders Coal Miners Back to Work for 80-Day Period," *New York Times*, Mar. 10, 1978; Ben A. Franklin, "Coal Miners Ignore Taft-Hartley Order; Pact Reported Near," *New York Times*, Mar. 14, 1978.

48. William Robbins, "Miners Gloomy as They Vote on New Contract," *New York Times*, Mar. 25, 1978; "Strike Is Over," *Bluefield Daily Telegraph*, Mar. 25, 1978; Alan Shearer, "Miller Rips Anti-Contract Ads, Sees Education Program Need," *Welch Daily News*, Mar. 25, 1978; Drew Von Bergen, "Long Strike Over; Work to Resume Monday Morning," *Welch Daily News*, Mar. 25, 1978; "Coal 'Peace Treaty' Is Signed," *Bluefield Daily Telegraph*, Mar. 26, 1978; "Safety Inspections Made; Mines Ready for Occupancy," *Bluefield Daily Telegraph*, Mar. 27, 1978; Sam Boyle, "Miners Answer Work Call," *Bluefield Daily Telegraph*, Mar. 28, 1978.

49. Congressional Research Service, *The Coal Industry*, 21–22.

50. U.S. Steel Corp., *Annual Report*, 1977, 31; 1978, 5.

51. Ibid., 1971, 2.

52. Ibid., 1974, 8.

53. Ibid., 1977, 4.
54. Congressional Research Service, *The Coal Industry*, 24.
55. Harvey, *Coal in Appalachia*, 73–74.
56. Garret Mathews, "Gary Is an Oasis, Employment-Wise," *Bluefield Daily Telegraph*, Sept. 2, 1979.
57. U.S. Steel Corp., *Annual Report*, 1977, 31.
58. Franklin, "Coal Strikers: Mountain Men Are Clannish, Combative"; James F. Clarity, "New Breed of Coal Miners Showing Defiance," *New York Times*, Sept. 1, 1977.
59. "Coalfield Jobs Being Eliminated in Wake of Strikes and Recession," *New York Times*, Dec. 19, 1978; "Coal Industry in a Slump As Utilities' Growth Lags," *New York Times*, Jan. 10, 1979.
60. Mathews, "Gary Is an Oasis, Employment-Wise."

Chapter 11

1. U.S. Steel Corp., *Annual Report*, 1989, cover, 2, 4.
2. Apelt, *The Corporation*, 401.
3. Mary Davis, "Outside Looking In," *Bluefield Daily Telegraph*, June 18, 1980.
4. State of West Virginia, *Annual Report of the Department of Mines*, 1980, 150; *1981 Keystone Coal Industry Manual*, 1316–17.
5. Davis, "Outside Looking In."
6. U.S. Bureau of the Census, *U.S. Census Population: 1980*, vol. 1, *Characteristics of the Population*, pt. 50, West Virginia (Washington, DC: U.S. Government Printing Office, 1982), 96.
7. Davis, "Outside Looking In."
8. "Hard Times Again in West Virginia," *Coal Age* (April 1980): 21, 25.
9. Ibid.
10. President's Commission on Coal, *Coal Data Book* (Washington, DC: Government Printing Office, 1980), introduction.
11. Ben A. Franklin, "Miners' Lives Found Better, But Job Is Most Dangerous," *New York Times*, Mar. 3, 1980.
12. "State Economy Touched by Steel Industry Gloom," *Welch Daily News*, Seventeenth Annual Coal Edition, Feb. 29, 1980.
13. U.S. Steel Corp., *Annual Report*, 1980, 4.
14. Energy Information Administration, *Historical Monthly Energy Review*, 170.
15. U.S. Steel Corp., *Annual Report*, 1980, 4.
16. State of West Virginia, Dept. of Mines, *Directory of Mines*, 1979, 165; 1980, 150; *1980 Keystone Coal Industry Manual*, 1145–46; 1981, 1316–17.
17. American Iron and Steel Institute, *Annual Statistical Report*, 1980, 38, 44, 92–93; 1985, 40, 50, 102–3.
18. U.S. Steel Corp., *Annual Report*, 1980, 2, 37; Ahlbrandt et al., *The Renaissance of American Steel*, 55.
19. West Virginia Coal Association, *Coal Facts 2003*, 34.
20. U.S. Steel Corp., *Annual Report*, 1980, 3, 5–6, 8, 10, 13–15, 18, 35, 38.
21. *1945 Keystone Coal Buyers Manual*, 341; 1951, 677; 1955, 672; 1960, 644; *1971 Keystone Coal Industry Manual*, 659; *1973*, 770; *1981*, 1316; *1982*, 1362;

246

"Yourston on Board at Gary," *Welch Daily News*, Nineteenth Annual Coal Edition, Feb. 26, 1982.

22. State of West Virginia, Dept. of Mines, *Directory of Mines*, 1980, 150; 1981, 140; *1981 Keystone Coal Industry Manual*, 1316–17; *1982*, 1362.

23. "Coal Miners Strike As Contract Expires," *New York Times*, Mar. 27, 1981; Kip Rudge, "Local Miners Dissatisfied with New Contract," *Welch Daily News*, Mar. 30, 1981; Andrew Gallagher, "Donnybrook: UMW President Church Faces Struggle in District 17," *Welch Daily News*, Mar. 30, 1981; Ben A. Franklin, "New Coal Contract Rejected by Miners; Long Strike Feared," *New York Times*, Apr. 1, 1981; Drew Von Bergen, "Rejected: UMW Rank-And-File Votes 'No' on Contract," *Welch Daily News*, Apr. 1, 1981.

24. Drew Von Bergen, "Pickets Form Lines at Non-Union Mines," *Welch Daily News*, Apr. 2, 1981; Ben A. Franklin, "Coal Miners Vote on New Contract; Early Returns Viewed as Favorable," *New York Times*, June 7, 1981.

25. Harvey, *Coal in Appalachia*, 127–28.

26. Drew Von Bergen, "Second Contract Agreement Is Reached," *Welch Daily News*, May 29, 1981; Seena D. Gressin, "Miners May Return to Work Monday," *Welch Daily News*, June 2, 1981; Kip Rudge, "McDowell Miners Are Back at Work," *Welch Daily News*, June 8, 1981; Kip Rudge, "Coal Operators Dodging ABC Pickets," *Welch Daily News*, June 11, 1981; Kip Rudge, "Local Developments: Several Pickets Lose Heart; Companies Comment," *Welch Daily News*, June 12, 1981; "Back to Work, Coal Moves Again," *Welch Daily News*, June 18, 1981; U.S. Steel Corp., *Annual Report*, 1981, 9.

27. U.S. Steel Corp., *Annual Report*, 1981, 1–2, 4, 6.

28. Robert J. Cole, "Coal Mines for Sohio," *New York Times*, Dec. 3, 1980.

29. Douglas Martin, "U.S. Steel, Sohio End Coal Talks," *New York Times*, Mar. 18, 1981; Agis Salpukas, "U.S. Steel in Sohio Deal," *New York Times*, Apr. 10, 1981.

30. Cole, "Coal Mines for Sohio."

31. Agis Salpukas, "Steel Industry Cashes in on Coal," *New York Times*, Sept. 25, 1980; Energy Information Administration, *The Changing Structure of the U.S. Coal Industry 1976–1986*, U.S. Dept. of Energy, 1986, vii–viii, 1–2, 12, 15, 27–30.

32. Salpukas, "Steel Industry Cashes in on Coal."

33. U.S. Steel Corp., *Annual Report*, 1981, 9.

34. Anna-Marie Hornick, "USS Gary Wants More Production," *Welch Daily News*, Nineteenth Annual Coal Edition, Feb. 26, 1982.

35. U.S. Steel Corp., *Annual Report*, 1981, 3, 5, 13–14.

36. Ibid., 4,6,10.

37. Apelt, *The Corporation*, 381–92; U.S. Steel Corp., *Annual Report*, 1981, 2.

38. U.S. Steel Corp., *Annual Report*, 1981, 2.

39. Ibid., 2, 36–37.

40. Apelt, *The Corporation*, 391–92.

41. William T. Hogan, *Steel in the United States: Restructuring to Compete* (Lexington, MA: Lexington Books, 1984), 29.

42. Apelt, *The Corporation*, 392.

43. U.S. Steel Corp., *Annual Report*, 1982, 10–11.

44. "Will the Marathon Deal Pay Off in a Downturn," *Business Week*, Apr. 26, 1982, 34–36.

45. American Petroleum Institute and the Energy Information Administration, "Statistical Summary," *The Oil and Natural Gas Producing Industry in Your State*, Sept. 1989, 14.
46. U.S. Steel Corp., *Annual Report*, 1982, 2.
47. Hoerr, *And the Wolf Finally Came*, 140.
48. U.S. Steel Corp., *Annual Report*, 1982, 2, 4, 8, 14.
49. "Will the Marathon Deal Pay Off in a Downturn," 35.
50. U.S. Steel Corp., *Annual Report*, 1982, 2, 18; "U.S. Steel's Debt-Shrouded Future," *Business Week*, Oct. 18, 1982, 154.
51. U.S. Steel Corp., *Annual Report*, 1982, 4.
52. Hoerr, *And the Wolf Finally Came*, 138–40.
53. U.S. Steel Corp., *Annual Report*, 1982, 1–2, 16; "U.S. Steel's Debt-Shrouded Future," 154.
54. U.S. Steel Corp., *Annual Report*, 1982, 1–2.
55. Ibid., 3, 22, 24.
56. American Iron and Steel Institute, *Annual Statistical Report*, 1985, 40, 50, 102–3.
57. U.S. Steel Corp., *Annual Report*, 1982, 24.
58. "Why Are America's Steel Plants Closing?" *U.S. Steel News*, July 1982, 1–6, 12, 17.
59. "U.S. Steel's Get-Tough Policy," *Business Week*, Aug. 30, 1982, 73–74; Hoerr, *And the Wolf Finally Came*, 16–20.
60. U.S. Steel Corp., *Annual Report*, 1982, 24.
61. "U.S. Steel Shrinks Steelmaking Further," *Business Week*, Nov. 15, 1982, 44.
62. Hoerr, *And the Wolf Finally Came*, 11–12, 153–55.
63. Ibid., 143.
64. "U.S. Steel's Debt-Shrouded Future," 154.
65. Hoerr, *And the Wolf Finally Came*, 2–13.
66. U.S. Steel Corp., *Annual Report*, 1982, 14, 48, 54.
67. Hall, *Steel Phoenix*, 32.

Chapter 12

1. House Committee on Banking, Finance and Urban Affairs, Subcommittee on Domestic Monetary Policy, *The Costs of Unemployment for Local Communities—Welch, W.Va.*, Hearing, 97th Cong., 2d sess., 1982, 93.
2. Kip Rudge, "Gary Miners Plan Fishing Trips," *Welch Daily News*, Apr. 14, 1982.
3. State of West Virginia, Dept. of Mines, *Directory of Mines*, 1981, 140; 1982, 152–53; *1982 Keystone Coal Industry Manual*, 1362; *1983*, 1356–57.
4. David Saltz, "Steel Slump Brings Coalfield Layoffs," *United Mine Workers Journal* (May 16–31, 1982): 1.
5. Pat Cecil, "U.S. Steel Sites to Close Indefinitely," *Bluefield Daily Telegraph*, Mar. 26, 1982.
6. Mary Davis, "U.S. Steel Shuts McDowell County Facilities," *Welch Daily News*, Apr. 13, 1982; "Gary Mine Operations Will Be Suspended," *Bluefield Daily Telegraph*, Apr. 13, 1982.

7. Energy Information Administration, *The Changing Structure of the U.S. Coal Industry 1976–1986*, 1, 9; Harvey, *Coal in Appalachia*, 43–46, 50.

8. Energy Information Administration, *The Changing Structure of the U.S. Coal Industry 1976–1986*, 1, 9; Harvey, *Coal in Appalachia*, 32, 34–40, 43–45; "UMW Unemployment Rate Set at 20%," *Coal Age* (July 1982): 11.

9. "UMW Unemployment Rate Set at 20%," 11.

10. State of West Virginia, Dept. of Mines, *Directory of Mines*, 1980, 18; 1981, 43; 1982, 51, 152–53; *1983 Keystone Coal Industry Manual*, 1356–57.

11. Davis, "U.S. Steel Shuts McDowell County Facilities," 1; "Coal in Brief: High Unemployment," *Coal Age* 87 (Oct. 1982): 41.

12. State of West Virginia, Dept. of Mines, *Directory of Mines*, 1980, 24–25; 1981, 44–45; 1982, 52–53.

13. "Sign Up Set for U.S. Steel Lay Offs," *Welch Daily News*, Apr. 8, 1982; "U.S. Steel Sign Up Set," *Welch Daily News*, Apr. 15, 1982; Kip Rudge, "Gary Miners Plan Fishing Trips," *Welch Daily News*, Apr. 14, 1982.

14. Saltz, "Steel Slump Brings Coalfield Layoffs," 1, 4; "Economic Impact of Gary Mines' Closing Worsens," *Bluefield Daily Telegraph*, June 6, 1982.

15. David H. Corcoran, "Governor Examines Gary Situation," *Welch Daily News*, May 4, 1982.

16. "Economic Impact of Gary Mines' Closing Worsens"; Beth Spence, "Coaltown Christmas," *Charleston (WV) Gazette-Mail Sunday Outlook*, Dec. 19, 1982.

17. Mary Davis, "Unemployed Miner Facing Change," *Welch Daily News*, May 10, 1982; Rudge, "Gary Miners Plan Fishing Trips."

18. "Economic Impact of Gary Mines' Closing Worsens"; "Employees of Closed U.S. Steel Mines Seek Other Jobs," *Bluefield Daily Telegraph*, May 2, 1982; Deborah Baker, "U.S. Steel Laying Off 700 McDowell Miners," *Charleston Gazette*, Apr. 14, 1982.

19. "Gary Tipple Repairs No Sign of Reopening of Mines," *Bluefield Daily Telegraph*, June 13, 1982.

20. Davis, "U.S. Steel Shuts McDowell County Facilities"; "Economic Impact of Gary Mines' Closing Worsens"; "Gary Shutdown Is Staggering Blow to Area Economy," *Bluefield Daily Telegraph*, Apr. 18, 1982; Rudge, "Gary Miners Plan Fishing Trips."

21. David Corcoran, "New U.S. Steel Superintendent Says 'Our Biggest Concern Is People,'" *Welch Daily News*, Twentieth Annual Coal Edition, Feb. 25, 1983.

22. Corcoran, "New U.S. Steel Superintendent Says 'Our Biggest Concern Is People'"; "Gary Tipple Repairs No Sign of Reopening of Mines."

23. Mary Davis, "Commission Refuses to Bail out Cities," *Welch Daily News*, Sept. 28, 1982.

24. "Gary Trying to Dig in Against Adversity," *Bluefield Daily Telegraph*, Oct. 17, 1982; Spence, "Coaltown Christmas"; "U.S. Steel Shutdown Weakens Economy in McDowell County," *Bluefield Daily Telegraph*, Oct. 9, 1982.

25. House Committee on Banking, Finance and Urban Affairs, *The Costs of Unemployment for Local Communities*, 1.

26. Ibid., 14, 17–19, 20, 22, 24–25, 28–31, 55–56, 63, 67, 95.

27. Ibid., 73–75.

28. Ibid., 30, 35, 39, 55–56, 59, 83–84.

29. Ibid., 102

30. Spence, "Coaltown Christmas."

31. Ibid.

32. Karen Kaplan, "Future Looks Better for Embattled Gary," *Bluefield Daily Telegraph*, Aug. 5, 1983.

Chapter 13

1. U.S. Steel Corp., *Annual Report*, 1983, 3, 56.

2. Ahlbrandt et al., *The Renaissance of American Steel*, 55–56.

3. U.S. Steel Corp., *Annual Report*, 1983, 1–3, 51–52, 54, 55.

4. American Petroleum Institute and the Energy Information Administration, "Statistical Summary, The Oil and Natural Gas Producing Industry in Your State," Sept. 1989, 14.

5. U.S. Steel Corp., *Annual Report*, 1983, 2–3, 11.

6. Ahlbrandt et al., *The Renaissance of American Steel*, 56–59.

7. Apelt, *The Corporation*, 418–19; "Grim Tradition," *Time*, Jan. 9, 1984, 48.

8. U.S. Steel Corp., *Annual Report*, 1983, 7.

9. Ibid., 48–49; "Grim Tradition," 48.

10. U.S. Steel Corp., *Annual Report*, 1983, 48–49; "Grim Tradition," 48.

11. U.S. Steel Corp., *Annual Report*, 1983, 48–49; "Big Steel's Big Chill," *Newsweek*, Jan. 9, 1984, 69.

12. U.S. Steel Corp., *Annual Report*, 1983, 48–49.

13. U.S. Steel Corp., *Annual Report*, 1983, 24; Apelt, *The Corporation*, 411–15; Hoerr, *And the Wolf Finally Came*, 20.

14. Garret Mathews, "'Blessed to Have a Job,' in Gary," *Sunday Bluefield Daily Telegraph Magazine*, Feb. 6, 1983.

15. Strat Douthat, "Miner Afraid to Get Sick," *Bluefield Daily Telegraph*, Feb. 13, 1983; Karen Kaplan, "U.S. Steel Official Says Company Not Ready to Open Gary Mine District," *Bluefield Daily Telegraph*, Mar. 30, 1983.

16. "State of Siege," *Time*, Apr. 25, 1983; William Robbins, "90% Jobless Rate Grinds West Virginia Coal Town," *New York Times*, Apr. 10, 1983.

17. Karen Kaplan, "Leading Coal Officials View Future of Pocahontas Coalfield," *Bluefield Daily Telegraph*, Mar. 30, 1983; Karen Kaplan, "U.S. Steel Official Says Company Not Ready to Open Gary Mine District," *Bluefield Daily Telegraph*, Mar. 30, 1983.

18. "Fall Resumption at Gary No Longer Likely," *Bluefield Daily Telegraph*, July 15, 1983.

19. Corcoran, "New U.S. Steel Superintendent Says 'Our Biggest Concern Is People.'"

20. "U.S. Steel Calls 300 Back to Work at Gary," *Welch Daily News*, July 25, 1983; Karen Kaplan, "Gary Miners to Be Called Back," *Bluefield Daily Telegraph*, July 26, 1983.

21. David H. Corcoran, "Thumbs up for U.S. Steel," *Welch Daily News*, July 26, 1983.

22. Desda Moss and M. J. Zuckerman, "Mine Recall Lifts Hope for 50% Jobless," *USA Today*, Aug. 4, 1983; Karen Kaplan," Future Looks Better for Embattled Gary," *Bluefield Daily Telegraph*, Aug. 5, 1983.

23. Ward Morgan, "Returnees Say Gary Coal Must Be Mined Cheaply for Call-back to Last," *Bluefield Daily Telegraph*, Aug. 10, 1983.

24. "85 Laid-Off Miners Called Back at Gary," *Welch Daily News*, Aug. 3, 1983.

25. Karen Kaplan, "Gary's Number 9 Mine Will Reopen in January," *Bluefield Daily Telegraph*, Dec. 7, 1983.

26. State of West Virginia, Dept. of Mines, *Directory of Mines*, 1983, 127; *1984 Keystone Coal Industry Manual*, 1284–85.

27. State of West Virginia, Dept. of Mines, *Directory of Mines*, 1973, 12; 1983, 60.

28. Elaine Thompson, "U.S. Steel to Close Mine Permanently," *Bluefield Daily Telegraph*, Dec. 29, 1983.

29. David H. Corcoran, "Proud of Men, Says U.S. Steel Head," *Welch Daily News*, Twenty-first Annual Coal Edition, Feb. 24, 1984.

30. U.S. Steel Corp., *Annual Report*, 1983, 17, 46.

Chapter 14

1. U.S. Steel Corp., *Annual Report*, 1984, 1–4.

2. American Petroleum Institute and the Energy Information Administration, "Statistical Summary," 14.

3. U.S. Steel Corp., *Annual Report*, 1984, 2, 20.

4. Warren, *Big Steel*, 335–36.

5. Apelt, *The Corporation*, 420–21, 426.

6. William Robbins, "Bank and U.S. Steel Targets of Pittsburgh Protest," *New York Times*, July 23, 1984.

7. William Robbins, "Pennsylvania Mill Town's Church Militants Defy Synod Anew," *New York Times*, Dec. 4, 1984.

8. "U.S. Steel Idles 300 More in Gary," *New York Times*, Aug. 31, 1984; "Indiana Sheriff Bars Evictions in Steel Area," *New York Times*, Nov. 27, 1984.

9. "Music of a Giant Steel Plant Fades in Pennsylvania Town," *New York Times*, Apr. 6, 1984; William Serrin, "Sad Johnstown Awaits Demise of a Steel Plant," *New York Times*, Apr. 21, 1984.

10. William Serrin, "A Steel Valley's Death: Memories and Despair," *New York Times*, Jan. 10, 1984.

11. Steven Greenhouse, "U.S. Steel Seeks a Rival at Cost of $975 Million," *New York Times*, Feb. 2, 1984.

12. David Pauty, Tracey L. Robinson, Lawrence Walsh, and Madlyn Resener, "Big Steel Grows Bigger," *Newsweek*, Feb. 13, 1984, 70; "U.S. Steel Sees Its Future in Even More Steel," *Business Week*, Feb. 13, 1984, 36–37; "High Hurdles Ahead for U.S. Steel and National," *Business Week*, Feb. 20, 1984, 31–32.

13. "There Could Still Be Life in Steel Mergers," *Business Week*, Mar. 26, 1984, 36–37; Hogan, *Steel in the United States*, 30–32.

14. U.S. Steel Corp., *Annual Report*, 1984, 11.

15. Ibid., 2–4, 11.

16. "Some Important 1983 Coal Events," *Welch Daily News*, Twenty-first Annual Coal Edition, Feb. 24, 1984.

17. David H. Corcoran, "District President Saunders Voices Mixed Feelings About 1983–84," *Welch Daily News*, Twenty-first Annual Coal Edition, Feb. 24, 1984.

18. David H. Corcoran, "Usher Plans to Ride High on Improving Economy," *Welch Daily News*, Twenty-first Annual Coal Edition, Feb. 24, 1984.
19. "U.S. Steel Coal Profile Will Change with Acquisition," *Coal Age* 89 (Mar. 1984): 15.
20. Daniel F. Cuff, "U.S. Steel Sells Coal Units to Arch," *New York Times*, Sept. 29, 1984; U.S. Steel Corp., *Annual Report*, 1983, 17; U.S. Steel Corp., *Annual Report*, 1984, 10.
21. Energy Information Administration, *Historical Monthly Energy Review*, 170–71.
22. U.S. Steel Corp., *Annual Report*, 1984, 49.
23. "U.S. Steel Coal Profile Will Change with Acquisition," 15.
24. "Steelmakers Take Their Coal to Market," *Coal Age* (Oct. 1984): 11–13.
25. Toni Locy, "An Economy at the Crossroads: West Virginia Coal," *Pittsburgh Press*, Mar. 25, 1984.
26. Toni Locy, "Anatomy of a Layoff: 'Bear' Presley," *Pittsburgh Press*, Mar. 25, 1984.
27. "Negotiators Take a Determined Stand," *Coal Age* (June 1984): 11; "Major Utilities Plan for a Coal Miners Strike Lasting into 1985," *Coal Age* (Aug. 1984): 15.
28. "Gary and Kanawha U.S. Steel Mines Merging," *Bluefield Daily Telegraph*, Sept. 2, 1984.
29. Bill Keller, "Mine Workers and Coal Operators Reach Agreement on Pact," *New York Times*, Sept. 22, 1984; Bill Keller, "Coal Pact Wins Miners' Support by a Big Margin," *New York Times*, Sept. 28, 1984.
30. Keller, "Coal Pact Wins Miners' Support by a Big Margin."
31. David H. Corcoran, "1,500 U.S. Steel Workers Idled," *Welch Daily News*, Sept. 27, 1984.
32. "Arch 'Acquires' to Diversify with Lynch District Purchase," *Coal Age* (Nov. 1984): 23; Keller, "Coal Pact Wins Miners' Support by a Big Margin"; "Miners Move on to the Unemployment Lines," *Coal Age* (Nov. 1984): 11.
33. David H. Corcoran, "Turner, Sidote, Moore Receive Awards at Annual Chamber of Commerce Dinner," *Welch Daily News*, Oct. 8, 1984.
34. "Unemployment Claims to Be Taken Tuesday at County Library," *Welch Daily News*, Oct. 8, 1984.
35. "Miners Move on to the Unemployment Lines," 11.
36. Norman Oder, "Layoffs Put Town on Slow Speed Again," *Charleston Gazette*, Sept. 29, 1984; Garret Mathews, "Gary Aftermath: 'If I Were Younger I'd Leave,'" *Bluefield Daily Telegraph*, Sept. 30, 1984.
37. Peter Perl, "Decline of Steel Industry Leaves Regretful Residents in Dying Town," *Washington Post*, Dec. 2, 1984.
38. Ibid.
39. Kelly Barth, "Miner a Celebrity since Appearance on Network News," *Bluefield Daily Telegraph*, Dec. 24, 1984; Perl, "Decline of Steel Industry Leaves Regretful Residents in Dying Town."
40. Kelly Barth, "Christmas in Gary," *Bluefield Daily Telegraph*, Dec. 24, 1984.

Chapter 15

1. Apelt, *The Corporation*, 429–32; U.S. Steel Corp., *Annual Report*, 1985, 1–3, 26, 57.
2. U.S. Steel Corp., *Annual Report*, 1985, 4, 18.
3. William Serrin, "Five Concerns End Joint Role in Steel Talks," *New York Times*, May 4, 1985.
4. William Serrin, "Clerics Split in Battle Over Steel Jobs," *New York Times*, Jan. 18, 1985; William Serrin, "Activists Protest at Door of Church," *New York Times*, Jan. 21, 1985; William Serrin, "Militant Steelworker: Ronald Weisen, He Is Pressing Big Steel to Reopen Plants," *New York Times*, Jan. 17, 1985.
5. William Serrin, "Pittsburgh Area Rallies to Save Blast Furnace," *New York Times*, Jan. 30, 1985; "Furnace Reopening Rejected," *New York Times*, Apr. 16, 1985.
6. Serrin, "A Steel Valley's Death: Memories and Despair"; Lindsey Gruson, "Steel Towns Discharge Police and Reduce Services Sharply," *New York Times*, Oct. 6, 1985.
7. David H. Corcoran, "U.S. Steel Mining May Lead Area Recovery," *Welch Daily News*, Twenty-second Annual Coal Edition, Feb. 28, 1985.
8. *1986 Keystone Coal Industry Manual*, 1204–5.
9. Corcoran, "U.S. Steel Mining May Lead Area Recovery."
10. *1986 Keystone Coal Industry Manual*, 1204–5.
11. U.S. Steel Corp., *Annual Report*, 1985, 50.
12. Ibid., 16.
13. Allan Holtz and Harold R. Kokal, "U.S. Steel Improves Fine Coal Yield," *Coal Age* (July 1985): 73.
14. "Better Times in Gary Evoke Memories of Town's Past," *Bluefield Daily Telegraph*, Mar. 10, 1985.

Chapter 16

1. William Serrin, "Steel Unionists Muster Strength to Meet Owners," *New York Times*, Jan. 17, 1986.
2. Jonathan P. Hicks, "USX Earnings Fell 92.2% in Period," *New York Times*, July 30, 1986.
3. USX Corp., *Annual Report*, 1986, 1, 4, 6.
4. American Petroleum Institute and the Energy Information Administration, "Statistical Summary," *The Oil and Natural Gas Producing Industry in Your State*, Sept., 1989, 14.
5. USX Corp., *Annual Report*, 1986, 6.
6. Steven Greenhouse, "LTV Problems Stir Concerns on Survival of Steel Industry," *New York Times*, July 28, 1986; Jonathan P. Hicks, "Big Steel Is Getting Smaller," *New York Times*, July 31, 1986.
7. USX Corp., *Annual Report*, 1986, 2.
8. "USX Closings Set; Strike Threat Cited," *New York Times*, July 24, 1986.
9. William Serrin, "A Chapter of Industrial History Closes with the Homestead Steel Works," *New York Times*, June 27, 1986.

10. USX Corp., *Annual Report*, 1986, 2; Jonathan P. Hicks, "U.S. Steel: New Name Ends an Era," *New York Times*, July 9, 1986.

11. "U.S. Steel Is Changing a Lot More Than Its Moniker," *Business Week*, July 21, 1986, 71.

12. William Serrin, "USX Plants Struck by Steel Workers," *New York Times*, Aug. 1, 1986.

13. Jonathan P. Hicks, "116-Day Strike at USX Affects Economy Little," *New York Times*, Nov. 24, 1986.

14. USX Corp., *Annual Report*, 1986, 16.

15. Energy Information Administration, *The Changing Structure of the U.S. Coal Industry 1976–1986*, 9.

16. "The Death Knell Tolls for America's Met Coal Industry," *Coal Age* (Apr. 1986): 19.

17. "U.S. Steel Faces Difficulties Developing Outside Coal Sales," *Coal Age* (July 1986): 19.

18. Ibid.

19. "Coal in Brief: Layoffs," *Coal Age* (Aug. 1986): 31; "Coal in Brief: U.S. Steel Cutbacks," *Coal Age* (Sept. 1986): 45.

20. Garret Mathews, "Hard Times 'Paralyzing' Gary Hollow," *Bluefield Daily Telegraph*, Sept. 26, 1986.

21. Ibid.

22. Elizabeth Fried, "U.S. Steel Layoffs Indefinite," *Bluefield Daily Telegraph*, Nov. 7, 1986; "U.S. Steel Shuts Alpheus Operations, Dismissing 1,000 Workers," *Coal Age* (Dec. 1986): 13.

23. "Reaction: 'Devastating,'" *Bluefield Daily Telegraph*, Nov. 7, 1986.

24. Elizabeth Fried, "Job Education Sessions Set," *Bluefield Daily Telegraph*, Nov. 7, 1986; David Bourne, "U.S. Steel Layoffs," *Bluefield Daily Telegraph*, Nov. 8, 1986; David Bourne, "Hopes Vanish at Alpheus," *Bluefield Daily Telegraph*, Nov. 8, 1986; "Many Appalachian Mining Jobs Are Gone for Good," *Coal Age* (Aug. 1987): 13.

25. David Bourne, "Miners Eye Purchasing Coal Assets," *Bluefield Daily Telegraph*, Nov. 22, 1986.

26. USX Corp., *Annual Report*, 1986, 24.

Chapter 17

1. USX Corp., *Annual Report*, 1987, 1–2.

2. Kenneth B. Noble, "Steel Union Locals Back USX Pact," *New York Times*, Jan. 19, 1987.

3. "Steelworkers Ratify USX Pact, Ending Stoppage," *New York Times*, Feb. 1, 1987.

4. USX Corp., *Annual Report*, 1987, 3, 18.

5. Ibid., 3, 18, 56-57.

6. Ibid., 23–25.

7. Ibid., 2–3, 8–17.

8. Ibid., 2, 26, 50.

9. *1988 Keystone Coal Industry Manual*, 1037.

10. Jules Loh, "Gary Becomes an 'Old Folks' Town as Younger Generations Vanish," *Bluefield Daily Telegraph*, Jan. 11, 1987.
11. "In Gary, Saving the Coal Mines Means Saving the Town," *Coal Age* (May 1987): 14; "Gary Enterprises Gets Federal Aid to Reopen Former U.S. Steel Mine," *Coal Age* (Oct. 1987): 21.
12. David Quick, "Gary Mines to Reopen," *Bluefield Daily Telegraph*, July 29, 1987; "Gary Enterprises Gets Federal Aid to Reopen Former U.S. Steel Mine," 21.
13. William Archer, "Sounds of Silence Disappear as Gary Mines Reopen," *Observer*, Oct. 14, 1987.
14. Quick, "Gary Mines to Reopen"; "Gary Enterprises Gets Federal Aid to Reopen Former U.S. Steel Mine," 21.
15. David Quick, "Gary No. 2: Workers May Be the Last Coal Generation," *Bluefield Daily Telegraph*, Sept. 13, 1987; Archer, "Sounds of Silence Disappear as Gary Mines Reopen."
16. *Maps and General Information: Mines of the United States Coal and Coke Company Situated in State of West Virginia*, July 1, 1937, n.p.
17. Quick, "Gary No. 2: Workers May Be the Last Coal Generation."
18. Ibid.
19. USX Corp., *Annual Report*, 1989, 1–2.
20. Apelt, *The Corporation*, 444–45.
21. Ahlbrandt et al., *The Renaissance of American Steel*, 43.
22. As quoted in Warren, *Big Steel*, 336–37.
23. Henry Paul, interview with author, July 2002.
24. "U.S. Steel Shuts Down Final McDowell Offices," *Bluefield Daily Telegraph*, Apr. 15, 1989; *1989 Keystone Coal Industry Manual*, 1207–8.
25. "Partners to Reopen Gary No. 9," *Coal Outlook*, May 7, 1990, 7.
26. Henry Paul, interview with author, July 2002.

Postscript

1. Warren, *Big Steel*, 317.
2. "U.S. Steel Negotiates with CONSOL?" *Coal Outlook*, Mar. 30, 1992, 4; "U.S. Steel Mining up for Sale," *Coal Outlook*, Apr. 13, 1992, 1.
3. "U.S. Steel and PinnOak Conclude Their Deal," *Pittsburgh Business Times*, July 2, 2003.
4. Mark Paxton, "Death Knell in the Coal Field," n.s., May 6, 1990, n.p.
5. *1990 Population and Housing Characteristics for West Virginia*, West Virginia State Census Data Center, Charleston, Aug. 1992, 10, 50.
6. U.S. Census Bureau, *2000 Census of Population and Housing, Summary Social, Economic, and Housing Characteristics, PHC-2-50, West Virginia* (Washington, DC: U.S. Government Printing Office, 2003).
7. Henry Paul, interview with author, July 2002.
8. Davis, "The Impact of the Coal Industry on McDowell County, West Virginia," 81–84.

Index